SUPERVISORS
Safety Manual

SUPERVISORS
Safety Manual

Better production without injury and waste from accidents

6th EDITION

National Safety Council

444 North Michigan Avenue • Chicago, Illinois 60611

PREFACE
To the 6th Edition

You, the first-line supervisor, are an extremely important person in an occupational hazard control program. Not only are you the direct link between management and the work force, but in order to produce quality goods and/or services, you are responsible for quality job training, development of good safety attitudes, and detection of hazardous conditions and unsafe work practices.

You must know the techniques of human relations and the fundamentals of loss control to prevent accidents. You, yourself, must be properly trained so that you can adequately review hazard control information with your workers, check personal protective equipment and safety devices, and investigate accidents that occur in your area of responsibility. The *Supervisors Safety Manual* is designed to provide this needed safety training.

The Manual reflects the expertise of various staff members of the National Safety Council. These people have worked with supervisors and safety professionals in establishing effective safety and health programs.

Now in its Sixth Edition, the Manual has been revised many times since its original publication in 1956. In this edition, several chapters from the Fifth Edition have been modified and updated and chapters discussing Loss Control for Supervisors, Communications, Electrical Safety, Accident Investigation, and Safety Inspections have been added.

The National Safety Council appreciates the cooperation of the many supervisors, safety directors, and other professionals who have helped in the preparation of this edition. Even though a lot of detailed information has been included, the purpose of the book is not to serve as a complete handbook. Rather, it is designed to emphasize important issues to be considered by the supervisors who are responsible for safety in their organization.

The information and recommendations contained in this Manual have been compiled from sources believed to be reliable, and represent the best current opinion on the subject. No warranty, guarantee, or representation is made by the National Safety Council as to the absolute correctness of sufficiency of any representation contained in this or other publications, and the National Safety Council assumes no responsibility in connection therewith. Nor can it be assumed that all acceptable safety measures are contained in this (and other publications), or that other or additional measures may not be required under particular or exceptional conditions or circumstances.

Staff credits for the Sixth Edition of this Manual are as follows:

Overall coordination: Carlton D. Piepho, Manager, Safety Training Institute.

National Safety Council contributors: Gerald E. Cunningham, Alex Kane, and Richard Morel.

Staff support: Al Carpenter, Al DiCicco, Barbra J. Dembski, Terry Grisim, Ronald Koziol, Martin Mulhall, Austin Phillips, Barbara Plog, Michael Pinto, and Phil Schmidt.

Editing and production: Frank McElroy, director; Jan Elliott, Carol North, and Nancy Seeger.

Cover design: Jake Kasparian.

Outside contributors:

Al Lundin, Regional Sales Manager
Mine Safety Appliances Co.
Elk Grove, Ill.
Chapter 9

Leonard C. Smith
Safety Consultant
Onalaska, Wis.
Chapter 3

Edgar Mendenhall
Mendenhall Technical Services
Bloomingdale, Ill.
Chapter 13

Richard C. Kidwell
Cooper Industries
Houston, Texas
Chapter 4

Marshall E. Petersen, P.E.
Prospect Engineering
Mount Prospect, Ill.
Chapter 14

CONTENTS

CONTENTS

ix

CONTENTS

uses, Nuisance GFCI tripping, Summary. Hazardous
Locations: Overview of classes and divisions, Equip-
ment requirements, Equipment marking. Common
Electrical Deficiencies: Electrical extension cords.
Safeguards for Home Appliances. Safety Program
Policy and Procedures: Policy, Supervisory responsibili-
ties, Employee responsibilities, Electrical safety policy.
Electrical Distribution System Review. Summary.

Fire Safety

14

Basic Principles: Understanding fire chemistry, Determining fire hazards, Informing the work force. Causes
of Fire: Electrical equipment, Friction, Special fire-
hazard materials, Welding and cutting, Open flames,
Portable heaters, Hot surfaces, Smoking and matches, **387**
Spontaneous combustion, Static electricity. Fire-Safe
Housekeeping. Alarms, Equipment, and Evacuation:
Fire alarms, What about extinguishers?, Follow up for
fire safety, Fire brigades, Special fire protection problems, Evacuation. Reviewing the Supervisor's Fire Job.

Chapter 1

Loss Control For Supervisors

The bottom line of all safety programs is accident prevention, more often called Loss Control. Many supervisors and managers, unfortunately, do not seriously consider accident prevention as being an important part of their jobs, until after an accident causing a serious injury or illness occurs. Then they investigate to determine why the accident occurred. This is not accident *prevention*—it is accident *reaction*. Certainly, if an accident occurs, we must investigate to find the causes and eliminate them so that a recurrence is prevented. However, as supervisors, our job is to *prevent* accidents, and their resultant toll in both human and cash losses, by controlling the hazards that produce them.

The approach to safety discussed in this manual will help you to avoid many potentially negative aspects of your safety job. It should lead to positive actions on your part and a positive measurement of how well you perform your safety duties. It will also put the emphasis on accident prevention, rather than accident reaction. In addition, you'll be prepared to prevent *all* accidents, not just those that result in serious injuries. By taking this approach, you will perform the safety portion of your supervisory job in the most efficient manner. And by doing it well, you'll have more time for the other important parts of your job.

Accidents and incidents

Let's define our terms before we go any further.

Accident. An accident is an unplanned, undesired occurrence in a sequence of events that results in personal injury or illness or death and/or property damage.

Let's examine this definition. Accidents are clearly unplanned events. When they occur, they also upset *your* plans. You may have had

1

several things planned, but when an accident occurs, it demands all of your attention. You must stop what you are doing and handle the many problems caused by the accident.

Incident. An incident is an unplanned, undesired event that adversely affects the completion of a task. All accidents are incidents (see Figure 7-1, page 133). A "near" accident or "near miss" is an example of an incident resulting in neither an injury nor property damage. A near accident has the *potential* to result in injury or property damage if its cause is not corrected. About 75 percent of industrial injuries are forecast by near accidents or near misses, so it's in our best interest to find and eliminate their causes to keep them from recurring.

For example, an employee feels the tingle of a slight electric shock while using a defective portable drill. This is a near accident as there is no injury or property damage. If the cause—the defective drill—is removed from service, a potential injury or fatality can be prevented. Therefore it is very important to have a system that encourages the reporting of near accidents so the cause can be determined and appropriate corrective action taken.

Hazards and their control

Hazard: A hazard is any existing or potential condition in the workplace which, by itself or by interacting with other variables, can result in the unwanted effects of death, injuries, property damage, and other losses.

There are several factors involved with this definition. First, potentially hazardous conditions, as well as those that exist at the moment, must be considered. Secondly, hazards may result not from independent failure of workplace components, but from one workplace component acting upon or influencing another.

Loss control: Loss control is accident prevention, achieved through a complete safety and health hazard control program. Loss control involves preventing employee injuries, occupational illnesses, and accidental damage to the company's property. It also involves preventing injuries, illnesses, and property damage accidents involving visitors and the public.

Hazard control: Hazard control can be defined as the function that is directed toward recognizing, evaluating, and eliminating (or at least reducing) the destructive effects of hazards emanating from human errors and from the situational and environmental aspects of the workplace.

A necessary part of the management process, a hazard control program includes programs, procedures, audits, and evaluations, as well as sound operating and design procedures, operator training, inspection and test programs, and communicating essential information about hazards and their control. A hazard control program coordinates shared responsibility among departments. There is a definite interrelationship between the worker, equipment, and the environment.

Many supervisors think that accidents are only those incidents that result in serious injuries. If a minor injury or property damage results, some supervisors are easily relieved and continue on with their routine. People with this attitude let the *result* of an accident determine their level of interest. We know that the result of an accident (the degree of loss resulting from it) is a matter of chance, and that it would be better to try to control the hazards that *lead* to accidents. That is why many safety professionals prefer the term "hazard control" to "loss control." If we ignore the warnings of minor and "near" accidents, we are neglecting an important part of our supervisory responsibilities.

We must look for the cause(s), regardless of the results. The hazardous condition or action that causes a "near" accident one time may cause a serious injury or fatality the next time. Likewise, the hazard that causes only minor property damage at one time may result in a serious property damage at another time.

AREAS OF RESPONSIBILITY

Let's look at the responsibilities of supervisory jobs. There are four major areas that supervisors must control:

1. Production control
2. Quality control
3. Cost control
4. Accident/Illness (loss) control.

Many of us willingly accept responsibility for the first three, but ignore or procrastinate about the fourth. This is because we have assumed that the responsibility for accident loss control belongs to a safety director or someone in the personnel department. This is an incorrect assumption. It is *our* job.

Loss control through accident prevention is not merely a job we do on some convenient Friday afternoon. It must be considered at all times. Ask yourself this question: When should supervisors perform safety inspections? If your answer is "once a week" or "once a month," you do not understand your responsibility. Informal safety inspections should occur every time you walk through your department. Although your pri-

Figure 1-1. The effective supervisor does a "safety inspection" every time he or she goes through the department or other area of responsibility.

mary purpose may be to check attendance or to determine whether or not supplies are adequate, you should be conducting a safety inspection at the same time. (See Figure 1-1.)

Be on the alert for hazards, anything that may cause an accident, such as tripping hazards, fire hazards, poorly stacked materials, poor housekeeping, safeguards missing from machines, and/or unsafe practices. Actually, accident prevention should be part of your job *all of the time*. These responsibilities cannot be separated from the other parts of your work. In fact, the best way to describe your job is to say that you are responsible for production with safety. If you view your job in this way, your accident prevention responsibilities will be handled quite spontaneously.

Safety record as performance measure

Many progressive and successful firms include the supervisor's performance of safety responsibilities as part of the performance evaluation. Production, quality, cost, and loss control are of equal importance in measuring job performance. These four areas of your responsibility

Figure 1-2. Responsibility for safety and accident prevention rests with top management who, in turn, share it with middle management and, through them, to first-line supervisors. Your manager will hold you accountable for accident prevention because he or she is also held accountable, and so on up the line.

are well integrated and cannot really be separated. Performing all four functions simultaneously is required all of the time.

Acceptance of a supervisory job requires taking responsibility for the safety of your people. This is true, regardless of whom you supervise—a group of machinists, assemblers, a construction crew, or an office staff. Every supervisor is responsible for the safety of his or her people.

Let's examine the concept of safety responsibility. Who is responsible for safety and accident prevention? Accident prevention is a line function (Figure 1-2). The top person in the organization is responsible and held accountable for loss control. The top manager cannot handle all of the details of every job, so he or she delegates responsibilities, along with commensurate authority, to various subordinates. Although top managers delegate tasks to the subordinates, they cannot delegate all of their responsibilities to others.

These responsibilities must be shared with middle managers. The middle manager, such as your boss, will delegate the responsibility for safety and accident prevention in your department to *you,* the first-line supervisor. You should be aware that your manager will hold you accountable for accident prevention because he or she is accountable in turn, to the top manager.

Let's define the principal terms we are using:

- *Responsibility* is having to answer to higher management for activities and results.

- *Authority* is the right to correct, command, and determine the courses of action.

- *Delegation* is sharing authority and responsibility with others. Even though we delegate responsibility, we cannot be completely relieved of it.

- *Accountability* is an active measurement taken by management to ensure compliance to standards.

So, the answer to our original question, "Who is responsible for safety?" is that we *all* are. People at every level of supervision and management in an organization are responsible for controlling losses due to accidents in their areas. Each of us should expect to have our performance in the areas for which we are responsible measured by our boss, because our boss is held accountable for us. In turn, your employees are accountable to you for performing their jobs in a safe manner.

The 'old approach' to safety

Let's take a closer look at the way many supervisors have measured their safety performances in the past. The measurement was made by lost-time accidents. As long as no one was injured seriously, supervisors felt that they were doing well. Many times minor injuries, property damage, or near-miss accidents were brushed aside and ignored.

In 1931, H.W. Heinrich* conducted an accident study that is now famous. He showed that for every accident resulting in a serious injury, there are approximately 29 resulting in only minor injuries and 300 with no resultant injuries (see Figure 1-3). You can see that if you react only to *major injury* accidents, you are ignoring 99.7 percent of the accidents that occur in your operation. Heinrich stressed the fact that the same things that cause a near-accident (incident) at one time can cause a major injury the next time.

If we look only at the major injuries in our department, we will miss many opportunities to find and eliminate the causes of near- and property-damage accidents.

---

*H.W. Heinrich. *Industrial Accident Prevention: A Scientific Approach.* New York: McGraw Hill, 1931.

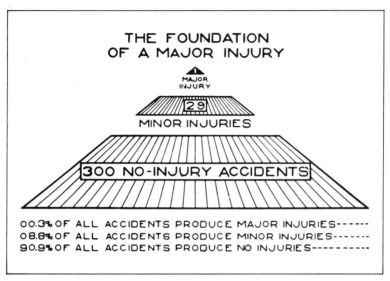

Figure 1-3. Heinrich's original illustration that showed the results of his accident study—that 99.7 percent of the accidents and near-accidents that occur do not result in a major injury.

From *Industrial Accident Prevention: A Scientific Approach,*
by H. W. Heinrich, copyright 1931 by McGraw Hill Book Co.
Used with permission.

Sometimes accidents are "no injury" accidents and we can find *and eliminate the causes* before a more serious accident occurs. Supervisors who do not look for property-damage accidents or near-accidents will not be eliminating accident causes as they should be.

If you only consider serious lost-time injuries when you measure your safety performance, you are not taking full responsibility for accident prevention. Having control requires being aware of the possibilities for all types of accidents and knowing how to prevent them appropriately.

THE COST OF ACCIDENTS

Another area of major concern to supervisors is the cost of accidents. Many people fail to realize how much accidents *really* cost. Accidents are expensive, in ways that are not always obvious; therefore, attention to loss control can improve your department's performance, and enhance your company's success.

Let's consider the question of "where does the money come from to pay for the results of accidents?" Some people think that organizations

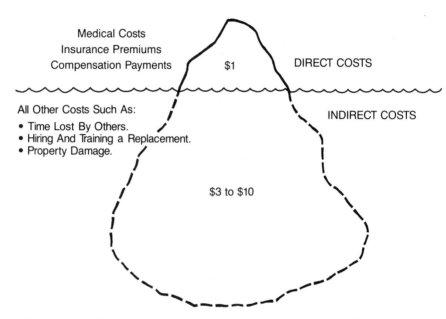

Medical Costs
Insurance Premiums
Compensation Payments

$1

DIRECT COSTS

All Other Costs Such As:
• Time Lost By Others.
• Hiring And Training a Replacement.
• Property Damage.

INDIRECT COSTS

$3 to $10

Figure 1-4. Accident costs can be compared to an iceberg—the more hidden (indirect) costs usually add up to much more than the obvious (direct) costs.

have excess money available to pay for the cost of accidents. However, we know that payment for accidents must come from profits.

A series of costly accidents can reduce profits radically. Accidents can cause obvious, direct costs, such as medical, hospital, rehabilitation expenses, Workers' Compensation payments, and higher insurance premiums, or even loss of insurability. But there are other, indirect costs— that are less obvious, and usually uninsured. These include the various disruptions of normal work procedures, such as employees being witnesses or helping the injured, or even the reduction in production that can result in the late delivery of products.

If profits are not sufficient, it may be necessary to defer the procurement of new equipment and facilities. You may frequently hear people try to minimize the costs of accidents by saying that they are covered by insurance. Insurance covers only a portion of the total accident cost and as accident loss experience increases, so will a company's insurance premiums. It is clear that directly and indirectly, accidents reduce profitability. Actually, the *total* costs of accidents are greater than many of us realize.

Accident costs can be compared to an iceberg (Figure 1-4). The part of the iceberg that we can see above the surface is like the smaller (direct)

ITEMS IN INDIRECT COST

Time lost by others

Costs of hiring and training a replacement

Lost efficiency

Overtime premium

Costs to investigate the accident

Report time

Possible lost orders

Tool and equipment damage

Lost equipment utilization

Spoilage

Lost production time

Figure 1-5.

portion of the total accident costs. An examination of a serious accident may give us a better understanding of total accident costs.

Suppose one of your people is seriously injured. Many people in the department would stop working. Some would rush to give first aid to the injured person. Another would call you to the scene. When you arrive to help the injured person, do the others immediately return to work? Not always. They may continue to help or just watch.

In this situation, all idle work time is a part of the accident costs. As soon as the injured person receives proper medical treatment, your next job is an accident investigation. You need to interview witnesses (see Chapter 7), isolate the area, and determine the causes. All of the time spent on accident investigation and making reports, as well as wages paid to witnesses, are included in the total costs.

If the injured person only misses work for a short time, you may be able to make up for the production loss by having the rest of the department work overtime. Overtime premiums paid are accident costs. On the other hand, if the injured person is gone for months, you may have to hire and train a replacement worker. The cost of hiring and training someone to replace your skilled operator can be prohibitive. The new operator's efficiency may be lower than that of the skilled person being replaced. If a machine is damaged in the accident and the job must be performed with less efficient equipment, further reduction of output will result. All of the reduced efficiency represents another indirect cost.

These are some of the factors adding to indirect costs. A more complete list is provided in Figure 1-5.

As with the example of an iceberg, we find that the indirect cost of accidents are usually greater than the direct costs. A conservative estimate is that for every dollar of direct accident costs, there are $3 of indirect costs. In his article in *Professional Safety,** Robert E. Sheriff showed that indirect costs may be four to ten times the insured costs. Frank Bird** calculates that for every $1 of direct costs, there may be $5 to $50 of uninsured ledger costs and $1 to $3 of uninsured miscellaneous costs.

We have established that there are many hidden costs due to accidents. Conversely, there are hidden savings in accident prevention, which is the reason that the phrase Loss Control is often used. Every accident you prevent saves direct *and* indirect accident costs and this money will remain in profits. Other benefits of accident prevention efforts include:

- People will not be injured or killed.
- Property and materials will not be destroyed.
- Production will flow more smoothly.
- You will have more time for the other major parts of your job.

A BETTER APPROACH TO SAFETY

It is best to include loss control as a regular part of your job and to expect to have this part of your performance measured. For example, you are expected to perform periodic safety inspections of the areas for which you are responsible (see Chapter 8). Your manager can verify that you conduct these inspections, check on the quality of the inspections, and determine how well you follow up on the items needing attention.

Similarly, other areas of your safety activities should be measured, such as housekeeping (discussed in Chapter 8). Pay attention to the issues involved with housekeeping and the details such as, (*a*) Are housekeeping inspections being performed on schedule? and (*b*) Is the supervisor taking positive action to improve housekeeping?

Safety and housekeeping inspections and the problems you discover are important, but what you do about them is more important. If a problem can be rectified by your people, assign the appropriate tasks as soon

---

*Robert E. Sheriff. "Loss Control Comes of Age," *Professional Safety,* September 1980.

**Frank E. Bird, Jr., and Robert G. Loftus. *Loss Control Management.* Loganville, Ga.: Institute Press, 1976.

Figure 1-6. Once you have trained an employee, you must monitor him frequently. If he is not working properly and safely, then he must be retrained.

as possible, so that the problem can be solved. If, on the other hand, service of maintenance personnel is required, issue a work order request immediately. Be sure to follow up, as needed, to see that the job is done. You may even find it necessary to have your boss help expedite the work by getting help from other departments.

Job instruction

You are responsible for training the workers in your area, and it's up to you to monitor their work habits. (Figure 1-6). One of the most effective ways to avoid accidents is to make sure that employees are following through with the safe work procedures in which they have been trained (see Chapter 5).

Some points to consider are:

- What is the quality level of the job instruction training (JIT)?
- How many people in the department are responsible for the training?
- Are all new employees trained?
- Are transferred employees trained?

Job safety analysis

You are also the one who looks for ways to improve operating proce-

11

dures in your area, while maintaining safe and healthy working conditions (see Chapter 5).

Some points to consider are:

- Are the assigned number of job safety analyses (JSAs) being performed?
- Is the quality improving?
- Are JSAs reviewed as operations are revised?
- How well are they being utilized?

Other measures

These are only a few of the positive approaches to loss control that you can take. You can probably add other items to the list. As you incorporate these actions into your normal routine, you will find that loss control work will be more easily accomplished.

As the number of accidents that occur in your department are reduced, things will run more smoothly. As a result, you will find that you have more time available to devote to the other parts of your job, such as production planning, quality improvements, and other cost controls.

Another positive measure is to have your people use the appropriate personal protective equipment (PPE). When new employees are trained, they should be informed about the needs for personal protective equipment. PPE, like eye protection, should be fitted; PPE, like some respiratory protective equipment, should be demonstrated so that the workers know how to use it properly. You should emphasize that people will be *expected* to wear and use it, as required.

It is easy to determine whether or not your people are following these rules. Whenever you enter your area, make an instantaneous check to see that the required personal protection equipment is being used. It is essential that any violations of these rules be dealt with at once. Your people must understand that this is a condition of their employment.

Anyone visiting your area must also comply with the requirements for wearing the proper equipment.

Help with your loss control work

Where can first-line supervisors turn for help and guidance with their safety activities? First, look to your supervisor for help. He or she should be most concerned with your control of losses. This is part of your supervisor's job-performance measurement, as well as your own. Your efforts in this area can play an important role in successful employment performance at the job for both of you.

The safety director or manager in your company can be another

Figure 1-7. Hazards should be "designed out" insofar as possible. The supervisor should make sure that engineers and designers are aware of problems that exist and that they take care of them.

source of help and can serve as a catalyst for your program. His or her job is to work with the management to plan the overall loss (hazard) control program and to assist supervisors in carrying it out. It is wise for you to cooperate and work closely with the safety director's program for your operation.

You, as a supervisor, can also work to eliminate hazards from entering your area in the first place. Directly involve yourself and cooperate with those who design machinery, equipment, controls, and safeguards that will be used in your area. (See Figure 1-7.)

SUMMARY

Let's review what we've covered in this chapter. Many supervisors evaluate their safety performance by the number of lost time accidents that occur in their departments. This is accident reaction. In order to do your job properly, you should *prevent* accidents from occurring. This approach puts you in control.

If accidents *do* occur, you should investigate to find and eliminate the causes. But investigate *all* accidents—serious injuries, minor injuries, property damage accidents—and near accidents (incidents). If you fail to eliminate the cause of one minor accident, it can cause a more serious accident the next time.

The responsibility to prevent accidents through a loss (hazard) control program is a line function. The top manager delegates the responsibility to your boss through the chain of command, and he or she, in turn, delegates responsibility to you.

However, even though managers *share* their responsibility with you, they cannot delegate it all to you.

Loss control is as important a part of your job as your production, cost, and quality control responsibilities. These parts of your work cannot be separated. They must all be fulfilled. We must *produce safely.* This will result from your handling accident prevention responsibilities naturally. Effective training is an important ingredient of loss control.

Accident costs amount to much more than most people realize. The direct costs represent only a small portion of the total. The indirect costs, including factors such as the time lost by others and that spent investigating and reporting, as well as the cost of repairing or replacing damaged equipment, can be prohibitive. It has been estimated that for every dollar of direct cost there are from *three* to *ten* dollars of indirect costs, and it could be much more!

In profit-making organizations, the occurrence of accidents takes money out of profits. Loss control saves money and keeps it in the profit column. In both nonprofit or profit organizations, accident costs may prevent the procurement of newer and better facilities or equipment.

Chapter 2

Communications

The success of your accident prevention efforts depends, to a great extent, on how well you communicate with your people. Your planning for avoidance of the problems accidents bring, your ideas for making the workplace safer, and the feedback you get about ways to improve operations depend on how well you communicate. Remember that communication involves not only what you send or say, but how well you receive or listen. It has been established that most supervisors and managers spend 50 percent more time on the job listening than they do speaking.

Communicating your ideas to people and giving them opportunities to share their ideas for improvement can help to increase the effectiveness of your accident prevention program. Good communications are vital to your success as a supervisor—they are essential to your accident prevention program. (See Figure 2-1.)

Definition —A good definition of Communication is: "Sharing information and/or ideas with others AND GETTING UNDERSTANDING."

The last three words are especially important. If there is no understanding, then we have failed to communicate. Remember that the receiver may not *agree* with what is being said, but he or she must *understand* it for communication to occur.

We must consider understanding as a vital part of our communications. Make sure that the communications you send can be understood. Conversely, develop ways to improve your understanding of the communications you receive. Question or obtain other clarification of oral communications or memos you receive so that your understanding will

Figure 2-1. Good communication is vital to an effective loss control program. Here the spoken word is strengthened by the leader when he writes the key points of the message on a large pad of paper. Sheets can be flipped over as required.

be enhanced. As you improve your techniques for understanding the communications you receive, you will develop skills in helping others to understand your communications.

Work diligently to improve your communication skills. It will be an asset in your accident prevention work. Good communication will pay dividends in all aspects of your supervisory job.

ELEMENTS OF COMMUNICATION

Sending the message

Communication involves sending messages. The simplest form of this is "one-way communication," one person sends a message and another receives it. This can be illustrated as follows:

SENDER ⟶ Information ⟶ RECEIVER

This type of communication has many problems:

1. Information flows in only one direction.

2. The receiver may not understand the sender's message.

3. The sender will not know if the message has been understood.

4. The receiver may not understand the message because the sender and receiver interpret words differently.

16

5. Lack of feedback keeps the sender from knowing whether or not the message has been received.

Feedback

Obviously, to be effective, a communication system must provide for feedback. The diagram can be expanded to include this:

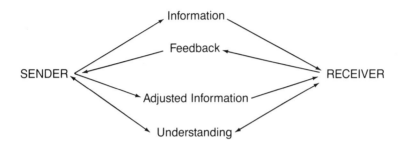

When you are communicating, whether orally or in writing, always provide for feedback. This is the only way for you to know that your message got through and was understood by the receiver.

Communication improves if the receiver has an opportunity to ask questions for clarification and to express how he or she understands the material being communicated. The sender can then realize that there has been a misunderstanding, and can adjust the communication accordingly. This way understanding is much more readily achieved. One-on-one, face-to-face, two-way communication is the best for us to use in the majority of situations that will arise on the job.

This second "ingredient" for improved communication, feedback, must be provided. After giving oral instructions for example, it is good to say, something like, "just to be sure I've covered the material completely, can you repeat what I just told you?" The response you get will tell you how well you've communicated. It is also wise to provide for feedback in your written communications; for example, include a closing sentence such as, "Please call me by Friday to give me your view of these proposals."

Getting good feedback can enhance understanding. The feedback and questions you get will also help you to improve the future communications you send. (See Figure 2-2.)

Communication filters

An important factor to consider when "sending" is always to communicate through the receiver's filters. Filters can be barriers to good communication, as shown here:

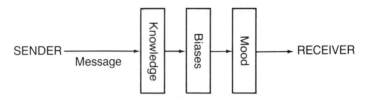

Some frequently encountered filters are:

Knowledge. To communicate effectively we must consider the level of knowledge of the receiver. It is essential to communicate at the appropriate level—not above or below it.

Bias. People are biased by everything that has happened to them.

Figure 2-2. Viewers of a slide-tape training program unit are asked to write down their comments and criticisms in order to provide feedback to help when the unit is later revised so that it will be even more effective in transmitting its message.

National Constructors Association

Their attitudes on most subjects are affected by these experiences. Biases have a definite bearing on a person's understanding of communications. In fact, biases may result in a person's listening to only part of what is being said. In extreme cases, people may "tune out" entirely.

Mood. This is one of the most serious filters to consider in communications. If listeners have something else on their minds at the time your communication is transmitted, they may not get the message at all. This is another reason for obtaining feedback from the receiver so we can *know* that our communication has been received. If, for example, you are instructing one of your people about the hazards on a task he is about to start, and you suspect the individual has something troubling him, ask for feedback. For example, ask the person to repeat the hazards back to you so you'll *know* he understands. A serious accident could result if you don't. It would be a mistake to ask, "Do you understand?" because the answer will be, "Yes." Rather ask people to repeat what you have told them. Similarly, you must not let *your* problems distract you so that you fail to listen to what people tell you about their jobs.

Think of your audience

In any of your communications, it will be most helpful to be empathic. Putting yourself in the position of your receiver enables you to better realize how well your communications are getting through to him or her. Whether it's oral instructions to one of your people (See Figure 2-3), a safety meeting you plan to lead, or a memo to your boss, thinking of your "audience" (your receiver) can help improve your communication. By mentally putting yourself in the place of your receiver, you will have a better understanding of how he or she will react and respond. Achieving understanding is the key to solid communication.

METHODS OF COMMUNICATION

Your choice of a communication method is important. In some situations, oral communications are appropriate, while in others, you may prefer to write your message. When giving job instructions, you can combine both methods. You may discuss the job procedures face-to-face, pointing out the hazards and showing the operator the safe job steps, giving him or her the Job Safety Analysis Form (see Chapter 5) as a reference and reminder of points covered orally. This example shows the value of oral and written communication.

Oral communications may take the form of a "tailgate" meeting, in which you discuss with several people a job they are about to start. During and after the discussion they can ask questions about the job. The

Figure 2-3. The supervisor must know the potential accidents and injuries associated with the use of both hand and portable power tools if he is to instruct his workers properly.

questions asked show you how well you explained the operations to them. If there are no questions, don't assume you've explained everything perfectly. You should then ask questions that will elicit answers that will reveal whether or not they understood what you said.

In some circumstances, you will prefer to use written communications. Generally, this will be when you are dealing with complicated or technical subjects. Written communications can be used as references in the future. Getting feedback is much more difficult with written communications than it is in face-to-face communication. You may want to follow up with verbal questions to be sure your receiver has a clear understanding of your written communications.

A good example of written communication is a Work Order Request sent to maintenance, asking the department to eliminate a problem you found on a safety inspection. You will probably want to follow up such a request orally to be sure that your request was understood and to determine when the job can be performed.

Our actions can communicate to our people

A lot of communication takes place without spoken or written words. People watch your actions very carefully. Because of this, the example you set is as important as the words you speak. If people hear you *say*, for example, that wearing personal protective equipment in your department is essential, but they see that *you don't wear it*, they get a contradictory message. Your actions tell them, "It's not important to wear personal protective equipment." People can usually interpret actions accurately, and will take your actions more seriously than your words.

When operating under pressure, be careful not to pass on those pressures to the people reporting to you. If they understand that you are under pressure and, as a result, take short-cuts and work in an unsafe manner, problems can occur. We must realize that our nonverbal messages are "read" and understood by people just as readily as the verbal communications we send.

Positive communication

Many supervisors make the mistake of failing to "communicate the positive." If their people do something that is not exactly right, supervisors must advise them of it at once. This is proper; however, when a job is done perfectly, many supervisors fail to communicate this to them. Why not take just a minute to praise them for their good work? You will find it will pay dividends in human relations. People know when they have done a job well. Your telling them lets them know that *you* know they did it well. Giving positive feedback to your people can improve their morale. By doing this you can make your supervisory work more effective. Remember the old cliché, "Praise in public, reprimand in private."

LISTENING EFFECTIVELY

Thus far we have concentrated only on the sending portion of communication. We have emphasized the importance of making messages clear, so that they will be understood. But no oral communication takes place unless someone listens with understanding. To be an effective leader, you must be a good listener. It is difficult to think of a profession that doesn't require good listening skills.

Certainly the first-line supervisor must be a skilled listener. In addition, each of us plays a number of roles in our family and social life. We interact with parents, children, spouses, friends, and neighbors. In each capacity, it is important to listen with understanding. How well do we listen? Some supervisors say, "My people just don't listen to me!" Employees, on the other hand, complain, "My boss says he has an open door policy, but what good does it do when I go in to his office and he doesn't really listen to me at all!" Fathers say, "My kids won't listen to me." But those kids of his say to their teachers, "Will you please listen to me? My Dad won't." Within the many roles we play in life, most of us can improve our listening skills.

Listening can be classified in three ways:

• *On-the-job listening.* Listening to the boss, people who report to us, other supervisors, and all others at work.

• *Social listening.* This refers to the listening we do off-the-job, outside the family circle. Listening to friends, neighbors, social acquaintances.

• *Family listening.* Listening to our spouses, children, parents and other family members and getting understanding.

Improving in all three areas of listening can help us become better communicators.

Steps in the listening process

There are four distinct steps in the listening process. Looking at each of them can help us to improve our listening skills.

• *Sensing.* The first step is purely mechanical. Did the listener hear the words that were spoken? If he or she can repeat the sense of the words, sensing has taken place.

• *Interpreting.* The next step begins to complicate the process. How did the listener understand the words spoken? Were the meanings of the words the same for both speaker and listener?

• *Evaluating.* At this stage the listener determines whether or not he or she agrees with what has been said. Before evaluation occurs, understanding must take place.

• *Responding.* In the final step, the listener responds to the message. Response may be a simple nod or shake of the head. It may be a simple, "I see." Before going to a lengthier response, the listener should be certain that the speaker has finished a particular point.

The importance of listening

How important is listening in your supervisory job? A manager spends about 70 percent of the work day communicating. Studies have classified this communication as follows:

Writing	9%
Reading	16%
Speaking	30%
Listening	45%

How well did our educational system prepare you for a job involving communication? Some parts of a twelve-year education were designed to teach reading and writing. These two combined represent only 25 percent of your communication job in business. You may have had one course in speech. Most schools have no courses in listening, but listening is involved in almost half of our communication time.

It's not surprising, therefore, that we don't listen as well as we should; we haven't had much listening training.

How good a listener are you? When asked that question, many of us rate ourselves as "average" or "below average" listeners. How much does the "average" listener retain of what he or she hears? Tests conducted at the University of Minnesota showed that immediately after hearing a 10-minute reading, the average listener retained 50 percent of the material read. Several days later the retention rate dropped to 25 to 30 percent. If we are, in fact, "average" listeners, we are retaining only 25 to 30 percent of the oral communications directed our way. We can do a lot to improve our listening, but we must work hard to do so.

Some of us are inclined to feel, "I may not listen well all the time, but when something really important is being said, I can *will* myself to listen better." It does not happen this way. It is when the average listener *wills* himself to listen, that he or she functions at the 25 to 30 percent level.

The cost of not listening

It would be difficult to estimate accurately how many accidents have been caused by poor listening. It is possible that the worker was not listening well when the supervisor discussed the hazards of a job and how to avoid them. Or perhaps the supervisor did not take the time to listen to what the worker mentioned as a problem the last time the job had run. The fact is that a better understanding of the problem on the part of supervisors and employees can reduce accident potential.

In addition to accidents, consider the costs of rework or scrap results from poor listening. Think of the costs of retyped letters, poor customer relations, and perhaps even the loss of business that could be traced to poor listening. When we consider the costs that occur when people do *not* listen, we can begin to appreciate the importance of improving listening skills.

Authorities say that we can double our listening ability, but that it will not occur overnight. If a non-runner began preparing for a 101 mile race, it would take a lot of practice to result in even gradual improvement toward achieving the goal. Similarly, we can find ways to improve our listening skills, but it will take time and diligent effort.

Barriers to effective listening

There are many factors that keep us from listening as well as we should. By looking at several of them, we may be able to determine some ways to improve in this important area. The barriers fall into two areas— word and emotional barriers.

Word barriers. Hearing certain words can shut off our ability to concentrate on what else is being said. People have different "turn-off" words or phrases. When one of these is spoken, the listener stops paying attention to what is being said and focuses on what the "turn-off" word brings to mind. For example, the word "death" is a turn off word for some people because it may remind them of a family tragedy that was emotionally disturbing. When that turn-off word is heard, the listener may stop listening for 15 seconds to 15 minutes. For some people, turn-off words are: lay-off, panic, mother-in-law, grievance, abortion, and pervert (Figure 2-4).

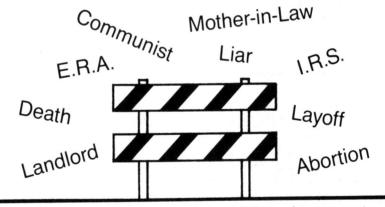

Figure 2-4. "Turn-off" words or phrases can stop the listener from concentrating on what else is being said for the next 15 seconds or even 15 minutes, during which time they recall the memories that the word brought forth.

What words turn off your listening? To improve your listening ability, you must discover your turn-off words, realize why these words "turn you off," and work to overcome the problem. When you hear one, concentrate on what else the speaker is saying to keep your mind from wandering to the thoughts that the turn-off words evoke. You are the only one who can reduce the effects of turn-off words on your listening ability.

Emotional barriers. The listener's emotions can also block listening. Anger is a good example. When a person becomes angry, he or she concentrates on the source of the anger, rather than on what is being said. People think of things to say that support their argument and often prepare questions to "trip-up" the person at whom the anger is directed. They may try to embarrass that person in front of others and during that time they are not listening to what is being said.

Anger is just one emotion that can be a barrier to listening. Others include prejudice, fear, suspicion, jealousy, over-enthusiasm, and distrust (Figure 2-5). Any one of these responses can keep us from listening to what is being said. To improve our listening we must overcome our emotional reactions. We must control our emotions and concentrate on what is being said, even though we may be angry at the speaker or suspicious of his motives. Keeping emotions under control can do a lot to improve listening skills.

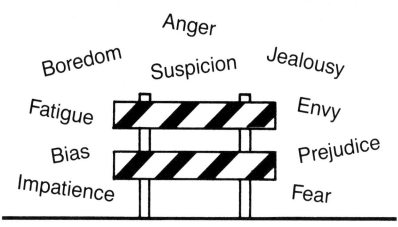

Figure 2-5. Emotional barriers, too, can block listening. We must keep our emotions under control if we are to get as much as possible from hearing someone speak who triggers these emotions.

Consider how emotions affect your listening during conversations with your people, your spouse, your union steward, and others.

Heated Discussion Rule

A good tool to use in situations in which anger may cloud your listening is the "Heated Discussion Rule." Of course, participants must agree to the provisions in advance. If the speaker in a meeting makes a

Figure 2-6. Finger-pointing is not the same as constructive criticism. If your criticism is built on a quiet, direct helpfulness that has a purpose to prevent error, correct mistakes, and build up confidence in all employees and their ability to do a job, then you are a supervisor.

From NSC *Petroleum Newsletter*

statement with which we disagree, we signal that we wish to speak. When the other person has completed his statements, he turns the discussion over to us. We may then make our statements, *provided* that we can first state the speaker's position and tell why he feels as he does about the matter. If the speaker agrees with our statement of his position, we may continue. This process *forces* us to listen in order to have a turn to speak.

When a heated discussion occurs (Figure 2-6), the points of disagreement often are not as serious as the "combatants" believe them to be. If each person would listen carefully to the other, he or she may find there is little difference in their positions. When responding in a sensitive situation, it is wise to begin by stating the other person's position. A good way to start is, "As I understand what you have said, you feel this way about the matter." Frequently we will find that our's and the other person's viewpoints are not so different. By listening to his or her supporting comments, rather than thinking of a rebuttal, we can do a lot to improve understanding.

Distractions

Another reason for failure to listen is that we allow distractions to disrupt our thoughts. External noises, such as machines or equipment operating, can affect our listening and other interruptions can derail our train of thought. Many times a personal problem can be a distraction, and interfere with listening. There are many possibilities for distractions, but we must overcome them so that we can listen attentively. We must keep these facts in mind when setting up communications with our people and try to keep distractions to a minimum,

There is a substantial difference between the rate at which people speak and the rate at which they listen. Most people speak at a rate of approximately 125 to 150 words per minute. Listening occurs at rates in excess of 600 to 700 words per minute. For some people that time differential interferes with good listening. Time is wasted because people think of other topics to bring up or they let their minds wander, occasionally returning to find where the speaker is. Consequently, only 25 to 30 percent of what was said is heard and remembered.

Improve your listening

On the other hand, the good listener thinks along with the speaker, mentally outlining his points and evaluating his credibility. The good listener will use the time differential to analyze the nonverbal messages being sent by the speaker to confirm that the two kinds of messages agree.

You can do a lot to improve your listening skills by making the maximum use of this time differential. It can enable you to improve your understanding of communications. The key to good communications is *achieving understanding.* Here are five general rules to improve your listening:

1. *Stop talking.* You can't listen while you are talking. In two-way communications, when you are the listener, stop talking so that you can listen to all that is being said.

2. *Empathize.* When you put yourself in the other person's place, you can get a better understanding of why he or she feels a certain way. Remember, understanding is the key to successful communications.

3. *Maintain eye contact.* This serves a dual purpose. First, it helps you to concentrate on what is being said and additionally it shows the speaker that you are listening.

4. *Share responsibility for communication.* The "receiver" is just as responsible as the "sender" for seeing that communication occurs.

5. *Get clarification.* When listening, if you do not understand any part of the communication, be sure to ask questions until you do.

SUMMARY

Good communication is essential for accident prevention. How well you "send," oral and written communications, and how well you "receive," by listening and reading, will determine your success.

Two-way, face-to-face communication is the best way to provide the understanding that is needed for strong communication to occur. Always think of the other person when engaging in any form of communication. Putting yourself in the other person's place will aid in getting the message across. Use written communication whenever the subject is technical, and/or if a listing or record is desirable.

In supervisory work, listening is a keystone to communication. Listening takes up about 45 percent of our communication time. We can all improve our listening skills—the average listener retains only 30 percent of what is said. Working to improve our listening abilities can result in our doubling those skills. To do so, we must overcome our word and emotional barriers, eliminate distractions, practice empathy, and share the responsibility for communications.

Chapter 3

Human Relations

A n examination of recent literature reveals that this is, indeed, an era of high technology. In some of the literature, this shift is referred to as the high-tech/high-touch era. What is abundantly clear is that high technology has an adverse impact on human relationships.

HUMAN RELATIONS CONCEPTS

Human relations concepts have not changed much over the years, so they are just as effective in today's high-tech society as they were back in the 1930s. What has changed drastically is the general lack of human interaction. The supervisor in the workplace is in an ideal position to promote and implement contacts between and among those people being supervised.

Background of motivation

Between 1924 and 1932, Elton Mayo, a clinical psychologist working at Harvard University Business School, conducted a series of experiments, carried out in the wiring rooms of Western Electric's Hawthorne Plant, located just west of Chicago. The research constitutes a landmark study. To determine whether there was any correlation between the amount of illumination in a workplace and productivity, Mayo turned up the lights. Production went up. When the lights were turned down, production went up again. Mayo conducted a second series of experiments varying the temperature, the length of rest periods, humidity, and other factors. No matter what was changed, productivity invariably went up. His conclusion: attention to employees, not work conditions, was the dominant influence on productivity. The result of these experiments is referred to as the Hawthorne effect and has established a base for a num-

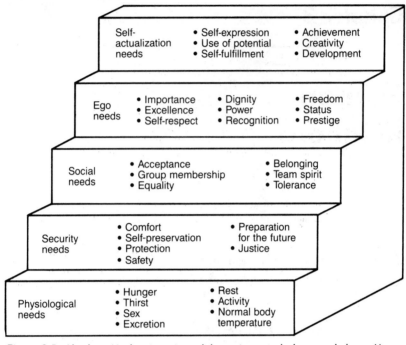

Figure 3-1. Abraham Maslow investigated the various needs that people have. He arranged them in his hierarchy, which groups tissue needs at the base and more intellectually satisfying needs near the top.

ber of studies in industrial social psychology. One of these, by Abraham Maslow, established that there is a hierarchy of needs among people (see Figure 3-1). At the base are physiological needs, including food, clothing, and shelter, often referred to as the tissue needs. In this society, adequate wages satisfy most basic needs, leaving the others to be met in different ways. That is why so much emphasis is placed on human relations as motivating factors in organization. Many of the tissue needs of employees can be satisfied in the work environment. There are a number of well-documented practices and procedures that are widely used to motivate employees toward increased production, greater job satisfaction, and less frustration. One does not have to be a psychologist to implement these practices, but just have a sincere desire to help.

Get out of the office

In studies done to determine what basic practices tend to make a company successful, it was found that the best companies implemented a network of informal, open communications. The first step for supervi-

Figure 3-2. Spend some time every day just listening to your employees. Moving about lets your people know that you are approachable and interested in them as individuals.

sors in establishing informal communications is to get out of the office. Institute an open-door policy. In some organizations, doors are not even permitted, since they are considered barriers to informal communications. Learn to be a good listener. Spend some time each day just listening to employees. Find out about their interests, their goals, and ambitions. Getting out of the office is an important first step in establishing a good base for human relations in any organization. Moving about lets your people know that you are approachable and interested in them as individuals. (See Figure 3-2.)

Let people know their work has value . . .

People want to know that their jobs have value—that their work is essential. People want jobs that provide opportunities for personal satisfaction and growth. Employees are more likely to have that feeling if they know where their job fits into the total pattern of the company. The job is often so small a part of the whole production that it is hard for workers to see where they fit in.

Supervisors can help by explaining the company's overall objectives and by showing people why their jobs are valuable to the company. The vital role that safety plays in the entire production picture must also be emphasized.

A supervisor might think that employees would realize that they would not be doing work unless it *had* value. But this is not always true. When people do the same thing over and over again—especially when a task does not produce a complete product—they can only keep a sense of the importance of the job when they have a clear idea of the final product of which their work is a part.

An individual usually feels a sense of accomplishment just by learning a job; but after years of doing the same thing, this feeling needs to be reinforced. People develop feelings that their efforts are swallowed up in the vast quantities of similar work turned out by others. In other words, their jobs lack meaning. As a supervisor, you can help these individuals by having friendly discussions centered around working conditions, growth possibilities, or the work itself.

. . . and that their work is appreciated

People want to know that their efforts are appreciated. To belittle a person's work is to belittle the person. Praise good work. The supervisor should give credit when it is due—but with caution. Giving a worker a slap on the back and saying, "Well done!" only means something if it is done sincerely, and not mechanically. Praise must also be given only for good work. Praise for work that the employee knows is poor will not only make the supervisor look foolish, but will also reduce the value of future praise, even when it is justified.

A beginner's work might not be up to the quality standards of an old timer, but beginners should be encouraged. Tell them that they are making progress (providing they are). You should give further instruction to help them attain acceptable work.

Although experienced workers generally know when work is good, they will be pleased, even so, to know that the boss knows it, too. Perhaps the best general rule is for supervisors to maintain a positive interest in the workers of their department. If you take such an interest, you will know what job each worker does, praise those who do well, and encourage those who are still learning or do not do quite as well as they should.

Praising workers for following safety practices will help to impress upon them how important you consider safety to be, as well as to encourage them to continue to do the job safely.

If people know their supervisor is not just looking for faults, but also will give them credit for good work, they will, in turn, have a better attitude toward their work. Workers are not likely to try to do more than the absolute minimum if they feel that what they do is not appreciated or recognized.

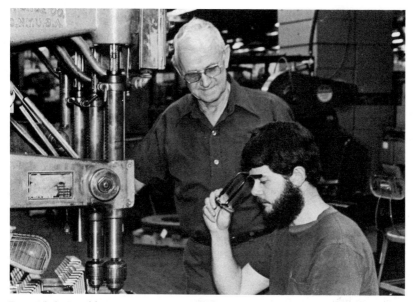

Figure 3-3. In addition to training your people in proper procedures and in using the right protective equipment, follow up to make sure that it is followed. The ultimate responsibility for safe, efficient operation is the supervisor's.

As a supervisor, you well know your own reactions when you are roughly handled by *your* supervisor. Often it makes little difference whether it is a decision, or general competence, that is questioned. Justified or not, criticism is a threat to one's self-respect. And, of course, a worker feels the same way.

The supervisor who attempts to maintain standards by using a "meet-them-or-else" attitude is more than likely to find people busily looking for ways to get around those standards. Explanations and encouragement, however, have been found to be more effective than laying down the law and demanding conformity, which usually meets with passive resistance.

Safety and security

People want to know what they are expected to do, also how to do their jobs safely and efficiently.

Supervisors are responsible, therefore, for seeing that their workers are thoroughly trained. This is essential to safe, efficient work, and contributes to the individual's feeling of security. Whether you do the training yourself or assign another to do it, the ultimate responsibility is yours. (See Figure 3-3.)

Injuries, work spoilage, and misused or broken equipment are almost certain to result when workers have been inadequately trained. Such casualties and production delays reflect on the individual, supervisor, and department—and reduce the security of all.

Workers who have had poor training and feel as though they have never mastered the job will continually be uncertain and hesitant. They may develop a sense of defeat and become uninterested in the job. This leads to dissatisfaction and poor work.

Training should include how to avoid getting hurt. Workers should know that the company wants to protect them against injury. They should know what they can do for their own protection. Accident prevention should be part of every worker's training. Special emphasis on safety is desirable because it creates an interest in safe practices for their own sake and helps satisfy the need for security.

Let people know they belong

People want to belong to their work group. That's why successful supervisors will do their best to create and maintain a feeling of group solidarity and friendliness. Watch for opportunities to talk with your group, and in talking to them, arouse group interest. Using words such as "we," "our department," and "our safety record" encourages group interest and a team spirit.

The supervisor, when seeing that people are left out or excluded from the group, can look for chances to include them. A small clique that excludes other members of the work group is harmful. The best way to combat this is to give all members the feeling of satisfaction that they belong to the larger group. The group feeling promotes good performance and safe practices.

Once the group accepts them, members discipline one another. Often, the group standards are higher than the standards of the individuals by themselves. The supervisor can appeal to people's pride in their safety record and in consistently following safe practices. One thing supervisors should *not* do, if they want to preserve a healthly group feeling, is to tell people, "You have got to . . ." or "Now listen, I want you to . . ." Supervisors, too, need to be accepted members of the group.

The supervisor must appeal to the self-interest of the group. When you appeal to each member to follow a line of action or a pattern of conduct, you must make sure that such action or conduct is for the member's and the group's own good.

Most people do not want to stand out as exceptions. They want to be liked by others so they try to think and act as others do. Individuals usually conform because of peer pressure.

This does not mean that individuals don't ever want to be considered as exceptional—to be singled out as having an unusual ability. A man may be proud of his brute strength, or a woman of her ability to produce more than anyone else in the department, and he or she may want others to recognize this. But even these workers will generally exercise their special talents only within limits allowed by their group.

People who consistently try to prove their abilities, however, probably do so because they feel they are not full members of the group. Some may consider lack of acceptance to be a real handicap. Others find this less important. By and large, though, people need to be part of the group. This desire can affect their actions.

The supervisor uses this desire for peer approval when training the new workers. If the group works safely and efficiently, the new member will be likely to work this way too. The fact that the new person wants to be a member of the group will be a powerful incentive to work safely and efficiently.

LEADERSHIP

Since the Hawthorne studies were made, a number of management leadership studies have been conducted. One of these, by Douglas McGregor (see "Useful References"), created the Theory X and Y concepts. Theory X assumes the average human has an inherent dislike of work and will avoid it if at all possible. People must, therefore, be controlled, directed, and/or threatened with punishment to get them to put forward effort to meet the goals of the organization.

In McGregor's Theory Y concept, the assumption is made that people do not inherently dislike work and threats of punishment are not the only means of getting people to work toward organizational goals. Such people learn not only to accept responsibility, but to seek it. Satisfaction results from reaching one's goals.

Leadership is complex. It is impossible to recommend a particular style. What works for a supervisor in one organization may be disastrous if applied in another. People are different; they do not seek the same goals and behave in different ways to achieve their goals. Consequently, good leadership depends, to a large degree, upon knowing the individual(s), the group, and the situation.

Leadership styles

Following are some leadership styles that are in vogue today. Some of these may be useful, depending upon perception of the problem. If you don't have a problem, count your blessings. There is no need to change styles.

Autocratic. A leader following McGregor's Theory X concept, whereby people are closely controlled and directed, is autocratic. Such leaders identify the problems, the objectives, and determine the course of action leaving subordinates with few opportunities to participate in the decision-making process. In some cases, such a leader may even use threats.

Benevolent/Autocratic. Such a leader will identify problems, set objectives, and make plans for subordinates. In some cases, this leader may ask for input that may or may not be followed. The flow of information is mostly downward and provides for rather limited freedom of subordinates.

Consultive. A consultive leader presents ideas, invites questions from subordinates, and considers their input. This style provides for a moderate number of opportunities for subordinates to participate by identifying problems and offering suggestions for solutions to such problems. A leader of this type considers alternative courses of action.

Participative. A leader following this style allows subordinates a great deal of freedom in the identification of problems and in suggesting solutions. The leader and the subordinates jointly set objectives, develop plans, and evaluate alternative courses of action. This style allows for a free flow of information.

Democratic. A supervisor following this leadership style would also be following McGregor's Theory Y concept. A democratic leader uses less authority and gives more freedom than the participative leader. A leader of this type aims to get the consensus of the group and may allow the group to override the leader's decision.

Free Rein — Permissive. A leader following this style may make few decisions, leaving this to subordinates. Such a leader makes no systematic effort to set objectives. Subordinates may do as they wish. In this type of leadership, the leader exercises little control and does not hold subordinates accountable for results.

Leadership qualities

Existing literature on leadership reveals that there are certain qualities expected of leaders in a work environment. (See Figure 3-4.) The following qualities appear *most often:*

1. Recognize and acknowledge that many of the ideas you use come from the people in your group. In this connection, many studies

Figure 3-4. The qualities of a leader are not strained. Twelve qualities that are most often expected are described in the text.

show that leaders do not originate all of the plans; in fact, with many good leaders, the majority of the ideas originate in the group. It is a common failure of new leaders to feel that they lose face if they accept suggestions from subordinates. On the other hand, experienced leaders know the value of having the group members feel that they are participating and that goals reflect their own ideas and contributions.

2. Show respect for employees, both as individuals and as a group. You should be sensitive to, and understand their needs.

3. The group wants a leader who will support, guide, train, and counsel.

4. As a leader you should be satisfied with the knowledge that you are right. Consequently, you should not feel that you have to prove that others are wrong.

5. Act as a buffer between employees and higher management by not passing on the pressures to those who work for you. This includes taking personal responsibility for the directions and orders you are required to give, even when they are not what you, personally, would like to do or would have chosen. You should never say, "The front office says we have to do this," because it gives others the feeling that you are shirking your responsibility.

6. Leave your personal problems and feelings out of your relationships with the group and its members by trying to maintain a calm, understanding approach at all times. A lack of emotional balance stirs up tension and stress in the group, particularly when you are grumpy, ir-

ritable, and irascible one day and pleasant, sensitive, and good humored the next.

7. Try to be fair at all times and play no favorites—always in keeping with good leadership.

8. Live up to what you say by setting the right example. The old cliché, "Don't do what I do; do what I say," does not work in on-the-job human relations.

9. Be available and understanding when people come in for help. Avoid the impression that you don't have time to help or to listen to problems. (When a supervisor is really under pressure and just can't take time at the moment, it is appropriate to say that and tell people you will be with them as soon as you can, providing that you actually live up to this promise.)

10. Although it is important for you to be accepted as one of the group, it is just as important not to go so far that your status as a leader is destroyed. Unfortunately, some leaders have tried so hard to belong, particularly in off-the-job get-togethers, that they have crossed that indefinable (but very real) line that separates leaders from those they lead. People realize that this line exists and that it has to be maintained; when it is not, status as a leader is destroyed.

11. The job climate must be such that there is a minimum of conflict and confusion which would generate fear and anxiety in group members with resultant inefficiency in operations.

12. You are a good one-on-one, face-to-face communicator. Good leadership and communication skills are strongly related. Being a good leader and able to supply the emotional, mental, and physical needs of those dependent on you is humanity at its finest.

Leadership effectiveness

Measure your effectiveness as a leader by how well you are meeting the goals and objectives of the organization. If you are satisfied, and the organization is satisfied with the performance of the other employees, there is no problem. If, however, what you are getting is not what you or the organization wants, there is a problem. Some specific areas to review for determining if the performance level meets organizational norms and standards are the following:

- Number of accidents
- Cost of accidents
- Cost of production
- Quality of production

- Quantity of production
- Absenteeism
- Employee turnover.

If you decide that you have a problem in any of the above areas, be advised that the problem will not go away and cannot be ignored. Supervisors have to decide on how to solve the problem. One solution might be to change your leadership style. Perhaps you need a more autocratic style to get results, or perhaps you have been too autocratic. In any event, supervisors have to make the decision, since they are in the best position to know the work environment, the situational factors involved, and the attitude of the people.

Preparing the worker for changes

With so many technological advances, many jobs change in character, and in some cases, drastically. Old jobs are abolished and new jobs are created. People should always be warned about job changes, as well as policy or organizational changes. If people are not informed until after the changes are made, they have no time to adjust. Change threatens employees' feelings of security. Supervisors should explain the reasons for changes and how decisions were reached. Not only do jobs change, but so do employees' work habits and feelings about jobs.

Change usually requires something new. Old skills may no longer be needed. This can lead to frustration; it may also make people feel unimportant and unwanted. When new skills are required, workers should be given an ample opportunity to learn them, providing that they have the capabilities.

People, in general, resist change. Providing advance knowledge of job changes helps to lessen resistance. Letting workers participate, whenever possible, in the decision leading up to the change will be even more effective. Participation makes people feel more important and increases their sense of security.

WORKERS WITH SPECIAL PROBLEMS

Most adults are reasonable and perform their jobs in a satisfactory manner. Job interviewing and screening helps place individuals in the proper work slot. In some instances, one may find a person who does not respond well to any of the usual motivation techniques. Such a person may show antisocial behavior and interrupt the work group. Another person may exhibit extreme anger or fear in commonplace situations. These people should be referred to the personnel department for help. It is the supervisor's job to know effective methods of motivating and dealing with normal people, but not with the mentally or emotionally disturbed.

To encourage individuals to improve their work, supervisors must have a good personal relationship with them. Although you must know a lot about people if you are to supervise them competently, it is not your responsibility to try to straighten out their private affairs or personality problems. Attempts to do this could cause more harm than good.

Temporary problems

In many cases, people are confronted with money or marital problems. These and other crises make them temporarily inattentive. Supervisors who know their people well can detect when a person is not acting normally. If supervisors are friendly and approachable, workers will, in many cases, say that they are not able to perform certain exacting or hazardous work for that day. Physical work, if not hazardous, is often just what a person needs to temporarily escape some personal problem. Such a reprieve will often allow the person to find a solution to the problem. Fortunately, much undesirable behavior is temporary. Behavior will vary from day to day, so supervisors should vary their approach so that workers have some leeway within the limits of doing safe, efficient work.

Talking reduces strong emotions

Although no one expects supervisors to become personnel counselors, supervisors can help to reduce strong emotions. Supervisors are in the best position to evaluate the emotional level of an individual worker and to do something about it.

Everyone is familiar with the emotional outbursts of people who have had a trying and upsetting experience. Such expressions of emotion may take many forms, from an outburst of invective or a torrent of tears to physical assault on inanimate objects. The end result is the same— relief from the intolerable tension, and emotional relaxation.

To reduce the intensity of such emotional responses, supervisors can engage in permissive listening, that is, giving employees an opportunity to talk about their problems. The freedom to say what the individual wants can reduce tension that might lead to distraction and accidents. It is important that supervisors not attempt to evaluate or judge an employee's remarks. An emotionally upset employee needs an opportunity to "blow off steam" without retaliation or evaluation.

The stresses that cause emotional upsets can occur within the work environment or away from it, but each kind has an effect on the other. A simple question such as "How are you today?" may well be sufficient to set off the verbalization of pent-up emotion. After the discussion, employees can often evaluate more clearly and realistically the things that upset them in the first place. This sensitive relationship between the supervisor and the worker is one of the supervisor's everyday functions. Diligent observation and effective and sensitive listening are the tools required.

The 'accident-prone' individual

Probably no phrase in accident prevention causes as much disagreement as the meaning of "accident proneness." Most definitions hinge upon the idea that an individual with certain personality traits is more likely than others to have accidents. When a person is said to be "accident prone," it generally means that some psychological characteristic he or she has predisposes that person toward having accidents.

Too often the term is loosely applied to anyone who has more accidents than others who do the same type of work. A person could, however, have more than his or her share of accidents because that person was never properly trained, or because of the need for new glasses, or because of working in cramped quarters, or for other reasons.

It is true that a small group of people often account for more than their expected share of accidents during a given period, but over a long period, the composition of the group changes—the accident repeaters of one period don't usually show up during the next time.

Unless it can be proven that accident repeaters have certain characteristics consistently linked to accidents, it is impossible to tell who is accident prone. It would be wonderful if such identification could be made, but at this time it is impossible.

THE ALCOHOL AND DRUG PROBLEM

The consequences of alcoholism and drug abuse to industry are realized in such hidden costs as lowered productivity, increased absenteeism, inefficiency, increased employee turnover, increased injury rates, and incidents arising from behavioral problems.

It is generally accepted that alcoholism and drug abuse adversely affect employee job performance and interfere with efficient company operations. Employees with these problems usually have increased absences from work and frequently engage in unsafe work practices. Their conduct at work can be disruptive and demoralizing to others, and can lead to excessive turnover.

Many companies believe that employees with alcohol or drug problems require professional assistance. Early recognition of these conditions and other emotional or behavioral problems by the employee's

Figure 3-5. The alcoholic can be crafty. If his secret bottle is removed, he may replace it with a medicine bottle—full of booze.

supervisor is essential to an effective program of evaluation, treatment, and rehabilitation. Concern with alcoholism and drug abuse is a basic management responsibility.

The employee's immediate supervisor is the first member of management most likely to observe unusual employee behavior, especially the possibility of alcoholism or drug abuse. (See Figure 3-5.)

Supervisors are expected, as part of their daily contacts with employees, to be familiar with their appearance, behavior, and work patterns, and to be alert for any changes. These could result from causes other than drug abuse—illness, properly prescribed drugs used as prescribed, and fatigue, to name a few.

Because behavioral problems may take many forms that are not necessarily clear-cut nor readily identifiable, recognition requires thoughtful observation and avoidance of hasty conclusions. Behavioral manifestations may or may not reflect a physical or an emotional difficulty with alcohol or drugs.

It is neither possible nor desirable for you to determine whether the changes you have observed are the result of emotional illness, physical illness, alcoholism, or drug abuse. As a supervisor, you are not expected to make a diagnosis; that is the responsibility of the medical department. Supervisors should be able to recognize gross changes in an employee's behavior that might indicate a problem for which help is needed.

Immediately noticeable extremes in behavior of a new employee may suggest to you that the individual has a problem that should receive medical attention or be brought to the attention of security personnel. With respect to employees who have been on the job for some time, however, marked changes in behavior and job performance are the key signals. Changes in the employee's appearance and certain physical manifestations may also be significant. Symptoms may arise suddenly or gradually, may be episodic or continuous.

Interaction of alcohol and drugs

Studies indicate that at any one time, from 10 to 20 percent of the population is taking prescription medication. Add to this the percentage of people using drugs illegally, and it becomes obvious that a substantial portion of our working population is exposed to the effects of drugs.

The combination of alcohol and drugs can produce a variety of effects that can severely impair a worker's judgment. Concentrations of alcohol and drugs remain in the bloodstream much longer than most users realize, and the effects may rise unexpectedly. Little scientific study has been conducted on the interaction of alcohol and drugs, but there is sufficient evidence to conclude that such a combination can lead to increased impairment of judgment and skill.

Alcohol and drugs on the job

In our society, some people have grown accustomed to the practice of having a cocktail, a bottle of beer, or some other alcoholic beverage at lunch. These individuals believe that a drink or two with lunch will not affect them. There may be no actual drinking *on* the job, but the effect of alcohol does not end with the meal.

Some individuals enjoy drinking, just as others enjoy eating, and no matter how often you speak about the hazardous effects of alcohol, the person who enjoys drinking will continue to do so. If you are a supervisor, it is your duty to make sure that workers reserve their drinking for off-duty hours. Also make sure that the effects of off-duty drinking do not accompany your employees on the job in the form of a hangover. Remember that a hangover may also impair working and driving.

One medical executive said that, unlike alcoholism, drug addiction is not amenable to ambulatory treatment. Whereas some companies report 60 to 75 percent success rate with alcoholic employees, rehabilitation of a drug addict is fraught with a high rate of relapse.

Countermeasures

Alcoholism and the sale and use of drugs by employees may not be problems in your company at this time, but will you be prepared to cope with these problems if and when they arise?

Alcohol. There is often a small group of heavy or problem drinkers most tempted to drink during working hours. Even if you are fortunate enough to have no workers who drink, remember that the problem drinker can still bring a hangover to work. Some studies also indicate that employees who are alcoholics have more accidents than non-drinkers. Countermeasures for dealing with alcoholism begin with education. Information on alcoholism and the effects of alcohol is readily available. Write for detailed information on alcoholism programs:

Alcohol and Drug Problems Association of North America (ADPA)
1101 15th St. N.W.
Washington, D.C. 20005

Supervisors should read as much information as possible in order to be familiar with alcoholism and its effects. One good way to inform your people about alcoholism and the problems it can create is through the five-minute safety talk. Drinking and driving can be discussed during the next safety meeting.

The next step in an alcohol program is the identification of problem drinkers under your supervision. Everyone is familiar with the drunk and can recognize the obvious signs of intoxication. Individuals who have been drinking on the job will probably give themselves away through unsteady actions, or by the noticeable odors. However, you should also watch for the apparently sober person with the continuous hangover, which may indicate a serious drinking problem.

Having identified a problem drinker, supervisors should examine the ways in which they can be helped. One way is counseling by people trained to deal with alcoholism. Check your community organizations, churches, and Alcoholics Anonymous for information on programs to assist alcoholics. (Telephone directories of many cities and towns list a number to call for information about meetings and about the program.)

Above all, supervisors must show the alcoholic that they care and have a true desire to help. Simply telling the alcoholic not to drink is like telling someone who enjoys eating not to eat. An admonition not to drink is not the solution. Alcoholism is an illness and must be handled by persons trained to deal with it. The alcoholic needs help.

Drugs. The current increase in the use of drugs is not confined to the younger segment of the population. The individual who often takes an overdose of aspirin or sedatives could, at times, be as much a problem as a heroin or cocaine addict.

One large company seriously considered the problem of employee drug abuse and designed a policy to cope with it. Having had a high rate of success in dealing with alcoholism, this company modified and updated its safety policy to include what it called "drug dependence." The drug abuse policy is as follows:

> In accordance with our general personnel policies, whose underlying concept is regard for the employee as an individual as well as a worker, we believe that:
>
> • Drug dependency is an illness and should be treated as such.
>
> • The majority of employees who develop a dependency on drugs can be helped to recover, and the company should offer appropriate assistance.
>
> • The decision to seek diagnosis and accept treatment for any suspected illness is the responsibility of the employee. However, continued refusal of an employee to seek treatment when it appears that substandard performance may be caused by an illness is not tolerated. Drug dependency should not be made an exception to this commonly accepted principle.
>
> • It is in the best interests of employees that, when drug dependency is present, it should be diagnosed as such and treated at the earliest possible stage.
>
> • Confidential handling of the diagnosis and treatment of drug dependence is essential.
>
> The objective of this policy is to retain employees who may have developed drug dependence by helping them to arrest its further advance before it renders them unemployable.

Identifying employees with drug problems is much easier if a company takes a positive approach. Since drug dependencies cause marked changes in work behavior patterns, personal relations, and emotional moods, supervisors should be alert for these changes in any employee. When an employee is suspected of drug usage or dependency, the supervisor should seek the assistance of the company staff or a community agency that deals with the problem and cure of drug dependency.

Your company must first establish a written policy, as did the company described above, when planning countermeasures to deal with drug abuse. This policy must be carefully prepared and made known to all employees in the same manner as company safety policy.

The next step is to locate community or area organizations that offer counseling to persons with drug dependency. Familiarize yourself with the types of drugs that can lead to dependencies and the effects these drugs may produce. There is a vast quantity of material available.

However, supervisors should not become drug detectives, constantly looking for pills and drug substances. Instead, they should watch for changes in the work behavior patterns, personal relationships, and emotional moods of their workers. Any of these changes in an employee may indicate an alcohol or drug problem.

Employee-assistance programs are being implemented by enlightened management to help employees with alcohol and other behavioral problems that interfere with job performance. Programs of this type enable a company to retain valued employees.

Such programs can assist the supervisor who feels an employee has a problem of this nature. For more detailed information on programs, contact:

Alcoholics Anonymous World Services
Grand Central Station, P.O. Box 459
New York, N.Y. 10163

National Institute on Drug Abuse
5600 Fishers Lane
Rockville, Md. 20857

SUMMARY

People have needs over and above those that money can satisfy. These needs should be met on the job, insofar as is possible, if employees are expected to work safely and efficiently. Everyone wants to feel that their work has value and that when performed well, is appreciated sincerely. Everyone also wants a sense of job security. Adequate wages and some permanence are basic to the feeling, but there are other factors too—factors over which the supervisor has a great deal of control.

People should know what to expect from you and what your reactions will be. They need to know that you do not play favorites and are fair.

Finally, a person needs to be part of the work group. A supervisor can help this group become a cooperating unit in which each member has a place. New members will be more readily accepted because old members will not see them as potential threats.

Above all, develop a sincere interest in and desire to help the employee with an alcohol and/or drug problem. Once you have developed these attitudes, you will want to help your employee solve this particular problem and again become a valuable asset to your organization.

All the answers cannot be given in one short chapter. In fact, no one could answer them all, especially when it comes to what a supervisor must say and do in every situation. But the supervisor who gains an understanding of those he or she supervises will become more skilled in handling all problems as they arise. Production will improve; accidents will decrease.

Chapter 4

Employee Involvement
In Safety

L oss control is management's responsibility. Top management formu-
lates policy. The supervisor interprets it and puts it into action for
the workers. The supervisor is responsible for carrying out management
policies in every way—and to the line worker the supervisor *is* the company. This was discussed in Chapter 1.

Supervisors constantly strive to develop good attitudes in their staff.
As a supervisor, you should train them in safe and healthful work practices. You should also try to convince them that management is sincerely
interested in safety. You must repeatedly emphasize that you *expect* safe
conduct. (See Figure 4-1.)

These approaches can represent problems in communications—in
getting through to people. Communication means much more than tack-
ing up posters, passing out rule books, and talking about safety and
health, as we read in Chapter 2. Success in safety and health depends on
the attitudes of both supervisor and employee and the dedication of top
management.

HOW TO PROMOTE SAFE WORKER ATTITUDES

The supervisor needs to use techniques that stimulate interest so that
safe work practices are encouraged. Some of these are described below.

Employee committees

One of the best ways to create and maintain interest is to get employees involved in running a safety committee.

An employee committee gives employees an opportunity to make a
personal contribution to the overall safety program. The committee must
be given time to do its work and should receive acknowledgement for

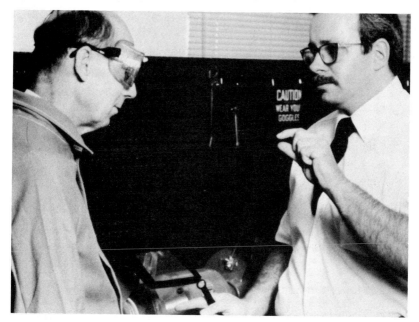

Figure 4-1. A supervisor's most important contribution is to effectively train and motivate his or her employees so they work safely.

successful efforts. The committee's duties should be spelled out in writing.

Certain fundamental principles contribute to the success of an employee safety committee. Here are some of them:

1. A need must exist within the department, to which the employee safety committee can make a contribution.

2. Although the supervisor delegates various functions to the committee, the responsibility for departmental safety belongs to the supervisor.

3. To carry out its assignments (inspecting, observing practices, investigating, and making recommendations) the committee must be given proper instructions, goals, and target dates.

4. Supervisors must communicate with other members of the department. The committee must not be used as a buffer.

5. All committee recommendations should receive careful consideration. Worthwhile recommendations should be implemented. When

the decision to adopt a recommendation is beyond the authority of the supervisor, it should be transmitted to a higher authority. If the final decision is negative, an explanation should be made to the committee.

6. The committee agenda should be limited to safety matters. The committee should not become involved in personnel actions or labor relations or in other matters not related to accident prevention.

7. Committee membership may be rotated so that over a period of time, all will have an opportunity to serve.

8. Written minutes of all meetings should be kept.

9. Meetings should be held regularly and attendance should be required.

The conventional order of business for a safety committee meeting is the following:

a. Record of attendance.

b. Approval of previous minutes.

c. Consideration of unfinished business.

d. Review of recent accidents, including near misses.

e. Reports on special assignments.

f. Reports of inspections.

g. Progress report on safety program.

h. Special features, such as a film, a talk or a demonstration by a specialist, slides or similar item.

i. Presentation of new business.

A top management representative should occasionally be invited to a meeting. This person can provide the front office point of view or explain new plans or policies. A summary of meeting content should be sent to management. Supervisors should make serving on a safety committee interesting, productive, and rewarding.

Safety posters

Safety posters alert people to safe practices. Supervisors should make use of posters and take responsibility for their selection, location, and maintenance.

Poster locations should be selected carefully. They should be dis-

Figure 4-2. Posters should be mounted near eye level; background should be uncluttered. At the left is a special hazard poster advocating use of special clothing; at right, a seasonal poster.

played in a prominent location that will not interfere with traffic, yet provide high visibility. They should be centered at eye level, about 63 in. (1.6 m) from the floor. They should be in well-lighted areas or mounted with their own light, if possible. (Never use a flashing light in a production area.) A good size for the poster board is 22 in. wide by 30 in. long (56 by 76 cm), or it may be smaller, just big enough to hold one poster. Standard National Safety Council posters are available in two sizes: "A" size—8½ by 11 in. (22 by 28 cm) and "B" size—17 by 23 in. (43 by 58 cm). Poster boards or frames should be attractively painted and covered with glass. One board is usually desirable in a workplace. In washrooms, locker rooms, or lunchrooms, several panels may be used effectively.

Materials posted should be displayed separately and kept free of clutter or other notices.

Changing posters and display materials frequently is preferred. Add a few new posters; circulate others. Selection and rotation of posters can be handled by the safety director. If supervisors select posters, they should choose those that keep employees' interest in safety alive. Posters may also provide notice of forthcoming holidays, and provide safety tips.

51

Special-purpose reminders

The National Safety Council's "POP" (point of problem) posters and safety stickers highlight particular hazards. POP posters are 4½ by 5½ in. (10.8 by 14.0 cm), and stickers are 2½ by 3¾ in. (6.4 by 9.5 cm). Both are self-sticking. (See Figure 4-3.)

Occasionally there is a message that must be permanently displayed, such as a poster describing correct use of fire equipment or respirators, or a warning of radioactive material. These posters should be mounted under glass or on heavy board to make them permanent. However, they should be reviewed regularly, to make sure they are not out-of-date.

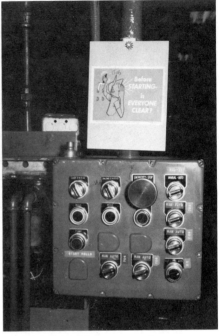

Figure 4-3. "POP" poster in place.

Poster contests can be used to create interest in safety and health.

Recognition organizations

Some organizations recognize people in the United States and Canada who have eliminated serious injuries, or who have minimized them by using certain articles of personal protective equipment. The award provides an excellent opportunity for publicity (see Figure 4-4).

Two of these recognitions are:

Wise Owl Club. Founded in 1947, this is the oldest of all such clubs. Membership is restricted to industrial employees and students who have saved their eyesight by wearing eye protection. Address inquiries to: Coordinator, Wise Owl Club, National Society to Prevent Blindness, 79 Madison Avenue, New York, N.Y. 10016.

The Golden Shoe Club. Awards are made to employees who have avoided serious injury because they were wearing safety shoes. Address inquiries to: Golden Shoe Club, 2001 Walton Road (P.O. Box 36), St. Louis, Mo. 63166.

Figure 4-4. Instructor (*left*) presents Wise Owl Club award to student in his general mechanic repair class. Student was cleaning the head of an engine when some pieces of metal flew out and cracked her safety goggles in several places.

National Society to Prevent Blindness

Safety contests

Safety contests are popular. Each year, about five million American workers participate in the industrial safety contests sponsored by National Safety Council members. More than nine billion work-hours are accounted for annually in the contest. Hundreds of awards are presented.

This effort is extremely worthwhile. Contests can be one of the most effective methods for creating interest in accident prevention. The supervisor who actively supports the company's contest or who starts a department contest is using one of the best motivations for safety known. (See Figure 4-5.)

Competition between departments, plants, divisions, or a number of companies within an industry may be held. In addition to the nationwide contest sponsored by the National Safety Council, there are contests sponsored by trade associations and local safety councils. It must be emphasized that safety contests are not a substitute for a good safety program. Safety contests have no other purpose than to create interest and participation in an organized safety program. If they fail to do this, they are meaningless.

Figure 4-5. Safe workhour contests can be between departments (*above*) or plants or industry (*right*). In department
contest, "Safety Dollars Barometer" records days without a
lost-time accident. At periodic intervals when there had been
no lost-time accidents, names of department employees are
drawn at random for cash awards.

Details. Contests are based generally on accident experience and are
conducted over a six month to one year period. Winners are determined
by relative standards, by performance improvement, or by other factors
agreed upon in advance. Many effective local contests are special campaigns that run for a specified time and are launched with advance publicity.

Interdepartmental contests are the most challenging for supervisors.
(National intercompany contests usually are directed by safety department personnel.) Since workers are more likely to have a personal interest in the standing of their own department, this type of competition has
been most successful.

Figure 4-6. After a year without a lost-time accident, home office gave plant manager a plaque (*above*) and all employees free coffee and doughnuts (*upper left*).

Worthington Division of McGaw Edison, Buffalo, N.Y.

When interdepartmental contests are conducted between dissimilar departments in one plant, difficulties created by differences in size, type of operation, and exposure to hazard must be considered.

• One solution is to compare the percentage of accident reduction in each department with a previous base period (usually the year before).

• Another method is to handicap high-hazard departments on the basis of the insurance rates for the different operations. If, for example, the rate per $100 of payroll is $3.00 for Department A, $2.00 for Department B, and $1.50 for Department C, factors for the units are 3, 2, and 1.5 respectively. To adjust the frequency rate of each department, divide the frequency rate by the handicap.

When two or more departments have perfect records, the department with the greatest number of work-hours since the last chargeable injury wins.

Whenever possible, every employee on a winning team should receive some sort of recognition or award. This will make "everyone a winner" and avoid angry feelings that may arise if only one person gets a large prize through a lottery or another type of drawing. The best prizes are those that everybody wins, although the prizes themselves may have little intrinsic value. Certificates, trading stamps, trophies, and plaques are good examples. (See Figure 4-6.)

For contest purposes, the basis for calculating occupational injury and illness incidence rates is given in the publication "Recordkeeping Requirements Under the Occupational Safety and Health Act of 1970," available from OSHA.

When departments have wide variations in the number of persons employed and in the kind of work performed, teams of 20 to 50 people can participate in intergroup competition. In order to equalize the variables, each team is made up of a proportionate number of people from high-, medium-, and low-hazard occupations. Interest is increased when teams are named after prominent football, baseball, or other sports teams, and the entire competition named after a league or a sports organization. Team names can be chosen by the group or drawn from a hat. Colored buttons designate team members.

Less formal contests among departments are also feasible. Contests can be held for good housekeeping, greatest improvement in housekeeping, or for wearing personal protective equipment. Housekeeping contest winners are determined by periodic, unbiased inspections.

Sometimes elaborate point systems are devised so that, in addition to helping win the department trophy, employees can also accumulate points for the department's performance. (See Chapter 8, "Safety Inspections.") Employees can select merchandise from a catalog on the basis of points accumulated. Sometimes trading stamps are used for this purpose.

Recognition. Methods for acknowledging employee cooperation are increasing with the use of personal no-accident awards, such as pencils, engraved buttons, billfolds, and similar articles. Some companies present awards to employees who have not suffered disabling injuries. This is discussed in Chapter 7, "Accident Investigation."

Some companies also recognize employees who have long-term safety records. They are presented with a watch and, occasionally, with a testimonial dinner.

If you think that these activities are trivial to the supervisor looking for solid ways of motivating interest in safety, you should be aware that they are highly successful, if properly conducted. Since the purpose of contests is to stimulate interest, there is virtually no limit to the ways in which contest and award presentations can be improved by added showmanship.

One way to make sure that a contest is handled properly is to provide positive recognition. Supervisors should reward their staff for good safety performances and not ridicule or publicize poor safety performance.

Suggestion systems

Periodically, people have ideas that can help the department or the company improve work methods or reduce work hazards. These ideas are frequently lost because there is no effective way to present them.

A well-organized suggestion system encourages employees to contribute ideas and stimulates their thinking about problem solving (see Figure 4-7). Employees may be rewarded by giving them a percentage of the savings resulting from increased production and absence or decrease in accidents and injuries. Solutions to safety problems are rewarded according to the importance of the idea that mitigated injuries.

Under the leadership of an executive, a committee receives and evaluates ideas. Some companies have suggestion departments to help them or use the services of professional organizations.

Special forms should be provided for submitting suggestions, and special boxes provided for their collection. Suggestions should be gathered frequently and receipt acknowledged promptly. Results of decisions made should be provided as soon as possible, and when a suggestion is not accepted, a brief explanation should be given.

Supervisors are usually not eligible to win awards for suggestions. However, they should let employees know that they will help them develop their ideas. Supervisors should also emphasize that suggestions will not be interpreted as criticisms, and that discrimination against the person making the suggestion will not occur.

A successful suggestion system must have a clear and precise operating plan that is understandable and scrupulously observed. Employees must know that the plan is fair, impartial, and potentially profitable. The results of useful suggestions submitted should be publicized, as well as the names, and photographs, when available, of those whose ideas were accepted. Supervisors can definitely encourage workers' participation by the ways in which they administer the suggestion system in their own departments.

Figure 4-7. Suggestions are encouraged by placing posters and suggestion form racks in employee lounges and cafeterias. Company distributes an information booklet that gives complete details of the suggestion plan. Company publicizes award-winners in newsletters and on bulletin boards.

Parke, Davis & Company

First aid courses

Companies that have conducted good first aid courses have found safety to be a conspicuous by-product. Some companies include first aid in their employment training program. The value of first aid training is most obvious in operations far removed from professional medical help. Another benefit is that these skills carry over to off-the-job emergencies.

Such training should be standard Red Cross courses or the Bureau of Mines courses. The need for personnel trained in first aid is spelled out in

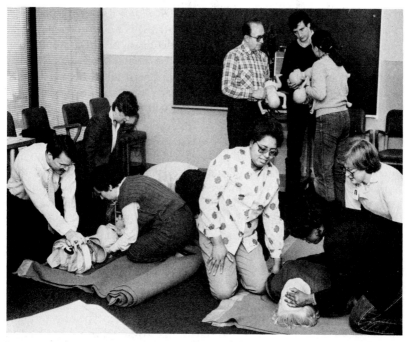

Figure 4-8. Cardiopulmonary resuscitation training is given to company personnel.

OSHA requirements if there is no infirmary, clinic, hospital, or physician in near proximity or reasonably accessible. (See Figure 4-8.)

Departmental safety meetings

Safety committee meetings are discussed at the beginning of this chapter. Here is additional information.

Department meetings can feature a film, videotape, chart talk or a subject related to the work of the group or to off-the-job safety. Models, exhibits, standard equipment and/or safety equipment can be displayed.

Visual aids with pictures and lettering on a wide variety of subjects that can be viewed by a group of 15 to 20 people can be easily obtained or produced. Here is how.

A supervisor can produce a homemade flip chart with little trouble or expense. Supplies required include approximately a dozen sheets of white paper (or a large pad), ranging in size from 18 by 24 in. to 24 by 36 in. (46 by 61 cm to 61 by 91 cm) that can be clamped to the top of a backing board, some markers (felt-tip, crayon, or colored chalk), and an outline of points to be discussed (see Figure 2-1 on page 16). Details are

59

given in NSC Industrial Data Sheet No. 564, *Nonprojected Visual Aids*.

A set of 35 mm color slides (or film strips) is a useful training aid. They can be purchased or produced. See details in NSC Data Sheet No. 574, *Projected Still Pictures*. The Council offers sets of professionally produced 35 mm slides covering a wide variety of industrial safety subjects. Each set has a reading script and many have audio-cassettes. Motion pictures are excellent for larger groups, if the projection equipment and viewing area are available.

All previously prepared visual aids are obviously just aids. They are effective training and motivating devices, but are not intended to communicate the entire message. Visual aids lose a lot of their value if they do not serve as a basis or a reinforcement for discussion. They should be selected because they are appropriate, not just because they are available.

A large meeting involving more than one department is valuable when company policies require explanation, or when general accident causes are discussed. Some meetings may be purely motivational, intended to create an awareness of hazards and stimulate accident prevention. Meetings are frequently held for presentation of safety awards.

The production huddle or toolbox talk is another type of meeting— an instruction session about a specific job. Although not restricted to safety, it focuses on the problem of safe work production. The supervisors who conduct these sessions and who give proper emphasis to safety may feel that they have had the best kind of safety meeting possible. Safety has now been "built in," which is the desired goal.

Public utility crews use this kind of meeting. They call it a "tailboard conference." Before tackling a job, the crew gathers around its truck and discusses the work. They layout the tools and materials required and agree upon which part of the job each person should handle.

These sessions are indispensible, especially in highly hazardous situations. Train and switching crews also use this type of gathering.

How to hold a meeting. A safety meeting, like any other, will be most successful when the person conducting it wants the audience to obtain useful information. Additionally, the goal should be that the audience gains an improved attitude toward the topic emphasized. If the supervisor understands human nature, this can be accomplished.

1. People do not like to attend meetings unless they expect to be interested or involved.

2. Most people can absorb only a few ideas at a time. The meeting should emphasize no more than three main ideas.

3. People become irritated and unresponsive when they are uncomfor-

Figure 4-9. An audio-cassette player and a slide projector are necessary for showing professionally produced 35 mm color slide sets. You can also shoot your own slides to make an entire show or to personalize a purchased program.

South Works, United States Steel Corp.

table. This occurs when they stand too long, are too warm or cold, look into strong light, listen over background noises, or if they feel ill at ease. Always consider the attendees when choosing the meeting location.

4. Good planning is necessary. The presenter should have a written outline of the subject and rehearse until he or she is comfortable with the subject. Visual aids used should be previewed, and all equipment should be checked to ensure that it is operating properly.

Talks should be rehearsed and timed. Exhibits should be checked to make sure they work properly.

Unless there is a good reason, such as an absorbing film, or some other good aid to provide interest, a safety session should not run longer than 30 minutes. Keep it short and simple. Only the most exceptionally appealing material warrants a one-hour session, even if the time is available. These estimates, of course, do not apply to instructional courses, but to group meetings.

The first question a supervisor may ask before he or she holds a safety meeting in the department is, "On what subject?" The safety director or safety department should be able to provide a multitude of ideas, either based on company experience or secured from the National Safety Council (see "Useful References" in the back of the book).

The supervisor who cannot answer the question, "What subject?," is one who has absolutely no safety problems either on or off the job. Think about your own problems and then look to those of your staff. You will not need to look long for a subject.

OFF-THE-JOB ACCIDENT PROBLEMS

The main goal of safety is to prevent accidents and injuries—either on or off the job. The off-the-job problem may be more simple, but it is larger. Refer to Table 4-A. In an average year, accidents away from work account for more than 70 percent of all deaths, and more than 55 percent of all injuries to workers. As company safety programs become more effective, deaths and injuries at work account for a smaller percentage of total injuries.

These figures are for all industries. In some industries, disabling injuries occur 10 to 20 times more often away from the job than on it. Although many companies are building outstanding safety records, their employees continue to suffer disabling injuries and death when away from work.

TABLE 4-A
ACCIDENT TOLL IN A TYPICAL YEAR

Place	Deaths	Disabling Injuries
All Accidents	91,000	8,800,000
At work	11,300	1,900,000
Away from work	79,700	6,900,000
Motor vehicle	44,600	1,600,000
Public non-motor vehicle	19,500	2,500,000
Home	20,000	3,000,000

Source: National Safety Council, *Accident Facts,* 1984 ed.

An employee is safer on the job because these four basic principles of accident prevention are continuously practiced:

1. Every effort is made to match the person to the job.

2. Employees are trained and motivated to do their jobs the safe way.

3. Tools, protective equipment, machines, and the work area are kept in first-class condition.

4. Materials are handled according to safe procedures; industrial hygiene is practiced; and machines are safeguarded.

When employees leave work for home, they leave behind a carefully constructed safety network. They become part of the general public and are exposed to the hazards on streets and highways, at home, and at play. They are responsible for themselves. Whether or not they have injuries depends on their abilities to supervise themselves and their families.

Companies have a continual responsibility to educate, motivate, and remind employees about the importance of following safe practices on and off the job. This responsibility is a major one. It is another area in which you must set an example.

Concern with off-the-job safety is important and is a sound investment. Firms that tackle the total problem of accident prevention claim that safety training is extremely successful because it reduces the incidence of injuries on and off the job.

Cost of off-the-job accidents

The cost of off-the-job accidents each year is about twice the $33.4 billion cost of on-job accidents (figures include property damage, as well as personal losses, wage losses, claims, medical and hospital costs, and administrative expenses). These accidents affect production output and upset schedules, because skilled workers have been lost.

If replacement workers must be hired, personnel department costs, wages spent for training, and reduced production must be accounted for. The cost of tools damaged or materials spoiled by new and inept workers must not be overlooked. Finally, wages paid to non-injured persons for nonproductive time, such as court appearances, hospital visits, and cleaning up, as the direct result of an off-the-job (OTJ) accident must be considered.

Personal trauma to the injured man or woman is often beyond measure. Emotional and physical suffering, loss of earning power, and an upset home environment—must all be dealt with.

Mental anguish may be as great a factor as physical impairment when a worker's efficiency is reduced upon returning to work. Worry and anxiety can lead to an alarming neglect of safety and result in an increase

Figure 4-10. Although they are frequently dismissed as bruising clichés in comedy cartoons, falls are actually the number one killer in the home. After traffic accidents, they are the largest single cause of accidental death in the United States—roughly 13 thousand fatalities a year.

of on-the-job accidents.

Safety-conscious employees work more days and are more efficient at work. They spoil fewer materials, do less damage to tools and machines, and have higher rates of production.

Humanitarian reasons for OTJ safety activities

Humanitarianism is, of course, a primary basis for safety. No one wants to see friends or associates suffer. OTJ safety activities help build good employee relations and develop good public relations. These activities are substantial evidence that a company believes in the dignity and worth of each employee.

Actually, a comprehensive OTJ safety program deserves the vigorous support of every company—large or small—no matter what product or service it produces, or how "safe" the company might be.

Measuring accident experience

The off-the-job frequency formula is the standard method of measuring and comparing OTJ accident experience.

$$\frac{\text{Number of OTJ injuries} \times 1,000,000}{312 \times \text{Number of employees}} = \text{OTJ frequency rate}$$

The formula is based on 312 exposure hours per employee per month. Here is why. An employee normally works eight hours a day, five days a week. The eight hours per day for sleeping are excluded. This gives a person eight hours of exposure per weekday and 16 hours on Saturday and Sunday. This adds to 72 exposure hours per week multiplied by $4^{1}/_{3}$ weeks per month, for a total of 312 exposure hours per month.

No adjustment need be made for overtime since it will be offset by holidays, vacations, and incidental absences.

For example, a plant with 10,000 employees has five OTJ injuries during one month. Each injury causes only one day's absence from work. The OTJ frequency rate for that month will be:

$$\frac{5 \times 1,000,000}{312 \times 10,000} = 1.60$$

To qualify for reporting, an OTJ injury must result in a person's losing at least one full day, either a working day or a holiday, weekend, or vacation. No medical opinion is needed. Fatal or permanent injuries must be included. No scheduled time charges are made for permanent partial disabilities or fatalities. Only the amount of lost-time injuries and fatalities are reported.

OTJ injuries are classified under three types: transportation, home, and public.

Transportation. Defined as injuries caused by, or resulting from accidents at places other than home involving a moving automobile, truck, bicycle, bus, streetcar, motorcycle, railroad, boat, airplane, or pedestrian. Classification also includes injuries occurring during boarding, alighting, or moving within vehicles.

Home. Injuries occurring at home or in the yard caused by vehicles, firearms, machinery, tools, fire, explosion, exposure to heat or cold, electricity, toxic material, fall, slip, improper lifting, hot object or material, sharp object, striking an object, overexertion, or animal, insect, or other causes.

Public. All other injuries caused by firearms, fire, explosion, fall,

Figure 4-11. "Defensive Driving" courses, such as those developed by NSC, are intended to teach better driving to millions of vehicle drivers. Many firms sponsor these courses to improve the skills of both on-the-job and off-the-job driving.

a.ip, striking objects (including stationary vehicles), animals or insects, fighting, assault, exposure to heat or cold, sports, toxic material (such as poison ivy), electricity, and others.

By having subdivisions in these three classifications, companies can evaluate the effectiveness of program areas, and pinpoint where and when the greatest efforts are needed.

Integrating OTJ with on-the-job safety programs

A company safety program cannot be completely effective unless it deals with the whole person—not just the person acting as a machine operator or a truck driver. People are not likely to be careful at work if they disregard safety as soon as they walk out the door or the plant gate. Conversely, if people are careful at home and on the highway, they are likely to be receptive to safety education at work.

This is why more and more employers are directing their attention to OTJ safety education, and are integrating it with on-the-job safety education. Here is how.

• Many organizations provide reading racks stocked with helpful literature for employees to take home.

• Some material is sent directly to an employee's home. Traffic, vacation, and home safety leaflets and other material are available. Over 2¹/₂ million copies of National Safety Council's *Family Safety and Health* are subscribed to by companies for their employees.

• Companies sponsor safety-oriented activities: the National Safety Council's Defensive Driving Program (Figure 4-11), Red Cross first aid courses, learn-to-swim campaigns, and even family night safety rallies.

Support for community and family safety programs reinforces a company's safety efforts. Company officials, supervisors, and employees should participate.

The supervisor's role in OTJ safety

OTJ safety activities affect the general well-being of employees, the operation of the company safety program, and the efficiency of the supervisor's own department. The methods used to promote these activities are the same as those used to promote on-the-job safety.

• As a supervisor, you must believe in and practice safety all the time, wherever you may be. You must recognize its importance to the well-being of your own family. You must set an example.

• The supervisor should determine whether an injury has kept a person away from work. You should encourage reporting of all accidents. Reporting near-misses can supply topics for safety discussions.

• Part of departmental and committee meetings can be devoted to discussing OTJ safety. Supervisors can talk to people individually.

• Bulletin boards can display vacation and holiday safety hints—and newspaper or magazine clippings that may be of interest to employees.

• The supervisor can support public and home safety activities. Local safety councils, churches, fraternal organizations, and youth groups need safety-minded volunteers.

Chapter 5

Safety Training

O ne of the more positive actions supervisors take in accident prevention is to provide safety training to their people. The effects of these efforts become readily apparent, and furthermore, they can be measured. That's a positive evaluation of your accident prevention work.

Many studies have been made to determine why people behave unsafely. Some of the reasons are that workers have:

- Not been given specific instructions in the operation

- Misunderstood the instructions

- Not listened to the instructions

- Considered the instructions either unimportant or unnecessary

- Disregarded instructions.

Any of the above can result in an accident. To prevent such an occurrence, it is essential that safety training work be conducted efficiently. In many cases, supervisors provide the training themselves. You may, in some instances, choose to delegate some of the training to other skilled people who report to you. In any event, make a follow-up check to determine that the training achieved its purpose. Supervisors have the final responsibility for the effectiveness of training efforts. On technical subjects, such as fire prevention or first aid, other qualified people may provide assistance and lend their expertise to the training effort.

Every person who conducts safety training needs a number of qualities:

- Thorough knowledge of the subject

- Desire to instruct

- Friendly and cooperative attitude

- Leadership qualities
- Professional attitude and approach
- Exemplary behavior.

This chapter covers several areas of safety training of special interest: (*a*) new employee indoctrination; (*b*) job safety analysis; (*c*) job instruction training; and (*d*) other methods of instruction.

Other subjects, such as proper lifting technique and the care and use of personal protective equipment, are covered in Chapters 10 and 9 respectively. Let's now examine the details of the subjects listed above.

NEW EMPLOYEE INDOCTRINATION

General provisions

One of the best ways of getting people involved in an accident prevention program is to provide a thorough indoctrination for new employees. One frequently hears of people having accidents the first day on a new job. In many instances, these employees had not been given proper instructions. A good indoctrination program for new employees should emphasize:

- General company rules and employee benefits. These topics are usually covered by the industrial relations or personnel department.

- Overall safety rules and accident prevention programs and policies. The safety director will usually cover this.

- Explanation of the specific hazards in the new employees' department and the applicable safety rules and practices to offset those hazards. This part of the indoctrination is the most important and should be conducted by you—the first-line supervisor. (See Figure 5-1.)

While on the job, supervisors can show new employees how certain hazards have been eliminated while others that could not be designed out of the operation have been guarded against. In some cases, personal protective equipment is the only answer. There are a number of benefits to be realized from such an explanation:

- New employees will see the precautions the company has taken to prevent accidents.

- Supervisors can emphasize the need for safety rules and give reasons why they must be followed.

- New employees should be encouraged to offer their ideas and suggestions for improved safety.

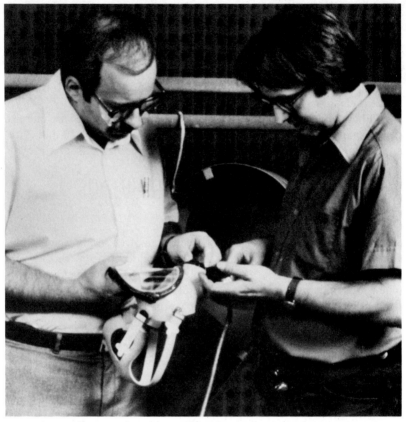

Figure 5-1. Both new and newly transferred employees should be indoctrinated in all applicable safety rules and practices necessary to perform their job both efficiently and safely.

• New employees, from the first day on the job, realize how important safety is everywhere in the plant.

Personal protective equipment

As various processes are discussed with new employees you, as supervisor, can show the personal protective equipment required. This is a golden opportunity to explain *why* such equipment is necessary. Showing and telling new people why they must wear eye protection, for example, will help to get their compliance with the rules. (See Figure 5–1 again.)

It is a good idea at this time to show new employees the care and cleaning of their personal protective equipment, and also the procedures to follow if it needs repair or replacement. So right from the first day on the job, new employees learn the importance of personal protective equipment and the fact that departmental rules regarding it will be strictly enforced. New employees also realize how important safety is as part of their new job. They will also come to appreciate your no-nonsense approach to accident prevention.

Safe operating procedures

Before new employees start their first assignment, supervisors should discuss the following procedures:

- *All* accidents must be reported immediately after injury, property damage, and near accidents (often called "near misses").

- Any unsafe conditions must be reported to supervisors at once.

- Equipment and tools, even though they are thought to be in good condition, should still be checked before using.

- No one is allowed to operate a piece of equipment without specific authorization and instruction from the supervisor.

- Job instruction includes applicable safety instructions as a matter of course.

Follow-up

A follow-up session with the employees should be scheduled several days after the indoctrination. This session will help to determine how good a job of training you have done. It also gives the new person another opportunity to raise questions regarding the job. Supervisors must encourage their people to bring up any questions they may have regarding accident prevention. This gets employees thinking about safety right from the start.

Many supervisors use a checklist of items to be covered in their indoctrination for new employees. A sample list is shown in Figure 5-2. It can be used as a basis for making your own checklist. In this way, you can be certain you have covered all the relevant items. Some firms ask new employees to sign the checklist and return it to personnel to verify that the points were covered.

Transferred employees

When people are not new employees but are transferred into your department, it is also necessary to conduct an indoctrination session with them. Using this process, you can cover specific problems that they have not encountered in their prior jobs within the company. It's better to alert transferred employees a second time to hazards than to take the chance that they are not aware of them.

NEW EMPLOYEE CHECKLIST

☐ Rules regarding lunch and break periods

☐ Personal protective equipment issued and why required on this job

☐ Procedure for obtaining, cleaning, repairing, replacing personal protective equipment and clothing

☐ What to do in the event of an injury/illness

☐ What to do in the event of a non-injury accident (incident)

☐ How to handle unsafe/unhealthy conditions

☐ How to report fires and other emergencies

☐ Personal cleanup rules and why

☐ Clean-up and housekeeping rules

Specific safety and health rules applicable to this department or area, including reasons for having the rules:

    ☐ No-smoking areas

    ☐ Special materials

    ☐ Hot work, entry, and other permits

    ☐ Fire drills and testing of warning signals

TOUR DEPARTMENT AND RELATED FACILITIES: DISCUSS HAZARDS

Where to keep personal belongings, such as lunch, outerwear, clothes changes (if required), and any required tools

Location of first aid and/or medical facilities

Location of fire extinguishers

Location of fire exit(s) and marshalling areas

        Employee's name and signature _____

        Discussed with _____

        Date _____

Figure 5–2. A sample checklist that can be used as part of a new employee indoctrination. By adding specific rules to this list and spelling out required personal protective equipment, the supervisor can complete it quickly. Each item is checked off as it is discussed with the new employee.

JOB SAFETY ANALYSIS

One of the best accident prevention tools to use is called a job safety analysis, or JSA. It has been used for a long time by many of the most effective supervisors. Job safety analysis is another of the positive tools in your arsenal for attacking accidents. It is also an area in which the positive action you take can be measured, resulting in improved safety performance.

JSA is a hazard hunt conducted by the two people best qualified to make operations safer. They are you—the first-line supervisor—and one of your skilled operators. In most instances, you two know more about the job than anyone else and can do more to spot hazards. Job safety analysis is a procedure by which jobs are broken down into steps. Each step is thoroughly checked for hazards. Solutions are then developed to eliminate or, if that's not possible, guard against the hazards. (See Figure 5-3.)

Priority of job selection

It is essential to establish a priority for the order in which to analyze jobs. What would be a logical way to select them?

First, select the jobs in which the most accidents occurred. And remember—consider *all* accidents—injury, property damage, and near accidents. If you choose the jobs to be analyzed in this way, you'll enjoy immediate accident prevention benefits.

Second, consider jobs that have a potential for severe accidents even though there may not have been any accidents yet. It is quite possible that everyone exercises great care when jobs of that type are running. Such jobs are splendid candidates for job safety analysis.

Third, study newly established jobs carefully. It is quite possible that a new job has hazards not previously encountered. Perhaps, personal protective equipment is needed. It is also possible that an old hazard will be removed in the new operation. In these instances, you would strive for wider application of the new process.

Any job for which you conduct a safety analysis should be reviewed in the event that a method or process changes. Again, look for hazards that may have been introduced or removed in the change.

Selection and briefing of operators

The best person to help on a hazard hunt is a skilled operator who knows the job thoroughly. In addition to having job knowledge, the person should have a good attitude toward safety and a good record.

INSTRUCTIONS FOR COMPLETING JOB SAFETY ANALYSIS FORM

Job Safety Analysis (JSA) is an important accident prevention tool that works by finding hazards and eliminating or minimizing them *before* the job is performed, and *before* they have a chance to become accidents. Use your JSA for job clarification and hazard awareness, as a guide in new employee training, for periodic contacts and for retraining of senior employees, as a refresher on jobs which run infrequently, as an accident investigation tool, and for informing employees of specific job hazards and protective measures.

Set priorities for doing JSAs: jobs that have a history of many accidents, jobs that have produced disabling injuries, jobs with high potential for disabling injury or death, and new jobs with no accident history.

Here's how to do each of the three parts of a Job Safety Analysis:

SEQUENCE OF BASIC JOB STEPS

Break the job down into steps. Each of the steps of a job should accomplish some major task. The task will consist of a *set* of movements. Look at the first set of movements used to perform a task, and then determine the next logical set of movements. For example, the job might be to move a box from a conveyor in the receiving area to a shelf in the storage area. How does that break down into job steps? Picking up the box from the conveyor and putting it on a handtruck is one logical set of movements, so it is one job step. Everything related to that one logical set of movements is part of that job step.

The next logical set of movements might be pushing the loaded handtruck to the storeroom. Removing the boxes from the truck and placing them on the shelf is another logical set of movements. And finally, returning the handtruck to the receiving area might be the final step in this type of job.

Be sure to list *all* the steps in a job. Some steps might not be done each time—checking the casters on a handtruck, for example. However, that task is a part of the job as a whole, and should be listed and analyzed.

POTENTIAL HAZARDS

Identify the hazards associated with each step. Examine each step to find and identify hazards—actions, conditions and possibilities that could lead to an accident.

It's not enough to look at the obvious hazards. It's also important to look at the entire environment and discover every conceivable hazard that might exist.

Be sure to list health hazards as well, even though the harmful effect may not be immediate. A good example is the harmful effect of inhaling a solvent or chemical dust over a long period of time.

It's important to list *all* hazards. Hazards contribute to accidents, injuries and occupational illnesses.

In order to do part three of a JSA effectively, you must identify *potential and existing hazards*. That's why it's important to distinguish between a hazard, an accident and an injury. Each of these terms has a specific meaning:

HAZARD—A potential danger. Oil on the floor is a *hazard.*

ACCIDENT—An unintended happening that may result in injury, loss or damage. Slipping on the oil is an *accident.*

INJURY—The *result* of an accident. A sprained wrist from the fall would be an injury.

Some people find it easier to identify possible accidents and illnesses and work back from them to the hazards. If you do that, you can list the accident and illness types in parentheses following the hazard. But be sure you focus on the *hazard* for developing recommended actions and safe work procedures.

RECOMMENDED ACTION OR PROCEDURE

Using the first two columns as a guide, decide what actions are necessary to eliminate or minimize the hazards that could lead to an accident, injury, or occupational illness.

Among the actions that can be taken are: 1) engineering the hazard out; 2) providing personal protective equipment; 3) job instruction training; 4) good housekeeping; and 5) good ergonomics (positioning the person in relation to the machine or other elements in the environment in such a way as to eliminate stresses and strains).

List recommended safe operating procedures on the form, and also list required or recommended personal protective equipment for each step of the job.

Be specific. Say *exactly* what needs to be done to correct the hazard, such as, "lift, using your leg muscles." Avoid general statements like, "be careful."

Give a recommended action or procedure for *every* hazard.

If the hazard is a serious one, it should be corrected immediately. The JSA should then be changed to reflect the new conditions.

Figure 5-3. The three principal parts of a job safety analysis are explained here.

It is important to explain the purpose of JSA to the operator you have selected. Also, point out the important role he or she is playing in overall accident prevention. Job safety analysis is an excellent way of getting your people involved in your safety program. It can get them to thinking, "They want *my* ideas," or, "They really care about what I think." Letting people know that you want and need their ideas will help to get the cooperation needed.

Breaking the job into steps

You and the operator can work together to break a job down into its various steps. Each step should begin with a verb and be as brief as possible. Remember, this is not a detailed industrial engineering analysis that covers every micro movement of the job.

For illustration, see how the job of Picking Apples is broken into steps. (See Figure 5-4.) The first job with the most steps is to obtain the proper tools or equipment. Make it a standard practice not only to select the proper tools, but to be certain that they are in good condition.

Once the proper tools and equipment have been selected, the remaining steps are shown in numbers 2 to 9. When making a JSA, list the job steps in sequence without concern, at the moment, for hazards or recommended procedures. These are attended to later.

In listing the job steps, avoid getting into either too much detail or too little. Too much detail will result in an unnecessarily large number of steps, while the opposite can result in the omission of some basic steps. Either extreme is undesirable. Strive for sufficient detail to cover the job. Number the job steps in sequence. Remember to begin each step with a verb and keep them short as possible.

When the job steps have been listed, return to the first step and ask the question: "What hazards exist in this step?" "What possible accidents could occur?" Some forms list the accident types. This helps the supervisor and operator as they consider possible hazards that may occur with each step. Any hazards they envision should be listed in the column headed "Potential Hazards" (shown in Figure 5-3 in the second column). The hazards should be numbered to agree with the step number. On some steps, there may be no hazard. So they would write "none" in the appropriate place in Column 2.

As hazards are envisioned, the JSA team will next consider the "Recommended Action or Procedure" to overcome or minimize risks. A list of control measures is shown on page 78. As you come up with other ideas, add them to your list. If the recommended procedure involves the use or the wearing of personal protective equipment, enter that in the third column, and in the box provided above the sequence column. In the

(Text continues on page 78.)

JOB SAFETY ANALYSIS	JOB TITLE (and number if applicable): PICKING APPLES	PAGE___ OF___ JSA NO.___	DATE:	☐ NEW ☐ REVISED
INSTRUCTIONS ON REVERSE SIDE	TITLE OF PERSON WHO DOES JOB:	SUPERVISOR:	ANALYSIS BY:	
COMPANY/ORGANIZATION:	PLANT/LOCATION:	DEPARTMENT:	REVIEWED BY:	
REQUIRED AND/OR RECOMMENDED PERSONAL PROTECTIVE EQUIPMENT:			APPROVED BY:	

SEQUENCE OF BASIC JOB STEPS	POTENTIAL HAZARDS	RECOMMENDED ACTION OR PROCEDURE
1. Get proper equipment (ladder, shoulder sack, baskets)		
2. Position ladder		
3. Climb ladder		
4. Pick apples and put in sack		
5. Descend ladder		
6. Empty apples into basket		
7. Move ladder to new position		
8. Repeat steps 2 through 7 until job is complete		
9. Put equipment away		

Figure 5-4. First break the job down into its various steps. Write them down in proper sequence. Don't do a detailed engineering analysis, however.

JOB SAFETY ANALYSIS

INSTRUCTIONS ON REVERSE SIDE

JOB TITLE (and number if applicable):

PAGE____ OF____ JSA NO____

DATE:

☐ NEW
☐ REVISED

TITLE OF PERSON WHO DOES JOB:	SUPERVISOR:
COMPANY/ORGANIZATION:	PLANT/LOCATION:

ANALYSIS BY:

DEPARTMENT:

REVIEWED BY:

REQUIRED AND/OR RECOMMENDED PERSONAL PROTECTIVE EQUIPMENT:

APPROVED BY:

SEQUENCE OF BASIC JOB STEPS	POTENTIAL HAZARDS	RECOMMENDED ACTION OR PROCEDURE
1. Get proper equipment (ladder, shoulder sack, baskets)		Select correct ladder
2. Position ladder	Ladder toppling	Place on level ground
3. Climb ladder	Fall	Hands on rails
4. Pick apples and put in sack	Fall	Do not lean over edge when picking apples
5. Descend ladder	Same as 3	
6. Empty apples into basket		
7. Move ladder to new position	Strain	Lift properly
8. Repeat steps 2 through 7 until job is complete		
9. Put equipment away		

Figure 5-5. Corresponding to each step, list the hazards that the worker could be exposed to. If you can envision no hazard(s), the leave the line blank or write "None" in the space. For each hazard listed in the second column, you must write down a recommended action or procedure to overcome it.

CONTROL MEASURES
TO MINIMIZE RISKS

Engineer the Hazard Out	Improve Lighting
Provide Guards	Exhaust Ventilation
Use Personal Protective Equipment	Improve Housekeeping
Isolate Process	Education and Training
Substitute Materials	

completed JSA (see Figure 5-5), the supervisor or the operator will be able to tell at a glance the kinds of personal protective equipment needed on the job.

When listing the Recommended Action or Procedure, be specific. A statement such as, "Be careful" is of no value. Rather, use such recommendations as, "Lift with your legs, not with your back." The Recommended Action or Procedure should be numbered to agree with the Steps and Hazards to which they apply.

When you have completed the form, test the procedure to make sure that no steps are left out and all hazards are listed. After this checkout, get the JSA typed and duplicated. The completed job safety analysis should always be available at or near the work area where the job is to be performed. In this way, it can be better used as an accident prevention tool.

Some firms have been successful in developing job safety analysis programs for their maintenance operations, as well as for production, another indication of its versatility.

Periodic review of job safety analysis

Whenever a job is changed, or the process is modified, you should review the JSA. A new hazard may have been introduced by the change, or an old hazard may have been removed. To be of maximum value as accident prevention tools, JSAs must be kept current. In addition, establish a minimum period before the JSAs are reviewed. Depending on the nature of your operations, this interval could be every 6 to 12 months.

Benefits of job safety analysis

Fewer accidents. You should have fewer accidents as a result of JSA efforts. Even if you performed only two JSAs a month, you would be able to cover the 24 most hazardous jobs during the first year in operation.

Employee involvement. Skilled operators will have a feeling of being involved in accident prevention work. By helping to prepare the JSA, skilled employees get the feeling that you really want to hear their ideas and care about what they think. Workers know that you recognize the value of the experience that they have had on the job. And when these individuals are given an opportunity to make working conditions safer for all people in the department, they become more involved. The new employees will look upon the completed JSA as training for their jobs. So from the first day new employees join the department, they will be aware of the extent of your concern for accident prevention. In addition, new workers will generally be more willing to offer their ideas to improve operations. You'll have them thinking safety right from the start.

Training the new employee

The job safety analysis can also be used to train new operators because it spells out the job steps, the hazards associated with each, and the recommended safe procedure. In addition, the personal protective equipment needed is listed at the top of the form. Use the job safety analysis for refresher training on jobs run infrequently, because this kind of job often results in accidents. Help to prevent those accidents by having operators review the JSA before they start a job that has not been done for some time.

Accident investigations

If an accident occurs on a job for which a JSA has already been prepared, it can be most useful during the accident investigation. The JSA with show either that you missed a hazard in your original analysis, or that the procedure prescribed was not being followed. In either event, you can take the appropriate action to rectify the situation.

In conclusion, think about the value of job safety analysis. Consider how much safer your operations can be. Job safety analysis is one of the best existing accident prevention tools.

JOB INSTRUCTION TRAINING

Once job safety analyses are operating in your department, get the benefits of job instruction training (JIT) as well. JIT is a technique for on-the-job training of particular tasks. Teaching new and/or transferred

JOB INSTRUCTION TRAINING (JIT)

HOW TO GET READY TO INSTRUCT

Have a Timetable—
How much skill you expect the operator to have, by what date

Break Down the Job— *
List important steps, pick out the key points. (Safety is always a key point.)

Have Everything Ready—
The right equipment, materials and supplies.

Have the Workplace Properly Arranged—
Just as the trainee will be expected to keep it.

*Use JSA, job safety analysis, breakdown to locate hazards.

**SAFETY TRAINING INSTITUTE
NATIONAL SAFETY COUNCIL**

HOW TO INSTRUCT

1. Prepare
Put trainee at ease.
Define the job and find out what he or she already knows about it.
Get the employee interested in learning the job.
Place in correct position.

2. Present

Tell, show, and illustrate one IMPORTANT STEP at a time.
Stress each KEY POINT.*

3. Try Out Performance

Have the employee do the job— coach him or her.
Have the employee explain each key point to you during the process.
Make sure the worker understands.
Continue until YOU know the worker knows.

4. Follow Up

Let the employee work independently.
Designate whom to go to for help.
Check frequently. Encourage questions.
Taper off extra coaching and close followup.

*Safety is always a key point.

Figure 5–6. Every supervisor should follow the JIT format when teaching job skills.

employees to do jobs safely and efficiently can improve operations immensely.

Either conduct the job training yourself or delegate it to an experienced operator who relates well to people. Because the responsibility for the quality of the training is vested in you, the supervisor, consider the following qualities when selecting instructors. They should have:

- Detailed knowledge of the job

- A strong desire to teach

- A demonstrated safety record

- Ability to communicate
- A friendly, cooperative attitude.

Getting ready to teach

Before beginning any job training, several things must be determined:

- *What kind of training is needed.* Find out what trainees already know. It is wasteful to provide training if it is not needed.

- *Set a time table.* On the basis of training needs, determine how much time it will take and plan accordingly.

- *Have all equipment and supplies ready.* To provide uninterrupted training, it is essential that all materials, supplies, fixtures, and other necessary items be readily available.

- *Have the workplace properly arranged.* In order to develop good housekeeping practices right from the start, make sure that everything is in place. Good housekeeping habits impressed on the trainee on the first day can set the pattern for good housekeeping practices on other jobs.

- *Have key points firmly in mind.* Key points are any items that will enable the operator to do the job better, safer, more quickly. Instructors then share their on-the-job experience by demonstrating the safe, efficient way to do the job.

Four-step instruction

Four-step job instruction was developed during World War II to help people do training who had not been schooled in instructional techniques. This method worked so well that many people who were trained adopted it and applied it to their instruction techniques. Today it is being used in many countries of the world. It is outlined in Figure 5-6 and examined below.

Step 1. Prepare the worker. New employees are especially nervous on the first day of the new job. So, it is essential that trainers put them at ease. Get them to relax. Define the job in detail and show the quality standards that must be met. It is best to show how and where the work being done will affect the quality of the finished product. Knowing the importance of a particular job as it relates to the finished product can do a lot for the morale of new workers and reduce the first-day tension. It is recommended that the trainer work alongside the trainee rather than across the work bench or machine. This enables the trainees to see the work exactly as they will on the job.

Step 2. Present the operation. Now the trainer demonstrates the job, one step at a time. Whenever possible, telling the trainees *why* a step is done in sequence will be most helpful because it is easier to remember *when* you know *why*. Trainees should be advised to raise any questions regarding any phase of the operation. Failure to ask questions could result in accidents. Key points should be stressed as they come up in the job steps.

Step 3. Try out performance. At this point in the training cycle, the instructor becomes coach and watches trainees perform. It is essential that a new employee describe each step as it is being completed. This will enable the instructor to determine whether or not the training was effective. In this step, patience and empathy are the most needed qualities. Patience is required when trainees learn slowly. Empathy is the ability to put yourself in the other person's shoes. Remember how you were on your first day on the job? Do you remember all the questions you had regarding the operation? The new individual probably has many of the same feelings and same questions. Try to anticipate those questions and be ready to answer them. There's an old saying in job training, "If the trainee hasn't learned, the instructor hasn't taught!"

Step 4. Follow up. When you have observed enough job cycles to be certain that new employees have mastered the operation, it's time to put the final step into operation. Let the workers demonstrate what they have learned. Again, express confidence that *quality* levels will be met. (In time, quantity levels will be met.)

It is a good idea to let trainees know where they can get help if you're not available. Continue to check back as often as is necessary. Encourage the trainees to ask questions at any time.

Which of the steps in job instruction training is the most important? Actually all four are essential to proper training of new operation:

1. Preparing the new worker;

2. Presenting the operations;

3. Observing new employees doing the operation;

4. Following up with on-the-job observation.

There it is—a simple four-step procedure for training new employees that helps to:

- Shorten the learning time

- Reduce scrap and rework

- Reduce injuries among new employees.

Many supervisors make the mistake of assuming that there is no need to use training techniques with transferred employees. Just because these people have worked in another area of the organization does not mean that they are skilled in your operations. Many accidents have occured because supervisors assumed that transferred workers knew more than they did.

Take advantage of accident prevention techniques. Use the job safety analysis (JSA) to discover and minimize hazards, then follow up with job instruction training (JIT) for both new and transferred people. The right way is always the safe way.

OTHER METHODS OF INSTRUCTION

The methods discussed so far have primarily been methods that are commonly used to teach job skills in on-the-job situations. However, there may be times when the supervisor will need to know how to make a presentation or teach in a classroom situation. You may be asked to teach a lesson that is part of an overall course, such as one designed to train employees to become welders or pipe fitters, or to conduct a periodic safety meeting. There may be other occasions when you find it advisable to call your group together to explain a new procedure or method. At such times, the lesson plan format will be useful.

The lesson plan

The supervisor should be familiar with lesson plans. They are the blueprint for presenting material contained in a course outline or for presenting a single unit of instruction. In addition to standardizing training, lesson plans help the instructor:

1. Present material in proper order.

2. Emphasize material in relation to its importance.

3. Avoid omission of essential material.

4. Run his or her classes on schedule.

5. Provide for trainee (student) participation.

6. Increase his or her confidence, especially if he or she is, in turn, learning how to instruct.

Names for the parts of a lesson plan may vary; even the order may not always be the same. The following, however, is a good example of arrangement for a lesson plan:

1. Title: Must indicate clearly and concisely the subject matter to be taught.

2. Objective:
   a) Should state what the trainee should know or be able to do at the end of the training period.
   b) Should limit the subject matter.
   c) Should be specific.
   d) May be divided into a major and several minor objectives for each session.

3. Training aids: Should include such items as actual equipment or tools to be used, and charts, slides, films, television, etc.

4. Introduction
   a) Should give the scope of the subject.
   b) Should tell the value of the subject.
   c) Should stimulate thinking on the subject.

5. Presentation:
   a) Should give the plan of action.
   b) Should indicate the method of teaching to be used (lecture, demonstration, class discussion, or a combination of these).
   c) Should contain suggested directions for instructor activity ("Show chart," "Write key words on chalkboard").

6. Application: Should indicate, by example, how trainees will apply this material immediately (problems may be worked; a job may be performed; trainees may be questioned on understanding and procedures).

7. Summary:
   a) Should restate main points.
   b) Should tie up loose ends.
   c) Should strengthen weak spots in instruction.

8. Test: Tests help determine if objectives have been reached. They should be announced to the class at the beginning of the session.

9. Assignment: Should give references to be checked or indicate materials to be prepared for future lessons.

Programmed instruction

Programmed instruction may be used as a supplement to classroom and on-job training. Using self-contained teaching materials, programmed instruction permits the trainee to set an individual pace and to absorb knowledge in easy-to-take bits. The learning process is reinforced by requiring the trainee to answer questions and correct his or her own errors before progressing with the course.

There are a number of programmed instruction courses available in such areas as safety training, vocational training, and communications; many of these courses use multi-media materials, such as tapes, slides, films, computers, video disks, and TV monitors (interactive video).

A complete list of courses and devices is available from The National Society for Performance and Instruction, Suite 315, 1126 16th Street, NW., Washington, D.C. 20036.

Independent study

Courses offered through correspondence schools are called home study or independent study courses.

Independent study courses combine the fundamentals of good training, guidance and counseling of a qualified instructor, with the convenience of studying at home or in supervised study sessions arranged by the company (often on company time).

A list of subjects taught by accredited private home study schools may be obtained from the National Home Study Council, 1601 18th Street, NW., Washington, D.C. 20009.

Extension programs of most major universities offer programs of all types through independent study and will furnish complete information upon written request.

Closed circuit TV

Closed circuit TV (CCTV) training uses television's "instant replay" techniques. The basic technique is to record the visual procedure and directions on videotape and then play it back later on a monitor. Once the process or manual skills, along with the instructions, are recorded, they can be replayed many times. Videotape can be used to record the steps in a job safety analysis, which can then be used to train employees in safe job procedures.

CCTV is extremely flexible; portions of the tape may be shown for review purposes where the job is not regularly performed. It also makes for uniform training since the job is presented in exactly the same manner to each trainee.

SUMMARY

Although training will not solve all the problems, it can go a long way toward helping to prevent accidents. In particular, the areas of training highlighted in this chapter can be assets to you in helping your people to perform safely. In new-employee indoctrination, start your people on the road to safe operations by discussing the details of all the hazards in your operation. The personal protection equipment provided emphasizes the concern for the workers' well-being.

Job safety analysis and job instruction training are both ways to prevent accidents. One helps you find and remove hazards, while the other teaches your employees to do the job safely and efficiently.

The other methods of instruction should be used as required, depending on the situation. The good supervisor attempts to fit the training method to the problem and not use the same technique to solve all problems. In many cases, the supervisor may find it advantageous to mix training methods, such as using programmed instruction along with on-the-job training to reach the highest level of learning in the shortest possible time.

Good training produces skilled and productive workers, as well as safe workers.

Chapter 6

Industrial Hygiene
And Noise Control

In addition to safety responsibilities, supervisors must make sure that there are no conditions in the work area that could be detrimental to health. Consequently, the more you know about industrial hygiene, the better supervisor you will be. This chapter supplies sufficient information to enable the first-line supervisor to recognize an environmental health hazard so that assistance can be requested. And, industrial hygienists, working with medical, safety, and engineering personnel, can supply that help.

Industrial hygienists define their work as "the recognition, evaluation, and control of environmental conditions that may have adverse effects on health, that may be uncomfortable or irritating, or that may have some undesired effect upon the ability of individuals to perform their normal work."

It is possible to group these environmental conditions or stresses into four general categories—chemical, physical, ergonomic, and biological. So that the supervisor can recognize potential industrial hygiene problems, each is discussed in some detail.

CHEMICAL

The first category is chemical. Chemical compounds in the form of liquids, gases, mists, dusts, fumes, and vapors may cause problems by inhalation (breathing), by absorption (through direct contact with the skin), or by ingestion (eating or drinking).

Inhalation

The major exposure to chemical compounds results from their being breathed after becoming airborne. Contaminants that can be inhaled into the lungs can be physically classified as gases, vapors, and particulate matter. Particulate matter can be further classified as dust, fume, smoke, aerosol, or mist.

Absorption

Absorption through the skin can occur quite rapidly if the skin is cut or abraded. Unfortunately, there are several compounds that can be either in liquid or gaseous form, or both, and may be absorbed through intact skin. Some are absorbed by way of the hair follicles and others dissolve in the fats and oils of the skin.

Examples of chemical compounds that can be hazardous by skin absorption are alkaloids; phenols; lead acetate; lead oleate; salts of lead, antimony, arsenic, bismuth, and mercury; nitrobenzene; nitrotoluene; aniline; and nitroglycerine. Other bad actors are triorthocresylphosphate, tetraethyl lead, and parathion and related organic phosphates. Compounds that are good solvents for fats may cause problems by being absorbed through the skin, although they are not as hazardous as those mentioned previously. Toluene and xylene are examples.

Ingestion

Ordinarily, people do not knowingly eat or drink harmful materials. It is true that toxic compounds capable of being absorbed from the gastrointestinal tract into the blood—an example is lead oxide—can cause serious problems if people working with them are allowed to eat or smoke in their work areas. Also, careful and thorough wash-ups are required before eating and at the end of every shift.

PHYSICAL CLASSIFICATION OF AIRBORNE MATERIALS

Because inhalation of airborne compounds or materials is so easy, it is necessary that the supervisor know their physical classifications.

Dusts

These are solid particles generated by handling, crushing, grinding, rapid impact, detonation, and decrepitation (breaking apart by heating) of organic or inorganic materials, such as rock, ore, metal, coal, wood, and grain.

Dust is a term used in industry to describe airborne solid particles that range in size from 0.1 to 25 μm (μm = 1/10,000 cm = 1/25,000 in.; μm is the abbreviation for micrometer).

A person with normal eyesight can detect individual dust particles as small as 50 μm (micrometers or microns) in diameter. Dust particles below 10μm in diameter cannot be seen without a microscope. However, high concentrations of suspended small particles appear as a haze or have the appearance of smoke.

Dusts settle to the ground under the influence of gravity. The larger the particle, the more quickly it settles. Particles larger than 10 μm in diameter settle quickly while those under 10μm remain suspended in air for much longer times.

It is these smaller particles that can penetrate into the inner recesses of the lung. They are called "respirable dusts." Nearly all the particles larger than 10 μm in diameter are trapped in the nose, throat, trachea, or bronchi from which they are either expectorated or swallowed.

Some larger size particles can also cause difficulty, however. Ragweed pollen, which ranges from 18-25 μm in diameter, can cause hay fever from its action in the upper respiratory tract. Other allergenic dusts, as well as some bacterial and irritant dusts, cause problems in the larger particle sizes.

Dust may enter the air from various sources. It may be dispersed when a dusty material is handled, for example, when lead oxide is dumped into a mixer, when talc is dusted on a product, or where asbestos-containing acoustical and/or fireproofing materials are being removed (see Figure 6-1). When solid materials are reduced to small sizes in such processes as grinding, crushing, blasting, shaking, and drilling, the mechanical action of the grinding or shaking device supplies energy to disperse the dust formed.

Fumes

A fume is formed when volatilized solids, such as metals, condense in cool air. The solid particles that make up a fume are extremely fine— usually less than 1.0 μm. In most cases, the hot material reacts with the air to form an oxide.

Examples are lead oxide fume from smelting, and iron oxide fumes from arc welding. A fume also can be formed when a material such as magnesium metal is burned or when welding or gas cutting is done on galvanized metal. Gases and vapors are *not* fumes, even if newspaper reporters often (and incorrectly) call them that.

Smoke

Carbon or soot particles less than 0.1 μm in size, which result from the incomplete combustion of such carbonaceous materials as coal or oil, are called "smoke." Smoke generally contains droplets, as well as dry particles. Tobacco, for instance, produces a wet smoke composed of

Figure 6-1. Because dangerous dusts can be dispersed into the air when asbestos-containing materials are removed from older installations, filter respirators, special clothing, and plastic bags to contain the materials must be used, along with proper removal procedures. Here, workers are being trained in the proper procedures, using nonasbestos-containing materials for practice.

Laborer's International Union of North America

minute tarry droplets. The size of the particles contained in tobacco smoke is 0.25 μm.

Aerosols

Liquid droplets or solid particles dispersed in air, that are of fine enough particle size to remain so dispersed for a period of time, are called aerosols.

Mists

Mists are suspended liquid droplets generated by condensation from the gaseous to the liquid state or by breaking up a liquid into a dispersed state, by splashing, foaming, or atomizing. Mist is formed when a finely divided liquid is suspended in the atmosphere. Examples are the oil mist produced during cutting and grinding operations, acid mists from electroplating, acid or alkali mists from pickling operations, paint spray mist from spraying operations, and the condensation of water vapor to form a fog or rain.

Gases

Normally gases are formless fluids that occupy the space or enclosure in which they are confined and which can be changed to the liquid or solid state only by the combined effect of increased pressure and decreased temperature. Gases diffuse. Examples are welding gases, internal combustion engine exhaust gases, and air.

Vapors

The gaseous forms of substances that appear normally in the solid or liquid state (at room temperature and pressure) are called "vapors." The vapor can be changed back to the solid or liquid state either by increasing the pressure or decreasing the temperature alone. Vapors also diffuse. Evaporation is the process by which a liquid is changed into the vapor state and mixed with the surrounding atmosphere. Solvents that will boil at relatively low temperatures, for example, acetone, will vaporize readily at room temperature.

Hazards involved

The hazard associated with breathing a gas, vapor, or mist usually depends upon the solubility of the substance. For example, if the compound is very soluble—such as ammonia, formaldehyde, sulfuric acid, and hydrochloric acid—it is rapidly absorbed in the upper respiratory tract and does not penetrate deeply into the lungs. Consequently, the nose and throat become so irritated that a person is driven out of the exposure area before he or she is in much danger from the toxicity of the gas. Nevertheless, exposures even for brief periods to high concentrations of these compounds can cause serious problems.

Compounds that are not soluble in body fluids cause considerably less pain than the soluble ones, and can penetrate deeply into the lungs. Thus, a serious hazard can be present, but not be immediately recognized. Examples of such gases are nitrogen dioxide and ozone. The immediate danger from these compounds in high concentrations is acute edema or, possibly later, pneumonia or circulatory impairment.

There are numerous chemical compounds that do not follow the general solubility rule. They are not especially soluble in water and yet are irritating to the eyes and respiratory tract. They can also cause lung damage and even death under the right conditions. One example is acrolein.

SOLVENTS

The widespread industrial use of solvents can cause major problems. The supervisor can assist the hygienist and safety professional in helping to maintain control over such exposure. Substantial exposures, fortunately, are usually controlled—spray painting booths are ventilated and degreasing tanks are exhausted. These do not, ordinarily, present serious hazards as long as everything goes well. It is the job of the supervisor to make sure that controls and personal protective equipment are properly maintained and are used at all times.

Small exposures—jobs that come up infrequently or that involve small amounts of solvents not covered by standard operating procedures—cause the most problems. The point to remember is not how much solvent is used at the jobsite, but how much solvent a person inhales. A close check must be kept on all minor uses of solvents. A solvent should be issued only after it has been determined that it can be used properly and safely. Industrial health authorities or your safety professional have information about what solvents to use and for what purpose. It is up to the supervisor to see that this information is used and that employees follow the recommendations.

Selection and handling

Getting the job done without hazard to employees or property is dependent upon the proper selection, application, handling, and control of solvents and an understanding of their properties.

The term "solvent" refers to those organic liquids commonly used to dissolve other organic materials. Some solvents are naphtha, mineral spirits, gasoline, turpentine, benzene, alcohol, and trichloroethylene.

A good working knowledge of the nomenclature and effects of exposure to solvents is helpful in making a proper assessment of damage or harm.

Nomenclature can be misleading and confusing. Consider, for example, the two solvents benzine and benzene. They are spelled nearly the same; they are pronounced the same; yet they are different with respect to their toxicity. To distinguish them more clearly, benzene, the more toxic of the two, is sometimes called *benzol*. The distinction is especially important because benzol is considered a carcinogen (a substance that tends to produce a cancer).

Another nomenclature problem that can cause confusion is the similarity of names for the various kinds of solvents in the chlorinated hydrocarbon family. Perchloroethylene, trichloroethylene, trichloromethane, and dichloromethane are a few examples of such solvents that have similar sounding names yet each has its own characteristic hazards.

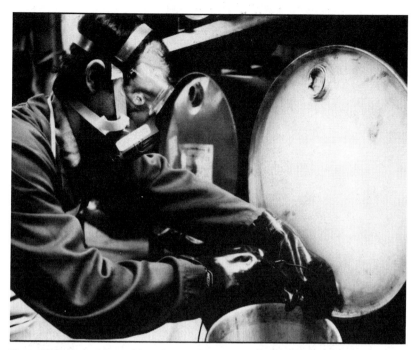

Figure 6-2. To avoid possible contact with toxic substances, this worker is wearing job-fitted gloves, apron, and long sleeves in addition to respirator and wraparound eye protection. The degree of hazard is determined not only by the toxicity of the substance itself, but also by the conditions of its use.

North Safety Equipment, A Division of Siebe North, Inc.

When you see chemical names on warning labels, it is best to discuss handling procedures with your industrial hygienist, safety professional, or chemist. The supervisor should study the labels placed on containers by the manufacturer. Labels should tell what precautions are necessary when the solvents are used. Information indicating health and fire hazards is extremely important. In fact, if a solvent is not properly labeled, it should not be used. The purchasing department should notify suppliers that improperly labeled solvents will not be accepted in the plant.

Many companies have developed hazardous materials control programs that are designed to help employees become aware of not only the hazardous properties of materials they work with, but also with the procedures and protective measures required for safe handling and usage (see Figure 6-2). Supervisors should be thoroughly familiar with such programs.

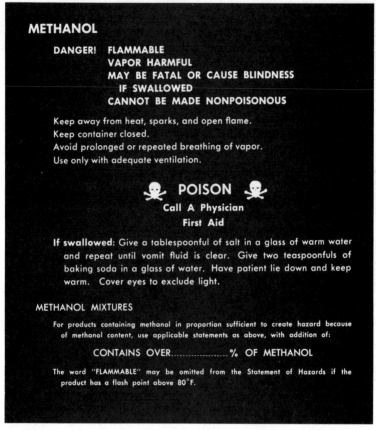

Figure 6-3. Hazardous chemical label conforming to American National Standard Z129.1 is shown here. For labeling of consumer products and for identification during shipment, consult appropriate federal regulations.

Degree of severity of solvent hazards

The severity of hazard in the use of organic solvents depends on the following facts:

How the solvent is used

Type of job operation (determines how the workers are exposed)

Work pattern

Duration of exposure

Operating temperature

Exposed liquid surface

Ventilation efficiency

Evaporation rate of solvent

Pattern of air flow

Concentration of vapor in workroom air

Housekeeping

The solvent hazard, therefore, is determined not only by the toxicity of the solvent itself, but by the conditions of its use—who, what, how, where, and how long. Precautionary labeling should indicate the major hazards and safeguards (see Figure 6-3).

For convenience, job operations employing solvents may be divided into three categories:

1. Direct contact is a consequence of hand operations. Emergency repair of equipment, spraying or packaging volatile materials without ventilation, cleanup of spills, and manual cleaning using cloths or brushes wetted with solvent are examples where employees may have direct contact with the solvent.

   It is important to remember that solvents can penetrate the skin and be absorbed into the body. Solvents are a leading cause of industrial dermatitis or skin diseases. Thus, properly selected gloves and clothing must be used in order to avoid a situation in which solvents come in contact with the skin.

2. Intermittent or infrequent contact is encountered when the solvent is contained in a semi-closed system where exposure can be controlled. Examples are paint spraying in an exhausted spray booth, vapor degreasing in a tank with local lateral slot exhaust ventilation, and charging reactors or kettles in a batch-type operation, where the worker is exposed only at infrequent intervals.

3. Minimal contact is characterized by remote operation of equipment totally isolated from the work area. This type of operation includes directing chemical plant operations from a control room, mechanical handling of bulk packaged materials, and other operations where the solvent is contained in a closed system and is not discharged to the atmosphere in the work area.

"Safety" solvents. It is unfortunate that the term "safety" solvent has been applied to some proprietary cold cleaners, because the term is not precise and subject to various interpretations. For example, a "safety" solvent may be considered by some users as nondamaging to the surfaces being cleaned. Other users may consider it to be free from fire or toxicity hazards. Depending on the conditions of use, neither of these criteria may be met by a so-called "safety" solvent.

Figure 6-4. A supervisor who believes he or she has a dust, fume, vapor, or radiation hazard should consult an industrial hygienist. Here an instrument for measuring carbon monoxide levels is being used to check warehouse atmosphere.

E. D. Bullard Company

These solvents are prepared as mixtures of halogenated hydrocarbons and petroleum hydrocarbons to be used for cold cleaning. Although the halogenated hydrocarbons are effective grease and oil solvents and generally have no flash or fire point, they are relatively expensive and may be toxic under adverse conditions. The petroleum hydrocarbons are effective solvents, low in toxicity, and inexpensive, but they have flash and fire points.

To combine the best qualities of each solvent, manufacturers mix them in an attempt to produce a cold cleaner that has a flash point higher than that of the flammable petroleum hydrocarbon. Such a mixture, however, can present both fire and toxicity hazards, depending on the evaporation rates of the solvents used. If the flammable liquid is more volatile than the nonflammable solvent, the vapors from the mixture can be highly flammable. Conversely, if the nonflammable solvent is more volatile, it can evaporate to leave a flammable liquid.

These considerations should always be kept in mind by users of such solvents. Never forget that, under the right conditions, the vapor from a "safety" solvent can be just as deadly as the vapor from an extremely toxic solvent.

If there is a chance that anyone might be exposed to hazardous substances in the workroom air, have the breathing zone checked carefully (see Figure 6-4).

PARTICULATES

Dusts and particulate matter (such as fumes) also fall in the chemical category. To properly evaluate dust exposures, one must know the chemical composition, particle size, dust concentration in air, method of dispersion, and many other factors described in this section.

With the exception of certain fibrous materials, dust particles must usually be smaller than 5 μm in order to enter the alveoli or inner recess of the lungs. See the cutaway illustration in Figure 6-6. Although a few particles up to 10 μm in size may enter the lungs occasionally, nearly all the larger particles are trapped in the nasal passages, throat, larynx, trachea, and bronchi, from which they are expectorated or swallowed and enter into the digestive tract.

A person with normal eyesight can detect dust particles as small as 50 μm in diameter. Smaller airborne particles can be detected individually by the naked eye only when strong light is reflected from them, as in a projector beam or a sunbeam. Dust of respirable size (below 10 μm) can be seen only with the aid of a microscope. Most industrial dusts consist of particles that vary widely in size, with the small particles greatly outnumbering the large ones. Consequently, with few exceptions, when dust can be seen in the air around an operation, there are probably more invisible dust particles than visible ones present.

Dispersion

In order for particulate matter to become airborne, some form of energy is required. A solid or liquid particle of sufficient mass will be thrown a considerable distance if ejected from its source with a high enough velocity. This type of dispersion is known as dynamic projection and is a result of the kinetic energy (which is one-half the mass times the square of the velocity) and is too small to overcome air resistance. The particle's forward velocity is thus minimized and it remains suspended in the containing air mass.

As a rough approximation, macroscopic particles (those large enough to be visible to the naked eye) are considered to be dispersed by dynamic projection. Microscopic particles (those visible only through a microscope) are considered to have a mass so small that their movement is dependent on the containing air mass. Contaminants such as the larger dust particles, mists, and sprays, which are dispersed by dynamic projection, can cause external injury such as acid burns, eye damage, and dermatitis. The microscopic particles may be dangerous to health, if inhaled.

Nonmetallic dusts

A number of occupational diseases result from exposures to such non-metallic dusts as silicia and asbestos. Although specialized knowledge and instruments are needed to determine the severity of a hazard, the supervisor can, however, recognize a danger spot and ask for expert help. If a supervisor is not alert, a lot of harm can be done.

Here are some of the things to watch for.

A process that produces dust fine enough to remain suspended in the air long enough to be breathed should be regarded as questionable until it can be proven safe. For example, a dust is produced in hard rock mines and by quarrying and dressing granite, which contains free silica. Silicosis is a lung disease caused by exposure to free silica.

The danger of lung disease from the grinding wheel itself disappeared when the natural sandstone wheel was replaced with the Carborundum wheel and the Alundum wheel. Neither produces silicosis; however, when they are used to grind castings that contain mold sand, the grinding operation can still present a silicosis hazard.

Methods of drilling rock with power machinery produce more dust than old-fashioned hand methods. This dust, however, is controlled by applying water to the drill steel so that the dust forms a slurry instead of being suspended in air.

Processes in which inorganic materials are crushed, ground, or transported are potential sources of dust. They should either be controlled by use of wet methods or should be enclosed and ventilated by local exhaust. Points where conveyors are loaded or discharged, transfer points along the conveying system, and heads or boots of elevators should be enclosed and, usually, exhaust ventilated.

Supervisors must be on the alert to see that someone does not cancel the effectiveness of built-in dust controls by tampering with them or by using them improperly. They must also insist that required respiratory equipment is worn by those workers who need supplementary protection.

Fumes

Welding, metalizing, and other hot operations produce fumes, which may be harmful under certain conditions.

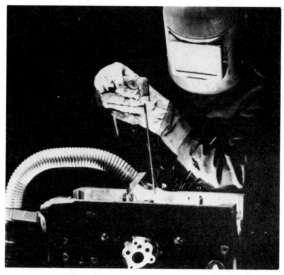

Figure 6-5. Flexible connection to high-velocity exhaust system draws off welding fumes at point of generation.

Eutectic Corporation

Arc welding volatilizes metal that then condenses—as the metal or its oxide—in the air around the arc. In addition, the rod coating is in part volatilized. These fumes, because they are extremely fine, are readily inhaled.

Iron pigment in the lung appears to have no effect in producing illness or disability. Its presence shows up in X-rays of the lungs and may lead to a mistaken diagnosis of silicosis.

More highly toxic materials—such as those formed when welding structures that have been painted with red lead, or when welding galvanized metal—may produce severe symptoms of toxicity rather rapidly, unless fumes are controlled with good local exhaust ventilation, or the welder is protected by respiratory protective equipment.

When pouring brass, zinc volatilizes from the molten mass and oxidizes in the surrounding air to produce a zinc fume, which (in high concentrations) may produce the rather nonspecific disease known as "metal fume fever" or "brass ague." If lead is present, it also will become airborne. As a result, brass foundry workers may incur a lead intoxication—chronic if the lead is present only in very small amounts, and acute if it is present in substantial amounts.

Most soldering operations, fortunately, do not require temperatures high enough to volatize an appreciable amount of lead. However, some

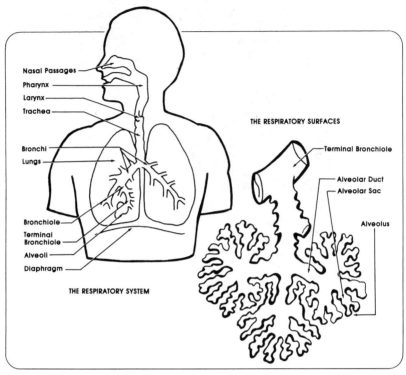

Figure 6-6. Cutaway shows the major parts of the respiratory system. *At right,* a lung lobule is shown greatly enlarged.

of the lead in the molten solder is oxidized by contact with air at the surface. If this oxide, often called dross, is mechanically dispersed into the air, it may produce a severe lead poisoning hazard.

In operations where this might happen, for example, soldering or lead battery making, prevention of occupational poisoning is largely a matter of scrupulously clean housekeeping to prevent the lead oxide from ever becoming dispersed into the air. It is customary to enclose melting pots, dross boxes, and similar operations, and to provide exhaust ventilation.

RESPIRATORY PROTECTION

It is important that supervisors have an understanding of the basic concepts of respiratory protection, if they are to properly protect their workers. A competent industrial hygienist or safety professional should decide what kind of respiratory protection is needed. However, the more supervisors know about respiratory hazards, and the types and selection of respirators, the better prepared they will be to make sure that employees are protected. Figure 6-6 shows the parts of the respiratory system, including an enlargement of the respiratory surface, or lung lobule.

Respiratory hazards

When a respiratory hazard exists or is suspected, the actual airborne concentration of the air contaminant(s) must be measured by an industrial hygienist. Sometimes determination can be made concerning the degree or type of respiratory hazard involved by using past experience with similar industrial processes.

For example, some typical industrial processes are the respiratory hazards that might result are listed here.

Manufacturing Process	*Possible Respiratory Hazards*
Brake shoe relining	Asbestos dust
Coke oven	Coal tar pitch dust and smoke
Core blowing	Phenol and/or formaldehyde vapor, triethylamine vapor
Degreasing	Methylchloroform vapors or other organic vapors
Foundry core knock out	Dust that contains silica
Grey iron mill room—grinding	Dust that contains silica
Machining	Oil mist
Mulling, core knock out, shakeout	Dust that contains silica
Oil quench	Smoke
Pickling	Mists that contain acid
Plating	Vapors or mists containing acids and/or chromates
Sanding and grinding on surfaces painted red, orange, or yellow	Dust containing lead and chromium
Solvent handling	Organic vapor
Spray painting	Airborne mist containing lead and chromium
	Solvent vapor
Welding through surfaces painted yellow, orange, or red	Fumes containing lead and chromium

A respiratory hazard about which the supervisor must constantly be aware is oxygen deficiency. This results when the air contains less than the normal percentage of oxygen found in the atmosphere. Oxygen is present in the atmosphere at about 21 percent. An environment is immediately hazardous to life and health when the oxygen level is 16 percent or lower.

The degree of hazard involved is also an important factor when analyzing respiratory hazards. Some respiratory hazards can produce environments immediately hazardous to life and health when the air contaminants are present in high concentrations. Oxygen deficiency, by its very nature, is immediately dangerous to life and health. Gasses and vapors can also be immediately dangerous to life and health, if they are present in high concentrations.

Selection of the proper respirator is important and is discussed in Chapter 9, "Personal Protective Equipment."

PHYSICAL AGENTS

The second category of environmental factors or stresses involves physical agents. Problems relating to such things as noise, ionizing radiation, nonionizing radiation, temperature extremes, and pressure extremes fall into this category. It is important that the supervisor watch for these hazards because they can have immediate or cumulative effects on employee health.

Noise

Noise—defined as unwanted sound—is a form of vibration that can be conducted through solids, liquids, or gases. The effects of noise include the following:

• Psychological effects, for example, noise can startle, annoy, and disrupt concentration, sleep, or relaxation.

• Interference with communication by speech, and as a consequence, interferes with job performance and safety.

• Physiological effects, for example, noise-induced loss of hearing, or aural pain, even nausea (when the exposure is severe).

Damage risk criteria. If the ear is subjected to high levels of noise for a sufficient period of time, some loss of hearing may occur. A number of factors can influence the effect of the noise exposure. Among these are:

Variation in individual susceptibility

Total energy of the sound

Frequency distribution of the sound

Other characteristics of the noise exposure, whether it is continuous,

TABLE 6-A
PERMISSIBLE EXPOSURES

Duration per Day Hours	Sound Level dB(A)*
8	90
6	92
4	95
3	97
2	100
1½	102
1	105
³/₄	107
½	110
¼	115-C**

*Sound level in decibels as measured on a standard level meter operating on the A-weighting network with slow meter response.
**Ceiling Value

intermittent, or made up of a series of impacts

Total daily time of exposure

Length of employment in the noisy environment.

Because of the complex relationships of noise and exposure time to partial loss of hearing and the many other possible contributory causes for hearing loss, it is difficult to give exact rules for protecting workers. However, criteria have been developed to protect against hearing loss in the speech frequency range. In fact, these criteria, known as the Threshold Limit Values (TLVs®) for noise, are observed by the U.S. Department of Labor under the Occupational Safety and Health Act; they have the force of law. See Table 6-A.

Normally, it is not possible for the supervisor to measure noise levels. This should be done by an industrial hygienist or a safety professional (see Figure 6-7) who then gives the supervisor the necessary data for establishing administrative controls or advises as to the necessity for hearing protection. Details and definitions of noise and its measurement, evaluation, and control are given in NSC's books *Fundamentals of Industrial Hygiene* and *Industrial Noise and Hearing Conservation*.

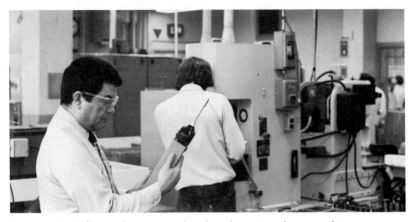

Figure 6-7. Professional uses octave band analyzer to make a sound survey.

General Radio Company

Rules of thumb. There are three nontechnical rules of thumb that supervisors can use to determine if a work area has excessive noise.

1. If it is necessary to speak in a loud voice or shout directly into the ear of a person in order to be understood, it is likely that the Exposure limit for noise is being exceeded.

2. If employees tell you that they have heard noises in their heads and ringing noises in their ears at the end of the work day, they are being exposed to too much noise.

3. If employees complain that speech or music sounds are muffled to them after leaving work, but sounds fairly clear in the morning before they return to work, there is no doubt about their being exposed to dangerous noise levels that can cause a partial loss of hearing that can be permanent.

Protecting hearing

The supervisor can prevent excessive exposure to noise by working closely with engineering personnel in attempting to reduce noise levels. If the noise cannot be reduced by engineering means, the supervisor can resort to administrative controls, rotating employees so that the time they spend in a noisy area does not exceed a specified limit. If this is not feasible, or if engineering controls cannot be installed for a long period of time, the supervisor must enforce the wearing of hearing protective devices. In this respect, as with all aspects of safety, the supervisor must set a good example. An effective hearing conservation program should address the following areas.

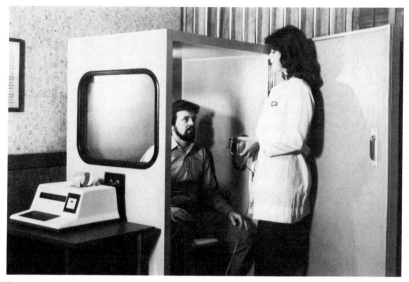

Figure 6-8. Audiometric booth provides the necessary background-noise-free environment for administering hearing tests—a vital part of a hearing conservation program.

Eckel Industries Inc.

Personal hearing-protective devices. The wearing of ear protectors must be enforced if the exposure is greater than 90 dBA or if the employee shows a significant hearing loss on a hearing test called an "audiogram." These requirements will become more stringent if the OSHA Hearing Conservation Amendment is put into effect.

Audiograms. The first audiogram is called the baseline audiogram, because it is the basis of comparison for subsequent yearly audiograms that are also required to assess hearing. Employees should be notified if a significant shift in hearing is discovered.

Testing is an important part of any hearing conservation program. To be successful, it requires the close cooperation of the supervisor. If possible, the supervisor should schedule employees so that their hearing can be tested before they are subjected to noise. A good time for testing hearing is, therefore, prior to work. If this is not possible and employees must be called off the job, the supervisor must make certain that the employees who are selected for hearing tests wear ear plugs or muffs prior to their test. This will help avoid the problem of possibly confusing what may be a temporary detrimental effect on hearing with a more serious long-term effect.

Tests must be conducted in a noise-free environment, such as a testing booth (see Figure 6-8).

Training The training program should be repeated annually and should cover such topics as the effects of noise on hearing; purpose, advantages, disadvantages, use, fitting and care of hearing protectors; and explanations of audiometric testing.

Supervisors whose workplaces have hearing conservation programs will find themselves responsible for front-line supervision of the use and care of personal hearing-protective devices. Setting an example by proper use of his or her own ear plugs or muffs is an important component of a successful program.

Ionizing radiation

Although ionizing radiation is a complex subject, a brief discussion is included here because it is one of the more dangerous physical agents. (Please refer to Figure 6-9.)

Gamma radiation from radioactive materials and X-radiation are highly penetrating and can produce damage. The amount of damage depends, in part, on the energy of the radiation and also on the relative sensitivity of the tissue.

Alpha and beta radiation are two other types of ionizing radiation. Alpha particles are heavy and thus do not travel far in air. Alpha particles are usually stopped by the skin. But, if particles are inhaled or ingested, they can do considerable internal damage. Beta radiation is lighter and thus travels farther. If a beta source is left on the skin, it can do damage. Some type of shielding material is necessary to protect from beta radiation.

High-energy protons and neutrons. In the handling of some types of radioactive materials and in the operation of the high-powered particle accelerators, bombardment by high-speed protons and by both high-speed and thermal neutrons must also be considered possible health hazards.

X-radiation is produced by high-potential electrical discharge in a vacuum and should be anticipated in evacuated electrical apparatus operating at a potential of 10,000 volts or more. Although X-radiation is certain to be produced in such apparatus, it is dangerous only if it penetrates the jacket of the apparatus and enters the inhabited part of the workroom.

If one is overexposed to the radiation of a comparatively low-voltage X-ray tube, dermatitis of the hand is generally the first result. It is characterized by a rough, dry skin, a wartlike growth, and dry, brittle

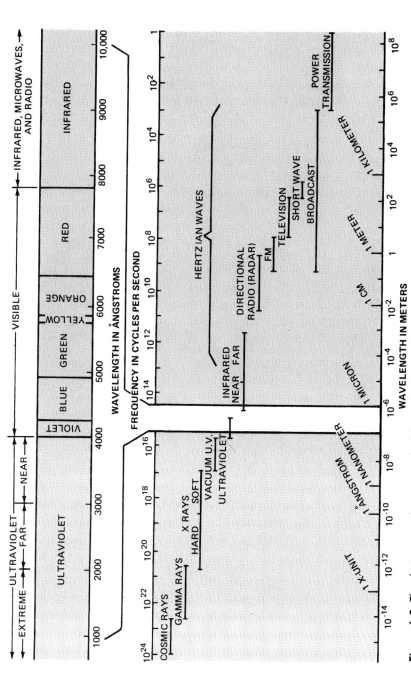

Figure 6-9. The electromagnetic spectrum. Ionizing radiations are shown on the lower portion; nonionizing radiations are illustrated on the expanded (upper) portion. Note that "cycles per second" is called hertz.

107

nails. With continuing exposure and somewhat more penetrating X-rays, bone destruction will develop.

Beta sources and X- and gamma-radiation are found in industry in some gages to measure thickness of various materials or in beta-source thickness gages. Sealed gamma sources and X-ray generators are seen in industry as various types of level gages, for example, to measure the level of a liquid inside a tank. They are also used to X-ray the welds where joints are joined.

These types of radiation all cause injury by ionizing the tissue in which they are absorbed. Such injuries differ widely in location and extent, but the determining factors are the ability of the particular radiation to penetrate through the tissues and the amount of ionization produced by a given physical amount of the radiation. Alpha radiation, for instance, is classed as 20 times as biologically effective as X-ray because the alpha particles are heavy and possess a great deal of ability to disrupt and ionize the tissue molecules with which they come in contact.

Although this discussion is concerned primarily with X-rays and gamma radiation because they are the best known, the same statements apply qualitatively to other types of penetrating radiation. The general method for preventing injuries from any penetrating radiations is separation from them, by distance or by shielding with heavy substances in sufficient quantity to reduce the radiation received to below the maximum permissible dose, and by limiting the time of exposure.

Rules for working with ionizing radiation will be set by industrial hygienists or health physicists. They must be strictly followed at all times to avoid the chance of radiation injuries and illnesses.

Nonionizing radiation

Electromagnetic radiation has varying effects on the body, depending largely on the particular wavelength of the radiation involved. Following, in approximate order of decreasing wavelength and increasing frequency, are some hazards associated with different regions of the nonionizing electromagnetic radiation spectrum.

Low frequency. The longer wavelengths—including power frequencies, broadcast, radio, short wave radio—can produce general heating of the body. The health hazard from these radiations is thought to be minimal, however, since it is unlikely that they would be found in intensities great enough to cause significant effect.

Microwaves have wavelengths of 3 m to 3 mm (100 to 100,000 megahertz, MHz). They are found in radar, communications, and diathermy applications. Microwave intensities may be sufficient to cause significant heating of tissues.

Effect is related to wavelength, power intensity, and time of exposure. Generally, the longer wavelengths will produce a greater temperature increase in deeper tissues than do the shorter wavelengths. However, for a given power intensity, there is less subjective awareness to the heat from longer wavelengths that there is to the heat from shorter wavelengths because of its absorption beneath the body's surface.

An intolerable rise in body temperature, as well as localized damage, can result from an exposure of sufficient intensity and time. In addition, flammable gases and vapors may ignite when they are inside metallic objects located in a microwave beam.

Power intensities from microwaves are given in units of watts per square centimeter (w/cm²). Areas having a power intensity that is greater than 0.01 watts per square centimeter should be avoided. In such areas, dummy loads should be used to absorb the energy output while equipment is being operated or tested. If a dummy load cannot be used, adjacent populated areas should be protected by adequate shielding.

Infrared radiation does not penetrate much below the superficial layer of the skin so that its major effect is to heat the skin tissues immediately below it. The health hazard upon exposure to infrared radiation depends on the frequency and strength of the radiation, the source, the exposure time and distance, and the susceptibility of the individual.

Ultraviolet radiation and visible radiation also do not penetrate appreciably below the skin; their effects are essentially heating on the surface. However, high-intensity visible radiation can severely damage the retina of the eye, even causing blindness in a relatively short exposure time. This is the reason behind the insistent warnings to the public about not staring directly at the sun during periods of partial solar eclipses.

The effects of ultraviolet light are generally more of a problem because ultraviolet can produce a severe burn with no warning whatsoever, and excessive exposure can result in significant damage to the eye lens. The automatic defense mechanism of closing the eyes or looking away usually prevents damage. It should be emphasized that this defense mechanism is not effective against visible light emitted by lasers.

Because ultraviolet radiation in industry is found around electrical arcs, they should be shielded by opaque materials. Opacity in the ultraviolet has no relation to opacity in the visible part of the spectrum. Ordinary window glass, for instance, is almost completely opaque to the ultraviolet although transparent to the visible. A piece of plastic dyed a deep red-violet may be almost entirely opaque in the visible part of the spectrum and transparent in the near ultraviolet.

Electric welding arcs and germicidal lamps are the most common strong procedures of ultraviolet in industry. The ordinary fluorescent lamp generates a good deal of ultraviolet inside the bulb, but is essentially absorbed in the glass bulb and its fluorescent coating.

The most common exposure to ultraviolet radiation is from direct sunshine. People who continually work outdoors in the full light of the sun may develop tumors on exposed areas of the skin. These tumors occasionally become malignant.

Ultraviolet radiation from the sun also increases the skin effects of some industrial materials. After exposure to compounds such as cresols, the skin is exceptionally sensitive to the sun. Even a short exposure in the late afternoon when the sun is low is likely to produce a severe sunburn. There are other compounds that minimize the effects of UV-rays. Some of these are used in certain protective creams, for example, sunblocks that are found in various suntan lotions.

VISIBLE RADIATION OR LIGHTING

Visible radiation, which falls about halfway up the spectrum of frequency and wavelength, concerns the supervisor because it can affect both the quality and accuracy of work. Good lighting invariably results in increased product quality with less spoilage and increased production. Good lighting contributes to sanitary, clean, and neat operations. (See Figure 6-10.)

What is good lighting? Many factors help to produce it—color of the light, direction and diffusion, and amount. The nature of illuminated surfaces is important. A dark gray, dirty surface may reflect only 10 or 12 percent of the incident light, while a light-colored, clean surface may reflect more than 90 percent.

Lighting should be bright enough to produce easy sight and directed so that it does not create glare. The level should be high enough to permit efficient sight. The *Accident Prevention Manual for Industrial Operations* lists the illumination levels and brightness ratios recommended for various occupational tasks by the Illuminating Engineering Society. The IES's *Practice for Industrial Lighting* is designated as American National Standard ANS1/IES RP7.

One of the more objectionable features of lighting is glare—brightness within the field of vision that causes discomfort or interferes with seeing. The brightness can be caused by either direct or reflected light. To prevent glare, keep the source of light well above the line of vision, or shield it with opaque or translucent material.

Figure 6-10. Company program saves energy and provides more light. Standard fluorescent units were replaced with lamps using 14 to 20 percent less energy and giving more lumens per watt. The program included fixture cleaning, which alone helped raise illumination levels an average of three times.

GTE Products Corporation

Objectionable glare can originate from a surface that reflects the image of the light source directly into the line of vision, for example, from polished control handles or machinery dials. You can dull reflections by having such surfaces matte (dull), rather than polished or smooth.

Almost as bad as this is an area of excessively high brightness in the visual field. A highly reflecting white paper in the center of a dark, nonreflecting surface, and a brightly illuminated control handle or dial on a dark or dirty machine are two examples.

To prevent this condition, keep surfaces light or dark with little difference in surface reflectivity. Color contrasts are all right, however.

Although it is generally best to provide even, shadow-free light, some jobs require contrast lighting. In these cases, keep the general or background light well diffused and glareless, and add a supplementary source of light directed to cast shadows as desired. Too much contrast in brightness between the work and its surroundings is distracting and harmful as is direct or reflected glare.

Lasers

Lasers emit beams of coherent light of a single color (or wavelength).

111

Contrast this with conventional light sources that produce random, disordered light wave mixtures of various wavelengths. The word *laser* is an acronym for Light Amplification by Stimulated Emission of Radiation. A laser is made up of light waves that are nearly parallel to each other (collimated), and that are all traveling in the same direction. Electrons of atoms capable of emitting excess energy in the form of visible light are "pumped" full of enough energy to force them into higher-energy-level orbits. These electrons quickly return to their normal-energy-level orbits but, in so doing, they emit a photon of visible light. The light waves that are given off are directed to produce the coherent laser beam.

The maser, the laser's predecessor, emits microwaves instead of light. Some companies call their lasers "optical masers."

Lasers are extremely versatile; they are being used in many ways and new applications are being developed every year. Lasers are used for welding microscopic parts, for welding heat-resistant exotic metals, for communications instruments, for all kinds of guidance systems, for various surgical procedures, in chemistry laboratories, and in other applications too numerous to mention.

Since the laser is highly collimated (has a small divergence angle), it can pack a large energy density in a narrow beam. Direct viewing of the laser should therefore be avoided. The work area should contain no reflective surfaces (such as mirrors or highly polished furniture) for even a reflected laser beam can be hazardous. Suitable shielding to contain the laser beam should be provided.

Biological effects. The eye is the organ most vulnerable to injury induced by laser energy. The reason for this is the ability of the cornea and lens to focus the parallel laser beam on a small spot on the retina.

Never directly observe a laser beam or its reflection with an optical aid, such as a binocular or a microscope. The fact that infrared radiation of certain lasers may not be visible to the naked eye contributes to the potential hazard. Eyes must be protected; see Figure 6-11.

Lasers generating in the ultraviolet range of the electromagnetic spectrum produce corneal burns rather than retinal damage, because of the way the eye handles ultraviolet light.

Other factors that have a bearing on the degree of eye injury induced by laser light are: (*a*) the pupil size—the smaller the pupil diameter, the smaller the amount of laser energy permitted to the retina; (*b*) the power of the cornea and lens to focus the incident light on the retina; (*c*) the distance from the source of energy to the retina; (*d*) the energy and wavelength of the laser; (*e*) the pigmentation of the subject; (*f*) the place on the retina where the light is focused; (*g*) the divergence of the laser light;

Figure 6-11. Eyes must be protected when working with lasers because the high concentration of energy in the narrow beam of light can easily damage eyesight.

AO Safety Products, Division of American Optical Corp.

and (h) the presence of scattering media in the light path.

TEMPERATURE EXTREMES

General experience shows that extremes of temperature affect the amount of work that people can do and the manner in which they do it. The industrial problem is more often that of exposure to high temperatures than to low temperatures.

The body is continuously producing heat through its metabolic process. Since the body processes are designed so that they can operate only within a narrow limit of temperature, they must dissipate this heat as rapidly as it is produced, if the body is to function efficiently and well. A sensitive and rapidly acting set of thermostatic devices in the body must also control the rates of its temperature-regulating processes.

Sweating

Sweating is the most important of the temperature-regulating and heat-dissipating processes. Almost all parts of the skin are provided with sweat glands that excrete a liquid (mostly water and a little salt) to the surface of the body. This process goes on continuously, even under conditions of rest.

In an individual who is resting and not under stress, the sweating rate is approximately 1 liter per day, which is evaporated in the air as rapidly as it is excreted. Under the stress of heavy work or high temperature, this sweating rate may increase to as much as 4 liters (approximately one gallon) in 4 hours. As much as 10 to 12 gm (150 to 190 grains) of salt per day will be lost with the water. Both the water and salt loss must be replaced promptly if good health is to continue. In terms of stress, an individual's ability to acclimate is variable and such stress is especially dangerous for those with heart problems.

If the sweat can be evaporated as rapidly as it can be formed, and if the heat stress is not such as to exceed the maximum sweating rate of which the body is capable, the body can maintain the necessary constant temperature.

The rate of evaporation depends on the moisture content of the surrounding air, the rate of air movement, and the temperature of the surrounding air. The industrial hygienist must simultaneously deal with all of these factors in any attempt to determine the effect of the thermal environment on humans.

Radiation

Radiation accounts for some of the body's equilibrium with its surroundings. If an object in the surroundings is far below body temperature, such as a glass window on a subzero day, a large amount of heat can be radiated from the person and the person may feel chilled even if the air in the immediate environment is fairly warm. Conversely, if an object in the surroundings, such as a furnace wall, is above body temperature, people can receive a large amount of heat by radiation, and it may be extremely difficult to keep them cool enough by the other available means.

Radiant heat is electromagnetic energy that does no heating whatsoever until it strikes some object, such as a person, where it is absorbed.

Merely blowing air around offers no relief—the only protection is to set up an invisible infrared shadow. This can be done by placing any kind of opaque shield or screen between the person and the radiating surface. This is discussed later under Preventing Heat Stress.

Conduction

Conduction through the clothing and dissipation into the air provides some cooling to the body. This usually is not an important means of cooling because the conductivity of clothing and the heat capacity of air are usually low.

Conduction and convection become an important means of heat loss when the body is in contact with a good cooling agent, such as water. For this reason, when people are exposed to cold water, they become chilled much more rapidly than when exposed to air at the same temperature.

Air movement cools the body by conduction and convection. But more importantly, moving air removes the layer of saturated air around the body (which is formed rapidly by evaporation of sweat) and replaces it with a fresh layer, capable of accepting more moisture.

Effects of high temperature

Effects of high temperature are counteracted by the body's attempt to keep the internal temperature down by increasing the rate of heart beat. The capillaries in the skin then dilate to bring more blood to the surface so that both the rate of cooling and, gradually, the body temperature, are increased.

If the thermal environment is tolerable, these measures will soon lead to an equilibrium where the heart rate and the body temperature remain constant. If this equilibrium is not reached until the body temperature is about 102 F (38.9 C), corresponding to a sweating rate of about 2 liters per hour, there is imminent danger of heatstroke.

Intermittent rest periods for persons necessarily exposed to extreme heat reduces this danger.

Heatstroke (also known as sunstroke) is not necessarily the result of exposure to the sun. It is caused by exposure to an environment in which the body is unable to cool itself sufficiently. Sweating stops and the body can no longer rid itself of excess heat. As a result, the body temperature rises, and reaches a point where the heat-regulating mechanism breaks down completely. The body temperature then rises rapidly.

The symptoms are hot dry skin, which may be red, mottled, or bluish, severe headache, visual disturbances, rapid temperature rise, and confusion, delirium, and loss of consciousness. The condition is recognizable by the flushed face and high temperature. The victim should be removed from the heat immediately and the body cooled as rapidly as possible, most readily by being wrapped in cool wet sheets. Studies show that for people admitted to hospital emergency rooms for heat stroke, the higher the body temperature upon admission, the higher the mortality rate. Since the condition may be fatal, medical help should be obtained as soon as possible.

Heatstroke is a much more serious condition than heat cramps or heat exhaustion, discussed next. An important predisposing factor is excessive physical exertion. The only method of control is to reduce the temperature of the surroundings or to increase the ability of the body to cool itself, so that body temperature does not rise. Heat shields, discussed under the next section, Preventing Heat Stress, are of value here.

Heat cramps may result from exposure to high temperature for a relatively long time, particularly if accompanied by heavy exertion, with excessive loss of salt and moisture from the body. Even if the moisture is replaced by drinking plenty of water, an excessive loss of salt may provoke heat cramps or heat exhaustion.

Heat cramps are characterized by the cramping of the muscles of either the skeletal system or the intestines. In either case, the condition may be relieved in a few hours under proper treatment, although soreness may persist for several days.

Heat exhaustion may result from physical exertion in a hot environment when vasomotor control and cardiac output are inadequate to meet the increased demand placed upon them by peripheral vasodilation. Its symptoms are a relatively low temperature, pallor, weak pulse, dizziness, profuse sweating, and cool moist skin.

Preventing heat stress

Most heat-related health problems can be prevented or, at least, the risk can be reduced. Following a few basic precautions should lessen heat stress.

• *Acclimatization* to heat by short exposures followed by longer periods of work in the hot environment can reduce heat stress. New employees and workers returning from an absence of two weeks or more should have a 5-day period of acclimatization. This period might begin with 50 percent of the normal workload and time exposures the first day and gradually build up to 100 percent on the fifth day.

• A variety of *engineering controls* including general ventilation and spot cooling by local exhaust ventilation at points of high heat production may be helpful. Evaporative cooling and mechanical refrigeration

Figure 6-12. Flexible, light-weight, aluminum proximity suit permits maintenance of hot equipment while refinery unit remains on stream.

are other ways to reduce heat. Cooling fans can also reduce heat in hot areas. Eliminating steam leaks will also help. Equipment modifications, the use of power tools to reduce manual labor, and using personal cooling devices or protective clothing (see Figure 6-12) are other ways to reduce heat exposure for workers.

• Such *work practices* as providing a period of acclimatization for new workers and those returning from two-week absences and making plenty of cool drinking water available—as much as a quart per worker per hour—can help to reduce the risk of heat disorders. Training first aid workers to recognize and treat heat stress and making the names of trained staff known to all workers is essential. Employers should also consider individual workers' physical conditions when determining their fitness for working in hot environments. Older workers, obese workers, and workers on certain types of medication are at greater risk for heat stress illnesses.

• Alternating *work and rest* periods, but with longer rest periods in a cool area, can help workers avoid heat strain. If possible, heavy work should be scheduled during the cooler parts of the day and appropriate protective clothing provided. Supervisors should permit workers to interrupt their work if they are extremely uncomfortable.

• *Employee education* is vital so that workers are aware of the need to replace fluids and salt loss by sweating, and so they can recognize dehydration, exhaustion, fainting, heat cramps, salt deficiency, and heat exhaustion and heat stroke as heat disorders. Workers should be advised to drink beyond the point of thirst. (Salt tablets are not recommended.) Workers should also be informed of the importance of weighing themselves daily before and after work to avoid dehydration.

ATMOSPHERIC PRESSURES

It has been recognized from the beginning of caisson work, dating back to about 1850, that those who work under greater-than-normal atmospheric pressures are subject to various ills. The main effect, decompression sickness (commonly known as the bends), results from the release of nitrogen bubbles into the circulation and tissues during decompression. The bubbles lodge at the joints and under muscles, causing severe cramps. To prevent this trouble, decompression is carried out slowly and by stages so that the nitrogen can be eliminated slowly, without the formation of bubbles.

Deep-sea divers are supplied with a mixture of helium and oxygen for breathing. Since helium is an inert diluent and is less soluble in blood and tissue than is nitrogen, it presents a less formidable decompression problem.

Under some conditions of work at high pressure, the concentration of carbon dioxide in the atmosphere may be considerably increased so that the carbon dioxide will act as a narcotic. Keeping the oxygen concentration high will minimize the condition, although not prevent it. This procedure is useful where the carbon dioxide concentration cannot be kept at a proper level.

Common troubles encountered by workers operating under compressed air are pain and congestion in the ears caused by the inability to ventilate the middle ear properly during compression and decompression. As a result, many workers under compressed air suffer from tem-

Figure 6-13. All confined areas, such as subsurface structures and tanks, must be tested for oxygen deficiency and toxic and flammable gases and vapors so that proper precautions can be taken. Crew shown here is testing for the presence of methane in the 440-mile (700 km) Angeles Tunnel, part of the Southern California water system project.

Mine Safety Appliances Company

porary and permanent hearing loss. The cause of this damage is considered to be obstruction of the eustachian tubes that prevents proper equalization of pressure on the middle ear.

The effects of reduced pressure on the worker are much the same as the effects of decompression from a high pressure. If pressure is reduced too rapidly, decompression sickness and ear disturbances similar to, if not identical with, the divers' conditions may result.

Persons working at reduced pressure are also subject to oxygen starvation, which can have serious and insidious effects upon the senses and judgment. There is a considerable amount of evidence showing that exposure for 3 to 4 hours to an altitude of 9000 ft (2.7 km) above sea level, without breathing an atmosphere enriched in oxygen, can result in severely impaired judgment. Even if pure oxygen is provided, the altitude should be limited to that giving the same partial pressure of oxygen as air at 8000 ft (2.4 km).

Reduced pressure is not the only condition under which oxygen starvation may occur. As discussed under Respiratory Protection earlier in this chapter, deficiency of oxygen in the atmosphere of confined spaces is commonly experienced in industry. For this reason, the oxygen content of any tank or other confined space should be checked before entry is made. Instruments, such as the oxygen analyzer, are commercially available for this purpose. (See Figure 6-13.)

Normal air contains approximately 21 percent oxygen by volume. The first physiologic signs of a deficiency of oxygen (anoxia) are increased rate and depth of breathing. Oxygen concentrations of less than 16 percent by volume cause dizziness, rapid heartbeat, and headache. One should never enter or remain in areas where tests have indicated such low concentrations unless wearing self-contained supplied-air respiratory equipment.

Oxygen-deficient atmospheres may cause inability to move and a semiconscious lack of concern about the imminence of death. In cases of sudden entry into areas containing little or no oxygen, the individual usually has no warning symptoms, but immediately loses consciousness and has no recollection of the incident if rescued and revived.

Atmospheric contaminants are discussed in the two following sections in this chapter, Threshold Limit Values and Standard Operating Procedures.

ERGONOMICS

The third category of environmental factors is ergonomic. Involved are human reactions to monotony, fatigue, repeated motion, and repeated shock.

The term "ergonomics" literally means the customs, habits, and laws of work. According to the International Labor Office, it is:

> . . . the application of human biological science in conjunction with the engineering sciences to achieve the optimum mutual adjustment of man and his work, their benefits being measured in terms of human efficiency and well-being.

The ergonomics approach goes beyond productivity, health and safety. It includes consideration of the total physiological and psychological demands of the job upon the workers.

In the broad sense, the benefits that can be expected from designing work systems to minimize physical stress on workers are:

- More efficient operation

- Fewer accidents

- Lower cost of operation

- Reduced training time, and

- More efficient use of personnel.

The human body can endure considerable discomfort and stress and can perform many awkward and unnatural movements—but only for a limited period of time. When, however, unnatural conditions or motions are continued for prolonged periods, the physiological limitations of the workers may be exceeded. To ensure a continuously high level of performance, work systems must be tailored to human capacities and limitations.

Biomechanics is that phase of engineering devoted to the improvement of the man-machine-task relationship in an effort to reduce operator discomfort and fatigue.

Biotechnology is a broader term. It encompasses biomechanics, human factors engineering, and engineering psychology. To arrive at biotechnological solutions to work-stress problems, the sciences of anatomy, physiology, psychology, anthropometry, and kinesiology need to be brought into play.

Areas of concern are:

- Strictly biomechanical aspects—the consideration of stress on muscles, bones, nerves, and joints

- Sensory aspects—the consideration of eye fatigue, color, audio signals, and the like

- External environment aspects—the consideration of lighting, glare, temperature, humidity, noise, atmospheric contaminants, and vibration

- The psychological and social aspects of the working environment.

Information obtained from studying these factors can be translated into tangible changes in work environments. Reducing fatigue and stress with redesigned hand tools, adjustable chairs and workbenches, better lighting, control of heat and humidity, and noise reduction are definitely rewarding improvements.

Mechanical vibration

A condition known to stonecutters as "dead fingers" or "white fingers," occurs mainly in the fingers of the hand used to guide the cutting tool. The circulation in this hand becomes impaired, and when exposed to cold, the fingers become white and lose sensation, as though mildly frostbitten. The condition usually disappears when the fingers are warmed for some time, but a few cases are sufficiently disabling that the individuals are forced to seek other types of work. In some instances, both hands are affected.

The condition has been observed in a number of other occupations involving the use of fairly light vibrating tools, such as the air hammers used for scarfing and chipping in the metal trades. The condition is produced by vibration while the fingers are held in a strained position and is aggravated by chilling of the fingers. Prevention of this condition is, of course, much more satisfactory than treatment.

Preventive measures include directing the exhaust air from airdriven tools away from the hands so that they will not become unduly chilled, use of handles of a comfortable size for the fingers, vibration-dampening measures or tool designs and, in some instances, substitution of mechanical cleaning methods for some of the hand methods that have produced most of the cases of white fingers. In many instances, simply preventing the fingers from becoming chilled while at work will eliminate the condition. Especially designed tools that reduce the vibration transmitted to the hand are also available.

Repeated motion

Repetitive motions or repeated shocks like those in sorting and assembling jobs often cause irritation and inflammation of the tendon sheaths of the hands and arms. The condition is generally known as tenosynovitis, and once established, it is painful and disabling.

The condition results from repeated excessive strain. It may occur in an employee who has been working at the same job for years who is suddenly asked to put in considerable overtime. It is most likely to occur to a new employee or to an employee transferred to a new job. Prevention of the condition is, of course, much more satisfactory than treatment.

For example, in the printing industry, cases of sore hands and wrists were prevented by lowering the surface of the jogging tables 2 in. (5 cm) so that the hands and wrists could fall into a relaxed position at the end of each motion.

The employees should be closely watched so that if they show signs of soreness in the backs of the hands, wrists, forearms, or shoulders, they can be transferred temporarily to other work or the job can be changed to reduce the strain.

Carpal tunnel syndrome is another disease of the hand and wrists associated with repetitive motions during which the wrist is in a bent position. These motions are thought to compress the nerve running through the wrist tunnel or the "carpal tunnel." This causes pain, numbness, tingling, and sometimes complete disability.

Splinting the wrists at night is one form of treatment. Some severe cases require surgery. Prevention of the condition is the most desirable solution. This may be accomplished by analyzing the work tasks to identify improper wrist angles and redesigning the job, the work layout, or the tools in order to eliminate these wrist positions, or to reduce the number of repetitions necessary.

BIOLOGICAL STRESSES

Biological stresses include any virus, bacteria, fungus, or any other living organism that has the capability to cause a disease in humans.

Tuberculosis

Tuberculosis and other infections are classified as occupational diseases when they are contracted by nurses, doctors, or attendants caring for tuberculosis patients, or during autopsy or laboratory work where the bacilli may be present.

Fungus infections

A number of occupational infections are common to workers in agriculture and in closely related industrial jobs. Grain handlers who inhale grain dust are likely to come in contact with some of the fungi that contaminate grain from time to time. Some of these fungi can and do flourish in the human lung, causing a condition called "farmer's lung."

Fine, easily spread fungi, such as rust and smut, can be contacted once the covering of infected grain is broken and may produce sensitization.

One example, coccidioidomycosis or Valley fever, is a disease caused by a fungus that is present in the soil in the southwestern states and the San Joaquin Valley in California. It causes a lung disease in humans called Valley fever, which may be either mild or severe. Because the spores are found in the soil, Valley fever outbreaks sometimes occur during excavation and construction work.

Byssinosis

Byssinosis occurs in individuals who have experienced prolonged exposure to heavy air concentrations of cotton dust. Flax dust also has been incriminated.

The exact mode of action of the cotton dust is unknown, but one or more of these factors may be important: (*a*) toxic action of micro-organisms adherent to the inhaled fibers; (*b*) mechanical irritation from the fibers, and (*c*) allergic stimulation by the inhaled cotton fibers or adherent materials. It takes several years of exposure before manifestations are noticed.

Anthrax

Anthrax is a highly virulent bacterial infection. In spite of considerable effort in quarantining infected animals and in sterilizing imported animal products, this disease remains a problem. With prompt detection and modern methods of treatment, it is less likely to be fatal than it was a few years ago.

Q fever

There have been reports of infection—Q fever—with rickettsial organism among meat and livestock handlers. It is similar to, but apparently not identical with, tick fever, which has been known for many years. The exact mode of transmission is not known, but there is evidence that Q fever may come from contacting freshly killed carcasses or droppings of infected cattle. Probably in the latter case, transmission is by inhalation of the infectious dust. Prevention undoubtedly depends upon recognition and elimination of the disease in the animal host.

Brucellosis

Brucellosis (undulant fever) has long been known as an infection produced by drinking unpasteurized milk from cows suffering from Bang's disease (infectious abortion). Since it can also be contracted by handling the animals or their flesh and is also transmitted by swine and goats, it is an occupational ailment of slaughterhouse workers, as well as of farmers, although more common among the latter. Here also, preventive measures are primarily proper testing and control of the animals to eradicate the disease.

Erysipelas

The other major bacterial infection to which slaughterhouse workers and fish handlers are subject is erysipelas, which seems to be especially virulent when contracted from the slime of fish.

Upper respiratory tract infections

Workers exposed to dusts from such vegetable fibers as cotton, bagasse (sugar cane residues), hemp, flax, or grain may develop upper respiratory tract infections ranging from chronic irritation of the nose and throat to bronchitis, complicated by asthma, emphysema, or pneumonia, or a combination . Dust from any of these fibers may also be a source of allergens, histamine, and toxic metabolic products of microorganisms.

THRESHOLD LIMIT VALUES

The three ways that chemicals enter the body are from inhalation, skin absorption, and ingestion or swallowing the chemical. In the workplace, inhaling the chemical is the most common.

Limits, called "Threshold Limit Values" (abbreviated as TLVs®), have been established for airborne concentrations of many chemical compounds. Since supervisors could be involved in discussing problems with their employees and industrial hygienists who are conducting surveys, they should understand something about the meaning of TLVs and the terminology in which concentrations are expressed.

The basic idea of the TLV is fairly simple. TLVs refer to airborne concentrations of substances and represent conditions under which it is believed that nearly all workers may be repeatedly exposed, day after day, without adverse effect. Because individual susceptibility varies widely, exposure of an occasional individual at (or even below) the threshold limit may not prevent discomfort, aggravation of a preexisting condition, or occupational illness. In addition to the TLVs set for chemical compounds, there are limits for physical agents, such as noise, microwaves, and heat stress.

The TLV may be a time-weighted average figure that would be acceptable for an 8-hour exposure. For some substances, such as an extremely irritating one, a time-weighted average concentration would not be acceptable, so a ceiling value is established. In other words, a ceiling limit means that at no time during the 8-hour work period should the airborne concentrations exceed that limit.

Establishment of values

Threshold Limit Values have been established for more than 600 substances, as well as for heat and cold stress, vibration, radiation, and biological exposure indexes. A group of well-qualified toxicologists, industrial hygienists, and doctors reviews the list annually and values are revised as necessary.

The data for establishing a TLV come from animal studies, human studies, and industrial experience. The limit may be selected for one of several reasons. It may be based on the fact that a substance is very irritating to the majority of people exposed to concentrations above a given level. The substance may be an asphyxiant. Other reasons for establishing a limit might be that the chemical compound is anesthetic, or fibrogenic, or can cause allergic reactions, or malignancy. Some TLVs are established because above a certain airborne concentration, a nuisance exists.

The concentrations of airborne materials capable of causing problems are quite small. Consequently, industrial hygienists use special terminology to define these concentrations. They often talk in terms of parts (of contaminant) per million (parts of air) when describing the airborne concentration of a gas or vapor. If measuring airborne particulate matter, such as a dust or fume, they use the term milligrams (of dust) per cubic meter (of air), or (mg/m^3) to define concentrations. Industrial hygienists also may use the actual number of particles present in one cubic foot of air being tested, in which case the descriptive term becomes millions of particles per cubic foot (mppcf). As an example of the small concentrations involved, the industrial hygienist commonly samples and measures substances in the air of the working environment in concentrations ranging from 1 to 100 ppm. Some idea of the magnitude of these concentrations can be appreciated when one realizes that 1 in. in 16 miles, one cent in $10,000, one ounce of salt in 62,500 lb of sugar, one ounce of oil in 7812.5 gal of water—all represent one part per million.

DERMATITIS

The four general categories into which industrial hygiene problems fall have been discussed in some detail, yet dermatitis has not been thoroughly discussed. Because skin problems in industry account for the single largest cost of all hygiene problems, they are important enough to be placed in a separate category. Individual problems usually can be traced to exposure to some kind of a chemical compound, or to some form of physical abrasion or irritation of the skin. Occupational skin diseases account for about 60 percent of all compensation claims for occupational diseases. Although rarely a direct cause of death, skin disorders cause much discomfort and are often hard to cure. (See Figure 6-14.)

Causes of occupational skin diseases are classified in these ways:

1. Mechanical agents—friction, pressure, trauma.

2. Physical agents—heat, cold, radiation.

3. Chemical agents—organic and inorganic. These are subdivided according to their action on the skin as primary irritants or sensitizers.

4. Plant poisons—several hundred plants and woods can cause derma-

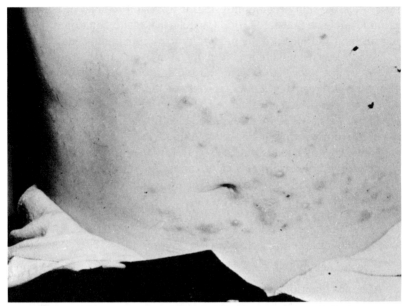

Figure 6-14. Chloracne is caused by clothing that has been soaked in cutting oils. It could have been prevented by after-work showers and daily change of work clothes.

titis. The best known example is poison ivy.

5. Biological agents—bacteria, fungi, parasites.

Even substances that are normally harmless will cause irritations of varying severity in some skins.

There are two general types of skin reactions: primary irritation dermatitis and sensitization dermatitis. Practically all persons suffer primary dermatitis from mechanical, physical, or chemical agents. Brief contact with a high concentration of a primary irritant or prolonged exposure to a low concentration will result in inflammation. Allergy is not a factor in these conditions. Sensitization dermatitis, the second type of reaction, is the result of an allergic reaction to a given substance. Once sensitization develops, even small amounts of the material may cause symptoms.

Some substances produce both types of dermatitis. Examples are organic solvents, formaldehyde, and chromic acid.

Occupational acne

Cutting fluids are frequently responsible for occupational acne. It all

127

starts when the skin becomes infected, it forms oil pimples or boils that resemble adolescent acne. Dirty oil, carelessness, and addition of germicides in the fluid increase the possibility of occupational acne.

To reduce the possibility, keep machines and areas around them strictly clean. Change cutting fluid at regular intervals. Have employees use protective creams or gloves, aprons, or face shields. Encourage employees who work in these areas to shower at the end of each shift. They should use warm water, mild soap, and a soft brush. They should be discouraged from wearing oil-soaked clothing.

Some types of skin are more susceptible than others, but most people will develop oil acne with sufficient exposure. Certain factors help account for some skin disorders. Any investigation of occupational skin disease should take into consideration:

1. Degree of perspiration

2. Personal cleanliness

3. Preexistence of skin disorders

4. Allergic conditions

5. Diet

Some sensitive skins may require special cleansers.

STANDARD OPERATING PROCEDURES

One of the primary functions of the supervisor is to develop standard operating procedures for jobs that require industrial hygiene controls, and to enforce these procedures once they have been established. Common jobs involving maintenance and repair of systems for storing and transporting fluids or entering tanks or tunnels for cleaning and repairs are controlled almost entirely by the immediate supervisor.

Entering tanks

As an example, there should be a standard operating procedure for entering tanks that has been established by a trained health and safety expert. Even if a tank is empty, it may have been closed for some time and developed an oxygen deficiency. As discussed earlier, the atmosphere must be tested for oxygen content and for the presence of any flammable gas, toxic particles, vapors, or gases. The space may have to be force ventilated before beginning and, perhaps, continuously during the work operation. It is unsafe to enter without self-contained breathing apparatus. If a tank was filled with solvent and has not been thoroughly cleaned, the atmosphere within is saturated with the solvent vapor. Even if the volatile

Figure 6-15. Person entering tank has his lifeline held by standby man who is similarly equipped. In addition, both are equipped with emergency egress unit (the small cylinder on the belt) in case air supply is accidently disconnected or stopped.

Scott Aviation, a Division of Figgie International, Inc.

solvent has been flushed with water and steam, the tank may still be hazardous. There are records of severe poisoning of workers who have entered "cleaned" tanks that were found to be relatively free of solvent vapor. In these instances, the disturbed scale released trapped solvents.

For these reasons, it is universal practice to provide approved respiratory equipment for persons entering tanks. An industrial hygienist or safety professional will advise you on which is the proper respirator for adequate protection. It is important to remember that air cleaning respirators (those *without* an air supply) must *never* be used in oxygen-deficient atmospheres. Because the inside of a washed tank looks relatively harmless, workers often neglect to use the equipment supplied. It is the supervisor's job to prevent workers from entering tanks without approved equipment and attached lifeline, or without a similarly equipped employee outside to assist if there are any serious difficulties encountered. (See Figure 6-15.)

Maintaining pumps and valves

The other job that can often lead to serious exposures to solvent vapors is maintenance of pumps, valves, and packed joints in solvent lines. Vapor from dripping packing glands may collect to form a fire and explosion hazard, as well as a health hazard.

The lower explosive limit for most flammable solvents is about 1½ percent. The Threshold Limit Value for less toxic solvents is about 1/10 of one percent. Control measures for solvent exposures try to keep the concentration below the Threshold Limit Value for health reasons. Although the fire hazard will be taken care of "automatically" in general areas, a dripping gland could still produce a flammable concentration in its immediate area.

Industrial hygiene controls

Finally, the supervisor should be aware of the various kinds of controls that are used to maintain a good healthy working environment.

The type and extent of these controls depend on the physical, chemical, and toxic properties of the air contaminant, the evaluation made of the exposure, and the operation that disperses the contaminant. The extensive controls needed for lead oxide dust, for example, would not be needed for limestone dust, since much greater quantities of limestone dust can be tolerated.

General methods of controlling harmful environmental factors or stresses include the following:

1. Substitution of a less harmful material for one that is dangerous to health. Be careful here to have a professional do this so that a more hazardous material is not mistakenly substituted.

2. Change or alteration of a process to minimize worker contact.

3. Isolation or enclosure of a process or work operation to reduce the number of persons exposed, or isolation of the workers in clean control booths.

4. Wetting down dust during working operations and clean up to reduce generation of dust in operations such as mining and quarrying.

5. Local exhaust ventilation at the point of generation and dispersion of contaminants.

6. General or dilution ventilation with clean air to provide a safe atmosphere. (Don't use dilution ventilation improperly for highly toxic chemicals; local exhaust ventilation is the way to control these.)

7. Personal protective devices, such as special clothing, and eye and respiratory protection. (These are discussed in Chapter 9.)

8. Good housekeeping, including cleanliness of the workplace, proper waste disposal, adequate washing and eating facilities, potable drinking water, and control of insects and rodents.

9. Special control methods for specific hazards, such as reduction of exposure time, film badges and similar monitoring devices, continuous sampling with preset alarms, and medical programs to detect intake of toxic materials.

10. Training and education to supplement engineering controls. (Training in work methods. Training in emergency response procedures—medical, gas release, etc.—to teach who should and should *not* respond in specific emergencies.)

As a supervisor, you play an important role in making sure that controls are effective. You must observe and study process changes, process enclosures, use of wet methods, local exhaust ventilation, and general ventilation carefully and systematically to make sure that they are functioning properly, or to determine if maintenance or repair work is needed. Even more important is the part you must play in controls relating to personal protective devices. The Occupational Safety and Health Act places the responsibility for enforcement of the wearing of such devices squarely upon supervisors. Consequently, if you do not enforce the use of protective equipment, such as hearing protectors and respirators, in areas where they should be worn, your company can be cited and penalized by OSHA.

Good housekeeping, special monitoring devices, and training and education also call for the full cooperation of the supervisor.

In fact, you, the supervisor, are the key person insofar as safety and industrial hygiene controls are concerned. Without your help and guidance, they will be of questionable value.

Chapter 7

Accident Investigation

A ccident investigation is a necessary and effective technique for preventing recurring or future accidents. If anything positive results from an accident, it is the opportunity to determine the causes and how to eliminate them. Thorough accident investigation can point out the problem areas within an organization. When these problems are resolved, a safer and healthier work environment will result. Accident investigation involves more than form-filling procedures. Well-managed organizations insist on quality accident investigations, just as they insist on efficient, quality production. Part of your performance evaluation is based on how well you handle this vital part of your job.

Accident reporting

As a basis for a good accident investigation program, it is essential that *all* accidents be reported. A common mistake occurs when only serious accidents are reported and investigated. In order to establish an effective accident reporting system it is important for you to cover it in your new-employee indoctrination program. At that time, you should emphasize to your people that *all* accidents must be reported—whether they result in personal injuries, illnesses, or property damage. In any circumstance, you must be advised at once. The "near-accident" or incident can also be significant, since it represents a warning. For example, when a tool is knocked off a platform that is missing toe boards, it might fall once without hurting anyone. However, it could have hit someone and resulted in a serious accident. Regardless of the outcome, this kind of incident should be reported and the causes must be investigated. If cause(s) are removed, serious accidents can be prevented. Immediate action regarding all accidents and incidents can prevent future mishaps.

Figure 7-1 shows the relationship between incidents and accidents.

Figure 7-1. Accidents are a part of a broad group of events that adversely affect the completion of a task. All of the events in this group are called incidents; those that do not result in injury and/or property damage are called "near misses" or near accidents.

All accidents are incidents and should be investigated. The supervisor is the person who most often investigates accidents and makes out reports. As the supervisor, you should have a special and personal interest in every accident that occurs in your department. In the interest of their future prevention, you must know and understand the underlying reasons for accidents.

Finding causes

The objective of any accident investigation is to determine the causes and recommend corrective actions that will eliminate or minimize them. Accident investigation should be aimed at fact finding, rather than fault finding; otherwise, the investigation may do more harm than good. As you investigate, avoid any emphasis on identifying the individuals who could be blamed for the accident. Looking for someone to blame reflects on your credibility and will usually reduce the amount and accuracy of the information you receive. This does not mean that oversights or procedures that were carried through incorrectly by employees should be ig-

133

nored, nor does it say that personal responsibility should not be determined, when appropriate. It means that the investigation should be concerned with only the facts. In order to do a quality job of investigating accidents, a supervisor must be objective and analytical.

There are many factors and causes of accidents. The theory of multiple causation states that it is the random combination of all of these factors that results in accidents. If this is true, additional information about accidents is always needed and helpful.

A report must do more than identify unsafe acts or hazardous conditions, because these are actually only symptoms of, or contributing factors to, accidents. For example, an accident report might explain that the accident was caused by oil being on the floor. Instead of simply noting that there was oil on the floor, the supervisor must determine how the oil got there. If there was an equipment lubrication leak, had the condition been previously reported? If poor maintenance was the cause, had that been reported? If so, when? If not, why not? These are the kinds of questions that must be asked and answered.

In this case, the oil on the floor was just a symptom of a larger problem. Generally, the methods by which procedures are carried through provide clues to other problems. Accident factors are usually symptoms of other basic or underlying problems. Inadequate maintenance, poorly designed equipment, untrained employees, and lack of policy enforcement or standard procedures (management control) are all causative factors (see Figure 7-2).

EMERGENCY PROCEDURES

A serious accident may not yet have happened in your organization, but it is essential that emergency procedures be established before one does occur. Having a clear plan for handling accidents can prevent the situation from getting out of control, and can actually save lives, protect property, and ensure a timely investigation. It is management's responsibility to see that there is a plan, and it is your responsibility to plan the specifics for your operation.

Your emergency procedures plan should specify all that needs to be done in case of an accident. It is important to list key names and phone numbers. Specific tasks should be assigned to individuals, and these people should know exactly what they are to do in an emergency. You may want to make a discussion of emergency procedures a topic of your safety meetings.

As the first-line supervisor, you will usually be the first management representative to arrive at the scene of an accident, so it is your responsibility to communicate about accidents of all kinds. Include in your plan-

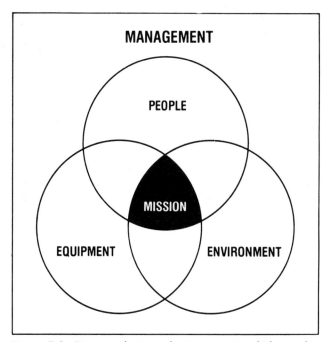

Figure 7-2. Diagram depicts a basic system in which people, equipment, and the environment are managed to accomplish a mission. Sometimes they work together in unplanned ways to produce accidents.

ning a method to notify, as required, people such as your boss, safety personnel, nurses, and first-aiders. Planning these things in advance will help make your actions more effective at the time of any accident.

Immediate action

The safety and health of employees and visitors must be your primary concern when an accident occurs. You must be sure that the injured employee gets immediate medical attention if an injury or illness occurs. Take all the necessary steps to provide for emergency rescue. In addition, take any actions that will prevent—or minimize the risk of—further immediate accidents.

Securing the accident site

Next, it is essential that you secure the accident site for the duration of the investigation, after rescue and damage control are complete. It may be necessary to barricade or isolate the accident scene with ropes, barrier tape, cones, and/or flashing lights that can be used to warn peo-

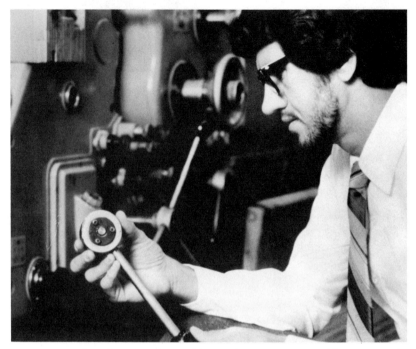

Figure 7-3. Collect physical evidence of the accident as soon as possible; For example, you may pick up a broken tool or machine part, or take a sample of a liquid spilled on the floor.

ple or otherwise restrict access to the area. In extreme cases, guards may be posted to make sure that no one is allowed to enter the accident scene.

Nothing should be removed from the accident site without the approval of the person in charge. The site should be maintained, as much as possible, just as it was at the time of the accident. The accident evidence needs to be examined. It can be preserved on film, recorded on tape, diagrammed, or sketched. Detailed notes must accompany the picture or drawing.

Preserving evidence

Time is of the essence when investigating accidents. The quicker you get to the scene of an accident, the less chance any details will be lost. A prompt and careful investigation of the scene will help to answer the questions of who, where, what, when, how, and why. For example, witnesses will remember more facts, and dangerous fluids that may evaporate or dusts that may be blown or swept away will still remain. Preserving evidence at the accident scene ultimately makes the investigative process much less frustrating (see Figure 7-3). Observing and recording fragile or perishable evidence, such as instrument readings, control panel settings, and details of weather and other environmental conditions, can result in an improved investigation procedure.

Photography

The camera is a useful tool for studying accidents. One that produces instant photographs is often preferred by someone with no photographic experience. A picture can be studied in detail at your leisure and often reveals items that might have been overlooked initially. General and specific scenes should be photographed in order to make comprehensive visual records. No one can predict in advance which data will be most useful, so photographs should be taken from many different angles. In addition, accurate and complete sketches and diagrams of the accident scene should be made. An old saying for accident photographers is "overshoot and underprint." This means to take every possible photo you might need, but make the necessary enlargements after you've studied the proof set.

Objects involved in the accident must be identified and measured to show the proper perspective. Including a ruler or coin in a close-up photograph will help to demonstrate the perspective nicely. Accurate measurements of various aspects of the area, equipment, and/or materials involved are useful. Measurements are vital to accident investigations, with or without photographs.

EFFECTIVE USE OF WITNESSES

If found and interviewed promptly, witnesses are your best source of information about the accident. Here are some useful tips for getting the most from them.

Identifying witnesses

Witnesses are, obviously, important sources of information when accidents are being investigated. They do not have to be eyewitnesses because anyone who heard or knows something about the event can offer useful information. Ask witnesses to identify and document the names of others who were in the area, so that all sources of vital information can be contacted. Determine who all of the witnesses are, as soon as you can.

Promptness

Witnesses should be interviewed one at a time and as soon as possible. The validity of a statement is highest immediately following the accident. A prompt interview minimizes the possibility for a witness to subconsciously adjust the story. Many things can happen to cloud a person's perspective, particularly if too much time elapses.

The opinions of others and reading stories about the accident can influence a witness. A person with a vivid imagination can create situations that did not actually happen. Again, time is an essential factor during accident investigation.

Interviewing witnesses

Whenever possible, interviews should be conducted at the accident site. This gives a witness an opportunity to describe and point out what happened, and being at the scene can also spark a person's memory. Tactful, skilled investigation will usually produce uninhibited cooperation from employees. Eliminating apprehension in a witness dispels the fear of incrimination, either of oneself or of others. You should remind the witness that you are seeking the facts of the accident and that you are not interested in placing blame.

Reenactment. Supervisors will frequently ask employees to show them "what they mean" or "how it happened." In some cases, reenactment has provided valuable information (see Figure 7-4). Expert investigators have learned to exercise definite precautions, however, whenever they ask someone to show or reenact an accident so that the accident doesn't happen again!

Before reenactment:

1. Ask employees to explain what happened first, before going through the motions. This preliminary explanation should give you additional insight about the accident. The last thing anyone wants is for the witness to repeat an act similar to the one that caused the accident.

2. Make sure that the witnesses thoroughly understand that they are to go through the motions of the accident without repeating the mistakes that caused the original accident.

Location. When it is not possible to interview people at the site, the area chosen should be free from distractions and away from other witnesses. Privacy is paramount. When people are discussing what they saw take place, they can influence other witnesses. This is to be avoided. Likewise, the person being interviewed should not be subjected to pressure or influence by anyone. Avoid using the supervisor's office for conducting interviews; sometimes, the witness or employee, generally a subordinate, finds the supervisor's office intimidating, inhibiting, and distracting.

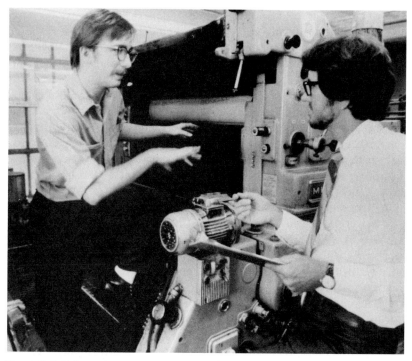

Figure 7-4. Talk to witnesses as soon as possible after the accident so they don't "adjust" their story. If you ask a witness to show you how the accident happened, make certain that the accident can't be repeated.

How to do it. When conducting a witness interview, establish a relaxed atmosphere. Be a good listener. Witnesses should be allowed to tell their stories without interruption or prompting. More detailed information can be sought after the full story has been told. Interruptions can derail a person's train of thought, influence their answers, and inhibit responses. Ask open-ended questions. The ways in which questions are phrased are very important. Avoid leading the witness. For example, asking the question, "Where was he standing?" is preferable to "Was he standing there?" Remember that your purpose is to determine the facts of the accident and you want as much information from the witnesses as is possible. As you ask questions, make sure that the specifics of who, what, where, how, and why are included. Here are some typical areas that you should explore: What about your employees' fellow workers? Were they factors? Did the worker's mental or physical condition contribute to the accident?

It is advisable for supervisors to take notes and record employee statements for later review. This should be done unobtrusively. In some cases, it is best to wait until the employee has finished explaining what happened before making notes or recording details. Supervisors should always repeat the information as they heard it, after the employee has finished. This reduces misunderstandings and often leads to further clarifications.

Employees who have been directly involved with the accident should be contacted first, followed by eyewitnesses and those who were in the nearby area. Discretion should always be exercised in situations where employees have been injured. Fellow workers might be in shock, incoherent, or have no memory of the accident. Sometimes the supervisor must postpone interviews until the employee or a witness who has been involved (in other words, the victim(s)) is in a more stable physical or emotional condition.

It is a good idea for you to solicit ideas from the employees interviewed regarding ways to prevent a recurrence of the accident. Many times they will have the best suggestions. This will also help them to feel involved with you and gives you an opportunity to recognize their willingness to participate.

The interview should end on a positive note. Thank each individual for his or her time, for the information supplied, and for the ideas offered.

REPORTS

The purpose of accident reporting is to alert and inform concerned people about the information and circumstances of an accident. The report should record in clear and concise language all of the appropriate circumstances of the accident, and the details of the subsequent investigation. Write down all causal factors that might have led to the accident. These factors will be in at least one, and possibly all four areas of: equipment, environment, personnel, and management.

Here are some typical questions to help you identify the accident causes. Was there an equipment procedure to detect the hazardous condition? Was the correct equipment, material, or tool used? Was it readily available? Was it properly used according to established procedure?

Refer to the "Accident Investigation Report," Figure 7-5. The report is designed primarily for the investigation of accidents involving injury, but also can be used for property damage accidents. In this event, simply write "D.N.A." (does not apply) across items 1 through 18 and fill out the remainder of the form.

In the event of an accident in which injury is involved, follow the instructions attached to the form and be sure all blocks on the form are filled out as completely as possible.

Filling out a report

The following instructions apply to using the Accident Investigation Report shown in Figure 7-5.

This report is designed primarily for investigation of accidents involving injuries, but also can be used to investigate occupational illnesses arising from a single exposure (for example, dermatitis caused by a splashed solvent or a respiratory condition caused by the release of a toxic gas).

All questions on this form should be answered. If no answer is available, or the question does not apply, the investigator should so indicate. Answers should be complete and specific. Supplementary sheets can be used for other information, such as drawings and sketches, and should be attached to the report. A separate form should be completed for each employee who is injured in a multiple-injury accident.

The report form meets the recordkeeping requirements specified in OSHA Form 101. The individual entries are explained below.

DEPARTMENT—Enter the department or other local identification of the work area to which the injured is assigned (for example, maintenance shop or shipping room). In some cases, this may not be the area in which the accident occurred.

LOCATION—Enter the location where the accident occurred if different from the employer's mailing address.

1. *Name of injured*—Record the last name, first name, and middle initial.

2. *Social Security Number*

3. *Sex*

4. *Age*—Record the age of the injured at the last birthday, not the date of birth.

5. *Date of accident or initial diagnosis of illness*

6. *Home address*

7. *Employee's usual occupation*—Give the occupation to which the employee is *normally* assigned (for example, assembler, lathe operator, or clerk).

8. *Occupation at time of accident*—Indicate the occupation in which the injured was working at the time of the accident. In some cases, this may not be the employee's usual occupation.

9. *Length of employment*—Check the appropriate box to indicate how long the employee has worked for the organization.

(Text continues on page 144.)

ACCIDENT INVESTIGATION REPORT

CASE NUMBER

COMPANY _____ ADDRESS _____

DEPARTMENT _____ LOCATION (if different from mailing address) _____

1. NAME of INJURED	2. SOCIAL SECURITY NUMBER	3. SEX ☐ M ☐ F	4. AGE	5. DATE of ACCIDENT

6. HOME ADDRESS

7. EMPLOYEE'S USUAL OCCUPATION

8. OCCUPATION at TIME of ACCIDENT

9. LENGTH of EMPLOYMENT
☐ Less than 1 mo.   ☐ 6 mos. to 5 yrs.
☐ 1-5 mos.   ☐ More than 5 yrs.

10. TIME in OCCUP. at TIME of ACCIDENT
☐ Less than 1 mo.   ☐ 6 mos. to 5 yrs.
☐ 1-5 mos.   ☐ More than 5 yrs.

11. EMPLOYMENT CATEGORY
☐ Regular, full-time   ☐ Temporary   ☐ Nonemployee
☐ Regular, part-time   ☐ Seasonal

12. CASE NUMBERS and NAMES of OTHERS INJURED in SAME ACCIDENT

13. NATURE of INJURY and PART of BODY

14. NAME and ADDRESS of PHYSICIAN

15. NAME and ADDRESS of HOSPITAL

16. TIME of INJURY
A. _____ A.M. P.M.
B. Time within shift
C. Type of shift

17. SEVERITY of INJURY
☐ Fatality
☐ Lost workdays—days away from work
☐ Lost workdays—days of restricted activity
☐ Medical treatment
☐ First aid
☐ Other, specify _____

18. SPECIFIC LOCATION of ACCIDENT

ON EMPLOYER'S PREMISES? ☐ Yes   ☐ No

19. PHASE of EMPLOYEE's WORKDAY at TIME of INJURY
☐ During rest period   ☐ Entering or leaving plant
☐ During meal period   ☐ Performing work duties
☐ Working overtime.   ☐ Other _____

20. DESCRIBE HOW the ACCIDENT OCCURRED

21. ACCIDENT SEQUENCE. Describe in reverse order of occurrence events preceding the injury and accident. Starting with the injury and moving backward in time, reconstruct the sequence of events that led to the injury.

A. Injury Event _____

B. Accident Event _____

C. Preceding Event #1 _____

D. Preceding Event #2, #3, etc. _____

Figure 7-5.

22. TASK and ACTIVITY at TIME of ACCIDENT	23. POSTURE of EMPLOYEE
A. General type of task _____	
B. Specific activity _____	24. SUPERVISION at TIME of ACCIDENT
C. Employee was working:	☐ Directly supervised ☐ Not supervised
☐ Alone ☐ With crew or fellow worker ☐ Other, specify _____	☐ Indirectly supervised ☐ Supervision not feasible

25. CAUSAL FACTORS. Events and conditions that contributed to the accident. Include those
identified by use of the Guide for Identifying Causal Factors and Corrective Actions.

_____
_____
_____
_____
_____
_____
_____
_____
_____
_____
_____
_____
_____

26. CORRECTIVE ACTIONS. Those that have been, or will be, taken to prevent recurrence. Include those
indentified by use of the Guide for Identifying Causal Factors and Corrective Actions.

_____
_____
_____
_____
_____
_____
_____
_____
_____
_____
_____
_____
_____

PREPARED BY _____

TITLE _____

DEPARTMENT_____ DATE _____

Developed by the National Safety Council

APPROVED _____

TITLE _____ DATE _____

APPROVED _____

TITLE _____ DATE _____

10. *Time in occupation at time of accident*—Record the total time the employee has worked in the occupation indicated in Item 8.

11. *Employment category*—Indicate injured's employment category at the time of the accident (for example, regular, temporary, or seasonal).

12. *Case numbers and names of others injured in same accident*—For reference purposes, the names and case numbers of all others injured in the same accident should be recorded here.

13. *Nature of injury and part of body*—Describe exactly the kind of injury, or injuries, resulting from the accident and the part, or parts, of the body affected. For an occupational illness, give the diagnosis and the body part, or parts, affected.

14. *Name and address of physician*

15. *Name and address of hospital*

16. *Time of injury*—In part B, indicate in which hour of the shift the injury occurred (for example, 1st hour). In part C, record the type of shift (for example, rotating or straight day).

17. *Severity of injury*—Check the highest degree of severity of injury. The options are listed in decreasing order of severity.

18. *Specific location of accident*—Indicate whether the accident or exposure occurred on the employer's premises. Then record the *exact* location of the accident (for example, at the feed end of No. 2 assembly line or in the locker room). Attach a diagram or map if it would help to identify the location.

19. *Phase of employee's workday at time of injury*—Indicate what phase of the workday the employee was in when the accident occurred. If "other," be specific.

20. *Describe how the accident occurred*—Provide a complete, specific description of what happened. Tell what the injured and others involved in the accident were doing prior to the accident; what relevant events preceded the accident; what objects or substances were involved; how the injury occurred and the specific object or substance that inflicted the injury; and what, if anything, happened after the accident. Include only facts obtained in the investigation. Do not record opinions or place blame.

21. *Accident sequence*—Provide a breakdown of the sequence of events leading to the injury. This breakdown enables the investigator to identify additional areas where corrective action may be taken.

In most accidents the *accident event* and the *injury event* are different. For example, suppose a bursting steam line burns an employee's hands or a chip of metal strikes an employee's face during a grinding operation. In these cases the accident event—the bursting of the steam line or the setting in motion of the metal chip—is separate from the injury event—the steam burning the employee's hands or the chip cutting the employee's face. The question is designed to draw out this distinction and to record other events that led to the accident event.

There also may be events preceding the accident event that, although not accident events themselves, contributed to the accident. These *preceding events* can take one of two forms. They can be something that happened that should not have happened, or something that did not happen that should have happened. The steam line, for example, may have burst because of excess pressure in the line (preceding event #1). The pressure relief valve may have been corroded shut, preventing the safe release of the excess pressure (preceding event #2). The corrosion may not have been discovered and corrected because a regular inspection and test of the valve was not carried out (preceding event #3).

To determine whether a preceding event should be included in the accident sequence, the investigator should ask whether its occurrence (if it should not have happened) or nonoccurrence (if it should have happened) permitted the sequence of events to continue through the accident event and injury event.

Take enough time to think through the sequence of events leading to the injury and to record them separately in the report. The information found in the Finding Causes section, earlier in this chapter, can be used to help identify management system defects that contributed to the events in the accident sequence. By identifying such defects, management may help to prevent many more types of accidents than the type under investigation. (See entry 25, below.)

In the example, the failure to detect the faulty pressure relief valve would lead to a review of all equipment inspection procedures. This review could prevent other accidents that might have resulted from failure to detect faulty equipment in the inspection process.

Additional sheets may be needed to list all of the events involved in the accident.

22. *Task and activity at time of accident*—In parts A and B, first record the general type of *task* the employee was performing when the accident occurred (for example, pipe fitting, lathe maintenance, or operating punch press). Then record the specific *activity* in which the employee was engaged when the accident occurred (for example, oiling shaft, bolting pipe flanges, or removing material from press). In part C, check the appropriate box to indicate whether the injured

employee was working alone or with a crew or fellow worker.

23. *Posture of employee*—Record the injured's posture in relation to the surroundings at the time of the accident (for example, standing on a ladder, squatting under a conveyor, or standing at a machine).

24. *Supervision at time of accident*—Indicate in the appropriate box whether, at the time of the accident, the injured employee was directly supervised, indirectly supervised, or not supervised. If appropriate, indicate whether supervision was not feasible at the time.

25. *Causal factors*—Record the causal factors (events and conditions that contributed to the accident) that were identified by use of the Finding Causes section earlier in this chapter, discussed under entry 21, above.

26. *Corrective actions*—Describe the corrective actions taken immediately after the accident to prevent a recurrence, including the temporary or interim actions (for example, removed oil from floor) and the permanent actions (for example, repaired leaking oil line). Record other recommended corrective actions; include any other corrective actions as requested.

NOTE: Users may add other data elements to the form to fulfill local or corporate requirements. Types of data elements that might be added include:

• Information on accident patterns that are typical of a particular industry or organization (for example, an establishment with many confined-space accidents might wish to add some questions on accidents of that type).

• Information required for special studies (for example, a study tracing the effectiveness of a specific corrective action).

• More detailed severity information (for example, the cost of the accident).

• Management data for use in performance reviews and in determining training needs.

• Exposure data for use in calculating incidence rates or injuries associated with certain activities. These data would be estimates or the actual number (or percent) of hours that the employees devote to the activity in a week, month, or year. Incidence rates based on the hours of exposure to specific activities can then be calculated. The use of incidence rates yields a fairer comparison of activities than methods comparing only the total number of cases associated with each activity.

SUMMARY

One of the most important parts of your accident prevention work is how you conduct accident investigations. *All* accidents and incidents should be investigated because today's "near miss" could result in tomorrow's serious injury, if the causes are not found and removed.

As the supervisor, you should investigate all accidents that occur in your area. The purpose of accident investigation is to determine the facts, and not to find blame. Remember that accidents may have many causes and it is your responsibility to find all of them.

It is important to have specific emergency procedures for potential accidents. In the event of an injury, while caring for the injured, take steps to prevent further accident or property damage. Protect the area so that the evidence is preserved. Take many photographs from all angles to aid the investigation. Identify the witnesses and interview them individually at the earliest possible time. Tell them the purpose of the interview, and thank them for their help when you have finished talking and listening. Be sure to get their suggestions for the prevention of any future accidents.

A properly completed accident report form and any necessary follow-up actions will conclude your accident investigation task.

Chapter 8

Safety
Inspections

When should a safety inspection be conducted? Without giving it too much thought, some supervisors would answer the question by saying, "The third Friday of each month." A much better reply would be, "I conduct safety inspections every time I go through my department." Although the primary reason for walking through your department may be to check attendance or to see if operational supplies are adequate, these functions can be easily combined with making safety inspections, as discussed on pages 3 and 4.

When a safety inspection has become part of your routine, you will have integrated the safety responsibilities of your job with the others. One part of a supervisory job should not be more important than another.

Safety inspections should be factored into every part of production, and they should be a regular and informal part of your standard operating procedure. This type of inspection is called *continuous,* and it requires that supervisors and their employees continually look for hazards.

FORMAL INSPECTIONS

In addition to continuous inspections, it is important to make formal inspections once a month, using a checklist (see Figure 8-1). (Note: In some operations, you may choose to make inspections more frequently.) These formal inspections can be the foundation for a strong loss control program.

There are three types of scheduled inspections:

• *Periodic inspections.* These include the inspection of specific items that are made weekly, monthly, semi-annually, or at other intervals.

Figure 8-1. Make periodic formal inspections; actual frequency depends on the equipment and its relative importance.

• *Intermittent inspections.* This type of inspection is performed at irregular intervals. Occasionally, an accident in another department that has involved a piece of equipment similar to that used in your department would lead to an intermittent (special) inspection of your equipment.

• *General inspections.* These inspections are designed to include all areas that do not receive periodic inspection, including parking lots, sidewalks, and fences.

Objective and purposes of inspections.

The objectives of an inspection program include:

- Maintaining a safe work environment through hazard recognition and removal.

- Determining that people are behaving and working in a safe manner.

- Determining that operations meet or exceed acceptable safety and government standards.

- Maintaining product quality and operational profitability.

The basic purpose of safety inspections is to detect potential accident causes (hazards) so that they can be corrected or safeguarded to prevent accidents. Just as inspections of the manufacturing process are important to quality control, safety inspections are of vital importance in loss control (accident prevention).

A safety inspection program should answer the following questions:

- What items need to be inspected?

- What aspects of each item need to be examined?

- What conditions need to be inspected?

- How often must items be inspected?

- Who will conduct the inspection?

In addition, prompt correction of substandard or hazardous conditions detected in an inspection demonstrates to everyone that management is seriously concerned with accident prevention. Furthermore, if you discover that workers are performing their jobs in an unsafe manner, you can determine what retraining may be necessary and take the appropriate actions.

Responsibility for inspection

It is generally agreed that the responsibility for employees' working conditions belongs to the first-line supervisor. This means that the primary safety inspections are clearly your responsibility. Because supervisors spend most of their time in their respective departments, they are the people who should be continuously monitoring working conditions.

Completion of a good safety inspection requires that you have: (*a*) knowledge of your organization's accident experience, (*b*) familiarity with accident potential and with the standards that apply to your area, (*c*) ability to make intelligent decisions for corrective action, (*d*) diplomacy in handling personnel and situations, and (*e*) clear understanding of your organization's operations—its workflow, systems, and products.

During routine inspections, it is important to check to see that (*a*) employees are complying with safety rules, (*b*) no physical hazards exist,

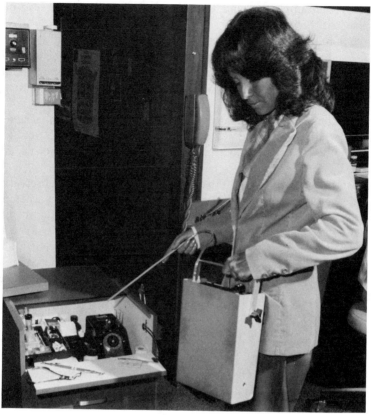

Figure 8-2. Using a highly sensitive gold film mercury detector, this technician can determine the levels of mercury vapor in the atmosphere and the sources of contamination. The inspector should always contact the supervisor both before and after the inspection, especially to check results of the inspection.

Jerome Instrument Corporation

(*c*) aisles and passageways are clear and proper clearances are maintained, and (*d*) material in-process is properly stacked or stored.

These spot-checks emphasize your commitment to safety. Regular formal inspections should also be conducted as frequently as company policy indicates.

Working with an outside inspector

Sometimes outside professionals are asked to complete an inspection. When this occurs, you should know when they will arrive so that you can be prepared to answer their questions and offer assistance. Any other people in charge, and all of your employees, should also be informed of the inspection.

Upon arriving, the inspector should contact you first, so that you can give him or her any information that is necessary for the inspection. This is especially important when conditions have been temporarily changed because of construction, maintenance, equipment downtime, or employee absence.

You may want to accompany the inspector, if there are no rules prohibiting this. However, sometimes the inspector may want to work alone (see Figure 7-2) and may, tactfully, make it clear that your presence is not needed.

An inspector is always expected to make independent observations, whether or not you participate in the tour. Even if you do not accompany the inspector, you must be consulted after the inspection because discussion about each recommendation should take place. The two of you need to agree on the importance of each recommendation. Obviously, an inspector should not focus on numerous trivial items just to make a report look good, but any observations about hazardous conditions must be reported.

Once you fully understand the problems and what changes need to be made, you may be able to initiate corrections quickly. Even if this is possible, the inspector's written report should include *all* items, but notations stating that you have agreed to make the adjustments quickly can be included. This way the record is clear, and it can also serve as a reminder to check for a particular condition during the next inspection.

Inspectors are required to report all hazardous conditions and you should try not to perceive the report as personal criticism. Remember that inspections are for fact-finding, not fault finding. They should always be kept on a high level of professionalism, and not be allowed to degenerate into issues of personality. Inspectors are expected to have attitudes that are firm, friendly, and fair.

You may want the inspector to help in making recommendations for the purchase of new equipment, reassignment of space, or transfer of certain jobs from one department to another. When these suggestions deal with safety, they should be included in the inspector's notes and, possibly, in the report.

After you have informed your employees about the inspection, be sure that they understand that the purpose is for fact-finding and that it should not be taken as a personal investigation. Explain that the inspector may need to observe them closely while they are working so that he or she can gain a clear understanding of how tasks are performed. An inspector should always ask the employee's permission to watch him or her at work. If this is all done appropriately, the inspection should be a worthwhile and smooth operation.

INSPECTION PLANNING AND CHECKLISTS

Many different types of inspection checklists are available for your use. Lists vary in length—from hundreds of items to only a few. Each type has its particular purpose (see Figure 8-3 and the following listing). These are some of the items that need to be inspected.

1. Environmental factors (illumination, dusts, gases, sprays, vapors, fumes, noise).

2. Hazardous supplies and materials (explosives, flammables, acids, caustics, toxic materials or by-products).

3. Production and related equipment (mills, shapers, presses, borers, lathes).

4. Power source equipment (steam and gas engines, electrical motors).

5. Electrical equipment (switches, fuses, breakers, outlets, cables, extension and fixture cords, grounds, connectors, connections).

6. Handtools (wrenches, screwdrivers, hammers, power tools).

7. Personal protective equipment (hard hats, safety glasses, safety shoes, respirators).

8. Personal service and first aid facilities (drinking fountains, wash basins, soap dispensers, safety showers, eyewash fountains, first aid supplies, stretchers).

9. Fire protection and extinguishing equipment (alarms, water tanks, sprinklers, standpipes, extinguishers, hydrants, hoses).

10. Walkways and roadways (ramps, docks, sidewalks, walkways, aisles, vehicle ways).

11. Elevators, electric stairways, and manlifts (controls, wire ropes, safety devices).

12. Working surfaces (ladders, scaffolds, catwalks, platforms, sling chairs).

13. Materials handling equipment (cranes, dollies, conveyors, hoists, fork lifts, chains, ropes, slings).

14. Transportation equipment (automobiles, railroad cars, trucks, front-end loaders, helicopters, motorized carts and buggies).

15. Warning and signaling devices (sirens, crossing and blinker lights, klaxons, warning signs).

16. Containers (scrap bins, disposal receptacles, carboys, barrels, drums, gas cylinders, solvent cans).

(Text continues on page 156.)

SAFETY INSPECTION CHECK LIST

PLANT OR DEPARTMENT _____

This list is intended only as a reminder. Once specific areas of responsibility have been determined, an inventory should be made of those items that can become unsafe or cause accidents. (Note also whether potential accident causes, marked "X" on previous inspection, have been corrected). These would include:

☒ Unsatisfactory   ☑ Satisfactory

1. EMPLOYEE HEALTH
- ☐ Noise
- ☐ Lighting
- ☐ Heating & ventilation
- ☐ Gases, fumes, vapors & dusts
- ☐ _____
- ☐ _____

2. HAZARDOUS MATERIALS
- ☐ Corrosive (acids-bases)
- ☐ Compressed gases
- ☐ Toxic materials or by-products
- ☐ Explosive-flammable
- ☐ Hazardous material warnings
- ☐ _____
- ☐ _____

3. PRODUCTION AND RELATED EQUIPMENT
- ☐ Point-of-operation
- ☐ Drive train guarding
- ☐ Operating controls
- ☐ Equipment maintenance
- ☐ _____
- ☐ _____

4. POWER SOURCE EQUIPMENT
- ☐ Engines and turbines
- ☐ Electric motors
- ☐ Hydraulic pumps
- ☐ _____
- ☐ _____

5. ELECTRICAL EQUIPMENT
- ☐ Switches
- ☐ Breakers
- ☐ Outlets
- ☐ Cables
- ☐ Extension and fixture cords
- ☐ Equipment grounding
- ☐ Temporary wiring
- ☐ _____
- ☐ _____

6. HANDTOOLS
- ☐ _____
- ☐ _____
- ☐ _____
- ☐ _____
- ☐ _____

7. PORTABLE TOOLS
- ☐ _____
- ☐ _____
- ☐ _____
- ☐ _____
- ☐ _____

8. PERSONAL PROTECTIVE EQUIPMENT
- ☐ Face shield
- ☐ Hearing protection
- ☐ Hard hats
- ☐ Safety glasses/goggles
- ☐ Safety shoes
- ☐ Respirators
- ☐ Protective gloves
- ☐ Protective clothing
- ☐ _____
- ☐ _____

9. PERSONAL SERVICE AND FIRST AID FACILITIES
- ☐ Drinking fountains
- ☐ Wash basins
- ☐ Soap dispensers
- ☐ Safety showers
- ☐ Eyewash fountains
- ☐ First aid supplies
- ☐ Stretchers
- ☐ _____
- ☐ _____

10. FIRE PROTECTION & EXTINGUISHING EQUIPMENT
- ☐ "Hot Work" permits
- ☐ Personnel trained
- ☐ Alarms
- ☐ Sprinklers
- ☐ Extinguishers
- ☐ Hydrants & wrench
- ☐ Available water supply
- ☐ Exits marked
- ☐ Fire doors
- ☐ Fire hose & adapters
- ☐ "No Smoking" or "Open Flame" signs
- ☐ Fire Detectors
- ☐ _____
- ☐ _____

11. WALKWAYS AND ROADWAYS
- ☐ Ramps
- ☐ Docks
- ☐ Sidewalks
- ☐ Walkways
- ☐ Aisles
- ☐ Vehicle ways
- ☐ Stairways
- ☐ Standard railings
- ☐ _____
- ☐ _____

12. ELEVATORS, ELECTRIC STAIRWAYS, AND MANLIFTS
- ☐ Gates & doors
- ☐ Controls
- ☐ Wire ropes/cables
- ☐ Safety devices
- ☐ Procedures posted
- ☐ Weight limits posted
- ☐ Elevator emergency call devices
- ☐ Inspection certificate posted
- ☐ _____
- ☐ _____

(continued on other side.)

Figure 8-3. A typical safety inspection checklist. Lists vary in length and detail, depending on what is being inspected and the purpose of the inspection.

13. WORKING SURFACES
- ☐ Ladders
- ☐ Scaffolds
- ☐ Catwalks
- ☐ Platforms
- ☐ Floors
- ☐ _____
- ☐ _____

14. MATERIAL HANDLING EQUIPMENT
- ☐ Cranes
- ☐ Dollies
- ☐ Conveyors
- ☐ Hoists
- ☐ Forklifts
- ☐ Chains
- ☐ Ropes
- ☐ Slings
- ☐ A-frame
- ☐ Front-end loaders
- ☐ _____
- ☐ _____

15. TRANSPORTATION EQUIPMENT
- ☐ Automobiles
- ☐ Railroad cars
- ☐ Trucks
- ☐ Motorized carts and buggies
- ☐ _____
- ☐ _____

16. WARNING AND SIGNALING DEVICES
- ☐ Sirens, bells
- ☐ Crossing and blinker lights
- ☐ Klaxons
- ☐ Warning signs
- ☐ Gas/vapor detectors
- ☐ _____
- ☐ _____

17. CONTAINERS
- ☐ Scrap bins
- ☐ Disposal receptacles
- ☐ Carboys
- ☐ Barrels
- ☐ Drums
- ☐ Gas Cylinders
- ☐ Solvent cans
- ☐ Tanks
- ☐ _____
- ☐ _____

18. STORAGE FACILITIES AND AREAS BOTH INDOOR AND OUTDOOR
- ☐ Bins
- ☐ Racks
- ☐ Lockers
- ☐ Cabinets
- ☐ Shelves
- ☐ Tanks
- ☐ Closets
- ☐ _____
- ☐ _____

19. STRUCTURAL OPENINGS
- ☐ Windows
- ☐ Doors
- ☐ Stairways
- ☐ Sumps
- ☐ Shafts
- ☐ Pits
- ☐ Floor openings
- ☐ _____
- ☐ _____

20. BUILDINGS AND STRUCTURES
- ☐ Floors
- ☐ Roofs
- ☐ Walls
- ☐ Fencing

- ☐ Hoppers
- ☐ Silos
- ☐ Ceiling
- ☐ _____
- ☐ _____

21. PHYSICAL LAYOUT
- ☐ Aisle markings
- ☐ Area designations
- ☐ Blind corners
- ☐ Utility color coding
- ☐ _____
- ☐ _____

22. HOUSEKEEPING
- ☐ Wash and locker rooms
- ☐ Toilets
- ☐ Yards and parking
- ☐ Storage and piling of materials
- ☐ Disposal of waste
- ☐ Pest control
- ☐ _____
- ☐ _____

23. CONFINED SPACE ENTRY PROCEDURES
- ☐ "Entry Permit" before entry into confined space
- ☐ Lifeline and observor
- ☐ Respiratory equipment
- ☐ Stand-by equipment
- ☐ _____
- ☐ _____

24. MISCELLANEOUS-Any items that do not fit in preceeding categories.
- ☐ _____
- ☐ _____
- ☐ _____
- ☐ _____

Signed _____   Date _____

Issued by

National Safety Council 444 North Michigan Avenue, Chicago, Illinois 60611
A NONGOVERNMENTAL, PRIVATELY SUPPORTED, PUBLIC SERVICE ORGANIZATION

17. Storage facilities and areas both indoor and outdoor (bins, racks, lockers, cabinets, shelves, tanks, closets).

18. Structural openings (windows, doors, stairways, sumps, shafts, pits, floor openings).

19. Buildings and structures (floors, roofs, walls, fencing).

20. Miscellaneous—any items that do not fit in preceding categories.

Generally, the longer checklists are keyed to OSHA standards. They are useful in determining the particular standards or regulations that apply to individual situations. Once the relevant standards are identified, the checklist can be tailored to your needs. In some organizations, the checklists are computerized for easy follow-up.

Checklists not only serve as reminders of what to look for, but they also serve as records of what has been covered in the inspection. They give direction to an inspection. They permit easy, on-the-spot recording of all findings and comments, before they are forgotten. If an inspection is interrupted, checklists provide a record of what has already been inspected. Without them, you may miss things or be unsure that you have covered everything. If you do not have a printed checklist, keep a blank pocket notebook with you at all times. That way you are always prepared to make notes during your continuous inspections.

Good checklists also help in follow-up inspections. Of course, merely running over a checklist does little to locate or correct problems. If you simply check off the items on the list, you are not conducting a safety inspection. The checklist is an *aid* to the inspection process; it is not an end in itself. A hazard observed during inspection must be recorded, even though it may not be included in the checklist.

An adequate checklist should also call attention to the following items and conditions:

• *Grounds*—Parking lots, roadways, and sidewalks need to be checked frequently for cracks, holes, and tripping hazards.

• *Loading and shipping platforms*—These areas get heavy use and need to be checked periodically for damage.

• *Outside structures*—Small, isolated buildings should be inspected with the same care as large plant facilities.

Floors

Floors, regardless of their construction, should be carefully inspected, especially in areas subject to heavy traffic. Slippery floors should receive special study. Here are several checkpoints.

• Is the surface wearing out too rapidly?

- Is shrinkage present?
- Is the surface damaged?
- Are there slippery areas?
- Are there holes or unguarded openings?
- Are there indications of cracks, sagging, or warping?
- Are replacements necessary because of deterioration?

Stairways

Stairways should be checked to determine whether:

- Treads and risers are in good condition and of uniform width and height.
- Handrails are secure and in good condition.
- Lighting on stairs is sufficiently bright.
- Always bear in mind that stairs are never to be used for storage.

Housekeeping

The general housekeeping throughout the facility must be checked regularly. Aisles should be marked off with painted lines and all materials must be kept out of aisles.

Fire

One of the greater hazards to an industrial plant is fire. Consequently, you must pay special attention to fire hazards. Periodic inspections of all types of fire protection equipment must be conducted.

Such inspections should review sprinkler systems, alarms, extinguishers, standpipes, hoses, and any other fire protection equipment. Fire inspections should be made of all exits from buildings, and emergency lighting systems. Be sure that the fire protection equipment is in the right place and not blocked.

Electrical installations

Electrical installations should be in accordance with the *National Electrical Code,* published as Standard ANSI/NFPA 70 by the National Fire Protection Association. (See Chapter 13, "Electrical Safety.")

Chains, ropes, and slings

Chains, wire and fiber ropes, and other equipment subject to severe strain in handling heavy equipment and materials should be inspected at regular intervals by a qualified individual. A careful record should be kept of each inspection.

Timing of inspections

Inspections should be scheduled when there is a maximum opportunity to view operations and work practices with a minimum of interruptions. Although the areas and routes for inspection should be planned in advance, it is important to vary the time and the day on which you conduct the formal inspections in order to check the widest possible variety of conditions.

It is a good idea to review *all* accidents that have occurred in the area prior to conducting an inspection. In addition to the regular checklists or formats used, supervisors should have a copy of previous inspection reports.

Reviewing these reports makes it possible to determine whether or not earlier recommendations to remove or correct hazards were followed.

INSPECTING WORK PRACTICES

Another important purpose of an inspection is to observe work practices. Are your employees following instructions for specific procedures and doing their jobs in the ways in which they were trained?

Here are some examples of the kinds of questions that should be considered during an inspection.

1. Are machines or tools being used without proper authorizations?

2. Is equipment being operated at unsafe speeds?

3. Are guards and other safety devices being removed or rendered as ineffective?

4. Are defective tools or equipment being used? Are tools or equipment being used unsafely?

5. Are employees using their hands or bodies instead of tools or push sticks?

6. Is overloading or crowding occurring, or are workers failing to stack materials properly?

7. Are materials being handled in unsafe ways, for example, is improper lifting occurring?

8. Are employees repairing or adjusting equipment while it is in motion, under pressure, or electrically charged?

9. Are employees failing to use (or using improperly) personal protec-

Figure 8-4. Workers should be responsible for inspecting their equipment and following good work practices. If they use checklists or job safety analyses, be sure that they are up to date and that each worker knows what is required.

tive equipment and/or other safety devices?

10. Are unsafe, unsanitary, or unhealthy conditions being created by the improper personal hygiene of employees, such as their use of compressed air for cleaning clothes, poor housekeeping, or smoking in unauthorized areas?

11. Are employees standing or working under suspended loads, scaffolds, shafts, or open hatches?

Communicating the results of work practice inspections

It is important to discuss the results of the inspections with any of the people involved. If poor work practices and bad habits have developed, you must advise employees of your observations immediately, explaining the correct ways in which the work should be done. Always remember to communicate the good news with the bad.

Many supervisors fail to communicate about the positive actions and practices that occur in their departments. It is always important to positively reinforce people who follow good work practices. Making comments such as, "I'm glad to see that you always check the condition of your tools before using them," is appropriate and encouraging to the workers. (See Figure 8-4.)

Additionally, if you have found it necessary to correct a person's actions, it is wise to follow up and acknowledge to them that you've seen improvement in their work patterns. It is always good policy to "communicate the positive" to your people.

The best guide to use for the manner in which the job should be done is a job safety analysis (see Chapter 5, "Safety Training"). It is strongly recommended that you use it when observing your people at work.

HOW OFTEN MUST INSPECTIONS BE MADE?

The frequency of inspections is determined by five factors:

1. *What is the loss severity potential of the problem?* The greater the loss severity potential, the more frequently an item or process should be inspected. A frayed wire rope on an overhead crane block has the potential to cause a much greater loss than a defective wheel on a wheelbarrow. The rope obviously needs to be inspected more frequently than the wheel.

2. *What is the potential for injury to employees?* If the item or a critical part should fail, how many employees would be endangered and how frequently? The greater the probability for injury to employees, the more often the item should be inspected. For example, a stairway used continuously needs to be inspected more frequently than one that is seldom used.

3. *How quickly can the item or part become hazardous?* The answer to this question depends on the nature of the part and the condition to which it is subjected. Equipment and tools that get heavy use usually become damaged, defective, or wear out more quickly than those used rarely. An item located in a particular spot may be exposed to greater potential damage than an identical item in a different location. The shorter the amount of time in which tools and equipment can become unsafe, the more frequently you should inspect them.

4. *What is the past record of failures?* Maintenance and production records and accident investigation reports can provide (*a*) valuable information about how frequently items have failed and (*b*) a description of the results in terms of injuries, damage, delays, and shutdowns. The more frequently a process or equipment has failed in the past and the greater the consequences, the more often that item needs to be inspected.

5. *Are there required inspections?* Some equipment in your department may have to be inspected at regular intervals. This could be required by regulation or as a manufacturer's recommendation. When inspec-

tions on such equipment are performed, be certain that they are documented properly.

RECORDING HAZARDS

You should identify and describe each hazard that is uncovered during an inspection. Machines and specific operations must be identified by their correct names. Locations must be accurately identified by name or number. Specific hazards must be described. Instead of noting "poor housekeeping" for example, the report should give the details: "Empty pallets left in aisles, slippery spots on the floor from oil leaks, a ladder lying across empty boxes, scrap piled on the floor around machines." Instead of merely noting "guard missing," the report should read, "Guard missing on shear blade of No. 3 machine, SW corner of Bldg. D."

Writing the inspection report

A clearly written report must follow each inspection. The report should specify the name of the department or area inspected (giving the boundaries or location, if needed), and the date and time of the inspection.

One way to begin the report is to copy items carried over from the last report that were not permanently corrected. Number each item consecutively. After listing the hazard, specify the recommended corrective action and establish a definite abatement date. Record the name of the person responsible for removing the hazard and the date by which the problem should be resolved.

FOLLOW-UP

Follow-ups will be necessary to correct any problems that have been discovered. Obviously, decisions will need to be made as to how to best rectify a problem situation. If the problem can be resolved by your people, assign someone to correct it promptly. For example, if materials are not properly stacked, ask one or more of your people to stack them safely. If, on the other hand, the condition cannot be corrected by your employees, you need to write a maintenance work order request so that the necessary actions can be taken.

Anything unsafe should be removed from service, in line with management policies. Not only should the hazard be removed, but the cause should be identified. For example, if the problem is an oil spill on the floor and it is wiped up, removal of the immediate problem does not remove the cause. If the oil leak came from a fork lift truck, it is essential that the truck be repaired to prevent oil spills in your or other departments. Wiping up the spill is necessary, but it does not correct the basic problem.

In some cases, intermediate action is necessary. If permanent correction of the problem will take time, consider temporary measures that will help to prevent an accident. Roping off the area, tagging or locking out equipment, or posting warning signs are examples of intermediate actions. They may not be ideal, but they are positive actions. When intermediate actions are taken, it is essential that follow-up permanent actions be made as quickly as possible.

Dangerous conditions should be reported to the appropriate person or management immediately. When this is required, make precise recommendations for removal or correction of the conditions.

Some of the general categories into which recommendations might fall include:

- Set up a better process
- Relocate a process
- Redesign a piece of equipment or tool
- Provide personal protective equipment
- Improve training procedures
- Improve maintenance procedures.

SAFETY LEADERSHIP

It is important to realize that your employees have keen inter. the actions you take to remove any hazardous conditions. When it is clear that you are actively making job conditions better and safer, your people will readily follow your lead. Quite often, they will offer positive ideas for further improvements, knowing that positive action will probably result. By performing your safety inspections in an appropriate manner, your leadership skills will also improve.

Chapter 9

Personal Protective Equipment

W hen a hazard is found in the workplace, every effort should be made to eliminate or control it by engineering. For instance, if there is a turret lathe, screw machine, or milling operation that produces large quantities of steel chips that fly all over an aisleway, the engineering control to be taken, short of eliminating the operation, is either to enclose the operation or provide a deflector to keep the chips from flying in the aisle. The best approach is to determine first whether the hazard can be engineered out of the operation.

Another way to reduce or control the hazard is to isolate the process. Can that dip tank be relocated? Can the spray booth be enclosed? Can that noisy machine operation be isolated, separated from the rest of the plant?

Personal protective equipment should be considered only as a last resort. Judicious use of such protective equipment sometimes, however, can greatly simplify operations in case of breakdowns or other emergencies.

CONTROLLING HAZARDS

People who must work in certain areas—where the hazards cannot be eliminated or controlled or where ordinary work clothes do not provide sufficient protection—should use personal protective equipment. This equipment can protect a person from head to toe.

In order to have an effective program on the use of personal protective equipment, supervisors should:

• Be familiar with required standards and requirements of the Occupational Safety and Health Act.

• Be able to identify hazards quickly.

Figure 9-1. There are many suppliers selling a wide range of safety equipment, but the only products to use are those that conform to nationally recognized standards. A safety professional can help to review these standards with you and compare the products that are available.

• Be familiar with the best safety equipment on the market to protect against the specific hazard(s).

• Know the company procedures for paying for and maintaining the equipment.

• Develop an effective method for persuading employees to dress safely and to wear the proper protective equipment.

Overcoming objections

Once you, the supervisor, know what and when personal protective equipment is needed, you are responsible for following up on its use. When people do not see the reason for using protective equipment, it is up to the supervisors to impress workers about its value and to help them to recognize the need for it. Getting some workers to use protective equipment may be one of the toughest jobs you face.

To fulfill this responsibility, supervisors must learn about safety equipment. Local safety meetings are a good source of information because equipment is usually on display and manufacturers' representatives are handy. Hundreds of firms exhibit at the National Safety Congress and Exposition held each fall. Company safety and personnel departments can also be helpful. There is a wealth of information on safety equipment—manufacturers' catalogs, trade literature, and the equipment issue of *National Safety and Health News,* published each March.

The safe rule to follow when specifying or buying safety equipment is to insist on the best, and deal only with reputable firms. Do not take a chance on inferior items just because they may be less expensive. (See Figure 9-1.) Protective equipment should conform to standards where they apply; standards for respiratory protective equipment are discussed later in this chapter.

One of the bigger problems supervisors have is to overcome the objections of some workers who have to wear such protective equipment. The following paragraphs should help in overcoming most objections, regardless of the type of protection involved. As you proceed through this chapter, which covers all types of personal protective equipment, refer back to these paragraphs for help in overcoming objections.

Most of the objections you will encounter are quite similar, whether employees are talking about eye, ear, or head protection, respiratory protective equipment, or protective clothing such as aprons, gloves, and even safety shoes.

You should be familiar with OSHA regulations, be able to recognize hazards, and know your equipment and your dealer so that you are thoroughly familiar with all types of protective equipment. One specific objection you will encounter is a worker's complaint about having to wear eye protection because it is uncomfortable. You have to point out to the worker that he or she has only one pair of eyes and that the wearing of safety glasses is a minor discomfort compared to the loss of the sight in an eye. But that is not all. Other questions arise as a consequence. Why are the glasses uncomfortable? Do they fit properly? Were they installed, measured, and properly fitted by a qualified person? Did the employee have any choice in the selection process? Reluctance to wearing eye protection is sometimes merely a matter of color. If employees are allowed to participate in the selection process, chances for their wearing eye protection voluntarily are enhanced.

When looking for reasons why employees do not wear the prescribed protective equipment, try to be objective and to see the entire picture. There are some things that are common to all types of protection. Proper fit has already been discussed. Another common factor is comfort. Make sure that the safety glasses, the ear protectors, the respirator, the aprons, gloves, and shoes are properly fitted. No one wants to wear something that does not feel or look good, that is not clean, or that constantly needs adjusting. (See Figure 9-2.)

Appearance is another factor to be considered. If the piece of equip-

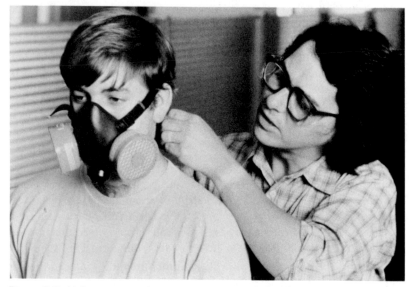

Figure 9-2. Make sure protective equipment is properly fitted and is as comfortable as possible to wear. Employees should be trained in the proper fit, use, and care.

ment does not look attractive—for example, big clumsy safety shoes as opposed to a snug steel-toed moccasins or wing-tip dress shoes—workers are turned off. So, in addition to a comfortable fit, workers are also concerned with appearance; if possible, let workers select their style (see Figure on page 206.)

The last item to be considered is the ease with which protective equipment can be cleaned and maintained. This is particularly important in the case of hearing and respiratory protection.

In summary, supervisors need to deal with qualified suppliers who can specify the appropriate equipment. They should make sure that it fits correctly, is attractive, and, especially, that there is a good cleaning and maintenance program so that the equipment is always sanitary.

As you review the various kinds of personal protective equipment referred to in this chapter, remember these few paragraphs. Using common sense, empathizing with your people, and understanding the basic principles about protective equipment will help you to overcome the objections.

Selling the need for PPE

Closely associated with overcoming objections is selling the need for personal protective equipment (PPE). Here a certain amount of salesmanship is required. It is obviously better to sell the workers on the need fo₁ wearing the protection than to threaten punishment. A threat is called motivation by fear, which is not nearly as effective as getting workers to understand the need for wearing the protective equipment. If your people can be made to see the need, the selling job is much easier. When looking at personal protective equipment, picture the human body and, starting with the head, analyze all of the hazards or the types of accidents that could possibly occur. For example, the head is vulnerable to injuries, such as bumps and abrasions, so think of what types of protection are needed: hard hats, bump caps, hair nets? Then move on to the eyes, the ears, throat and lungs (respiratory protection), arms and legs, torso, hands and toes. In this checklist fashion, you will be reminded of all the hazards that can occur and the protection that is required.

The remainder of this chapter covers protection of the head, eyes and face, feet and legs, ears, fingers and hands, and the torso. Respiratory protective equipment, safety belts and harnesses, protection against ionizing radiation, and safe work clothing are discussed, as are methods of paying for certain equipment and getting employees to use it properly.

PROTECTING THE HEAD

Safety hats are needed on jobs where a person's head is menaced by falling or flying objects or by bumps (Figure 9-3). American National Standard Z89.1, *Requirements for Protective Headwear for Industrial Workers,* gives specifications that a protective hat must meet.

Impact resistance is essential. Where contact with energized circuits is possible, only hats that meet the requirements of Class B, ANSI Z89.1, should be worn. These hats should have no conductive fittings passed through the shell. Class B hard hats are tested at 20,000 volts.

A brim all around the hat provides the most complete protection for the head, face, and back of the neck. In a situation where the brim would get in the way, the cap type may have to be worn.

In addition to these, there is another type of head protection. Known as "bump hats" or "bump caps," these are used only in confined spaces where the exposure is limited to bumping. Bump hats should never be used on construction sites or shipyards, or on other locations where exposure to any hazard is greater than bumping the head against an obstruction. They do not meet the requirements of ANSI Z89.1

Fabrication

Plastic, molded under high pressure, is most frequently used for safety hats. It resists impact, water, oil, and electricity. Glass fibers impregnated with resin is preferred because of its high strength-to-weight ratio, high dielectric strength, and resistance to moisture. Hats with re-

167

Figure 9-3. A three-day headache (and some minor bruises on back and shoulders) was all this communication lineman received when a 500-pound, 25-foot pole fell on his head. The brunt of the blow was caught by this company-issued safety hat. The impact pushed the lineman's head against the ground and split the hat (as shown here). The pole came to rest on the lineman's left shoulder.

flective trim are available on special order and give added protection against traffic accidents that occur when employees work at night or in darkened areas.

The hard outer shell of the hat is supported by a suspension—a cradle attached to a headband that keeps the shell away from the head and provides limited protection against falling objects. This must be adjusted in order to fit well. Extra cradles and headbands should be kept on hand and should be replaced whenever they show signs of deterioration or soiling.

If bands and cradles are not replaced, the band, cradle, and shell should be washed in warm, soapy water and then rinsed. Steam cleaning is also effective. Thirty days is the recommended maximum interval between cleanings. Hats and suspensions should be thoroughly cleaned before being reissued. Regular replacement of the suspension, at least once a year, is recommended.

No attempt should be made to repair the shell of a hat once it has been broken or punctured. A few extra shells should be kept on hand as replacements. Do not let people drill holes in their safety hats to improve ventilation or let them cut notches in the brims. Such practices destroy the ability of the hat to protect the wearer.

Auxiliary features

Liners are available for cold weather use. Do not let workers remove the safety hat suspension in order to wear the hat over parka hoods. This practice completely destroys the protection given by the hat, and has led to tragic results.

A chin strap is useful when the wearer may be exposed to strong winds, on oil derricks, for example.

An eye shield of transparent plastic can be attached to some hats. The shield is secured under the brim and lies flat against the brim when not in use.

Brackets to support welding masks or miners' cap lamps are available on some safety hats. Other mounting accessories for hearing protection, and eye and face protection are available.

Color. White, yellow, red, green, blue, brown, and black are the standard hat colors. Other colors are available on special order. Colors that go all the way through the laminated shell are permanent. Painting is not recommended because paint may contain solvents that can make the shell brittle.

Often distinctive colors or designs are used to designate the wearer's department or trade, especially in companies or plants where certain areas are restricted to a few selected employees.

Hair styles vs. hard hats

In some cases, hair styles may be incompatible with wearing hard hats. You, as the supervisor, will have to convince people that it is more important (indeed it may be required) to wear hard hats than to have stylish hairdos.

In certain industries, for example, in food-processing plants, in addition to wearing bump caps, the worker is also required to cover all facial hair—beards and mustaches—with hair nets. This is a requirement of the FDA and is done for sanitary reasons. Here, supervisors have an additional job cut out for them; they must explain the reasons for this protection to the workers.

Overcoming objections was mentioned at the beginning of this chapter. In the case of hard hats, there are a few more that will probably surface. In winter, one complaint is that the hats are too cold. A liner or skull cap large enough to come down over the ears can also be worn. The suspension must not be removed. Some people complain that hats give them headaches. This is possible until the employee becomes accustomed to wearing it. However, there is usually no physiological reason for a properly fitted hat to cause a headache.

Safety hats are slightly heavier then ordinary hats, but this difference is not noticed after a while if the headboard and suspensions are properly adjusted, unless there are other causes—physiological or psychological.

PROTECTING THE EYES

Industrial operations expose the eyes to a variety of hazards, such as flying objects, splashes of corrosive liquids or molten metals, dusts, and harmful radiation. Eye injuries not only disable a person, but they often disfigure the face. Per-injury cost is high to both employee and employer.

Flying objects cause most eye injuries—metal or stone chips, nails, or abrasive grits. The National Society to Prevent Blindness lists the chief causes of eye injury as:

- Flying objects (especially those set in motion by hand tools)
- Abrasive wheels (small flying particles)
- Corrosive substances
- Injurious light or heat rays
- Splashing metal
- Poisonous gases or fumes

Operations in which hardened metal tools are struck together, where equipment or material is struck by a metal handtool, or where the cutting action of a tool causes particles to fly, usually require the user of the tool and other workers exposed to flying particles to wear eye protection. The hazard can be minimized by using nonferrous, "soft" striking tools and shielding the job with metal, wood, or canvas.

Safety goggles or face shields should be worn when woodworking or cutting tools are used at head level or overhead with the chance of particles falling or flying into the eyes.

Occasionally, the need for eye protection is overlooked on such jobs as cutting wire and cable, striking wrenches, using hand drills, chipping concrete, removing nails from scrap lumber, shoveling material to head level, working on the leeward side of a job, using wrenches and hammers overhead, and on other jobs where particles or debris may fall.

Contact lenses

Contact lenses of the hard corneal type or the newer soft, large hydrophilic type are becoming more commonly used, and the supervisor should understand the potential problems related to each. First, it is important to know whether an individual with contact lenses can tolerate them comfortably for 10 hours or more each day. Second, where there are appreciable amounts of dust, smoke, or irritating fumes or liquid irritations that could splash into the eyes, contact lenses are not recommended. Often a judgment must be made, however, as to the degree of potential hazard, because some persons obtain better correction with contact lenses and, therefore, need them. These persons should wear the proper safety spectacles or goggles over their contacts when in an area where any sort of potential eye hazard exists.

Even though safety glasses can be worn over contact lenses, an impact blow to the safety glasses can forcefully push the contact lenses, or fragments of them if they shatter, against or into the eyes, and result in severe eye injury. One rarely noticed regulation under the OSHAct prohibits the wearing of contact lenses in contaminated areas with respirators; see §1910.134(e)(5)(ii) of OSHA regulations.

The National Society to Prevent Blindness, through its Advisory Committee on Industrial Eye Health and Safety, has issued the following position statement:

> Because of the increased risk to the eyes, the National Society to Prevent Blindness strongly advises that the use of contact lenses of any type by industrial employees while at work should be prohibited, except in rare cases. The Society recommends that any exception be verified in writing to the employer by the physician or optometrist who sanctions such use in a specific industrial sense; their use without eye and/or face protective devices of industrial quality should not be permitted.

Equipment types

Goggles and other kinds of eye protection are available in many styles, and with the protective medium of heat- or chemically treated glass, plastic, wire screen or light-filtering glass. Supervisors should be familiar with the various forms of eye protection and should know which ones are the best for each job (see Table 9-A). Protective equipment for the eyes includes the items below, described in greater detail in the paragraphs that follow:

Cover goggles

Splash-resistant goggles

Protective spectacles

Dust goggles

Spectacles with side shields

Miners' goggles

Cup goggles

Melters' goggles

Welders' goggles

Cover goggles are frequently worn over ordinary spectacles. Lenses that have not been heat or chemically treated are easily broken. A cover goggle protects against pitting, as well as breaking.

Cover goggles include the cup type with heat-treated lenses and the wide-vision type with plastic lenses. Both are used for heavy grinding, machining, shipping, riveting, working with molten metals, and similar heavy operations. They offer the advantage of being wide enough to protect the eye socket and distribute a blow over a wide area.

Tempered lenses are being more frequently used in ordinary eye-corrective spectacles used for street wear, but many of them do not even meet the requirements of the Food and Drug Administration Standard,* which became effective December 31, 1971, and which are not as demanding as the ANSI Standard. Although they do provide additional protection against ordinary exposure, they are inadequate for industrial exposure; therefore, only lenses meeting the American National Standard should be worn for such exposures.

Wearers can have their correction ground in heat-treated lenses. A refractionist (opthalmologist or optometrist) should do the fitting and should know the job on which eye protection is to be worn. The specialist should also know the working distance, especially for those whose accommodation is not good (such as often happens in middle age), or for those whose work distance is very close. Some companies require that bifocal lenses be used in those safety glasses that require this correction. This eliminates the risk of having a wearer lift his glasses up whenever he must see close up or far away, depending on the correction.

(Text continues on page 176.)

_____

*Food and Drug Administration, Department of Health and Human Services, Arlington, Va. 22202.

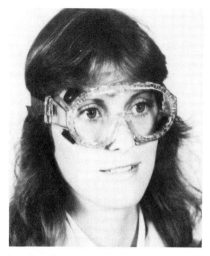

4a. Goggles are available for people with smaller faces to provide a better fit. One style has impact- and dust-resistance; another, chemical splash protection.

Sellstrom Manufacturing Company

4b. Goggles attached to this safety hat can be shoved up and stored on the hat when they are not required to fend off splashing substances that could otherwise harm the eyes.

Uvex Winter Optical Inc.

4c. Prescription safety glasses are worn under a face shield, which is attached to a bump cap. A bump cap is not a safety hat and is only used when the heat might bump against something.

Aden Safety, Airco, Inc.

4d. Safety cap has hanger for attaching hearing protection and face shield. Worker also wears goggles for added protection against eye hazards.

Mine Safety Appliances Company

Figure 9-4. Various types of eye and face protection.

TABLE 9-A. EYE AND FACE PROTECTIVE EQUIPMENT TO BE WORN FOR VARIOUS TYPES OF EXPOSURES

	Gases, fumes, mists	Molten metal splash (melting point above 2,100 F.)	Molten metal splash (melting point below 2,100 F.)	Liquid splash, eye hazardous	Liquid splash, irritating only	Dusts	Frontal impact only, light to moderate	Light to moderate impact (belt sanding, most machining operations, etc.)	Heavy impact (chipping, grinding, etc.)
Spectacles (3mm glass or plastic lenses)									
" with sideshields									
Spectacles (0.050-inch plastic lenses)									
" with sideshields									
Eyecup goggles, basic (3mm lenses)									
" with fine-mesh screens									
" with shielded/baffled ports		High viscosity only	High viscosity only						
Rigid or semirigid mask goggles (3mm lens)									
" with fine mesh screens or baffled ports									
Rigid or semirigid mask goggles (0.050-inch lens)									
" with fine mesh screens or baffled ports									

Flexible-fitting mask goggles (3mm or 0.050-inch lens)

" with fine-mesh screens

" with shielded/baffled ports

" unventilated

Foundrymen's goggles (3mm lenses)

" with fine-mesh screens

Gas-tight goggles

Special fabric-cup dust goggles

Rubber-frame chemical goggles, baffled vents

" unventilated

Plastic-visor face shield (0.040-inch)

" with crown and chin protectors

Wire-mesh visor face shield (0.0295-inch mesh)

High viscosity only

High viscosity only

Recommended, Optimum Protection

Permissible

Permissible but has features not needed for hazard cited

Protective spectacles without side shields may be worn only when it is unlikely that particles will fly toward the side of the face. However, spectacles with side shields are recommended for all industrial use. Side shield spectacles are recommended for all industrial use. Side shield spectacles should always be worn where there is additional side exposure.

Frames must be rigid enough to hold lenses directly in front of the eyes. The nose bridge should be adjustable or universal. Frames should also be fitted by a specialist.

Splash-resistant goggles, with soft vinyl or rubber frames, protect eyes against splashes of corrosive chemicals and exposure to fine dusts or mists. Lenses can be heat-treated glass or acid-resistant plastic. For exposures involving chemical splashes, they are equipped with baffled ventilators on the sides. For vapor or gas exposures, they must be nonventilated. Some types are made to fit over spectacles.

Leather mask dust goggles should be worn by employees who work around noncorrosive dusts, for example, in cement and flour mills. The goggles have heat-treated or filter lenses. Wire-screen ventilators around the eye cup provide air circulation.

Miners' goggles for underground work and other locations where fogging is a serious problem are made of corrosion-resistant wire screen, coated a dull black to reduce reflection.

Melters' goggles come in spectacle and cup types with cobalt blue glass in graded shades. Lenses with color in the upper half and clear glass in the lower half are also available. Frames are of leather or plastic to protect the face from radiant heat.

Welders' goggles with filter lenses are available for such operations as oxyacetylene welding, cutting, lead burning, and brazing. Table 9-B is a guide for the selection of the proper shade numbers. These recommendations may be varied to suit the individual's needs.

Goggle frames. All goggle frames should be of corrosion-resistant material that will neither irritate nor discolor the skin, that can withstand sterilization, and that are flame-resistant or nonflammable. Metal frames should not be worn around electrical equipment or near intense heat.

To permit the widest range of vision, goggles should be fitted as close to the eyes as possible without the eyelashes touching the lens. The lenses should have no appreciable distortion or prism effect. Some specifica-

TABLE 9-B. SELECTION OF SHADE NUMBER
FOR WELDING FILTERS

Welding Operation	Suggested Shade Number*
Shielded Metal-Arc Welding, up to 5/32 in. (4 mm) electrodes	10
Shielded Metal-Arc Welding, 3/16 to 1/4 in. (4.8 to 6.4 mm) electrodes	12
Shielded Metal-Arc Welding, over 1/4 in. (6.4 mm) electrodes	14
Gas Metal-Arc Welding (Nonferrous)	11
Gas Metal-Arc (Ferrous)	12
Gas Tungsten-Arc Welding	12
Atomic Hydrogen Welding	12
Carbon Arc Welding	14
Torch Soldering	2
Torch Brazing	3 or 4
Light Cutting, up to 1 in. (25 mm)	3 or 4
Medium Cutting, 1 to 6 in. (26 to 150 mm)	4 or 5
Heavy Cutting, over 6 in. (150 mm)	5 or 6
Gas Welding (Light) up to 1/8 in. (3.2 mm)	4 or 5
Gas Welding (Medium) 1/8 to 1/2 in. (3.2 to 12.7 mm)	5 or 6
Gas Welding (Heavy) over 1/2 in. (12.7 mm)	6 or 8

*The choice of a filter shade may be made on the basis of visual acuity and may therefore vary widely from one individual to another, particularly under different current densities, materials, and welding processes. However, the degree of protection from radiant energy afforded by the filter plate or lens when chosen to allow visual acuity will still remain in excess of the needs of eye filter protection. Filter plate shades as low as shade 8 have proven suitability radiation-absorbent for protection from the arc-welding processes.

In gas welding or oxygen cutting where the torch produces a high yellow light, it is desirable to use a filter lens that abosrbs the yellow or sodium line in the visible light of the operation (spectrum).

NOTES:

1. All filter lenses and plates shall meet the test for transmission of radiant energy prescribed in ANSI Z87.1-1979, *Practice for Occupational and Educational Eye and Face Protection.*

2. All glass for lenses shall be tempered, substantially free from striae, air bubbles, waves, and other flaws. Except when a lens is ground to provide proper optical correction for defective vision, the front and rear surfaces of lenses and windows shall be smooth and parallel.

3. Lenses shall bear some permanent distinctive marking by which the source and shade may be readily identified.

Source: *U.S. Code of Federal Regulations,* Title 29—Labor, Chapter XVII, Part 1910, Occupational Safety and Health Standards, § 1910.252(e)(2)(i), and Part 1926, Safety and Health Regulations for Construction, § 1926.102(a)(5).

tions are covered by American National Standard Z87.1, *Practice for Occupational and Educational Eye and Face Protection.*

Figure 9-5. Part of company's eye protection program includes instruction as to why wearing eye protection is important and what to do to care for the eyes. Glasses should be fitted and adjusted by trained personnel.

Cleaning after use. Eye protection equipment must be sterilized before being reissued to different employees. The proper procedure is to disassemble it, as much as possible, and wash with soap or detergent in warm water. Rinse thoroughly.

Replace defective parts.* Immerse all parts in a solution containing germicide, deodorant, and fungicide. Do not rinse, but hang to dry in air. Then place the parts in a clean, dustproof container—a plastic bag is good.

Some companies keep extra goggles in the main supply department. Others keep them in individual departments, along with a stock of parts. A third practice is to have an eye protection cart with a trained attendant who makes the rounds of the company to clean, adjust, repair, or replace eye protection on the job (see Figure 9-5). Many companies have stations that dispense cleaning liquid and tissues to encourage frequent cleaning as soon as possible after they get smudged or dirty. Carrying cases or

---

*If a lens has more than just the most superficial scratch, nick, or pit, it should be replaced. Such damage can materially reduce protection afforded the wearer.

storage cabinets also help promote care of eye protection.

The following are other important considerations regarding the care of eye protection equipment and overcoming employee complaints.

Glasses should never be put down with the lenses facing down because they could be scratched, pitted, or pick up dirt. They should not be kept in a bench drawer or tool box, unless the goggles are in a sturdy case. Cleaning stations or materials should be easily available.

A lens "fog" problem can usually be eliminated by use of one of the many commercial antifog preparations. In hot weather, a person can wear a sweatband to keep perspiration off his goggles. It takes a little effort to keep the goggles clean, but the effort required is no excuse for people to go without goggles and risk losing an eye.

Some people protest that goggles give them a headache; it is true that goggles that do not fit well can produce headaches. Goggles should fit so that the right and left eyes of the wearer look through the center of the right and left lenses respectively. The nose bridge should rest flush on the bridge of the nose. The head strap on cup goggles should be adjusted for just enough tension to hold them securely, and the strap should be worn low on the back of the head.

On spectacle goggles, each bow should hook behind the ear close to the head, touching the ear all along, not just at one or two points. The spatula-type temple bow should, similarly, contact the head along its entire length, not just at one point. Correct fit is important.

If workers still complain of headaches, even though their goggles fit properly, the supervisor should direct them to the doctor, since there may be another cause for the headaches. Plano (uncorrected) spectacles usually have no effect on the normal eye, but people with minor eye defects may complain that they are uncomfortable.

Face protection

Many types of personal protective equipment shield the face (and sometimes also the head and neck) against light impact, chemical or hot metal splashes, heat radiation, and other hazards. (See Figure 9-6.)

Face shields of clear plastic protect the eyes and face of a person who is sawing or buffing metal, sanding or light grinding, or handling chemicals. The shield should be slow burning and must be replaced if warped or scratched. A regular replacement schedule must be set up because plastic tends to become brittle with age.

The headgear and shield should be adjustable to the size and contour of the head, and easy to clean. Many types permit the wearer to raise the shield without removing the headgear.

Plastic shields with dichroic coating or metal screen face shields de-

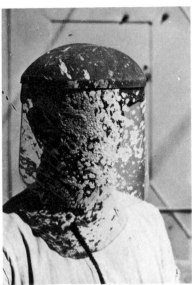

Figure 9-6. *Left:* Metal-screen face shield protects furnace personnel and others exposed to radiant heat. *Right:* To protect the entire face against light impact and chemical splash, a face shield should be provided. This shield stopped a splash of boiling caustic.

flect heat from a person and still permit good visibility. They are used around blast furnaces, soaking pits, heating furnaces, and other sources of radiant heat.

Babbitting helmets protect the head and face against splashes of hot metal, rather than against heat radiation. The helmet consists of a window made of extremely fine wire screen, a tilting support, an adjustable headgear, and a crown protector and chin protector (if required). They are also used around other molten metal applications.

Welding helmets, shields, and goggles protect the eyes and face against the splashes of molten metal and the radiation produced by arc welding (see Figure 9-7). Helmets should have the proper filter glass to keep ultraviolet and visible rays from harming the eyes. A list of shade numbers recommended for various operations is given in Table 9-B. Workers' eyes vary due to age, general health, and the care given to them. Two persons may require different shaded lenses when doing the same job.

Cracked or chipped filter lenses must be replaced, otherwise they will permit harmful rays to reach the welder's eyes.

180

The shell of the helmet must resist sparks, molten metal, and flying particles. It should be a poor heat conductor and a nonconductor of electricity. Helmets that develop pinholes or cracks must be discarded. Helmets should have headgears that permit workers to use both hands and to raise the helmet to position their work.

Most types of helmets have a replaceable, heat-treated glass or plastic covering to protect the filter lens against pitting and scratching. Some helmets have a lift-front glass holder that permits the welder to give his work a rapid inspection without lifting or removing the helmet.

Impact goggles should be worn under helmets to protect welders from flying particles when the helmets are raised. The spectacle type with side shields is recommended as minimum protection from flying materials, adjacent work, or from the popping scale of a fresh weld.

Welder's helpers should have proper welding goggles or helmets to wear while assisting in a welding operation or while chipping flux away after a bead has been run over a joint. The danger of foreign bodies becoming lodged in the eye is great for workers performing this latter operation without protection.

A hand-held shield can be used where the convenience of a helmet is not needed, such as for inspection work, tack welding, and other operations requiring little or no welding by the user. Frame and lens construction are similar to that of the helmet.

Welding goggles are available with filter glass shades up to No. 8. If darker shades are required, then complete face protection is needed because of the danger of skin burns. When shades darker than No. 3 must be used, side-shields or cup goggles are recommended.

Acid-proof hoods that cover head, face, and neck are used by persons exposed to severe splashes from corrosive chemicals. This type of hood has a window of glass or plastic that is securely joined to the hood to prevent acid from seeping through. Hoods made of rubber, neoprene, plastic film, or impregnated fabrics are available for resistance to different chemicals. Consult manufacturers to find the protective properties of each material.

Hoods with air supply should be worn for work around toxic fumes, dusts, mists, or gases. These hoods provide a supply of clean, breathing-quality air, which excludes toxic materials and maintains worker comfort. To support the hose, the worker should wear a harness or belt.

Transparent face shields, supported from a head harness or headband, are used when there is limited exposure to direct splashes of corro-

 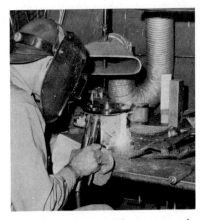

Figure 9-7. *Left:* The lift front on this welding helmet permits the welder to inspect the work without raising the helmet. Stationary plate of clear impact-resistant glass affords eye protection if light chipping is required. *Right:* Sturdy, nonflammable helmet with specified cover and filter plates protects this welder against sparks, flying particles, and injurious rays. Note local ventilation exhaust.

sive chemicals. Splash-resistant cup goggles should be worn under the shield for added protection.

EAR PROTECTION

Excessive noise should be reduced by engineering changes and administrative controls, whenever possible, as outlined in Chapter 6, "Industrial Hygiene and Noise Control." Ear protection should be used only as a last resort.

Although there is some disagreement as to the maximum intensity of sound to which the human ear can be subjected without damage to hearing, the standards of the Occupational Safety and Health Act should be used as a minimum level of protection. Under the OSHAct the permissible noise exposure for an 8-hour duration is 90 dB, measured on an A-weighted scale that corresponds to the response of the human ear. This level may be increased slightly as the duration of exposure decreases. (Review the discussion in Chapter 6.)

On the decibel scale, zero is the threshold of hearing for a sensitive ear, and 130 dB is the threshold of pain. The decibel is a ratio-type scale. If the sound pressure is doubled, it increases 6 dB; if halved, it decreases 6 dB. If cut to one-tenth, it decreases 10 dB; if cut to one-one hundredth, it decreases by 20 dB. The human ear is not as sensitive as a sound-measuring device; it often interprets a 10 dB drop in intensity as being "half as loud."

It takes specialized equipment and trained personnel to analyze a noise exposure and a specialist or company medical department to recommend the types of ear protection that will be most effective. (See Figure 9-8.)

Amount of protection

Commercially available earplugs, if properly fitted and used, may reduce noise reaching the ear by 25 to 30 dB in the higher (more harmful) frequencies. They will give ample protection against sound levels of 115 to 120 dB. Earmuffs of the better type can reduce noise an additional 10 to 15 dB, making them effective against sound levels of 130 to 135 dB.

Combination of earplugs and muffs give 3 to 5 dB more protection. In no case, however, will total attenuation (sound reduction) be more than about 50 dB, because conduction of noise through the bones of the head becomes significant at this point.

The best ear protection is the one that is accepted by the individual and is worn properly. Properly fitted protectors can be worn continuously by most persons and will provide adequate protection against most industrial noise exposures.

Insert ear protectors

Insert protectors are, of course, inserted into ear canals and vary considerably in design and material. Materials used are pliable rubber, soft or medium plastic, wax, and cotton. *Rubber and plastic* are popular because they are inexpensive, easy to keep clean, and give good performance. *Wax* tends to lose its effectiveness during the work day because jaw movement changes the shape of the ear canal and this breaks the acoustical seal between ear and insert. Wax inserts may be objectionable for use in dirty areas because they must be shaped by hand. They should be used only once. *Cotton* is a poor choice because of its low attenuating properties and because it must be hand formed. Glass down, so-called "Swedish cotton," is being used with success by some.

Still another type of ear plug that is popular is one that is molded to fit each ear. After being allowed to set, it will hold its form. Because each person's ear canal is shaped differently, these plugs become the property of the individual to whom they were fitted. These plugs, of course, must be fitted by a trained, qualified person.

Because of the pressure required to fit a rubber or plastic earplug into the ear canal so that the noise does not leak around the edges (as much protection as 15 dB could be lost), points of pressure develop, and they may cause discomfort. To overcome this problem, plugs should be fitted individually for each ear. A good seal cannot be obtained, however,

Figure 9-8. Hearing protectors include cup or muff devices that cover the external ear *(shown at rear)*, superaural protectors that do not plug the ear canal but rather block it at the entrance *(to left of center)*, and both preformed and formable earplugs *(front row)*.

without some initial discomfort. There will be no lasting reactions as a result of using earplugs if they are made of soft material and kept clean. Hard rigid materials could injure the ear canal.

Skin irritations, injured ear drums, or other harmful reactions are exceedingly rare when properly designed, well-fitted, and clean ear protectors are used. They should cause no more difficulty than does a pair of well-fitted safety goggles. If fitting continues to be a problem, casts can be made of the ear canals and a plastic plug can be custom made for each.

Overcoming objections. Although some people object to earplugs because they believe they will not be able to understand conversation, tests show that when the noise level is higher than about 85 dB, speech is more easily understood with earplugs in place than without them. At worst, a person wearing earplugs is like one who is moderately hard of hearing, rather than deaf.

Supervisors should be aware of noise hazards in their departments. They should also be able to demonstrate the correct use of earplugs when other forms of control are not practical.

Muff devices

Cup or muff devices cover the external ear to provide an acoustic barrier, the effectiveness of which varies with the size, shape, seal material, shell mass, and suspension of the muff. Head size and shape also influence the effectiveness. Liquid- or grease-filled cushions give better noise suppression than plastic or foam rubber. Muffs are made in a universal type or a head, neck, or chin size. Hearing protection kits are also available that can be used with hard hats.

In the past few years, some employees have listened to radios with earphones. You, as the supervisor, should make sure that these are not worn in the shop. In addition to the possibility of damage to the ears from excessive noise levels, they are not safe in a working environment. They are not safe because your people may not be able to hear oncoming plant trucks, vehicular traffic, other workers, or any number of industrial noises. Most Air Force bases have banned their use for this reason.

RESPIRATORY PROTECTIVE EQUIPMENT

Respiratory equipment can be regarded as emergency equipment, or equipment for occasional use. Of course, if there are contaminants present, they should be removed at the source or the process should be isolated. Since leaks and breakdowns do occur, however, and since some operations expose a person only briefly and infrequently, respiratory equipment should be available. The user shall be instructed and trained in its proper use and its limitations.

Selecting the respirator

Air contaminants range from relatively harmless substances to toxic dusts, vapors, mists, fumes, and gases that may be extremely harmful. Respiratory protection is required in certain areas or during certain operations when engineering controls are not available to reduce airborne concentrations of contaminants to a safe level. Engineering controls might not be present because they are technically infeasible, or the hazardous operation might be done infrequently, making controls impractical. Respiratory protection is also needed while engineering controls are being implemented.

When equipment is needed, the chemical or other offending substance must be determined, and the extent of the hazard evaluated. With this information, the respirator that protects against the particular hazard can be selected. Before respiratory equipment is ordered, it is best to discuss the type of exposure with the company safety or industrial hygiene department, and with manufacturers and dealers.

Only respirators approved by the National Institute for Occupational Safety and Health (NIOSH) and the Mine Safety and Health Administration (MSHA) are acceptable. A NIOSH-MSHA-approved

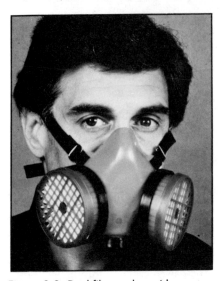

Figure 9-9. Dual-filter and cartridge system can use particulate filters, chemical cartridges, or aerosol filters, or a combination, to provide the wearer with a wide variety of breathing protection depending upon the hazard to which he is exposed. Air-purifying devices must not be used in atmosphere immediately dangerous to life, such as those deficient in oxygen.

H. S. Cover Co, Division of HSC Corp.

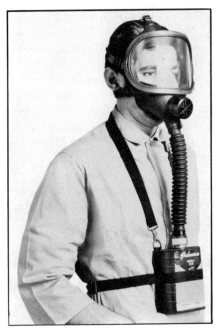

Figure 9-10. Canister-type gas mask has full-face piece which allows wide vision and wearing of prescription safety glasses underneath.

Pulmosan Safety Equipment Corp.

respirator is assigned an approval number prefixed by the letters TC, indicating that is has been tested and certified by NIOSH and MSHA for the air contaminant at the concentration range stated.

This approval assures that the design, durability, and workmanship of equipment meet minimum standards. Worker safety, freedom of movement, vision, fit, and comfort of facepiece and headpiece, the ease with which the filter and other parts can be replaced, the dust tightness of the apparatus, freedom from leakage, and resistance to flow of air when the wearer is inhaling and exhaling are tested.

Types of equipment

Respiratory equipment includes air purifying devices (see Figures 9-9 and -10) (mechanical filter respirators, chemical cartridge respirators, combination mechanical filter and chemical cartridge respirators, and masks with canisters), air-supplied devices (air line respirators, Figure 9-11), and self-contained breathing apparatus (see Figure 9-12).

Air purifying devices remove contaminants from air as it is being

Figure 9-11. This air line respirator can be disposed of instead of cleaned, and is approved for use in such applications as painting, buffing, bagging, clean room operations, and nuclear work. Supply air must be from uncontaminated source.

3M Company

Figure 9-12. This constant-flow, oxygen rebreathing self-contained breathing apparatus (SCBA) delivers up to four hours of service in oxygen-deficient or toxic environments.

National Draeger, Inc.

breathed. They can be used only in environments containing sufficient oxygen to sustain life. Air purifying devices are only effective in the limited concentration ranges for which they were designed, and must never be used where contaminant levels exceed the respirator manufacturer's accepted protection factor. These respirators generally consist of a soft, resilient facepiece and some kind of replaceable filtering element. Several types of air purifying respirators, however, are available as completely disposable units. Various chemical filters can be employed to remove specific gases and vapors, while mechanical filters remove particulate contaminants. Air purifying devices are never used in environments that are immediately hazardous to life or health.

Mechanical filter respirators must protect against exposure to nuisance dusts and pneumoconiosis-producing dusts, mists, and fumes. Examples of nuisance dusts are aluminum, cellulose, cement, flour, gypsum, and limestone.

Pneumoconiosis comes from three Greek words that mean "lung," "dust," and "abnormal condition." The generally accepted meaning of the word is merely "dusty lung." The kind of dust inhaled determines the type of condition or injury. Many organic dusts are capable of producing lung diseases, but not all these diseases are classified as pneumoconioses because they don't represent a "dusty condition" of the lung.

187

In rare cases, so much dust has been inhaled that it causes mechanical blockage of the air spaces. Flour dust has been known to do this. Some dusts are essentially inert and remain in the lungs indefinitely with no recognizable irritation, and a few (like limestone dust) may gradually dissolve and be eliminated without harm. Another type of filter respirator is approved for toxic dusts, such as lead, asbestos, arsenic, cadmium, manganese, selenium, and their compounds.

Protection against mists, for example, chromic acid, and exposure to such fumes as zinc and lead, are given by mechanical filter respirators specifically approved for such exposures. The filter, usually made of paper or felt, should be replaced frequently, for if it becomes clogged, it restricts breathing or becomes inoperative. This can happen as frequently as several times a shift.

A mechanical filter respirator is of no value as protection against solvent vapors, injurious gases, or oxygen deficiency. To use it under these conditions is a common, but serious, mistake.

Chemical cartridge respirators have either a half-mask facepiece or a full-mask facepiece connected to one or more small containers (cartridges) or sorbent, typically activated charcoal or soda lime (a mixture of calcium hydroxide with sodium or potassium hydroxide) for absorption of low concentrations of certain vapors and gases. These concentrations are approximately, 100 ppm organic vapors; 10 ppm chlorine, 50 ppm hydrogen chloride, 50 ppm sulfur dioxide (acid gases); 300 ppm ammonia; and 100 ppm methyl amines. The life of the cartridges can be relatively short. For protection against mercury vapors, the nominal container life is eight hours. After use, the cartridges must be discarded.

These respirators must not be used in atmospheres immediately dangerous to life or health, such as those deficient in oxygen.

A gas mask consists of a facepiece or mouth piece connected by a flexible tube to a canister (Figure 9-10). Inhaled air, drawn through the canister, is cleaned chemically. Unfortunately, no one chemical has been found that removes all contaminants. Therefore, the canister must be chosen to meet the exposure.

Gas mask canisters are identified by their color as to type of exposure.*

Black—organic vapors
White—acid gases

---

*American National Standard Z88.2, *Practices for Respiratory Protection.*

Yellow—organic vapors and acid gases

Green—ammonia gas

Brown—organic vapors, acid gases, and ammonia gases

White with green strip near bottom—hydrocyanic acid (hydrogen cyanide) gas

White with yellow stripe near bottom—chlorine gas

Blue—carbon monoxide

Purple—radioactive materials, except tritium and noble gases

Red with grey stripe near top—universal. All of the above atmospheric contaminants.

Gas masks have definite limitations on their effectiveness. Both gas concentration and length of time influence this. Gas masks, like chemical cartridge respirators, do not protect against oxygen deficiency, however.

When the canister is used up, it should be removed and replaced by a fresh one. Even if they have not been used, canisters should be replaced periodically. Manufacturers will indicate the maximum effective life.

Gas masks must be quickly available for emergencies. For example, in an ice plant where an ammonia leak is likely, masks should be placed either just inside or just outside the exit doors so that they can be reached quickly.

Masks should be stored away from moisture, heat, and direct sunlight. They should be inspected regularly.

Hose masks, with or without a blower, should not be used in atmospheres immediately dangerous to life or health (IDLH).

Supplied air devices deliver breathing air through a hose connected to the wearer's facepiece. The air source used is monitored frequently to make sure that it does not become contaminated. The most common contaminant monitored is carbon monoxide.

The air line respirator can be used in atmospheres not immediately dangerous to life or health, especially where working conditions demand continuous use of a respirator. Each person should be assigned his or her own respirator.

Air line respirators are connected to a compressed air line. A trap and filter should be installed in the compressed air line ahead of the mask to separate oil, water, grit, scale, or other matter from the air stream. When line pressures are over 25 psig (170 kPa), a pressure regulator is required. A pressure release valve, set to operate if the regulator fails, should be installed.

To get clean air, keep the compressor intake away from any source of contamination, for example, internal combustion engine exhaust. The compressor should have a carbon monoxide alarm in order to guard against the carbon monoxide hazard from overheated lubricating oil or from engine exhaust. The most desirable air supply is provided by a non-lubricated or externally lubricated medium-pressure blower, for example, a rotary compressor.

If workers need to move from place to place, they may find that the air hose is a nuisance. The supervisor must realize that this will reduce their efficiency. Care must be also exercised to prevent damage to the hose; for example, it should not be permitted to be in oil.

The abrasive blasting helmet is a variety of an air line respirator designed to protect the head, neck, and eyes against the impact of the abrasive, and to give a supply of breathing air. The air quality requirements are the same as those described for air line respirators.

The helmet should be covered both inside and out with a tough, resilient material. This increases comfort and still resists the abrasive. Some helmets have an outer hood of impregnated material and a zippered inner cape for quick removal. A glass window, protected by a 30- to 60-mesh fine-wire screen or plastic cover plate, should be provided. Safety glass, used to prevent shattering under a heavy blow, should be free of color and glass defects.

A lighter-weight helmet is approved for the less-severe applications of spraying paint, buffing, bagging, and working in clean rooms (see Figure 9-11).

Self-contained breathing apparatus provides protection for various periods of time by providing a portable air supply, which is usually worn by the user. The wearer of a self-contained breathing apparatus is independent of the surrounding atmosphere; therefore, this kind of respiratory protective equipment must be used in environments where air contaminants are immediately harmful to life. This equipment is frequently used in mine rescue work and in firefighting (see Figure 9-12).

The four principal types of self-contained breathing apparatus are (a) oxygen rebreathing; (b) self-generating; (c) demand; and, (d) pressure-demand. The length of time these units may be used is limited strictly by NIOSH/MSHA specifications.

Self-contained breathing apparatus should be worn only by workers who are physically fit and well trained. They should be retrained at least every six months in order to maintain efficiency.

Because of the extreme hazard, no one wearing self-contained breathing apparatus should work in an irrespirable atmosphere unless other persons similarly equipped are standing by, ready to give help.

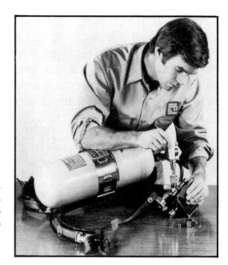

Figure 9-13. Some manufacturers offer training programs to assure that purchasers know how to properly fit, use, and maintain their respirators.

Mine Safety Appliances Company.

Protection factors are a measure of the overall effectiveness of a respirator. These factors, based on tests and on professional judgment, range from 5 to 10,000. The maximum use concentration for a respirator is determined by multiplying the TLVs of the substance to be protected against by the protection factor. For example, a respirator with a protection factor of 10 for acetic acid would protect a worker against concentrations up to 10 times its TLV. Since the TLV of acetic acid is 10 ppm, the worker would be protected in atmospheres containing acetic acid concentrations as high as 100 ppm. (TLVs were explained in Chapter 6.)

Cleaning the respirator

Respirator facepieces and harnesses should be cleaned and inspected regularly (Figure 9-13). If several persons must use the same respirator, it should be disinfected after each use in order to comply with OSHA regulations. Methods of disinfection include:

1. Immersion in a weak solution of quarternary ammonium compound, followed by a warm-water rinse. This solution is not normally injurious to skin or to rubber.

2. Washing in warm soapy water and rinsing for at least one minute in clean water of 120 F (49 C) minimum temperature.

The supervisor should inspect respirators at intervals to check for damage or improperly functioning parts, such as headbands or valve seats.

A most important consideration in respirator use is proper fit. In addition, supervisors must explain why it is so important to wear the respiratory protection, how it works and, in general, make sure that workers wear the proper respirator for the operation in question (see Figure 9-2).

If the respirator is removed at intervals, dust settles on it. When the respirator is replaced, these dust particles are transferred to the skin and cause irritation. To prevent this, the wearer should keep the respirator on constantly when in a contaminated atmosphere.

PROTECTING THE TORSO

The most common protection for the abdomen and trunk is the full apron. Aprons are made of various materials. Leather or fabric aprons, with padding or stays, offer protection against light impact and against sharp knives and cleavers, such as those used in packinghouses. Asbestos coats and aprons are often used by those who work around hot metal or other sources of intense conductive heat.

An apron worn near moving machinery should fit snugly around the waist. Neck and waist straps should be either light strings or instant-release fasteners in case the garment is caught. There should be a fastener at each end of the strap to prevent severe friction burns should the strap be caught or drawn across the back of the neck. Split aprons should be worn on jobs that require mobility on the part of the worker. Fasteners draw each section snugly around the legs.

Welders are often required to wear leather vests or capes and sleeves, especially when doing overhead welding, as protection against hot sparks and bits of molten metal.

On jobs where employees must carry heavy and angular loads, pads of cushioned leather or padded duck are used to protect the shoulders and back from injury.

SAFETY BELTS AND HARNESSES

Safety belts and harnesses with lifelines attached should be worn by those who work at high levels or in closed spaces where the air supply may not be adequate (particularly if they are wearing self-contained breathing apparatus or supplied air devices), and by those who work where they may be buried by loose material or be injured in confined spaces. This discussion, however, does not include seat (vehicular safety) belts or linemen's belts.

Both normal and emergency belts are available. Normal use involves comparatively light stresses applied during regular work—stresses that rarely exceed the static weight of the user. Emergency use means stopping an individual when he or she falls—every part of the belt may be sub-

Figure 9-14. A multi-purpose full body harness with two small shoulder D-rings for lowering and lifting and one D-ring in the center of the back for fall arrest, if required.

Rose Manufacturing Company

jected to an impact loading many times the weight of the wearer.

A window cleaner's belt, for example, is subjected to a moderate load most of the time it is used. It will be subjected to a severe loading, however, if the worker falls when only one terminal of the belt is attached. A belt for a person who leans back as he works should, therefore, have two D-rings, one on each side of the belt, to which a throw rope or lanyard can be attached. The rope is then anchored.

A harness-type safety belt is better at distributing the shock of an arrested fall. The shock is distributed over shoulders, back, and waist, instead of being concentrated at the waist; a two-line harness (see Figure 9-14) distributes the lifting and lowering stresses better than a one-line harness. The harness permits a person to be lifted with a straight back rather than bent over a waist strap. This makes rescue easier if the victim is unconscious, buried, or must be taken out through a manhole. Wherever a job requires use of self-contained breathing apparatus or supplied air devices, a harness and lifeline should also be used, if it would assist in escape.

If long free falls are possible, the harness should be designed to distribute the impact force over the legs and chest as well as the waist. A shock absorber or decelerating device, which brings the falling person to a gradual stop, lessens the impact load on both the equipment and the person. To prevent a long fall, the line should be tied off overhead and should be as short as movements of the worker will permit.

A boatswain's swing chair is used when the entire weight of a worker must be supported vertically as, for example, when raising or lowering a person along a wall. The chair has one strap (sometimes with a board attached) to sit on, and a waist strap fastened on each side so the worker can either stand or sit, but cannot fall out of the seat. The chair and fittings must conform to OSHA regulations.

Ladder safety devices. Fixed ladders more than 24 ft (7.5 m) high must have some device to prevent a climber from falling. Baskets and ladder guards are useful in some cases, but cost or space may require a ladder safety device, which consists of a body belt and a clamp that rides a wire rope or rigid device on the ladder. The clamp engages a safety device that locks on the rope or ladder when the climber slips or misses a step (ANSI A14.3-1984, *Safety Requirements for Fixed Ladders*).

Safety requirements for other types of ladders can be found in the following ANSI Standards:

Portable Ladders, Wood	ANSI A14.1-1982
Portable Ladders, Metal	ANSI A14.2-1982
Job-Made Ladders	ANSI A14.4-1979
Portable Ladders, Reinforced Plastic	ANSI A14.5-1982

Fabrication

Belts made of natural or synthetic materials are furnished by most manufacturers. Nylon belts, straps, and harnesses, while widely used, may not be satisfactory under some chemical conditions. Special types of belting are available for certain environments—wax-treated belts resist paint solvents or mildew, neoprene-impregnated belts resist acids and oil products. Be sure to consult the manufacturers before ordering.

Safety belts are designed to give a little when stress loaded. If a person does fall and stress a belt, the belt should be taken out of service and replaced.

There are several kinds of devices that are used to attach the belt to a lifeline that serve to reduce the stress of a fall; these minimize both the injury to the user and the damage to the belt.

Lifelines

Manila ropes of ³/₄-in. (1.9 cm) diameter, or nylon rope of ¹/₂-in. (1.3 cm) diameter is recommended for lifelines. Nylon is more resistant to wear or abrasion than is manila (abaca). It is more elastic (absorbing shocks and sudden loads better) and has high tensile strength (wet or dry). Nylon is tough, flexible, and easy to handle. Because it resists mildew, it can be stored wet.

Breaking strength is always measured in a straight-line pull on the rope. Half-inch (1.3 cm) diameter manila rope breaks at approximately 2650 lb (1200 kg), half-inch diameter nylon rope is rated at 6400 lb (2900 kg), ($\pm$ 5 percent). Using a safety factor of 5 for manila and 9 for nylon gives safe load strengths of 530 lb (240 kg) and 710 lb (320 kg), respectively.

Manila rope ³/₄-in. (1.9 cm) in diameter breaks at approximately 5400 lb (2450 kg), giving a safe load strength of 1080 lb (490 kg). When lowload-limit shock absorber is used, ³/₄-in. manila rope or ¹/₂-in. nylon rope is considered strong enough for most lifelines. Without a shock absorber, even ³/₄-in. manila may not be strong enough to arrest a long fall.

Wire rope should not be used for lifelines where free falls are possible, unless a shock-absorbing device is also used. The rigidity of steel greatly increases the impact loading. Steel is, furthermore, hazardous around electricity.

Knots reduce the strength of all ropes. The degree of loss depends upon the type of knot and the amount of moisture in the rope. See Table 9-C. (More information is given in Chapter 10, "Materials Handling and Storage.")

Inspection and care of belts and lines

Safety belts and lines should be looked over each time before using. At least once every three months, belts should be examined by a trained inspector.

Belts. Web belts should be examined for worn and torn fibers. When a number of the outer fibers are worn or cut through, the belt should be discarded.

Belt hardware should be examined and worn parts replaced. If the belt is riveted, each rivet should be carefully inspected for wear around the rivet hole. Dirt and dust should be brushed carefully from belts to prevent fiber damage. Broken or damaged stitching may require belt replacement.

Web belts may be washed in warm, soapy water, rinsed with clear water, and dried by moderate heat. If these belts are worn under unusual

TABLE 9-C
APPROXIMATE EFFICIENCY OF
MANILA ROPE HITCHES

	Percent
Full strength of dry rope	100
Eye splice over metal thimble	90
Short splice in rope	80
Timber hitch, round turn, half hitch	65
Bowline, slip knot, clove hitch	60
Square knot, weaver's knot, sheet bend	50
Flemish eye, overhand knot	45

Source: Oregon Safety Code for Places of Employment.

conditions, or if a dressing is to be used, consult the manufacturer.

Lines. The outer surface of rope lines should be examined for cuts and for worn or broken fibers. Manila rope should be discarded if it has become smaller in diameter or has acquired a smooth look. Inner fibers of manila rope should be examined for breaks, discoloration, and deterioration. If it shows any of these signs, the rope should be discarded.

A steel wire rope should be examined for broken strands, rust, and kinks that may weaken it. Ropes must be kept clean, dry, and rust free. They should be lubricated frequently, especially before use in acid atmospheres or before exposure to salt water. After such use, wire rope should be carefully cleaned and again coated with oil.

Flotation devices

Operations that require working on off-shore rigs, merchant vessels, barges, tugs, and so forth require flotation devices according to U.S. Coast Guard-promulgated standards. In these cases, the supervisor should make certain that this equipment meets all applicable standards, that it is in good condition, and, most important, that it be worn when required (see Figure 9-15). There have been near-accidents and, indeed, drownings that could have been easily prevented had this personal protective equipment been worn.

PROTECTION AGAINST IONIZING RADIATION

Ionizing radiation, dangerous because of its serious biological effects, need not be feared if it is respected and if suitable precautionary measures are taken. NSC's *Fundamentals of Industrial Hygiene* has

Figure 9-15. Wearing of a vest-type life preserver meeting U.S. Coast Guard standards should be required for anyone working over, on, or near water locations that expose them to the risk of drowning.

U.S. Coast Guard, First Coast Guard District

much information on the topic and many references.

Standards for protection against radiation, specified in OSHA regulations, reference the Nuclear Regulatory Commission regulations spelled out in *Code of Federal Regulations*, Title 10 "Energy," Part 20, should be followed.

Rubber gloves for handling radioactive materials, disposable clothing, suits with supplied air, and approved respiratory devices are some of the items of specialized equipment that are needed. Under no circumstances should contaminated clothing be worn into clean areas. Thorough washing with soap and water is usually the best general method for decontamination of the hands and other parts of the body, regardless of the contaminant.

Before supervisors or employees work with radioactive materials, they should check with the medical and safety departments. The supervisor must be absolutely assured in writing that all people will be adequately protected *before* any tests are made or procedures changed that involve radioactive materials or isotopes. Supervisors should see that medical clearances and other authorizations, in addition to badges and dosimeters, are issued to all personnel assigned to work in areas restricted for radioisotope use.

Monitoring radiation

Employees should be continuously monitored for exposure to radiation. At work, they should wear film badges that are developed and replaced at regular intervals, depending on the radiation intensity level to which they are exposed. The film badge records the total exposure for a given period, but does not indicate the precise time during the period when the exposure occurred.

For better protection, each person should also wear two pocket dosimeters. These show the dosage received during any part of a work period so that the individual can check at any time for exposure. The dosimeter does not provide a permanent record, but is essential for safety during work periods. It is read at least once, usually at the end of a shift. It can be reset by means of a dosimeter charger. Radiation accidents resulting in overexposures should be immediately reported to the medical director.

PROTECTION AGAINST CHEMICALS

Protecting workers in and around chemicals is of paramount importance. Many chemical substances to which employees are exposed can be irritating and result in serious burns on the body, hands, arms, and legs. You, as the supervisor, have the responsibility of evaluating operations using chemicals and determining what is needed in the area of personal protective equipment or proper clothing.

If you need help for this task, get in touch with your safety department, insurance company safety engineer, protective equipment supplier, or chemist. The best way to protect people is by wearing proper and safe clothing designed specifically for the chemicals involved. Keep in mind, however, that if the chemical can be replaced with a less toxic one, this is always the way to go. If it cannot be eliminated, replaced, or if the operation cannot be isolated, then your only recourse is protective clothing. This is discussed below.

SAFE WORK CLOTHING

Ordinary work clothing, if clean, in good repair, and suited to the job, may be considered safe. "Safety clothing" refers to garments designed for specific, hazardous jobs where ordinary work clothes do not give enough protection against such minor injuries as abrasions, burns, and scratches.

Good fit is important. Most work trousers or slacks are made extra long to provide for shrinkage and to fit tall workers. Trousers that are too long must be shortened to proper length, preferably without cuffs. If cuffs are made, they should be securely stitched down so the wearers cannot catch their heels in them. Cuffs should never be worn near operations that produce flying embers, sparks, or other harmful matter.

Neckties, long or loose sleeves, gloves, and loose-fitting garments (especially about the waist) create a hazard, because they are easily caught in moving (or revolving) machine parts.

All types of jewelry are out of place in a shop—rings, bracelets, and wristwatches can cause serious injury. A finger may be torn off if a ring catches on a moving machine part, or on a fixed object when the body is moving rapidly. Necklaces, key chains, and watch chains also constitute hazards near moving machinery. Metal jewelry worn around electrical equipment, including batteries, can be dangerous.

Clothing soaked in oil or flammable solvent is easily ignited and is a definite hazard. Remember that skin irritations are often caused by continued contact with clothing that has been soaked with solvents or oils.

If oil or dust gets in the hair, a cap should be worn to guard against dirt and infections and to keep hair looking nice. A cap may also help protect a person from moving parts of machines that cannot be completely guarded. More about this later.

Materials for protective clothing

A number of protective materials are used in making clothes to protect workers against various hazards. Supervisors should be familiar with these materials.

Aluminized and reflective clothing has a coating that reflects radiant heat. Aluminized asbestos or glass fiber is used for heavy-duty suits, and aluminized fabric for fire-approach suits. (See Figure 9-16.)

Asbestos is used as protection against intense conducted heat and flames. When used with a radiation barrier of reflective material, asbestos offers protection in firefighting and rescue work; however, it must always be treated so as not to give off airborne fibers.

Flame-resistant cotton fabric is often used as a hair covering for people who work near sparks and open flames. Although the fabric is durable, the flame-proofing treatment may have to be repeated after one to four launderings.

Flame-resistant duck, used for garments worn around sparks and open flames, is lightweight, strong, and long wearing. It is not considered adequate protection against extreme radiation heat.

Glass fiber is used in multi-layered construction to insulate clothing. The facing is made of glass cloth or of aluminized fabric.

Impervious materials (such as rubber, neoprene, vinyl, and fabrics coated with these materials) protect against dust, vapors, mists, mois-

Figure 9-16. Reflectorized, ventilated clothing protects the worker against excessive heat.

PPG Industries

ture, and corrosives. Rubber is used often because it resists solvents, acids, alkalis, and other corrosives. Neoprene resists petroleum oils, solvents, acids, alkalis, and other corrosives.

Leather protects against light impact. Chrome-tanned leather protects against sparks, molten metal splashes, and infrared and ultraviolet radiation.

Synthetic fibers (such as acrylics and low-density polyethylene) resist acids, many solvents, mildew, abrasion and tearing, and repeated launderings. Because some fabrics generate static electricity, garments should not be worn in explosive or high-oxygen atmospheres, unless they are treated with an antistatic agent.

Water-resistant duck is useful for exposures to water and noncorrosive liquids. When it is aluminum-coated, the material also protects against radiant heat.

Wool may be used for clothing that protects against splashes of molten metal and small quantities of acid and small flames.

Permanent press. With such extensive use of the permanent press garments, care must be taken to determine whether or not it is flammable.

PROTECTING FINGERS, ARMS, PALMS, AND HANDS

Fingers and hands are exposed to cuts, scratches, bruises, and burns. Although fingers are hard to protect (because they are needed for practically all work), they can be shielded from any common injuries with such proper protective equipment as the following:

1. Asbestos gloves and treated terrycloth gloves protect against burns and discomfort when the hands are exposed to sustained conductive heat.

2. Metal mesh gloves, used by those who work constantly with knives, protect against cuts and blows from sharp or rough objects.

3. Rubber gloves are worn by electricians. They must be tested regularly for dielectic strength.

4. Rubber, neoprene, and vinyl gloves are used when handling chemicals and corrosives. Neoprene and vinyl are particularly useful when petroleum products are handled.

5. Leather gloves are able to resist sparks, moderate heat, chips, and rough objects. They provide some cushioning against blows. They are generally used for heavy-duty work. Chrome-tanned leather or horsehide gloves are used by welders.

6. Chrome-tanned cowhide leather gloves with a steel-stapled leather patches or steel staples on palms and fingers are often used in foundries and steel mills.

7. Cotton fabric gloves are suitable for protection against dirt, slivers, chafing, or abrasion. They are not heavy enough to use in handling rough, sharp, or heavy materials.

8. Coated fabric gloves protect against moderately concentrated chemicals. They are recommended for use in canneries, packing houses, food service, and similar industries.

9. Heated gloves are designed for use in cold environments, such as deep freezers, and can be part of a heated clothing system. Other

Figure 9-17. Foam-insulated gloves offer flexibility, comfort, and wet grip in cold applications.

Edmont Division of Becton Dickenson and Company

types designed for such work are insulated with foam, and most such gloves are water-proof (see Figure 9-17).

Specially made electrically tested rubber gloves, worn under leather gloves to prevent punctures, are used by linemen and electricians who work with high-voltage equipment. A daily visual inspection and air test (by mouth) must be made. Make sure that rubber gloves extend well above the wrist so that there is no gap between the coat or shirt sleeve and glove. The shortest glove is 14 in. (42 cm).*

People do not mind wearing gloves when the dangers of not wearing them are apparent. When workers no longer have to worry about cutting their hands, and when they can grip materials better because of gloves, production increases. Still, if employees become lax in wearing their

---

*See NSC Industrial Data Sheet No. 598, "Flexible Insulating Protective Equipment for Electrical Workers."

gloves, frequent reminders are necessary.

The supervisor should be aware that gloves may be a hazard when worn around certain machining operations. Their use in these areas should be prohibited.

Hand leathers or hand pads are often more satisfactory than gloves for protecting against heat, abrasion, and splinters. Wristlets or arm protectors are available in the same materials as gloves.

Protective creams may be used to protect skin against many irritants when protective equipment is not practicable. Creams are available in water-soluble or water-resistant types, and in several grades for different exposures.

Water-soluble creams protect against cutting oils, paints, lacquers, and varnishes. Water-resistant types are used where the cutting oil or cooling lubricant has more than 10 percent water content. Soap and warm water will remove creams of this type.

For protective cream to be effective, coatings should be renewed frequently. Remember that creams do not protect against highly corrosive substances.

Certain operations, for example, plating, may require arm protectors. These should follow the same pattern as those prescribed for gloves. Arm protectors should be made of materials that overcome such hazards as acids, heat, or whatever else is encountered. These protectors should be fastened in such a way so as to prevent them from falling off. Again, equipment dealers can provide invaluable service.

PROTECTING THE FEET AND LEGS

About a quarter of a million disabling occupational foot injuries take place each year. This points to the need for foot protection in most industries, and the need for supervisors to see that their workers wear it.

All safety shoes have toes reinforced with a toe cap. The three classifications are shown in Table 9-D. The toe box will actually stand up under weights greater than those specified. In one case, a 10-ton roller passed over a man's toes. The toes were not crushed even when the toe box was broken.

Safety shoes have other protective features, as well as reinforced toes (see Figure 9-18).

Many shoe manufacturers and jobbers cooperate with companies to set up shoe sale departments. They provide experienced people to see that shoes are properly chosen for the hazard involved and are properly fit-

TABLE 9-D
MINIMUM REQUIREMENTS FOR SAFETY-TOE SHOES

Classification	Compression Pounds	Impact Foot Pounds	Clearance Inches
75	2,500	75	16/32
50	1,750	50	16/32
30	1,000	30	16/32

Note: 1 pound force = 4.45 newtons
    1 foot pound force = 1.36 joules
    1 inch = 2.54 centimeters

Source: American National Standard Z41-1983, *Safety-Toe Footwear.*

ted. Some companies keep shoes on hand for sale; others conduct business by mail. An employer can arrange for purchase of shoes at local outlets. Some dealers have a mobile shoe service—a truck equipped as a shoe store and manned by an experienced fitter. The responsibility for proper care of safety shoes ordinarily rests with the employees.

Metal-free shoes, boots, and other footwear are available for use where there are specific electrical hazards or fire and explosion hazards.

"Congress" or gaiter-type shoes are used to protect people from splashes of molten metal or from welding sparks. This type can be removed quickly to avoid serious burns. These shoes have no laces or eyelets to catch molten metal.

Reinforced or inner soles of flexible metal are built into shoes worn in areas where there are hazards from protruding nails and when the likelihood of contact with energized electrical equipment is remote, for example, in the construction industry.

For wet work conditions, in dairies and breweries, rubber boots and shoes, leather shoes with wood soles, or wood soled sandals are effective. Wood soles have been so generally used by workers handling hot asphalt that they are sometimes called "pavers' sandals."

Safety shoes with metatarsal guards should always be worn during operations where heavy materials, such as pig iron, heavy castings, and timbers are handled. They are recommended whenever there is a possibility of objects falling and striking the foot above the toe cap. Metal foot

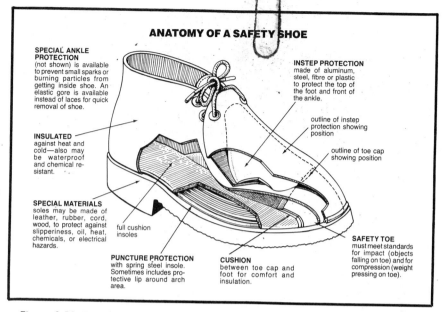

Figure 9-18. Features of a safety shoe—much more than merely a hard toe.

guards are long enough to protect the foot back to the ankle, and may be made of heavy gage or corrugated sheet metal. They are usually built onto the shoe.

Overcoming objections. Safety shoes used to be hot and heavy, and people often complained that they were uncomfortable. Current designs now make some safety shoes as comfortable, practical, and attractive as ordinary street shoes. The steel cap weighs about as much as a pair of rimless eyeglasses or a wrist watch. The toe box is insulated with felt to keep the feet from getting too hot or cold. Some shoes have inner soles of foam latex, which consist of tiny "breathing cells."

Some people object to wearing safety shoes because they do not cover the smallest toes. However, studies show that 75 percent of all toe fractures happen to the first and second toes. In most accidents, the toe box takes the load of the impact for the entire front part of the foot.

Another objection commonly voiced is that if the toe box were crushed, the steel edge would cut off the toes. Actually, accidents of this type are rare. In the majority of cases, safety shoes give sufficient protection. Freak accidents may happen, against which there is no sure protection. But, in any event, a blow that would crush the toe cap would certainly smash someone's toes if he or she were not wearing foot protection.

Figure 9-19. All equipment must meet safety standards, but that is not enough. Employees need fit and comfort, even the right styling in some cases. If the shoe fits, wear it.

Letting the employees select their shoe style encourages cooperation (see Figure 9-19).

Leg protection

Leggings which encircle the leg from ankle to knee and have a flap at the bottom to protect the instep, protect the entire leg. The front part may be reinforced to give impact protection. Such guards are worn by persons who work around molten metal. Leggings should permit rapid removal in case of emergency. Hard fiber or metal guards are available to protect shins against impact.

Knee pads protect employees whose work, like cement finishing or tile setting, requires much kneeling.

Ballistic nylon pads are often used to protect the thighs and upper leg against injury from chainsaws.

Foot and leg protectors are available in many different materials. The type selected depends on the work being done. Where molten metals, sparks, and heat are the major hazards, asbestos or leather is best. Where acids, alkalis, and hot water are encountered, natural or synthetic rubber or plastic, resistant to the specific exposure, can be used.

206

PAYING FOR PROTECTIVE EQUIPMENT

Companies differ in their personal protective equipment payment policies. Usually companies that require extremely clean operations will furnish laundered coveralls, aprons, smocks, and other garments.

Personal items, such as safety shoes and prescription safety glasses, are often sold on a share-the-cost basis. Some firms maintain safety shoe stores for their employees.

Other items considered necessary to the job are often supplied free to the employee. A welder's helmet and welder's gloves are good examples.

Ordinary work clothes and work gloves are, however, usually purchased by the employee.

It is better economy to assume the cost of necessary equipment than to risk possible injury by not having proper equipment when and where it is needed.

Chapter 10

Materials Handling
And Storage

Almost every supervisor, at one time or another, has had to handle materials on the job. Materials handling may be done manually or with mechanical equipment, but either way, materials handling can be a source of occupational injury. These same problems exist off the job and have the same results—injuries, suffering, and the loss of time.

MATERIALS HANDLING PROBLEMS

It has been estimated that manual handling of materials accounts for about 25 percent of all occupational injuries. These injuries are not limited to the shipping department or the warehouse, but come from all operations, because it is impossible to run a business without moving or handling materials. Moreover, such injuries are not limited to back strains, but can occur to legs or feet (by dropping whatever one is handling), or they can occur to the fingers, hands, and palms. The importance of proper materials handling techniques is glaringly apparent when all factors are considered.

Common injuries are strains and sprains, fractures, and bruises. These are primarily caused by unsafe practices—improper lifting, carrying too heavy a load, incorrect gripping, failing to observe proper foot or hand clearances, and failing to use or wear proper equipment and/or personal protective equipment and clothing.

The cause of materials handling accidents often can be traced to poor job design. Take a look at your operations and ask these questions about present operating practices.

- Can the job be so engineered that manual handling of materials is eliminated? (See Figure 10-1.)

Figure 10-1. Manual handling can be engineered out of both manufacturing and maintenance operations.

1a. Lift truck with carton clamps doesn't require pallets.

Industrial Truck Division,
Clark Equipment Co.

1b. Battery changes are made easy by having slot in overhead guard which accommodates a hoist chain for battery removal.

Towmotor Corporation, a subsidiary of
Caterpillar Tractor Co.

• How do materials such as chemicals, dusts, rough and sharp objects hurt the people doing the handling?

• Can employees be given handling aids—properly sized boxes, adequate trucks, or hooks—that will make their jobs safer? (See Figure 10-2.)

• Will protective clothing, or other personal equipment, help to prevent injuries?

These are by no means the only questions that might be asked, but they serve as a start and an overall appraisal.

Other causes of materials handling accidents are unsafe lifting procedures. As mentioned above, these injuries can occur on any part of the

Figure 10-2. Two handling aids for drums.

2a. A wheeled and tiltable drum cradle facilitates uprighting and moving such containers.

2b. Two-wheeled handtruck has an attachment for gripping drum. Tilting leverage can be applied by operator's foot to the treadle.

Liftomatic Material Handling, Inc.

body, such as the back, hands, and feet. It is beneficial for everyone to adhere to safe lifting and handling techniques when lifting objects manually is required. Safe lifting techniques are discussed next.

MANUAL HANDLING METHODS

Since the largest number of injuries occurs to the fingers and hands, people need instruction in how to pick up and put down heavy, bulky, or long objects. Some general precautions are in order. (See Figure 10-3.)

1. Inspect materials for slivers, jagged edges, burrs, rough or slippery surfaces.

2. Get a firm grip on the object.

3. Keep fingers away from pinch points, especially when putting materials down.

4. When handling lumber, pipe, or other long objects, keep hands away from the ends to prevent them from being pinched.

5. Wipe off greasy, wet, slippery, or dirty objects before trying to handle them.

6. Keep hands free of oil and grease.

In most cases, gloves, hand leathers, or other hand protectors can be worn to prevent hand injuries. Their use must be controlled if they are to be worn around moving machinery.

In other cases, handles or holders can be attached to the objects themselves, for example, handles for moving auto batteries, tongs for feeding material to metal-forming machinery, or wicker baskets for carrying control laboratory samples.

Feet and legs, primarily the toes, sustain a share of materials handling injuries. One of the best ways to avoid these injuries is to insist that people wear foot protection—safety shoes, instep protectors, and ankle guards.

The eyes, head, and trunk of the body can also be injured. When opening a wire-bound or metal-bound bale or box, people should wear eye protection, as well as stout gloves. They should take special care to prevent the ends of the bindings from flying loose and striking the face or body. The same precaution applies to coils of wire, strapping, or cable. If a material is dusty or toxic, the person handling it should wear a respirator or other suitable personal protective equipment. Workers also need training in handling heavy objects. See the following directions for lifting and carrying.

Lifting and carrying

Obviously, the best means to reduce back injuries is to try to eliminate manual lifting. If this cannot be done, another way is to reduce exposure. This can be achieved by cutting weight loads, using mechanical aids, and rearranging the workplace. In spite of all these efforts, manual lifting cannot be entirely eliminated. The basic rules and instructions to be followed include:

1. Never let workers overexert themselves when lifting. If the load is thought to be more than one person can handle, assign another person to the job.

2. Lift gradually, without jerking, to minimize the effects of acceleration.

3. Keep the load close to the body.

4. Lift without twisting the body.

5. Follow the six-step lifting procedure described on pages 212 and 213.

In reference to the six-step lifting procedure, remember that some researchers, working in the area of safe lifting, now feel that it is better to let workers choose the lifting position that is most comfortable for them.

(Text continues on page 214.)

Proper Way To Lift

Lifting is so much a part of everyday jobs that most of us don't think about it. But it is often done wrong, with bad results: pulled muscles, disk lesions, or painful hernia.

Here are six steps to safe lifting.

1. Keep feet parted—one alongside, one behind the object.
2. Keep back straight, nearly vertical.
3. Tuck your chin in.
4. Grip the object with the whole hand.
5. Tuck elbows and arms in.
6. Keep body weight directly over feet.

FEET should be parted, with one foot alongside the object being lifted and one behind. Feet comfortably spread give greater stability; the rear foot is in position for the upward thrust of the lift.

BACK. Use the sit-down position and keep the back straight —but remember that "straight" does not mean "vertical." A straight back keeps the spine, back muscles, and organs of the body in correct alignment. It minimizes the compression of the guts that can cause hernia.

Figure 10-3.

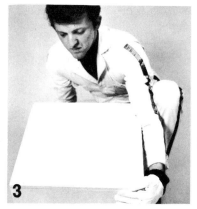

ARMS AND ELBOWS. The load should be drawn close, and the arms and elbows should be tucked into the side of the body. When the arms are held away from the body, they lose much of their strength and power. Keeping the arms tucked in also helps keep body weight centered.

PALM. The palmar grip is one of the most important elements of correct lifting. The fingers and the hand are extended around the object you're going to lift. Use the full palm; fingers alone have very little power. Glove has been removed to show finger positions better.

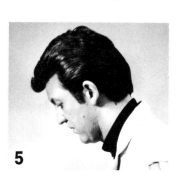

CHIN. Tuck in the chin so your neck and head continue the straight back line and keep your spine straight and firm.

BODY WEIGHT. Position body so its weight is centered over the feet. This provides a more powerful line of thrust and ensures better balance. Start the lift with a thrust of the rear foot.

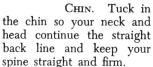

These researchers do not feel that the straight back procedure should be stressed, especially when handling bulky objects. All agree that the elbows and arms should be tucked in to keep the load as close to the body as possible. This reduces the stress on the back. Exercise to develop the abdominal muscles is recommended to the greatest extent possible. A number of supervisors whose employees do frequent manual lifting have instituted a five-minute warm-up period before starting a new shift. When bulky objects are to be handled, or when objects are to be carried on the shoulder, train your people in safe techniques for specific situations.

To place an object on a bench or table—First put the object on the edge and push it far enough onto the support to make sure it does not fall. Release it gradually. Move it into place by pushing it with the hands and body. This method prevents fingers from getting pinched.

To raise an object above shoulder height—Lift the object first to waist height. Rest the edge of the object on a ledge, stand, or hip. Shift the hand position so that the object can be boosted after the knees are bent. Straighten out the knees as the object is lifted or shifted to the shoulders.

To change direction—Point the foot in the direction of travel before picking up the load. Do not twist your body. In repetitive work, the person and the material should both be positioned so that the body will not twist when moving the material.

If the object is too heavy to be handled by one person—Get help. When two or more people are handling the same object, one should call the signals. Everyone on the lift should know who the head person is and should give warning if any one of the crew is about to relax his or her grip.

Handling specific shapes

Boxes, cartons, and crates are best handled by grasping them at alternate top and bottom corners and drawing one corner between the legs. Any box, carton or crate that appears either too large or too heavy for one person to handle should either be handled by two persons, or with mechanical handling equipment, if possible.

When two persons handle a crate, box, or carton, it is preferable that they be nearly the same size so that there is almost an even load to carry. The carriers must be able to see in front of the load so that they don't run into pedestrians, plant trucks, machines, walls, or equipment.

Figure 10-4. Lifts that are too heavy or too large for one person should be made by two, if use of mechanical handling equipment is not feasible.

Bags or sacks are grasped in the same manner as boxes. If a sack is to be raised to shoulder height, it should be raised to waist height first, and rested against the belly or hip before it is swung to the shoulder. It should rest on its side.

Additionally, if two persons are to lift a large bag or sack, they should be nearly the same size. This facilitates the job and keeps the load balanced. The two should lift at the same time, on an agreed signal.

Barrels and drums. Workers need special training to handle barrels and drums safely. If two people are assigned to upend a full drum, they should use the following procedure.

- Stand on opposite sides of the drum and face one another.

- Grasp both chimes (rolled edges at both ends of the drum) near their high points. Lift one end; press down on the other.

- As the drum is upended and brought to balance on the bottom chime, release the grip on the bottom chime and straighten it up with the drum.

When two people are to overturn a full drum, they should use this procedure.

• Make sure that there is enough room. Cramped quarters can result in badly injured hands.

• Stand near one another, facing the drum. Grip the closest point of the top chime with both hands. Rest palms against the side of the drum, and push until the drum balances on the lower chime.

• The two workers step forward a short distance, and each person releases one hand from the top chime in order to grip the bottom chime (see Figure 10-4). They ease the drum down to a horizontal position until it rests solidly on its side.

If one person is to overturn a drum, he or she should:

• Make sure there is enough room.

• Stand in front of the drum, reach over it, and grasp the far side of the top chime with both hands. (A short person can grasp the near side of the chime, if this is easier.) If the drum is tight against a wall or against other drums, pull on the chime with one hand and push against the wall (or other drum) with the other hand for additional control.

• Pull the top of the drum toward you, until it is balanced on the edge of the lower chime.

• Transfer both hands to the near side of the top chime. Keep the hands far enough apart to avoid their being pinched when the drum touches the floor.

• Lower the drum. Keep the back straight, inclined as necessary. Bend the legs so that the leg muscles take the strain.

If one person is to upend a drum, reverse this procedure. Actually, if one person must handle a drum, he or she should have a lifter bar that hooks over the chime and gives powerful leverage and excellent control. Barrel and drum lifters are commercially available. To roll a barrel or drum, push against the sides with the hands. To change direction of the roll, grip the chime. Do not kick the drum with your feet.

To lower a drum or barrel down a skid, turn it and slide it on end. Do not roll it. To raise a drum or barrel up a skid, two workers stand on opposite sides of the skid (outside the rails, not inside, and not below the object being raised). Then, roll the object up the incline.

Handling drums and barrels can be hazardous, even when using utmost care. Special handling equipment and tools (approved by the safety professional or safety department) should be available to make this job safer and easier (see Figure 10-2).

Long objects, like ladders, lumber, or pipe, should be carried over the shoulder. The front end should be held as high as possible to prevent its striking other employees, especially when turning corners. When two or more people carry an object, they should place it on the same shoulder, respectively, and walk in step.

MATERIALS HANDLING EQUIPMENT

Hand tools

Many hand tools are available for specific jobs and for specific materials. They should be used only for their designated purpose. Further, hand tools should always be kept in peak condition for best results and safety reasons. For instance, if a chisel is used, it should be sharp and also be free of burrs. A mushroom-headed chisel should never be used.

Crowbars are probably the most common hand tools used in materials handling. Select the proper kind and size for the job. Because the bar can slip, people should never work astride it. They should position themselves to avoid being pinched or crushed if the bar should slip or the object moves suddenly. The bar should have a good "bite" and not be dull or broken. When not in use, crowbars should be hung on a rack or otherwise placed so they cannot fall on or trip someone.

Rollers are used for moving heavy or bulky objects. Workers should be careful not to crush fingers or toes between the rollers and the floor. They should use a sledge or bar, not their hands and feet, to change direction of the object. They should avoid unnecessary turns by making sure the rollers are properly placed before moving. Compressed gas cylinders must never be used as rollers.

Handles of tongs and pliers should be offset so hands and fingers will not be pinched.

Hooks. Hand hooks used for handling material should be kept sharp so that they will not slip when applied to a box or other object. The handle should be strong and securely attached and shaped to fit the hand. The handle and the point of long hooks should be bent on the same plane so that the bar will lie flat when not in use and not constitute a tripping hazard. The hook point should be shielded when not in use.

Shovels. Shovel edges should be kept trimmed, and handles should be checked for splinters. Workers should wear safety toe shoes with

Figure 10-5. Various types of hand carts are available for moving various shapes and sizes of objects.

5a. Operators should wear gloves and safety shoes.

Advance Lifts, Inc.

5b. Carts are available for one- or two-hand operation. Cradle-type framework of this model helps when moving drums or barrels.

sturdy soles. Their feet should be well separated to provide balance and spring in the knees. The leg muscles should take much of the load.

To reduce the chance of injury, the ball of the foot—not the arch—should be used to press the shovel into clay or other stiff material. If the instep is used and the foot slips off the shovel, the sharp corner of the shovel may cut through the worker's shoe and into the foot.

Dipping the shovel into a pail of water occasionally will help to keep it free from sticky material. Greasing or waxing the shovel blade will also prevent some kinds of material from sticking. When not in use, shovels should be placed upright against a wall, or kept in racks or boxes.

Hand trucks—nonpowered

Two-wheeled hand trucks look as though they would be easy to handle, but there are safe procedures that must be followed.

1. Keep the center of gravity of the load as low as possible. Place heavy objects below lighter objects.

2. Place the load well forward so the weight will be carried by the axle, not by the handles.

3. Position the load so it will not slip, shift, or fall. Load only to a height that will allow a clear view ahead.

4. Let the truck carry the load. The operator should only balance and push.

5. Never walk backwards with a hand truck.

6. When going down an incline, keep the truck in front of you. When going up, keep the truck behind you.

7. Move the trucks at a safe speed. Do not run. Keep the truck under control.

A truck that is designed for a specific purpose should only be used for that purpose—a curved bed truck should be used for handling drums or other circular materials, and a horizontal platform truck for handling acetylene or compressed gas cylinders. Foot brakes can be installed on wheels of two-wheeled trucks so that operators need not place their feet on the wheel or axle to hold the truck. Handles should have knuckle guards, unless they are adequately narrower than the distance between the outside of the wheel axle or the chisel, whichever is greater. (See Figure 10-5.)

Four-wheeled truck operation follows rules similar to those for two-wheeled trucks. Extra emphasis should be placed on proper loading, however. Four-wheeled trucks should be evenly loaded to prevent tip-

Figure 10-6. When operations require continual use of a hand truck, it is probably time to switch to a battery-powered "walkie." Operators must be trained to run the trucks safely. Riding on this type of truck is forbidden.

Industrial Truck Division, Clark Equipment Co.

ping. Four-wheeled trucks should be pushed rather than pulled, except for trucks with a fifth wheel and a handle for pulling.

Trucks should not be loaded so high that operators cannot see where they are going. If there are high racks on the truck, two persons should move the vehicle—one to guide the front end, the other to guide the back end. Handles should be placed at protected places on the racks or truck body so that passing traffic, walls, or other objects will not crush or scrape the operator's hands. Truck contents should be arranged so that they will not fall or be damaged in case the truck or the load is bumped.

General precautions. Truckers should be warned of four major hazards: (*a*) running wheels off bridge plates or platforms; (*b*) colliding with other trucks or obstructions; (*c*) jamming hands between the truck and other objects; and, (*d*) running wheels over feet.

When not in use, trucks should be parked in a designated area, not in the aisles or in other places where they constitute tripping hazards or traffic obstruction. Trucks with drawbar handles should be parked with handles up and out of the way. Two-wheeled trucks should be stored on the chisel with handles leaning against a wall or the next truck.

Powered hand trucks

The use of powered hand trucks, controlled by a walking operator, is increasing (see Figure 10-6). The principal hazards are (*a*) the operator can be caught between the truck and another object, and (*b*) possible collisions with objects or people.

The truck should be equipped with a dead-man control, wheel guards, and an ignition key that can be taken out when the operator leaves the truck. Operators must be trained not to use trucks unless authorized. Training should follow the operating instructions included in the truck manufacturer's manual. General instructions are:

1. Do not operate the truck with wet or greasy hands.

2. Lead the truck from right or left of the handle. Face direction of travel. Keep one hand on the handle.

3. When entering an elevator, back the truck in to keep it from getting caught between the handles and the elevator walls. Operate the truck in reverse whenever it must be run close to a wall or other obstruction.

4. Always give pedestrians the right of way.

5. Stop at blind corners, doorways, and aisle intersections to prevent collisions.

6. Never operate the truck faster than normal walking pace.

7. Only handle flammable or corrosive liquids when they are in approved containers.

8. Never ride the truck, unless it is specifically designed for the driver to ride (see Figure 10-7).

9. Never permit others to ride on the truck.

10. Do not indulge in horseplay.

These general rules for operators of powered hand trucks should also be followed by operators of power trucks. All such training must be documented.

Powered industrial trucks

In order to comply with OSHA regulations, only physically qualified and trained operators are allowed to operate powered industrial trucks.

Training programs should include safe driving practices, as well as supervised experience driving on a training course. Emphasis should be placed on safety awareness. Trained and authorized drivers should have badges or other identification of authorization to drive, and they should display them at all times. This will help to meet OSHA requirements.

Power trucks have either a battery-powered motor or an internal-combustion engine. Trucks should be maintained according to the manufacturers' recommendations. All trucks acquired on or after February 15, 1972, must meet the design and construction requirements established in the "American National Standard for Powered Industrial Trucks, Part II, ANSI B56.1–1969."* Modifications and additions that affect capacity and safe operation shall not be performed by the customer or user without the manufacturer's prior written approval. All nameplates and markings must be accurate, in place, and legible. Eleven different designations of trucks or tractors are authorized for use in various locations.**

Battery-charging installations must be located in areas designated for that specific purpose. There must be facilities for flushing and neutralizing spilled electrolyte, and fire protection for protecting charging apparatus from damage by trucks. There must also be adequate ventilation for dispersal of gases or vapors from gassing batteries. Racks used to support batteries must be made of materials that are resistant to spark generation or be coated or covered to achieve this objective.

A conveyor, overhead hoist, or equivalent equipment must be used for handling batteries (see Figure 10-1b). Reinstalled batteries must be properly positioned and secured in the truck. A carboy tilter or siphon must be used for handling electrolyte. Acid must always be poured into water; water must never be poured into acid—it overheats and splatters. During charging operations, vent caps must be kept in place to avoid electrolyte spray. Make sure that vent caps are functioning. Battery or compartment cover or covers must be open to dissipate heat.

Precautions must be taken to prevent open flames, sparks, or electric arcs in battery-charging areas. Tools and other metallic objects must be kept away from the tops of uncovered batteries.

Employees charging or changing batteries must be authorized to do the work, trained in the proper handling, and required to wear protective

---

*Since the date this OSHA regulation 29–CFR–1910.178(a) (3) was promulgated, the standard has been redesignated ANSI/ASME B56.1–1983, *Safety Standard for Powered Industrial Trucks—Low Lift and High Lift Trucks.*

**Powered Industrial Trucks,* ANSI/NFPA 505–1981.

Figure 10-7. This powered hand truck is designed for riding by operator only.

Industrial Truck Division, Clark Equipment Co.

clothing, including face shields, long sleeves, rubber boots, aprons, and gloves. Smoking is prohibited in the charging area.

Refueling. All internal combustion engines must be turned off before refueling. Refueling should be in the open or in specifically designated areas, where ventilation is adequate to carry away fuel vapors. Liquid fuels, such as gasoline and diesel fuel, must be handled and stored in accordance with the National Fire Protection Association *Flammable and Combustible Liquids Code,* NFPA 30; liquefied petroleum gas fuel (or LP-gas) must be stored in accordance with the National Fire Protection Association *Handling of Liquefied Petroleum Gases,* NFPA 58. LP-gas tanks must be secured with *both* straps while on the truck so as not to shake loose with possible serious results. Smoking must not be permitted in the service areas and signs must be posted to that effect.

General rules for driving powered industrial trucks in the majority of

223

operations follow. For each operation, a specific set of rules should be drawn up by the supervisor.

1. All traffic regulations must be observed, especially plant speed limits.

2. Safe distances must be maintained—approximately three truck-lengths from the truck in front. Trucks must be kept under control at all times, so that an emergency stop, if necessary, can be made in the clear distance ahead.

3. The right-of-way must be yielded to ambulances, fire trucks, and other vehicles in emergency situations.

4. Other trucks traveling in the same direction must not be passed at intersections, blind spots, or other dangerous locations.

5. Drivers are required to slow down and sound horns at cross aisles and other locations where vision is obstructed. If the forward view is obstructed, because of the type of load being carried, drivers are required to travel with the load trailing behind them.

6. Railroad tracks must be crossed diagonally whenever possible, and parking within 8 ft (2.5 m) of the center of the nearest railroad track bed is prohibited.

7. Drivers are required to keep their eyes on the direction of travel, and have a clear view of the path of travel at all times. They should never back up without looking. Be especially careful on loading docks (see Figure 10-8).

8. Grades are to be ascended or descended slowly and loaded trucks must be driven with the load upgrade on grades in excess of ten percent. Unloaded trucks must be operated on all grades with their load-engaging means downgrade. On all grades, load and load-engaging means are to be tilted back if applicable, and raised only as far as necessary to clear the road surface.

9. Trucks must always be operated at a speed that will permit them to stop in a safe manner. Drivers are required to slow down on wet and slippery floors. Stunt driving and horseplay are not tolerated.

10. Dockboards or bridgeplates are to be driven over carefully and slowly and only after they have been properly secured. Their rated weight capacity must never be exceeded.

11. Approach elevators slowly and stop at least 5 ft (1.5 m) from the gate. Obey elevator operator's signals, and enter at a right angle, and only after the elevator is properly aligned. Once on the elevator, neutralize the controls, set the brakes, shut off power, and then step off the truck.

Figure 10-8. The operator of this lift truck received only a minor laceration of his right leg when he drove off this 54-inch high dock used for storage of material racks awaiting repair. The primary cause of the accident was the operator's failure to negotiate the edge of the dock because he was unfamiliar with the controls of the truck. Better training in safe vehicle operation was one positive result of this accident.

12. While negotiating turns, speed must be reduced to a safe level by means of turning the hand steering wheel in a smooth, sweeping motion. When maneuvering at a low speed, the hand steering wheel must be turned at a moderate and even rate.

13. Never run over loose objects on the roadway surface.

14. Only stable or safely balanced loads shall be handled and extra caution must be exercised when handling off-center loads.

15. Only loads within the rated load capacity of the truck shall be handled, and long or high (including multiple-tiered) loads that may affect capacity must be adjusted.

16. Load-engaging means must be placed under the load as far as possible and the mast is carefully tilted backward to stabilize the load.

17. Extreme care must be exercised when tilting the load forward or backward, particularly when placing items on high tiers. Tilting forward with the load-engaging means elevated is not permitted except to pick up a load. Elevated loads must not be tilted forward, except

225

Figure 10-9. When loading or stacking, operator should use only enough backward tilt to stabilize the load.

Allis-Chalmers *Engineering Review*

when the load is in a deposit position over a rack or stack. When stacking or tiering, use only enough backward tilt to stabilize the load. (See Figure 10-9.)

18. When operating in close quarters, keep hands out of the way so they cannot be pinched between steering controls and projecting stationary objects. Keep legs and feet inside the guard or the operating stations of the truck.

19. Do not use the reverse control on electric trucks for braking.

20. Park trucks only in designated areas—never in an aisle or doorway, obstructing equipment or material. Fully lower the load-engaging means, neutralize the controls, shut off the power, and set the brakes. Remove the key (or connector plug) when leaving a truck unattended. If the truck is parked on an incline, block the wheels.

Much research was conducted during 1982 and 1983, and at least one

Figure 10-10. Safety platform hoisted by forklift positions workers for ease in removing and replacing heavy load-retaining bars in freight car door openings. Old method required workers to mount individual stepladders and balance heavy bar carefully between them.

From NSC *Glass and Ceramics Newsletter*

manufacturer of industrial power trucks was convinced that safety belts should be installed for the protection of the drivers. In tests, it was found that if a truck tipped over, the driver was safer sitting on the seat rather than attempting to jump clear. The danger in attempting to jump clear of the truck is that the driver can be struck by some part of the truck body or overhead guard. This could result in serious injuries or death. This same manufacturer went so far as to offer to replace the old seats on some trucks and substitute those with safety belts.

Depending on its use, a power truck should have a dead-man control, and should be equipped with guards, such as hand-enclosure guard or a canopy guard. A lift truck should also have upper and lower limit switches to prevent overtravel. No power truck should be used for any purpose other than that for which it was designed.

A forklift should not be used as an elevator for employees (for example, in servicing light fixtures or when stacking materials), unless a safety pallet, with standard railing and toe boards, is fastened securely to the forks (see Figure 10-10). Failure to use safety pallets has resulted in many serious accidents.

Combustion by-products. When internal-combustion engine trucks are operated in enclosures, the concentration of carbon monoxide should

227

not exceed the limits specified by local or state laws, and in no case should the time-weighted average concentration exceed 50 ppm (parts per million) for an 8-hour exposure. The atmosphere must contain a minimum of 19 percent oxygen, by volume. (Air usually contains 20.8 percent oxygen, by volume.) (See Figure 6-4, page ●●)

Many companies equip their fuel-powered trucks with catalytic exhaust purifiers to burn the carbon monoxide before it reaches the atmosphere. Some power trucks are designated for use in locations where flammable gases or vapors are present in the air in quantities sufficient to produce explosive or ignitable mixtures, or which are hazardous because of the presence of combustible dust or easily ignitable fibers or flyings. Only trucks approved and marked for such areas are to be used. (See ANSI/NFPA Standard 505, *Powered Industrial Trucks*, for classification of types.)

Loads. Operators should refuse to carry unstable loads. If material of irregular shape must be carried, it should be placed so that it will not fall off, and be blocked, tied, or otherwise secured. A load should, if possible, be crosstied after being neatly piled. An extra counterbalance should never be placed on a forklift to facilitate handling overloads, because it puts added strain on the truck and endangers the operator and nearby employees. It is difficult to operate an overloaded truck safely.

Operators of powered industrial trucks should not drive up to anyone standing in front of a bench or other fixed object, or allow anyone to stand or pass under the elevated portion of any truck, whether loaded or empty. Unauthorized personnel are not permitted to ride on trucks; even if authorized, they are permitted only when they are in the space provided. The placing of arms or legs between uprights of the mast or outside the running lanes of the truck, by operators or authorized riders, is prohibited.

Raise or lower loads at the point of loading or unloading, not during travel. Operators should be trained to look before raising a load, so that they will not strike structural members of the building, electric wiring or cables, or piping (especially that carrying gases or flammable fluids).

Operators must make sure that there is sufficient headroom under overhead installations, such as lights, pipes, and sprinkler systems, before driving underneath them. Overhead guards must be used as protection against falling objects. It should be noted, however, that an overhead guard is intended to offer protection from the impact of small packages, boxes, bagged materials, and so forth, representative of the job application, but not to withstand the impact of a falling capacity load. Load backrest extensions must be used whenever necessary to minimize the possibility of the load or part of the load falling toward the rear.

Figure 10-11. To keep loose dockplates from "walking" or sliding when in use, this shipping dock worker places a pin to hold the plate to the truck.

When using a scoop or shovel attachment on a front-end loader, operators should be told to work the front of the pile and not to undercut. Overhangs are dangerous.

Floors on which power trucks travel should be kept in peak condition. They should have a load capacity great enough to support both truck and load. The combined weight of the heaviest truck and load should not exceed one-fifth of the design strength of the floor. For example, a floor originally designed to bear 1,000 pounds per square foot (psf) or 5,000 kg/m^2—should not be allowed to bear more than 200 pounds per square foot. Maximum floor loadings should be prominently displayed.

The 5 to 1 ratio, although not extremely conservative, is important in establishing a low risk. A conservative safety factor provides an adequate margin of protection to offset possible miscalculations due to inadequate structural data, and misinformation about age, condition of floor members, type of floor, and other details.

Dock plates

Dock plates (bridge plates) that are not built in should be fastened down in order to prevent them from "walking" or sliding when used. Either the plate can be nailed down or holes can be drilled and pins or bolts dropped through them (see Figure 10-11).

Plates should be large enough and strong enough to hold the heaviest load, including the equipment. A factor of safety of five or six should be used. Plates can have the edges turned up, or have angle iron welded to the edges, in order to keep trucks from running over their edges. Plates should be kept in good condition, without curled corners or bends. They should be kept clean and dry—clear of snow and ice, and free of oil and grease. They are often protected from the weather by means of a canopy.

To use a plate, employees should slide it into place, not drop it. It must be kept under control and not allowed to bounce. Large plates are best set in place by mechanical equipment, or if that is not available, a sufficient number of people should be assigned to the job. Handholds or other effective means must be provided on portable dock plates to permit safe handling.

The wheels of trucks or trailers backed up to the dock should be blocked or chocked to prevent movement when power trucks are loading or unloading. When not in use, dock plates should be placed safely to avoid tripping hazards. They should not be stored on edge so they can fall over. Powered dockboards must meet the requirements of Commercial Standard CS 202, *Industrial Lifts and Hinged Loading Ramps*, published by the U.S. Department of Commerce. For details of loading highway trucks and cars, see later sections in this chapter.

Conveyors

No one is allowed to ride on conveyors. Highly visible warning signs must be posted. If people must cross over conveyors, bridges should be provided to eliminate people crawling across or under the conveyor.

In the case of certain roller conveyors, it is possible to provide a hinged section that opens up, thus providing a place to walk through without having to climb over. The hinged section should be returned to its original position as soon as the individual has crossed the conveyor. Care must be taken to make sure that no merchandise is on the roller conveyor when using the hinged section.

Gravity conveyors, usually the chute or roller type, should be equipped with warning devices or protective devices to prevent hands from being caught in descending material, or from being jammed between material and the receiving table. If the conveyor jams up, try first to free it from the top side. If it becomes necessary to enter the chute to free a jam, the person who enters it should wear a lifeline and have another person stationed at the top of the chute to assist in case of emergency. People should be made aware of these hazards and trained to cope with them safely.

Pinch points on conveyors—gears, chain drives, and revolving shafts—should be guarded. People must not remove these guards. Should the conveyor need servicing, the power should be shut off and the switch locked out.

Pneumatic or blower conveyors must be shut off and locked before inspections or repairs are made, in order to keep material from being blown into the worker's face or into the working area. If an inspection or service door must be opened while a system is operating, the inspector should wear goggles and, if necessary, respiratory equipment. Inspection ports, equipped with transparent coverings made of durable, nonflammable, shatter-resistant material, permit inspections without stopping the operation.

Screw conveyors should be completely enclosed whenever possible. Their principal danger is that workers may try to dislodge material or free a jam with their hands or feet, and then be caught in the conveyor. Screw conveyors should never be repaired unless the power is off and the switch is locked out. Any exposed sections should be covered with a metal grate, with openings no larger than 1/2 inch (13mm), or with a solid plate. The cover should be strong enough to withstand abuse. Before removing any cover, grating, or guard, padlock the main disconnect in the OFF position. Do not rely on interlocks. Never step or walk on covers, gratings, or guards.

Cranes

All overhead and gantry cranes must meet the design specifications of the American National Standard *Overhead and Gantry Cranes*, B30.2; all mobile, locomotive, and truck cranes must meet the American National Standard *Mobile and Locomotive Truck Cranes*, B30.5.

Although many types of cranes are used in industry, safe operating procedures are much the same. Standard signals (see Figures 10-12 and -13) should be thoroughly understood by both operator and signalman. The supervisor should assign only one signalman for each crane, and tell the crane operator to obey only this person's instructions. People working with or near a crane should keep out from under the load, be alert at all times, and watch warning signals closely. At a warning signal, they should move to a safe place immediately.

No crane should be loaded beyond its rated load capacity, and the weight of all auxiliary handling devices, such as hoist blocks, hooks, and slings, must be considered as part of the load rating. Substantial and durable rating charts with clearly legible letters and figures are to be fixed to the crane cab in a location clearly visible to the operator while seated at the control station.

Hoist chain or hoist rope must be free of kinks and twists and must

HAND SIGNALS-BOOM CRANES

RAISE THE LOAD	LOWER THE LOAD	SWING LOAD IN DIRECTION FINGER POINTS
RAISE LOAD SLOWLY	LOWER LOAD SLOWLY	TRAVEL IN DIRECTION SIGNAL MAN FACES
RAISE THE BOOM	LOWER THE BOOM	RAISE THE BOOM AND HOLD THE LOAD
RAISE BOOM SLOWLY	LOWER BOOM SLOWLY	STOP
RAISE THE BOOM AND LOWER THE LOAD	LOWER THE BOOM AND RAISE THE LOAD	DOG EVERYTHING

Figure 10-12. Standard two-hand signals are suitable for use with locomotive and other boom cranes.

not be wrapped around the load. Loads must be attached to the load block hook by means of a sling or other approved device. Care must be taken to make certain that the sling clears all obstacles. The load must be well secured and properly balanced in the sling or lifting device before it is lifted more than a few inches. Before starting to hoist, make sure that multiple part lines are not twisted around each other. (See Figure 10-14.)

Hooks should be brought over the load slowly to prevent swinging. During hoisting operations, see to it that there is no sudden acceleration or deceleration of the moving load, and that the load does not come in contact with any obstructions.

Cranes must not be used for side pulls, unless specifically authorized by a responsible person who can determine that the stability of the crane

Figure 10-13. Standard one-hand signals for overhead traveling and bridge cranes.

is not endangered, and that the various parts of the crane will not be overstressed. There must be no hoisting, lowering, or traveling while any employee is on the load or hook, and the operator must not carry loads over people's heads. On overhead cranes, a warning signal must be given when starting the bridge and when the load or hook comes close to, or over, any person's head.

Brakes must be tested each time a load approaching the rated load is handled, and loads must not be lowered below the point where less than two full wraps of rope remain on the hoisting drum. When two or more cranes are used to lift a load, one qualified, responsible person must be in charge of the operation. He or she must analyze the operation and instruct all personnel involved about the proper positioning, rigging of the load, and all other movements. An operator must not leave his position at the controls while the load is suspended. All necessary clothing and personal belongings must be stored in the cab, so as not to interfere with access or operation. Tools, oil cans, waste, extra fuses, and other necessary articles must be kept in a toolbox and not carelessly left in or around the cab. There must be a hand fire extinguisher kept in the cab. Access to the cab must be by fixed ladder, stairs, or platform, but no steps over

Figure 10-14. Fifteen-foot, 34-in. width cargo sling is used to lift a highly finished 17-ton King roll for a paper calendar. Wide area of sling in contact with the roll subjects its delicate surface to only 27 lb pressure per square inch.

The Wear-Flex Corporation

gaps exceeding 12-in. (30 cm) are allowed.

The upper load limit switch of each hoist must be tried out under no-load conditions, at the beginning of each operator's shift. If the switch does not operate properly, a qualified person must be notified immediately. The hoist limit switch that controls the upper limit of travel of the load block must never be used as an operating control.

Inspections. Cranes in regular service must be inspected periodically, at intervals dependent upon the nature of the critical components of the crane and the degree of its exposure to deterioration or malfunction. Daily inspections must be made of all control mechanisms for maladjustments, including deterioration or leakage in air or hydraulic systems.

Frequent inspections at daily to monthly intervals, or as specifically

234

recommended by the manufacturer, must be made of: (*a*) all control mechanisms for excessive wear of components or contamination by lubricants or other foreign matter, as well as all safety devices for malfunction; (*b*) crane hooks for deformations or cracks, for hooks with cracks or having more than 15 percent in excess of normal throat opening or more than a 10-degree twist from the plane of the unbent hook; (*c*) rope reeving not in compliance with manufacturer's recommendations; (*d*) electrical apparatus for malfunctioning and excessive deterioration, dirt, and moisture accumulation.

Periodic inspections, from one- to twelve-month intervals or as specifically recommended by the manufacturer, cover the complete crane. These inspections include the items listed under frequent inspections, and in addition, include such items as (*a*) deformed, cracked, or corroded members in the crane structure and hook; (*b*) loose bolts or rivets; (*c*) cracked or worn sheaves and drums; (*d*) worn, cracked, or distorted parts, such as pins, bearings, shafts, gears, rollers, and locking devices; (*e*) excessive wear on brake and clutch system parts linings, pawls, and ratchets; (*f*) load, boom, angle, and other indicators over their full range to detect significant inaccuracies; (*g*) gasoline, diesel, electric, or other power plants for improper performance or noncompliance with safety requirements, excessive wear of chain-drive sprockets, and excessive chain stretch; and (*h*) travel steering, braking, and locking devices for malfunction and excessively worn or damaged tires. Determine if they constitute a hazard and, if so, correct them. Records must be kept; see OSHA requirements.

Prior to initial use, all new and altered cranes must be checked periodically and frequently. Cranes that are not in regular service and have been idle for a period of one month or more, but less than six months, must be in accordance with those items outlined for frequent inspections. Cranes that have been idle for a period of six months or more must be given a complete inspection in accordance with the OSHA requirements and standby cranes must be inspected at least semiannually. Cranes that have been exposed to adverse environmental conditions must be inspected more frequently.

All ropes must be given a thorough inspection at least once a month, and a full written, dated, and signed report of rope condition must be kept on file where it is readily available to appointed personnel. Any deterioration, resulting in appreciable loss of original strength, such as reduction of rope diameter below nominal diameter, due to loss of core support, internal or external corrosion, or wear or breakage of outside wires, and the degree of distribution or concentration of such broken wires; corroded or broken wires at end connections; or severe kinking, crushing, cutting, or unstranding, must be carefully noted and determination made as to whether further use of the rope would constitute a hazard.

All rope that has been idle for a period of a month or more, due to shutdown or storage of a crane on which it is installed, must be given a thorough inspection before being placed in service. This inspection should identify all types of deterioration and shall be performed by a responsible person whose approval is required before the rope is further used. A written, dated report of the rope condition shall be available for inspection.

On limited-travel ropes, heavy-wear and/or broken wires may occur in sections that come in contact with *(a)* equalizer sheaves or other sheaves where rope travel is limited, or *(b)* saddles. Particular care must be taken to inspect all ropes at these locations. Furthermore, extra care must be taken in the inspection of all non-rotating ropes.

These safety rules for electric overhead cranes are suggested by one crane manufacturer:

1. Only regularly authorized operators should use cranes.

2. When on duty, operators should remain in the crane cabs ready for prompt service.

3. Before traveling, make certain the hook is high enough to clear all obstacles.

4. Under no circumstances should one crane bump another.

5. Examine the crane at every shift for loose or defective gears, keys, runways, railings, warning bells, signs, switches, sweep brushes, ropes, cables, and other parts. Report defects. Keep the crane clean and well lubricated.

6. No one should go to the top of a crane without first opening the main switch, placing a warning sign on it, and locking it out. Operators should unlock the switch and remove the sign promptly when they come down.

7. After completion of a repair job, make sure that bolts, tools, and other materials have been removed, so that damage to machinery will not result when the crane is re-started, and so that there is nothing that can fall off the crane. Keep tools, oil can, and other loose objects in a box provided for that purpose.

8. Do not carry a load over workers' heads on the floor. Sound a gong or siren when necessary. No one shall ride the load or the crane hook.

9. If the power goes off, move controller to off position until power is again available.

10. Make sure that the fire extinguisher on the crane is in good condition, and if used, that it is refilled immediately thereafter.

11. Never let an operator who is ill or not physically fit run a crane.

12. Do not drag slings, chains, or ropes. After the load is taken off, do not move the crane until the hook is lowered and the hook-on person has hooked the chain or rope.

13. If the operator feels that it is unsafe to move a load, a check with the supervisor should be made.

14. Be sure that when an operator leaves the cage, he or she leaves the main switch open. A magnetic crane must be empty and its controller turned off.

15. When an outside crane is parked at the end of a shift, the brake should be set or the crane should be chained to the track.

16. Operators should know that if their crane fails to respond correctly, they should call the supervisor. Attempting to get out of difficulty by repeated operation may make the condition worse, not better.

Railroad cars

Spotting of railroad cars is usually done by switch-engine crews. If it is necessary for employees to move a railroad car, the supervisor should consider the following factors:

- Facilities or equipment available to move the car.
- Distance the car must be moved.
- Number of cars to be moved.
- Whether the track is level or on a grade.

After weighing these factors, the supervisor can decide whether to get power equipment, or move the car by hand, or take material to (or from) the car's location. If possible, use power equipment to move the car.

If a car must be spotted or moved without power equipment, a car mover (operated by only one person) can be used. If it takes two workers to move a car, then each one should have a car mover and they should work on opposite wheels. All hand-actuated car movers should be equipped with knuckle guards. A stationary car puller, if available, should be used.

When opening doors of boxcars, all persons should be alert to the danger of their fingers being caught, or freight falling out. A bar or ratchet hoist or puller should be used. Do not use trucks to open car doors because damaged doors may fall from runners.

Metal transfer plates must be securely anchored with bolts, and gangplanks and skids securely placed before using. Operators of mechanized equipment should avoid bumping doors or door posts. Metal bands should be removed or cut to avoid dangling ends. Special equipment, such as DF bars, should be stacked at the ends of car when empty, and the car doors closed and latched before the car is moved.

Specially equipped cars with movable bulkheads have instructions in the car that must be followed. When bulkhead partitions are difficult to move, examine the rollers to determine the reason for binding to avoid having the bulkhead fall on those working in the car.

Highway trucks

When loading or unloading highway trucks, set the brakes and place wheel chocks under the rear wheels to prevent these trucks from rolling (see Figure 10-15). Use a fixed jack to support a semitrailer that is not

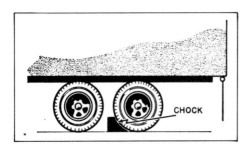

CHOCK

Figure 10-15. Preferred position for placing chock.

coupled to a tractor in order to prevent upending of the semitrailer, if a powered industrial truck operates in it. For more details of truck and truck terminal safety, see National Safety Council's *Motor Fleet Safety Manual*.

Motorized equipment

Heavy-duty trucks, mobile cranes, tractors, bulldozers, and other motorized equipment used in the production of stone, ore, and similar materials and also in construction work have been involved in frequent, and often serious, accidents. In general, prevention of these accidents requires:

- Safe equipment
- Systematic maintenance and repairs

- Safety training for operators

- Safety training for repair personnel.

Operation. Manufacturer's manuals contain detailed information on the operation of equipment. Recommended driving practices are similar to those necessary for the safe operation of highway vehicles. However, off-the-road driving involves certain hazards that require special training and safety measures. The modern heavy-duty truck or off-the-road vehicle is a carefully engineered and expensive piece of equipment and warrants operation only by drivers who are qualified physically and mentally and have had training and experience. For safety, driving standards should be especially high.

The time that is required for prospective drivers or operators to become thoroughly familiar with the mechanical features of the equipment, safety rules, driver reports, and emergency conditions varies. In no case, should even an experienced driver be permitted to operate equipment until the instructor or supervisor is satisfied with his or her abilities. After workers have been trained, supervisors have the important responsibility of seeing that drivers continue to operate in the ways in which they were instructed.

Equipment. Safe operation of heavy equipment begins with the purchase specifications. A good policy is to specify safeguards over exposed gears, safe oiling devices, handholds, and other devices when the order is placed with the manufacturer. In any case, before equipment is put into operation, it should be thoroughly inspected and necessary safety devices installed and checked.

Both operators and repair personnel, whether experienced or not, should know the recommendations of the manufacturer pertaining to lubrication, adjustments, repairs, and operating practices. All should be required to observe them. A preventive maintenance program is essential for safety and efficiency. Frequent and regular inspections and prompt repairs provide effective preventive maintenance.

In general, the operator is responsible for inspecting such mechanical conditions, as hold-down bolts, brakes, clutches, clamps, hooks, and similar vital parts. Wire ropes should be lubricated (see manufacturer's instructions); for inspections, see the section that follows.

Many of the basic safety measures recommended for trucks also apply to motor graders and other earth-moving equipment. All machines should be inspected regularly by the operator, who should promptly report any defects. The safety and efficiency of equipment are increased by adherence to periodic maintenance.

ROPES, CHAINS, AND SLINGS

There are special safety precautions that apply to using ropes, rope slings, wire rope, chains and chain slings, and storing chains. The supervisor should know the properties of the various types and the precautions that pertain to both use and maintenance. For additional help regarding ropes, chains or slings, consult the supplier.

Fiber ropes

Fiber rope is used extensively in handling and moving materials. The rope is generally made from manila (abaca), sisal, or nylon. Manila or nylon ropes give the best uniform strength and service. Other types of rope include those made from polyester or polypropylene or a composite of both that are adaptable to special uses.

Sisal is not as satisfactory as manila because the strength varies in different grades. Sisal rope is about 80 percent as strong as manila. Manila rope is yellowish with a somewhat silvery or pearly luster. Sisal rope is also yellowish, but often has a green tinge and lacks the luster of manila. Its fibers tend to splinter and it is rather stiff. The safe working loads and breaking strengths of the rope that you are using should be known and the limits must be observed.

Maintenance tips. Precautions should be taken to keep ropes in good condition. Kinking, for example, strains the rope and may overstress the fibers. It may be difficult to detect a weak spot made by a kink. To prevent a new rope from kinking while it is being uncoiled, first lay the rope coil on the floor with the bottom end down. Then pull the bottom end up through the coil and unwind the rope counter-clockwise. If it uncoils in the other direction, turn the coil of rope over and pull the end out on the other side.

Rope should not be stored unless it has first been cleaned. Dirty rope can be hung in loops over a bar or beam and then sprayed with water to remove the dirt. The spray should not be so powerful that it forces the dirt into the fibers. After washing, the ropes should be allowed to dry, and then be shaken to remove any remaining dirt.

Rope must be thoroughly dried out after it becomes wet, otherwise it will deteriorate quickly. A wet rope should be hung up or laid in a loose coil in a dry place until thoroughly dry. Rope will deteriorate more rapidly if it is alternately wet and dry than if it remains wet. Furthermore, rope should not be allowed to freeze.

Rope should be stored in a dry place where air circulates freely. Small ropes can be hung up, and larger ropes can be laid on gratings so air can get underneath and around them. Rope should not be stored or used in an area where the atmosphere contains acid or acid fumes, because it will quickly deteriorate. Signs of deterioration are dark brown or black spots.

Sharp bends should be avoided whenever possible because they create extreme tension in the fibers. When cinching or tying a rope, be sure the object has a large enough diameter to prevent the rope from bending sharply. A pad can be placed around sharp corners.

If at all possible, ropes should not be dragged because dragging abrades the outer fibers. If ropes pick up dirt and sand, abrasion within the lay of the rope will rapidly wear them out. Lengths of rope should be joined by splicing. A properly made short splice will retain approximately 80 percent of the rope's strength. A knot will retain only about 50 percent. See details in Chapter 9, under Lifelines.

Ropes should be inspected at least every 30 days, more often if they are used to support scaffolding on which people work. The following procedure will assist in the inspection of natural fiber rope:

1. Check for broken fibers and abrasions on the outside.

2. Inspect fibers by untwisting the rope in several places. If the inner yarns are bright, clear, and unspotted, the strength of the rope has been preserved to a large degree.

3. Unwind a piece of yarn 8-in. (20 cm) long and ¼-in. (0.6 cm) diameter from the rope. Try to break this with your hands. If the yarn breaks with little effort, the rope is not safe.

4. Inspect rope used around acid or caustic materials daily. If black or rusty brown spots are noted, test the fibers as described in steps 1, 2, and 3, and discard all rope that fails the tests.

5. As a general rule, rope that has lost its pliability or stretch, or in which the fibers have lost their luster and appear dry and brittle, should be viewed with suspicion and replaced. This is particularly important if the rope is used on scaffolding or for hoisting where, if the rope breaks, workers may be seriously injured or property may be damaged.

Rope slings

Because of the high tensile strength needed for a sling, fiber rope slings should be made of manila only. Below are some precautions to be observed in using manila-rope slings.

1. Make sure that the sling is in good condition and of sufficient strength. Take into account the factors of the splice and the leg angles of the sling. Hooks, rings, and other fittings must be properly spliced.

2. Reduce the load by one-half after the sling has been in use for six months, even though the sling shows no sign of wear.

3. If the sling shows evidence of cuts, excessive wear, or other damage, destroy it.

Whether fiber or wire rope slings are used, certain general precautions should be taken. (These were given under Fiber ropes—Maintenance tips, listed earlier.) In addition, it is best to keep the legs of slings as nearly vertical as possible (see Figure 10-16).

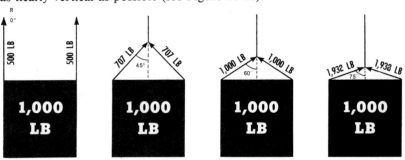

Figure 10-16. Increasing the sling angle (the angle of the sling leg with the vertical) increases the stress on each leg of the sling, even though the load remains constant. The stress on each leg can be calculated by dividing the load weight by the cosine of the angle.

Wire rope

Wire rope is used widely instead of fiber because it has greater strength for the same diameter and weight; its strength is constant either wet or dry, it has constant length under varying weather conditions, and greater durability. Wire rope is made according to its intended use. A large number of wires give flexibility. Fewer strands with fewer wires are less flexible.

A wire rope used for general hoisting should not be subjected to a working load greater than one-eighth its breaking strength—a factor of safety of 5. Greater factors of safety (6 or 7, for example) are always desirable for extra security. Ropes should be thoroughly inspected at least once a month, and written, dated, and signed reports kept on file. OSHA regulations spell out the details of this inspection. A tag attached to a sling can identify it and also indicate load capacity (see Figure 10-17).

Wire rope should be lubricated at regular intervals to prevent rust and excessive wear. Sheaves for rope should be as large as possible. The less flexible the rope, the larger the sheave or drum diameter must be, otherwise the rope will be bent too sharply. (See Table 10-A.) Rope

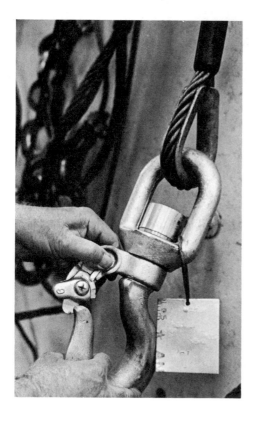

Figure 10-17. Tag indicates sling's load capacity. Note safety latch on hook. Visually inspect hooks daily. Replace cracked ones, and those with 15 percent in excess of normal throat opening or more than ten degrees twist from plane of unbent hook.

should be wound in one layer only. Using several layers will mash or jam the rope and shorten its life.

Sheaves and drums should be aligned as much as possible to prevent excessive wear of rope. Reverse bending of rope, in which rope is bent first in one direction and then in the other, should be avoided, as this wears out wire rope faster than anything else. Fittings should be properly selected and attached if they are to be safe. Some of the principal wire rope attachments are illustrated in Figure 10-18, and include:

- Babbitt- or zinc-coated connections
- Wedge sockets
- Swagged attachments
- Thimble-with-clip connections
- Three-bolt clamps
- Spliced eye-and-thimble connections
- Crosby clips.

The crosby clip is probably the most commonly used fitting. It is im-

243

TABLE 10-A
TREAD DIAMETERS OF SHEAVES AND DRUMS

Rope Classification	Average Recommended	Minimum
6 × 7 ....72 times rope diameter		42 times rope diameter
6 × 19 ....45 " " "		30 " " "
6 × 37 ....27 " " "		18 " " "
8 × 19 ....31 " " "		21 " " "

portant that these clips be installed properly. Wedge sockets are dependable and will develop approximately 75 or 90 percent of the strength of the rope. Swagged attachments are satisfactory for small diameter (¼- to 1-in. or 0.6 to 2.5 cm) ropes.

Wire rope should be spliced only by workers who have been trained to do it properly. Splices should be tested to twice the load they are expected to carry. Again, any questions should be referred to the supplier or manufacturer.

Chains and chain slings

Alloy steel chain, approximately twice as strong—size for size—as wrought-iron chain, has become standard material for chain slings. One advantage is that it is suitable for high-temperature operations. Continuous operation at temperatures of 800 F (420 C) (the highest temperature for which continuous operation is recommended) requires a reduction of 30 percent in the regular working load limit. For intermittent service, these chains can be used at temperatures as high as 1,000 F (540 C), but at only 50 percent of the regular working load limit. (See Table 10-B.)

An alloy steel chain should never be annealed when the chain is being serviced or repaired, because the process reduces the hardness of the steel, and this, in turn, reduces the strength of the chain. Wrought-iron chain, on the other hand, should be annealed periodically by the manufacturer (or persons specially trained in the operation) if it is used where failure might endanger human life or property.

Impact loads, caused by faulty hitches, bumpy crane tracks, and slipping hookups, can materially add to stress in the chain. The impact resistance of heat-treated alloy steel chain does not increase in proportion to the strength of the chain. Under a full working load, it will fail before fully loaded wrought iron, or heat-treated carbon steel chain will.

Chain slings should preferably be purchased complete from the manufacturers, and whenever they need repair, they should be returned to their manufacturer. The manufacturer should also be queried about de-

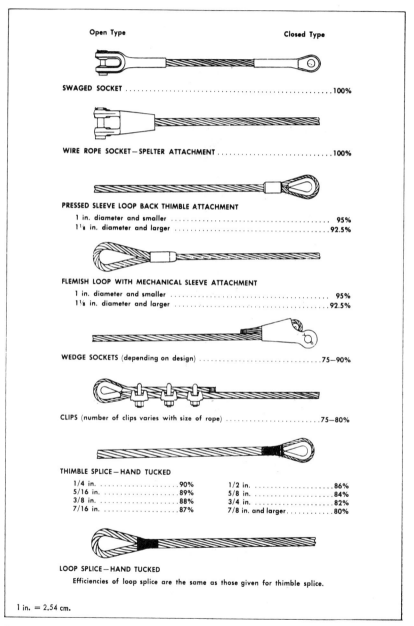

Figure 10-18. Efficiencies of wire rope fittings, in percentage of strength of rope.

TABLE 10-B
WORKING LOAD LIMITS AND BREAK TEST LIMITS
FOR ALLOY STEEL CHAIN*

Nominal Size of Chain Bar in Inches	Working Load Limits in Pounds	Minimum Break Test in Pounds
1/4	3,250	10,000
3/8	6,600	19,000
1/2	11,250	32,500
5/8	16,500	50,000
3/4	23,000	69,500
7/8	28,750	93,500
1	38,750	122,000
1 1/8	44,500	143,000
1 1/4	57,500	180,000
1 3/8	67,000	207,000
1 1/2	79,500	244,000
1 3/4	94,000	325,000

1 in. = 2.54 cm; 1 kg = 2.2 lb.

*Source: *Specification for Alloy Steel Chain,* American Society for Testing and Materials, A-391-58. The strengths for wrought iron chain are slightly less than half these figures.

tails of strength and specifications of the slings.

Load and wear. Chains should not be overloaded—the working load limit and break test limit for alloy steel chains are given in Table 10-B. Some of the principal causes of chain failure are:

1. Brittleness caused by cold working of the metal surface

2. Failure of the weld

3. Repeated and severe bending or deformation of the links

4. Metal fatigue

5. Brittleness caused by defects in the metal

6. Tensile failure—full elongation of the links.

How much wear a chain can stand is determined by its use, the original factor of safety, and the loads the chain is expected to carry. A regular schedule of checking and calipering the links should be set up for each chain, depending on usage. (See Table 10-C.)

To check elongation, chain should be calipered in gage lengths of 1 to

TABLE 10-C
CORRECTION TABLE FOR THE REDUCTION
OF WORKING LOAD LIMITS OF CHAIN DUE TO WEAR*

Nominal Original Chain Size, Inches		Reduce working load limits of chain by the following percent when diameter of stock at worn section is as follows:		
		5 Percent	*10 Percent*	*Remove from Service*
¼	0.250	0.244	0.237	0.233
⅜	0.375	0.366	0.356	0.335
½	0.500	0.487	0.474	0.448
⅝	0.625	0.609	0.593	0.559
¾	0.750	0.731	0.711	0.671
⅞	0.875	0.853	0.830	0.783
1	1.000	0.975	0.949	0.895
1⅛	1.125	1.100	1.070	1.010
1¼	1.250	1.220	1.190	1.120
1⅜	1.375	1.340	1.310	1.230
1½	1.500	1.460	1.430	1.340
1⅝	1.625	1.590	1.540	1.450
1¾	1.750	1.710	1.660	1.570
1⅞	1.875	1.830	1.780	1.680
2	2.000	1.950	1.900	1.790

1 in. = 2.54 cm.

*From American National Standard B30.2, *Safety Code for Cranes, Derricks, and Hoists.*

3 (preferably 5) feet when new, and a record of that should be kept. The chain (or sling) should be discarded if it shows a stretch (includes link wear) of more than 5 percent. Some states specify that a chain must be destroyed or discarded when any 3-ft (0.9 m) length is found to have been stretched one-third of a linklength.

A broken chain should never be spliced by inserting a bolt between two links. Neither should one link be passed through another and a nail or bolt inserted to hold them.

Use. Before making a lift, workers should check the chain—there should be no kinks, knots, or twists. Workers should lift the load gradually and uniformly and make sure that it is not merely attached to the tip of the hook. They should never hammer a link over the hook as this will also stretch the hook and stretch the links of the chain. When lowering a crane load, brakes should be applied gradually to bring the load to a smooth stop.

Each chain should be tagged to indicate its load capacity, date of last inspection, date of purchase, and type of material from which the chain was made. This information must not be stamped on the lifting links, however, as stamping can cause stress points that weaken the chain.

Chain attachments (rings, shackles, couplings, and end links) should be made of the same material to which they are fastened. Hooks should be made of forged steel or laminated steel, and should be equipped with safety latches. Replace hooks that have been overloaded, or loaded on the tips, or have a permanent set greater than 15 percent of the normal throat opening. (See Figure 10-17.)

Storing chains. Proper chain storage serves two purposes. It preserves the chain and promotes good housekeeping. Chains are best stored on racks inside dry buildings that have a fairly constant temperature. Chains should be stored where they will not be run over by trucks or other mobile equipment, and where they will not be exposed to corrosive chemicals.

Storage racks and bins should be constructed in such a way that air circulates freely around the chain and keeps it dry. Power equipment should be used to lift large and heavy chains. Attempting to lift a chain manually can cause an injury.

The supplier or manufacturer can arrange a time to give you on-location instructions on the care, use, inspection, and storage of chains. By instructing some of your maintenance workers on chains, you will be in a better position to evaluate your own needs.

MATERIALS STORAGE

Both temporary and permanent storage of materials must be neat and orderly. Materials piled haphazardly or strewn about increase the possibility of accidents. The warehouse supervisor must direct the storage of raw materials (and sometimes processed stock) kept in quantity lots for a length of time. The production supervisor is usually responsible for storage of limited amounts of materials and stock for short periods close to the processing operations. Planned materials storage minimizes (a) handling required to bring materials into production, and (b) removing finished products from production to shipping.

When supervisors plan materials storage, they should make sure that materials do not obstruct fire alarm boxes, sprinkler system controls, fire extinguishers, first aid equipment, lights, electric switches, and fuse boxes. Exits and aisles must be kept clear at all times.

There should be at least 18-in. (0.5 m) clearance below sprinkler heads to reduce interference with water distribution. This clearance should be increased to 36-in. (0.9 m), if the material being stored is flammable.

Aisles that carry one-way traffic should be at least three feet wider than the widest vehicle, when loaded. If materials are to be handled from the aisles, the turning radius of the power truck also needs to be considered. Employees should be told to keep materials out of the aisles and out of loading and unloading areas, which should be marked with white lines.

Storage is facilitated and hazards are reduced by using bins and racks. Material stored on racks, pallets, or skids can be moved easily and quickly from one work station to another. When possible, material piled on skids or pallets should be crosstied.

In an area where the same type of material is stored continuously, it is a good idea to paint a horizontal line on the wall to indicate the maximum height to which material may be piled. This will help to keep the floor load within the proper limits and the sprinkler heads in the clear.

Containers and other objects

Because packing containers vary considerably in size and shape, height limitations for stacking these materials vary. The weight of the container itself must also be figured when keeping within the proper floor-loading limit.

Sheets of heavy wrapping paper placed between layers of cartons will help to prevent the pile from shifting. Better still, crosstying will prevent shifting and sagging and permit higher stacking. Wirebound containers should be placed so that sharp ends do not stick into the passageway. When stacking corrugated paper cartons on top of each other, remember that increased humidity may cause them to slump.

Bagged materials can be crosstied with the mouths of the bags toward the inside of the pile, so contents will not spill if the closure breaks. Piles over 5-ft (1.5 m) high should be stepped back one row. Step back an additional row for each additional 3-ft (0.9 m) of height. Sacks should be removed from the top of the pile, not halfway up or from a corner. Sacks should be removed from an entire layer before the next layer is started. This keeps the pile from collapsing and possibly injuring people and damaging material.

Small-diameter bar stock and pipe are usually stored in special racks, located so that when stock is removed, passers-by are not endangered. The front of the racks should not face the main aisle, and material

Figure 10-19. Bar stock and large-diameter pipe should be piled in layers separated by strips of wood or by iron bars. Storage should not extend into the aisles.

should not protrude into the aisles. When the storage area is set up, the floor load, which this type of storage entails, should be considered.

Large-diameter pipe and bar stock should be piled in layers separated by strips of woods or by iron bars. If wood is used, it should have blocks at both ends; if iron bars are used, the ends should be turned up. Again, the floor must be considered. (See Figure 10-19.)

Lumber and pipe have a tendency to roll or slide. When making a pyramid pile, operators should (*a*) set the pieces down rather than dropping them; and (*b*) not use either hands or feet to stop rolling or sliding material. These practices can cause serious injury.

Sheet metal usually has sharp edges. It should be handled with care, using leathers, or leather gloves, or gloves with metal inserts. Large amounts should be handled in bundles by power equipment. These should be separated by strips of wood to facilitate handling when the material is needed for production and to lessen chances of shifting or sliding of the piles of material.

Tinplate strip stock is heavy and razor sharp. Should a load or partial load fall, it could badly injure anyone in its way. Two measures can be taken to prevent spillage and injuries: (*a*) band the stock after shearing, and (*b*) use wooden or metal stakes around the stock tables and pallets that hold the loads. It is the responsibility of the supervisor and all who handle the bundles to band loads properly and see that the stakes are

Figure 10-20. The operator should always stand to one side when tensioning the strapping. In this way, if the strap breaks or slips, he will be out of the direct line of the strapping if it recoils.

Packaging Division, Signode Corporation

in place when the load is on the table.

Packing materials, such as straw, excelsior, or shredded paper, should be kept in a fire-resistant room, equipped with sprinklers and dustproof electric equipment. Materials received in bales should be kept baled until used. Remove only enough material for immediate use, or for one day's supply. Packing materials should be taken to the packing room and placed in metal (or metal-lined wood) bins, the covers of which have fusible links so they will close automatically in case of fire. To prevent injury in case a counterweight rope should break, the weight should be boxed in.

Steel and plastic strapping, which may be flat or round, require that the worker be trained in both application and removal. In all cases, the worker should wear safety goggles or glasses with side shields, and leather-palm gloves (see Figure 10-20). Heavy strap may require the wearing of steel-studded gloves.

Barrels or kegs stored on their sides should be placed in pyramids, with the bottom rows securely blocked to prevent rolling. If piled on end, the layers should be separated by planks. If pallets are used, they should be large enough to prevent overhang.

Hazardous liquids

Acid carboys are best handled with special equipment, for example, carboy trucks. Boxed carboys should generally be stacked no higher than two tiers, never higher than three. Not more than two tiers should be used for carboys of strong oxidizing agents, such as concentrated nitric acid or concentrated hydrogen peroxide. The best method of storage is in specially designed racks.

Before carboy boxes are handled, they should be inspected thoroughly to make sure that nails have not rusted or that the wood has not been weakened by acid. Empty carboys should be completely drained and their caps replaced.

The safest way to draw off liquid from a carboy is to use suction from a vacuum pump or a siphon started by either a rubber bulb or an ejector. Another method is to use a carboy inclinator that holds the carboy at the top, sides, and bottom, and returns the carboy to an upright position automatically when released. Pouring by hand or starting pipettes or siphons by mouth suction to draw off the contents of a carboy should never be permitted.

Portable containers. When liquids are handled in portable containers, the contents should be clearly labeled. Substances should be stored separately in safety storage cabinets that meet pertinent OshAct and NFPA 30 requirements (see Figure 10-21). Purchasing agents should specify to suppliers that all chemicals are properly labeled showing contents, hazards, and precautions. Labels are discussed in Chapter 6, "Industrial Hygiene and Noise Control."

Drums containing hazardous liquids should be placed on a rack, not stacked. It is best to have a separate rack for each type of material. Racks permit good housekeeping, easy access to the drums for inspection, and

Figure 10-21. Safety storage cabinets for portable containers of acids and corrosives. Meeting NFPA 30, *Flammable and Combustible Liquids Code,* makes cabinet also suitable for storing containers of up to five-gallon capacity of flammable liquids.

Eagle Manufacturing Co.

easy handling (see Figure 10-22). Racks allow drums or barrels to be emptied through the bung. Self-closing spigots should be used, particularly where individuals are allowed to draw off their own supplies. If there is a chance that spigots might be hit by material or equipment, drums should be stored on end and a pump used to withdraw the contents. Drums containing flammable liquid, and the racks that hold them, should be grounded, and the smaller container into which the drum is being emptied should be bonded to the chime of the drum by a flexible wire with a C-clamp at each end.

Storage areas for liquid chemicals should be naturally well ventilated. Natural ventilation is better than mechanical, because the mechanical system may fail. The floor should be made either of concrete or of some other material treated to reduce absorption of the liquids. The floor should be pitched toward one or more drains that are corrosion-resistant and easily cleaned.

Where caustics or acids are stored, handled, or used, emergency flood showers or eyewash fountains should be available. Operators should be provided with chemical goggles, rubber aprons, boots, and gloves, and other protective equipment necessary to handle the particular

253

Figure 10-22. Storage rack reduces hazards, aids identification, and permits easy grounding of each drum. Note grates on the drip pans in front of the storage racks. The whole storage area has explosion-proof electrical equipment.

liquid. (See Chapter 9, "Personal Protective Equipment.")

Each type of hazardous material requires either special handling techniques or special protective clothing. In all cases, the supervisor or the purchasing agent should consult the safety professional or the safety department for handling precautions.

Additional measures to take when handling hazardous liquids:

1. Wear proper protective equipment.

2. Keep floors clean; do not allow them to become slippery.

3. Drain all siphons, ejectors, and other emptying devices completely before removing them from carboys.

4. To dilute acid, always add it to water, never add water to acid. Add the acid slowly and stir constantly with a glass implement.

5. In case of an accident, give first aid: flush burned areas with lots of water. Call a doctor immediately.

6. Do not force hazardous chemicals from containers by injecting compressed air. The container may burst or the contents may ignite.

7. Do not try to wash or clean a container unless its label specifically re-

quires that it be cleaned before it is returned.

8. Do not store hazardous chemicals in glass or other containers near heat or steam pipes, or where strong sunlight will strike them. The contents may expand and may cause a fire or explosion. Bottles may focus sunlight to ignite a fire in nearby combustibles.

9. Do not stir acids with metal implements.

10. Do not store chemicals or solvents in dark or poorly lit areas because the wrong chemical may be selected.

11. Do not pour corrosives from a carboy by hand.

12. Do not move a carboy unless it is securely capped.

Pipelines to outside storage tanks are safer if large quantities of liquid chemicals or solvents are used, because they reduce and localize any spillage. When hazardous liquids are used in small quantities, only enough for one shift should be kept on the job. In many cases, local ordinances limit the amount of hazardous materials that can be stored or processed inside a building. The main supply should be stored in tanks located in an isolated place.

Pipelines should be color-coded and labeled to identify their contents. Basic colors for identification of contents of pipes by class and methods of providing specific identification that your company uses should be understood. Should outside contractors work in the area, they should be adequately informed of piping system contents and any hazards.

When a valve is to be worked on, it should be closed, and the section of pipe in which it is located should be thoroughly drained before the flanges are loosened. Appropriate personal protective equipment must be worn by workers.

As a temporary measure, the opening between faces of a flange may be covered with a piece of sheet lead, and this wrapped around to make a sleeve while the flange bolts are being loosened and the faces separated. If the flanges do not separate readily, a strong nail can be driven through the lead shield into the flange joint to part it.

Workers should loosen the flange bolts farthest away first, so that the pipe will drain away from them. A blind (or blank) should be inserted between the flanges as soon as they are parted. If a line is opened often, a two-ended metal blank can be permanently installed on a flange bolt so that the blank can be pivoted on the bolt when the flanges are parted. One end of the blank is shaped in the form of a gasket, to permit flow of liquid. The other end is blind and is swung to cover the pipe opening when the flanges are unbolted and parted.

255

Figure 10-23. Rack is designed for safe storage of compressed gas cylinders.

Tank cars should be protected on sidings by derails and by blue stop flags or blue lights before they are loaded or unloaded. Hand brakes should be set and wheels chocked. Before the car is opened, it should be bonded to the loading line. The track and the loading or unloading rack should be grounded and all connections checked regularly. Chemical tank cars should be unloaded through the dome rather than through the bottom connection.

Gas cylinders

There are many regulations regarding the storage and handling of gas cylinders. Several government agencies and private organizations and their standards should be consulted—OSHA, National Fire Protection Association, Compressed Gas Association, and others. Care should be taken to comply with all local government codes as well.

Compressed gas cylinders should be stored on end on a smooth floor. All cylinders should be chained or otherwise fastened firmly against a wall, post, or other solid object. Different kinds of gases should be either separated by aisles or stored in separate sections of the building or storage yard. Empty cylinders should be stored apart from full cylinders. (See Figure 10-23.)

Keep storage areas away from heavy traffic. Containers in storage should be located in a place where there is minimal exposure to excessive temperature, physical damage, or tampering. Never store cylinders of flammable gases near flammable or combustible substances. Before cylinders are moved, check to make certain all valves are closed. Always close the valves on empty cylinders. Never permit a hammer or wrench to be used to open valves. As stated before, cylinders should never be used as rollers to move heavy equipment. Handle all cylinders with care—a cylinder marked "empty" just might not be.

To transport cylinders, use a carrier that does not allow excessive movement, sudden or violent contacts, and upsets. When a two-wheeled truck with rounded back is used, chain the cylinder upright. Never use a magnet to lift a cylinder. For short-distance moving, a cylinder may be rolled on its bottom edge, but never dragged. Cylinders should never be dropped or permitted to strike one another. Protective caps must be kept on cylinder valves when cylinders are not being used.

When in doubt about how to handle a compressed gas cylinder, or how to control a particular type of gas once it is released, ask the safety professional or the safety department.

Combustible solids

Bulk storage of grains and granular or powdered chemicals or other materials presents hazards of fire and explosion. Many materials that are not considered hazardous in solid form often become combustible when finely divided. Some of these are carbon, fertilizers, food products and by-products, metal powders, resins, waxes and soaps, spices, drugs and insecticides, wood, paper, tanning materials, chemical products, hard rubber, sulfur, starch, and tobacco. Though it is long, this list is by no means complete, and it mentions only the general categories of materials that may generate explosive dusts.

To avoid dust explosions, prevent formation of an explosive mixture or eliminate all sources of ignition. Either the dust must be kept down, or enough air supplied to keep the mixture below the combustible limit. Good housekeeping and dust-collection equipment will go far toward preventing disaster. Formation of layers of dust on floors and other structural parts of a building should not be allowed. A dust explosion is a series of explosions, or a progression of explosions. The initial explosion is small, but it shakes up dust that has collected on rafters and equipment so that a second explosion is created. This usually continues until the result is the same as if a large explosion had taken place.

Wearing protective equipment is important when dusts are toxic. Such equipment may range from a respirator to a complete set of protective clothing. The Council, or a state or local safety agency, can recommend the proper type of protective clothing for specific jobs. See the recommendations in Chapter 9, "Personal Protective Equipment."

Bins in which solids are stored should have a sloping bottom to allow the material to run out freely and to prevent arching. For some materials, especially if they are in process, the bin should have a vibrator or agitator in the bottom to keep the material flowing.

If large rectangular bins, open at one side, are entered with power shovels or other power equipment, workers should take care not to undercut the material, and thereby endanger themselves if arched material should suddenly give way. Where practical, tops of bins should be covered with a 2-in. (5 cm) mesh screen, or at least by a 6-in. (15 cm) grating (or parallel bars on 6-in. centers) to keep people from falling into the bins.

Tests for oxygen content and for presence of toxic materials should be made before anyone enters a bin or tank for any purpose. If such tests indicate the need for protection, people should use air-supplied masks, in addition to a safety belt and lifeline, before entering. Filling equipment should be made inoperative so that it cannot be started again, except by the worker after leaving the bin or by the immediate supervisor after checking the worker out of the bin. When a person is working in a bin, he or she should have a companion employee, equipped to act in case of emergency, stationed on top of the bin. Bins should be entered from the top only.

If flammable vapors, dusts, or other flammable air contaminants are found, workers should use only spark-resistant equipment and electrical equipment that is approved by a recognized testing laboratory.

Chapter 11

Machine Safeguarding

The first step in any operation—to assure continued production, employee safety and health, a good profit margin, and reduced equipment damage—is to engineer the hazards out of a job. However, there are times when redesign, replacement, or finding a better way is not feasible or practical, or perhaps the technical knowledge is not sufficiently advanced. It is then that safeguarding must be used to protect employees, equipment, and material from injury and damage.

As a supervisor, you are responsible for directing people to manufacture a product or provide a service, and, at a profit. Whenever mechanical equipment or production machinery is involved, you are also responsible for running it efficiently.

• When equipment is shut down for any unscheduled reason, production capacity and cost of operation are directly affected.

• When an employee is injured while operating machines or equipment, production capacity and cost of operation are again affected. Poorly designed, improperly safeguarded, or unguarded machinery or equipment is an ongoing threat to production capacity and to the well-being of employees.

An injury can take operators away from their jobs for a long time, sometimes permanently. They must be replaced if the department is to keep going. Even if a qualified person is transferred from another department, eventually a new person must be hired. Finding, hiring and training the right person also takes time. Training and the delay cost money.

Where do safeguards come into this picture? Everywhere. Because no matter how much training or experience a person may have, there is no way to keep that person's mind focused on work every minute.

Figure 11-1. An expanded-metal screen guard encloses the V-belt drive between this 200 hp explosionproof motor and the 5-cylinder pump unit.

Service Pipe Line Co., Tulsa, Okla.

What about the deceptive machine—the one that appears so easy to run that the supervisor allows semiskilled, or even unskilled persons to operate? The one that is so "simple" that the supervisor does not even train the operator? Often the results are drastic—in personal injury, machine and material damage.

Safeguarding reduces the possibility of human error, and mechanical failure. It is vital that supervisors have a complete understanding of the principles of safety, so that these concerns are obvious to workers.

PRINCIPLES OF GUARDING

Guarding is frequently thought of as being concerned only with the point of operation or with the means of power transmission (see Figure 11-1). Although guarding these hazards is required, guarding can prevent injuries from other causes, both on and around machines and from equipment and damaged material.

Guards or barriers can prevent injuries from these sources:

1. Direct contact with exposed moving parts of a machine—either points of operation on production machines (power presses, machine tools, or woodworking equipment), or power-transmitting parts of mechanisms (gears, pulleys and sheaves, slides, or couplings). (See Figure 11-2.)

Figure 11-2. See-through guard installed next to circular saw protects hands when operator aligns material for a cut, and protects eyes from flying sawdust or pieces of broken blade or sawteeth.

From NSC *Forest Industries Newsletter*

2. Work in process, for example, pieces of wood that kick back from a power ripsaw, or metal chips that fly from tools or from abrasive wheels.

3. Machine failure, which usually results from lack of preventive maintenance, overloading, metal fatigue, or abuse.

4. Electrical failure, which may cause malfunctioning of the machine, or cause electrical shocks or burns.

5. Operator error or human failure caused by lack of knowledge or skill, also by distraction, worry, zeal, anxiety, misunderstanding, indolence, deliberate chance-taking, anger, illness, fatigue, and so on.

Positive prevention of injury-producing accidents on machinery can be assured through the installation of safeguards or through engineering revision and redesign. Injury-producing accidents are inevitable when equipment with moving parts is operated without guards or is operated with incomplete or ineffective guards.

The experience of more than six decades of organized accident prevention proves that it is unwise to rely entirely on education and training of operators or their cooperation. Many factors affect a person's attitude and judgment, and the ability to concentrate. Skilled persons who have emotional or physical problems cannot pay strict attention to their production responsibilities and cannot give their best effort.

Benefits of safeguarding

Possibly the primary benefit of proper safeguarding, in the eyes of the supervisor, is that it reduces the possibility of injury. Another important benefit is that it may improve production. When operators are afraid of their machines or are afraid of getting close to moving parts, they obviously cannot pay strict attention to their production responsibilities. Once the fear has been removed, workers can concentrate on the operation at hand and often are more productive.

Well-designed and carefully maintained safeguards assure workers that management means what it says about the sincere desire to prevent accidents. When employees realize that their employers really are interested, they will be more inclined to contribute to the safety effort.

Whenever moving parts are left exposed, other objects may fall into them or get caught and damage the machine or material in process. Such damage can cause expensive shutdowns and loss of raw materials or finished products.

A proper safeguarding program can mean much in terms of employee morale, especially when the workers who will have to use the safeguards are consulted before the safeguards are made or bought. Employees often have good ideas that contribute to both safety and economy. Even if they have no suggestions, employees feel flattered at having been consulted. As a result, they take a personal interest in the project, and are, therefore, less likely to remove the guards or barriers or fail to replace them. Finally, a proper safeguarding program will help reduce litigations from accident and noncompliance and help to comply with state and federal regulations.

The first part of this chapter discusses guarding points of operation and power-transmitting parts of machinery or equipment. Part II discusses safeguarding of mechanisms. Part III covers types of guards and their maintenance.

PART I—SAFEGUARD DESIGN

It is easier to establish effective methods for safeguarding power transmissions than it is for guarding points of operation, because power transmissions are more standardized. The American National Standard *Safety Code for Mechanical Power-Transmission Apparatus,* B15.1, applies to all moving parts of mechanical equipment. Point-of-operation guarding can be found in American National Standards for specific machinery, such as the following safety requirements:

Bakery Equipment, Z50.1

Construction, Care, and Use of Drilling, Milling, and Boring Machines, B11.8

Construction, Care, and Use of Grinding Machines, B11.9

Construction, Care, and Use of Lathes, B11.6

Construction, Care, and Use of Mechanical Power Presses, B11.1

Construction, Care, and Use of Metal Sawing Machines, B11.10

Construction, Care, and Use of Power Press Brakes, B11.3

Safety Standard for Stationary and Fixed Electric Tools, ANSI/UL-987

Safety Standard for Mechanical Power Transmission Apparatus, ANSI/ASME B15.1

Most states and OSHA regulate the safeguarding of mechanical equipment. Occupational Safety and Health Standards, Part 1910, Subpart "O" covers safeguarding of machinery and equipment. It is, of course, a violation of law to ignore these regulations.

Whether safeguards are built by the user or purchased from manufacturers, they should meet certain performance or design standards, if they are to be effective. If a company does not have a safety professional, it should be able to get the advice of an insurance company safety engineer, state factory inspector, consulting engineer, or local safety council engineer as to what design is most effective in safeguarding a specific operation. The National Safety Council offers guidance to members. The National Safety Council's *Accident Prevention Manual for Industrial Operations—Engineering and Technology* Volume, *Guards Illustrated,* and *Power Press Safety Manual* give many ideas in addition to those given here.

To be generally acceptable, a safeguard should:

1. Conform to or exceed applicable American National Standards and requirements of OSHA and/or the state inspection department having jurisdiction.

2. Be considered a permanent part of the machine or equipment.

3. Afford maximum protection, not only for the operator and those performing lubrication, but also for passersby.

4. Prevent access to the danger zone or point of operation during operation.

5. Not weaken the structure of the machine.

6. Be convenient. Guards must not interfere with efficient operation of the machine, cause discomfort to the operator, or complicate light

maintenance and/or cleaning the area around the machine.

7. Be designed for the specific job and specific machine. (Provisions must be made for oiling, inspection, adjusting, and repairing of the machine parts.)

8. Be resistant to fire and corrosion. Be easy to repair.

9. Be strong enough to resist normal wear and shock, and durable enough to serve over a long period with minimum maintenance.

10. Not be a source of additional hazards, such as splinters, pinch points, sharp corners, rough edges, or other injury sources.

If possible, a safeguard covering rotating parts should be interlocked with the machine itself so that the machine cannot be operated unless the safeguard is in place. On some equipment, this may be required by OSHA.

A safeguarding problem

When installations are contemplated, persons in the organization who have a specific interest in them should be consulted. The opinions of the operators of the machine, supervisors, setup and maintenance personnel, millwrights, oilers, and electricians should be sought. Check manufacturers; frequently the company has equipment safeguards available that are superior to any others that might be installed; see the discussion under Built-in Safeguards. Also, consult manufacturers if a proposed guard or barrier changes the original design of the equipment.

Pertinent regulatory codes should be studied before definite action is taken. Every safeguard, whether installed when machinery is purchased or constructed afterward, must meet or exceed state, local, and OSHA federal regulations. Since state and OSHA regulations at best provide only minimum requirements, the supervisor or the person responsible for buying, constructing, or maintaining guards should be familiar with the applicable ANSI Standards and Subpart "O" (or other applicable portion) of OSHA requirements, Part 1910.

A safeguarding program should include all equipment in the establishment. It is clear that additional protection may be required under the following conditions:

• Where the protection is clearly below that recommended or required by an ANSI Standard or the state or federal authority having jurisdiction.

• Where the protective devices are in need of repair or replacement.

A good safeguarding program is a strong selling point when promoting observance of other preventive measures. If hands and arms are pro-

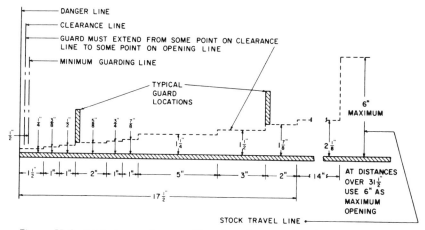

Figure 11-3. Point-of-operation guard locations. Barriers placed to touch dashed line will wedge hand or forearm. The danger line is the point of operation. The clearance line marks the distance required to prevent contact between the guard and the moving parts. Minimum guarding line is ½in. from the danger line.

From OSHA requirements 29 CFR 1910.217.

tected by guards or barriers, it makes more sense to shield eyes, feet, ears, and other parts of the body. Like a pair of safety glasses on a person's face, a safeguard is a warning signal—a constant reminder to workers that they are near a potential hazard.

Maximum size openings

An important factor to consider in the design of safeguards is the maximum size of openings. If a barrier is to provide complete protection, the openings in it must be small enough to prevent a person or object from getting into the danger zone. If for operational purposes, an opening must be larger than that specified by the standard (see Figure 11-3), further protection must be provided.

Types of safeguards

A great many standardized devices, as well as improvised barriers, enclosures, and tools have been developed to protect machine operators, particularly their hands, at point-of-operation areas. Table 11-A presents concise descriptions of the nature, action, advantages, and limitations of a variety of such safeguards and devices.

Sheet metal, perforated metal, expanded metal, heavy wire mesh or stock may be used for types of guards. The best practice is to follow the

265

TABLE 11-A.
POINT-OF OPERATION PROTECTION

Type of Guarding Methods	Action of Guard	Advantages	Limitations	Typical Machines on Which Used
		ENCLOSURES OR BARRIERS		
Complete, simple fixed enclosure	Barrier or enclosure which admits the stock but which will not admit hands into danger zone because of feed opening size, remote location, or unusual shape.	Provides complete enclosure if kept in place. Both hands free. Generally permits increased production. Easy to install. Ideal for blanking on power presses. Can be combined with automatic or semiautomatic feeds.	Limited to specific operations. May require special tools to remove jammed stock. May interfere with visibility.	Bread slicers Embossing presses Meat grinders Metal square shears Nip points of inrunning rubber, paper, and textile rolls Paper corner cutters Power presses
Warning enclosures (usually adjustable to stock being fed)	Barrier or enclosure admits the operator's hand but warns him before danger zone is reached.	Makes "hard to guard" machines safer. Generally does not interfere with production. Easy to install. Admits varying sizes of stock.	Hands may enter danger zone—enclosure not complete at all times. Danger of operator not using guard. Often requires frequent adjustment and careful maintenance.	Band saws Circular saws Cloth cutters Dough brakes Ice crushers Jointers Leather strippers Rock crushers Wood shapers
Barrier with electric contact or mechanical stop activating mechanical or electric brake	Barrier quickly stops machine or prevents application of injurious pressure when any part of the operator's body contacts it or approaches danger zone.	Makes "hard to guard" machines safer. Does not interfere with production.	Requires careful adjustment and maintenance. Possibility of minor injury before guard operates. Operator can make guard inoperative.	Dough brakes Flat roll ironers Paper box corner stayers Paper box enders Power presses Paper calenders Rubber mills
Enclosure with electrical or mechanical interlock.	Enclosure or barrier shuts off or disengages power and prevents starting of machine when guard is open; prevents opening of guard while machine is under power or coasting. (Interlocks should not prevent manual operation or "inching" by remote control.)	Does not interfere with production. Hands are free; operation of guard is automatic. Provides complete and positive enclosure.	Requires careful adjustment and maintenance. Operator may be able to make guard inoperative. Does not protect in event of mechanical repeat.	Dough brakes and mixers Foundry tumblers Laundry extractors, driers, and tumblers Power presses Tanning drums Textile pickers, cards

Type of Guarding Method	Action of Guard	Advantages	Limitations	Typical Machines on Which Used
		AUTOMATIC OR SEMIAUTOMATIC FEED		
Nonmanual or partly manual loading of feed mechanism, with point of operation enclosed	Stock fed by chutes, hoppers, conveyors, movable dies, dial feed, rolls, etc. Enclosure will not admit any part of body.	Generally increases production. Operator cannot place hands in danger zone.	Excessive installation cost for short run. Requires skilled maintenance. Not adaptable to variations in stock.	Baking and candy machines Circular saws Power presses Textile pickers Wood planers Wood shapers
		HAND-REMOVAL DEVICES		
Hand restraints	A fixed bar and cord or strap with head attachments which, when worn and adjusted, do not permit an operator to reach into the point of operation.	Operator cannot place hands in danger zone. Permits maximum hand feeding; can be used on higher-speed machines. No obstruction to feeding a variety of stock. Easy to install.	Requires frequent inspection, maintenance, and adjustment to each operator. Limits movement of operator. May obstruct work space around operator. Does not permit blanking from hand-fed strip stock.	Embossing presses Power presses
Hand pull-away device	A cable-operated attachment on slide, connected to the operator's hands or arms to pull the hands back only if they remain in the danger zone; otherwise it does not interfere with normal operation.	Acts even in event of repeat. Permits maximum hand feeding; can be used on higher speed machines. No obstruction to feeding a variety of stock. Easy to install.	Requires unusually good maintenance and adjustment to each operator. Frequent inspection necessary. Limits movement of operator. May obstruct work space around operator. Does not permit blanking from hand-fed strip stock.	Embossing presses Power presses

requirements of the OSHA and ANSI Standards when material for new guards or barriers is selected. Figures 11-4 through -7 show examples.

If moving parts must be visible, transparent impact plastic or safety glass can be used where the strength of metal is not required. Guards or barriers may be made of aluminum or other soft metals where resistance to rust is essential or where iron or steel guards can cause damage to the machinery. Wood, plastic, and glass fiber barriers have the advantages of usually being inexpensive, but they are low in strength where compared

Type of Guarding Methods	Action of Guard	Advantages	Limitations	Typical Machines on Which Used
		TWO-HAND TRIP		
Electric	Simultaneous pressure of two hands on switch buttons in series actuates machine.	Can be adapted to multiple operation. Operator's hands away from danger zone. No obstructions to hand feeding. Does not require adjustment. Can be equipped with continuous pressure remote controls to permit "inching." Generally easy to install.	Operator may try to reach into danger zone after tripping machines. Does not protect against mechanical repeat unless blocks or stops are used. Some trips can be rendered unsafe by holding with the arm, blocking or tying down one control, thereby permitting one-hand operation. Not used for some blanking operations.	Dough mixers Embossing presses Paper cutters Pressing machines Power presses Washing tumblers
Mechanical	Simultaneous pressure of two hands on air control valves, mechanical levers, controls interlocked with foot control, or the removal of solid blocks or stops permits normal operation of machine.			
		MISCELLANEOUS		
Limited slide travel	Slide travel limited to 1/4 in. or less; fingers cannot enter between pressure points.	Provides positive protection. Requires no maintenance or adjustment.	Small opening limits size of stock.	Foot power (kick) presses Power presses
Electric eye	Electric eye beam and brake quickly stop machine or prevent its starting if the hands are in the danger zone.	Does not interfere with normal feeding or production. No obstruction on machine or around operator.	Expensive to install. Does not protect against mechanical repeat. Generally limited to use on slow speed machines with friction clutches or other means to stop the machine during the operating cycle. Can be circumvented.	Embossing presses Power presses Rubber mills Squaring shears Press brakes
Special tools or handles on dies	Long-handled tongs, vacuum lifters, or hand die holders which avoid need for operator's putting his hand in the danger zone.	Inexpensive and adaptable to different types of stock. Sometimes increases protection of other guards.	Operator must keep his hands out of danger zone. Requires usually good employee training and close supervision.	Dough brakes Leather die cutters Power presses Forging hammers
Special jigs or feeding devices	Hand-operated feeding devices of metal or wood which keep the operator's hands at a safe distance from the danger zone.	May speed production as well as safeguard machines. Generally economical for long jobs.	Machine itself not guarded; safe operation depends upon correct use of device. Requires good employee training, close supervision. Suitable for limited types of work.	Circular saws Dough brakes Jointers Meat grinders Paper cutters Power presses Drill presses

with steel. These materials do, however, resist the effects of splashes, vapors, and fumes from corrosive substances that would react with iron or steel, and reduce its strength and effectiveness.

Built-in safeguards

The best guard or barrier is the one provided by the manufacturer of a machine. For many years, most standard machinery manufacturers designed first-class, serviceable safeguards for their equipment, available when specified on a purchase order. The manufacturer's safeguards are usually designed to be an integral part of the machine and are therefore superior to those made on-site, in appearance, convenience of arrangement, and functional value.

Failure to implement principles of correct machine safeguarding may stem from a belief that partial or makeshift barriers can do the job well enough, or from a reluctance to spend the additional money required for built-in safeguards. Neither reason is valid.

The disadvantages of makeshift safeguards are obvious. Such safeguards give a false sense of security and may, therefore, be more harmful than no safeguard at all. They require the operators to be constantly alert in order to make up for the guard's inadequacy and thus give little protection against human failure. Makeshift guards are often flimsy and are certain to become damaged and ineffective, sometimes within a short period after installation, and sometimes on purpose.

Usually, it is just as easy to install an effective barrier as it is to use one with limited protection. A completely effective safeguard is one that eliminates the hazard completely and permanently and can withstand handling and normal wear and tear.

Too often, even today, machinery is purchased and installed without the necessary safeguards to protect the operator and nearby workers. Frequently, the excuse given is that purchase of a machine is a capital expense and is closely budgeted, while construction of a barrier on a machine by the maintenance department after purchase is a maintenance item and, therefore, more acceptable because it is an operating cost. As a result, a large number of companies buy stripped-down machinery and make safeguards after the machinery has been installed.

This is poor economy. Machine safeguards can be provided by the manufacturer more cheaply, because the costs—for example, the cost of patterns—are spread over a number of machines. Aside from cost-savings, of course, the hazards presented by an unguarded machine make a powerful argument in favor of specifying safeguards from the manufacturer at the time a machine is ordered.

In summary, the advantages of securing as much built-in protection

Figure 11-4. Sheet metal guard completely encloses flywheel and belt to prevent possible injury to employees who work in the area around power press.

From NSC *Electronic and Electrical Equipment Newsletter*

Figure 11-5. Expanded metal guard protects people from the sweeping arms of a wrapping and tying machine.

From NSC *Electronic and Electrical Equipment Newsletter*

Figure 11-6. Transparent impact plastic chip and splash guard on turret lathe can be moved out of the way when required.

From NSC *Electronic and Electrical Equipment Newsletter*

as possible from the manufacturer are as follows:

1. The additional cost of safeguards designed and installed by the manufacturer is usually lower than the cost of installing safeguards after a machine has been purchased.

2. Built-in safeguards conform more closely to the contours of the machine.

3. A built-in safeguard can strengthen a machine, act as an exhaust duct or oil retainer, or serve some other functional purpose, thereby simplifying the design and reducing the cost of the machine.

4. Built-in safeguards generally improve production and prevent damage to equipment or material in process.

Like the installation of safeguards, substitution sometimes can mean elimination or reduction of machine hazards. Substitution of direct-drive machines or individual motors for overhead line-shaft and transmission decreases the hazards inherent in transmission equipment (assuming that some older line-shaft installations still remain). Speed reducers can replace multicone pulleys. Remote controlled automatic lubrication can eliminate the need for employees to get dangerously close to moving parts.

Figure 11-7. Total enclosure of moving parts is important. V-belt and pulley on vacuum pump are completely guarded. Hinging is for ease in maintenance.

Match machine or equipment to the operator

Thus far in this chapter, the discussion has emphasized safeguarding transmission parts or points of operation. Safe operation of machinery, however, involves more than eliminating or covering hazardous moving parts. The overall accident potential of the machine operation must be considered. These basic questions should be asked:

- Is there a materials handling hazard?

- Are the limitations of a person's manual effort—lifting, pushing, and pulling—recognized?

- Is the design of existing or proposed safeguards based on physiological factors and human body dimensions?

All physical or design features of a production machine and the workplace should be evaluated as though the machine were an extension of a person's body and can only do what that person wants it to do.

To match the machine or equipment to the operator, consider the following factors:

- *The workplace.* Machines and equipment should be arranged so that the operator does a minimum amount of lifting and traveling. Conveyors and skids to feed raw stock, and chutes or gravity feeds to remove finished stock should be considered.

- *The work height.* The work station should be of optimal height in relation to stand-up or sit-down methods of operation, whichever is used. The proper height and type of chair or stool must be determined. Elbow height, actually, is the determining factor in minimizing worker fatigue. In general, an effective work level is 41 in. (1 m) from floor to work surface, with a chair height from 25 to 31 in. (0.6 to 0.8 m).

- *Controls.* Machine speed and on-off controls should be readily accessible. Position and design of machine controls—such as dials, push buttons, and levels—are important. Controls should be standardized on similar machines. Then operators can be switched back and forth, as necessary, without having to use different controls.

- *Materials handling aids* should be provided to minimize manual handling of raw materials and in-process or finished parts, both to and from machines. Overhead chain hoists, belts or roller conveyors, and work positioners are typical examples.

- *Operator fatigue* at a machine station usually results from a combination of physical and mental activities. It is not always the result of energy expenditure alone. Excessive speed-up, boredom from monotonous operations, and awkward work motion or operator position also contribute to fatigue.

- *Adequate lighting* and other environmental considerations.

- *Excessive noise* is more than just an annoyance. It can be a real hazard because it can cause permanent hearing damage. Methods of protecting workers are given in Chapters 6 and 9 and are covered by OSHA regulations.

PART II—SAFEGUARDING MECHANISMS

There are certain basic mechanisms which, if exposed, always need safeguarding. Such mechanisms are found in almost any department that uses machinery and equipment. For purposes of discussion, these mechanisms, which incorporate the primary hazards involved in machinery, are discussed here under the following headings:

- Rotating mechanisms
- Cutting or shearing mechanisms
- In-running nip points
- Screw or worm mechanisms
- Forming or bending mechanisms

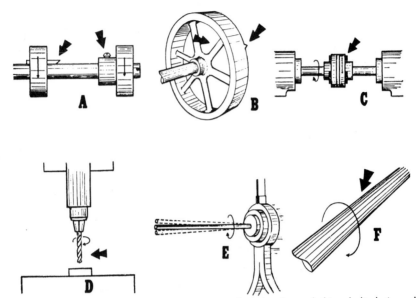

Figure 11-8. Rotating mechanisms can seize and wind up loose clothing, belts, hair, and the like. They should, therefore, be guarded. Left to right, they are: (A) projecting key and setscrew, (B) spokes and burrs, (C) coupling bolts, (D) bit and chuck, (E) turning bar stock, and (F) rotating shaft.

- Impact mechanisms.

A piece of equipment may involve more than one type of hazardous exposure. For instance, a belt-and-sheave drive is a hazardous rotating mechanism and also has hazardous in-running nip points.

Rotating mechanisms

A rotating part (see Figure 11-8) is dangerous unless it is safeguarded. Mechanical power transmission apparatus represents the large percentage of this type of hazardous mechanism. Although relatively few injuries are caused by such apparatus, the injuries often are permanently disabling. Transmission equipment should, therefore, be safeguarded as effectively as possible.

Small burrs or projections on a shaft can easily catch hair or clothing, or grab hold of a cleaning rag or apron and drag a person against and around the shafting. Vertical or horizontal transmission shafts, rod or bar stock projecting from lathes, set screws, flywheels and their cross members, drills, couplings, and clutches are common hazardous rotating machine parts.

Shafting, flywheels, pulleys, gears, belts, clutches, prime movers, and other types of power transmission apparatus usually seem safe by virtue of their location. However, many accidents happen in places where such apparatus is located—places "where no one ever goes." The supervisor, the oiler, and maintenance people go into these seldom-entered places. For their safety, the hazards in such areas should also be safeguarded.

When a flywheel, shaft, or coupling is located in such a way that any part of it is less than 8 ft (2.4 m) (ANSI/ASME B15.1-1984) above a floor or work platform, it must be safeguarded in one of several methods set forth in the federal standards.

For example, exposed pulleys, belts, and shafting with rotating parts within 8 ft of the floor should have substantial safeguards designed to protect employees from all possible contact. The underside of belts running over passageways or work areas should be protected by screening so that they can cause no harm if they break.

Enclosures should be removable, or provided with hinged panels, and interlocked to facilitate inspection, oiling, or repairing of the parts of the mechanism, but enclosures should be taken off only when the machine is stopped and the power disconnect is locked in the OFF position, and then preferably only by the supervisor's special order. Machines should never be operated until the enclosures have been properly replaced and secured.

Ends of shafting projecting into passageways or into work areas should be cut off or protected by nonrotating caps or safety sleeves. Hangers should be securely fastened and well lubricated. Setscrews with slotted or hollow heads should be used instead of the projecting type. Couplings should be protected to prevent contact not only with coupling, but the exposed rotating shafts also.

Exposed gears should be entirely enclosed by substantial barriers or protected in some other equally effective way. Sheet metal is preferable. The inrunning side of the gearing should be treated with special care. Removable barriers should be equipped with interlocks and the power disconnect locked in the OFF position for inspection and maintenance. Wood barriers can be used where excessive exposure to water or chemicals might cause rapid deterioration of metal barriers. These can also deteriorate so it would pay to monitor their condition.

It is essential to enclose the gearing in power presses because the large forces involved may cause overloading, which, in turn, can cause fatigue cracks to start in the shaft or gear. The fact that gears have split in half, and have fallen, indicates the need for strong enclosures.

Clutches, cutoff couplings, and clutch pulleys with projecting parts 8 ft or less from the floor should also be enclosed by stationary safeguards. Some clutches within the machine may be considered "guarded by loca-

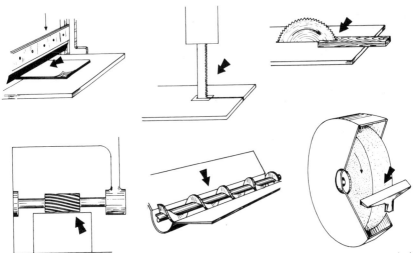

Figure 11-9. Common cutting or shearing mechanisms. Protection should be provided for all variations of such hazards.

tion," since they are out of normal reach, but if any possibility of contact exists, a complete enclosure should be provided.

Cutting or shearing mechanisms

The hazards of cutting or shearing mechanisms (see Figure 11-9) lie at the points where the work is being done, and where the movable parts of the machine approach or cross the fixed parts of the piece or machine. Guillotine cutters, shear presses, band and circular saws, milling machines, lathes, shapers, and abrasive wheels are typical of machines that present cutting or shearing hazards.

Saws. A circular saw must be safeguarded by a guard that covers the blade at all times to at least the depth of the teeth. The hood must adjust itself automatically to the thickness of the material being cut in order to remain in contact with it. The hood should be constructed in such a way that protects the operator from flying splinters or broken saw teeth. A table saw should be equipped with a spreader or splitter. It should also have an anti-kickback device to prevent materials from being thrown back at the operator.

All portions of a band saw blade must be enclosed or otherwise safeguarded except the working portion of the blade between the bottom of the guide rolls and the table. The enclosure for the portion of the blade between the sliding guide and the upper saw wheel guard should be self-

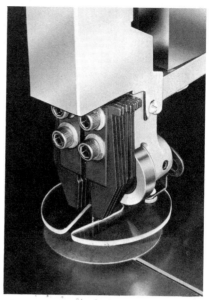

Figure 11-10. Blade safeguards. *Left:* Enclosure and guide for a 36-in. band saw. *Right:* Transparent orange plastic finger guard on a band saw.

adjusting, if possible. Band saw and band knife wheels should be completely enclosed, and the barrier should be constructed of heavy material, preferably metal. (See Figure 11-10.)

A swing cutoff saw should be equipped with a complete enclosure for the upper half of the saw. The lower half must be designed so it will ride over the fence and drop down on the table or on the work being cut. Also a counterweight or other device should automatically return the saw to the back of the table when the saw is released at any point in its travel. Limit chains or other equally effective devices should be provided to prevent the saw from swinging past the table toward the operator. Saw blades should be kept sharp at all times to prevent force feeding and the development of cracks.

Cutters on a milling machine should be shielded by an enclosure that provides positive protection for the operator's hands. A rotary cutter or slitter should have a barrier that completely encloses the cutting disks or knives to make it impossible for the operator to come into contact with the cutting edges while the machine is in motion.

Shears. The knife head on both hand- and power-operated shears should be equipped with barrier to keep the operator's fingers away from the cutting edge. The barrier should extend across the full width of the table and in front of the hold-down. This barrier may be fixed or it may automatically adjust to the thickness of the material to be cut.

If material narrower than the width of the knife blade is being cut, adjustable finger barriers should be installed that will protect the open area at the sides of the material being sheared so that the operators cannot get their hands caught at the sides under the blade. The barrier may be slotted or perforated to allow the operator to watch the knife, but the openings should not exceed 1/4 in. (6 mm), according to ANSI B11.1, and should preferably be slotted vertically to provide maximum visibility. A cover should be provided over the entire length of the treadle on the shears, leaving only enough room between the cover and the treadle for the operator's foot. This device prevents accidental tripping of the machine if something should fall on the treadle.

Grinding wheels. Since the abrasive grinding wheel is a common power tool and since it is often used by untrained persons, it is the source of many injuries. Stands for grinding wheels should be heavy and rigid enough to prevent vibration and should be securely mounted on a substantial foundation. The wheels should neither be forced on the spindle nor should they be too loose.

A person trained in correct and safe procedures should be in charge of wheel installations. Before a wheel is mounted, it should be carefully examined for cracks or other imperfections that might cause it to disintegrate.

The work rest should be rigid and set no farther away than 1/8 in. (3 mm) from the face of the wheel so that the material cannot be caught between the wheel and the rest. Wheels should be kept true and in balance.

Each wheel should be enclosed with a substantial hood made of steelplate to protect the operator in case the wheel breaks. The threaded ends of the spindle should be covered so that clothing cannot get caught in them. Hoods should be connected to effective exhaust systems to remove chips and prevent harmful dust from entering the grinding operation.

The manufacturer's recommended wheel speed should be adhered to at all times. Eye and face protection should be provided and properly fitted. Respirators should be used if considerable dust is generated, or if a poisonous or dangerous material is used and the air contaminants cannot be properly exhausted. Respirators should be frequently cleaned and sterilized. Respirators should not be issued for use by more than one employee.

It is important that grinding wheels be properly stored and handled to prevent cracking or other damage. They should be stored in a dry place where they will not absorb moisture and should be kept in racks, preferably in a vertical position. The manufacturers of the wheels can supply additional information on proper storage and handling methods.

Buffing and polishing wheels should be equipped with exhaust hoods to catch particles thrown off by the wheels. Not only do hoods protect the operator—they also prevent accumulation of particles on the floor and in the area. Eye or face protection should be provided for operators. They should not wear gloves and loose clothing. Protruding nuts or the ends of spindles, which might catch on the operator's hands or clothing, should be covered by caps or sleeves.

Wire brush wheels. The same machine setup and conditions that apply to polishing and buffing wheels apply to brushes. The speed recommended by the manufacturer should be followed scrupulously.

The hood on scratch wheels should enclose the wheel as completely as the nature of the work allows and should be adjustable so that the protection will not be lessened as the diameter of the wheel decreases. The hood should cover the spindle end, nut, and flange protection. Personal protective equipment is especially important in the operation of scratch wheels because wires can break off.

The materials should be held at the horizontal center of the brush. The wire tips of the brush should do the work. Forcing the work into the brush only results in *(a)* merely wiping or dragging the wires across the material, with no increase in cutting action, *(b)* increased wire breakage, and *(c)* a tendency for the work to become snagged. Small pieces should be held in a jig or fixture. More details about abrasive wheels, buffers, and scratch brushes are given in the next chapter.

Inrunning nip points

Whenever two or more parallel shafts that are close together rotate in opposite directions (see Figure 11-11), an inrunning nip point is formed. Objects or parts of the body may be drawn into this nip point and be crushed or mangled. Typical examples of nip points are found on rolling mills, calenders, chains and sprockets, conveyors, belts and sheaves, racks and pinions, and at points of contact between any moving body and a corresponding stationary body.

Nip points should be made inaccessible by fixed barriers (see Figure 11-12), or should be protected by instantaneous body-contact cutoff switches with automatic braking devices. The inrunning side of rolls like those used for corrugating, crimping, embossing, printing, or metal graining should be protected by a barrier arranged so that operators can feed material to the machine without catching their fingers between the

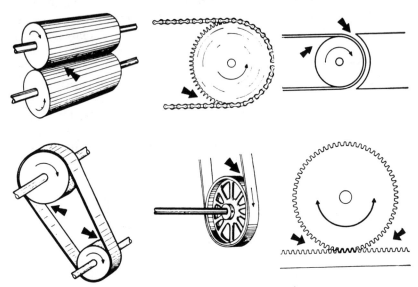

Figure 11-11. Typical inrunning nip points that require guarding.

Figure 11-12. Bar guards nip point of paper rewinder. Guard has adjustable cams so it always protects the inrunning nip point as diameter of the upper roll changes.

rolls or between the barrier and the rolls.

Calenders and similar rolls should be protected by a device arranged so that the operator can immediately stop the rolls at the feed point by means of a level, rod, or treadle. Otherwise, the nip should be guarded by an automatic electronic device that will stop the rolls if anything but stock approaches the intake points. Enclosures are usually the most satisfactory way to protect chains and sprockets, racks and pinions, belts and pulleys (or sheaves), and drive mechanisms for conveyors.

Screw or worm mechanisms

The hazards involved in the operation of screw or worm mechanisms are the shearing action set up between the moving screw and the fixed parts of the housing. Screw or worm mechanisms are generally used for conveying, mixing, or grinding materials. Examples are: food mixers, meat grinders, screw conveyors, dry material mixers and grinders of various types.

Screw conveyor covers should not be used as a walkway. If they must be walked on, additional protection should be provided. Corrosion and/or abrasive material in this type of conveyor can erode the metal from the underside of the conveyor cover so that a person might, without thinking, step through it.

Covers should also be provided for all mixers. The cover should be hinged to prevent removal and should have an interlock that will cut off the power source to stop action immediately when the cover is raised. Power switches for such machines should be locked out during maintenance or cleaning operations.

When screw conveyors are constantly fed while in motion and the use of an interlocked cover is impractical, a heavy screen or mesh guard or grid should be provided so that no opening large enough for a person to fall through is left when the cover is removed for product inspection.

Rigid grids should cover the openings on grinder hoppers. Such coverings should be large enough to permit materials to be fed to the grinder, but small enough to prevent any part of the operator's body from touching the cutting knives or the worm. Removable hoppers should be interlocked so that the grinders cannot be operated when the hoppers are removed.

Other safeguards for screw or worm mechanisms may include mechanical and electrical devices that require the operator to use both hands on the controls. Operating controls should be located so that they cannot be activated while any part of the body is in a position to be caught in the machine. The points of operation in many instances can be guarded by regulating the size, shape, and location of the feed opening.

Forming or bending mechanisms

The use of power, foot, and hand presses for stamping and forming pieces of metal and other materials has grown rapidly. Hand and finger injuries on these presses, as they are commonly operated, have become so frequent that misuse or abuse of these machines constitutes one of the most serious sources of mechanical problems in accident prevention.

Factors that make the problem difficult are variations in operations and operating conditions—in the size, speed, and type of press; in the size, thickness, and kind of pieces to be worked; in construction of dies; in degree of accuracy required in the finished work; and in length of run. It is unwise to simply depend on the skill of the operator for protection.

The supervisor who wants to make certain that operating methods are safe will insist that the die setter not only set the dies for a new run and test the machine for proper operation, but also set and adjust all other safeguards. The supervisor then will ask the operator to run the machine a few strokes to make sure the safeguards are in place and the adjustments are correct. The supervisor sees to it that operators know that each of these steps must be completed before starting a production run.*

A procedure that omits any of these steps provides no guarantee that the dies are in alignment, that the kickout is working properly, that the clutch is in proper condition, or that the guard (if it is removable) is in place and operating. Supervisors with long experience in hazard control customarily require the machine setup crew to fill out a tag as written evidence that the procedure was thorough and complete for each setting.**

Each job poses questions. Whether fixed guards, pull-away devices, two-hand devices, or electric-eye trips are to be used depends upon such factors as the kind of stock (piece, strip, roll), type of feed (hand, slide,

---

*This procedure applies equally to shearing mechanisms: for example, guillotine cutters, veneer chippers, paper-box corner cutters, leather dinking machines. As a group, these and similar machines present the worst kind of point-of-operation hazards, yet supervisors often believe that safeguarding them would slow down production. The right safeguards, properly designed and utilized, will not only cover the hazard, but will usually increase production.

** OSHA Regulation §1910.217 (e) (1) states, "Inspection, maintenance, and modification of presses—Inspection and maintenance records. It shall be the responsibility of the employer to establish and follow a program of periodic and regular inspections of his power presses to insure that all their parts, auxiliary equipment, and safeguards are in a safe operating condition and adjustment. The employer shall maintain records of these inspections and the maintenance work performed."

Figure 11-13. Power press safety prop prevents accidental dropping of ram during die change or maintenance. In the setup shown here, electrical interlock plug (arrow) must be disconnected before the prop can be positioned, thus deactivating the electrical circuit of the press.

dial, automatic), and type of knockout or ejection (mechanical or pneumatic).

Power presses sometimes repeat a cycle unexpectedly (usually referred to as a double trip), due to machine failure of one kind or another. The guard, therefore, must be designed to prevent injuries that could result from such occurrences. A common action responsible for the loss of fingers is the impulsive reach for misplaced stock after the press has been tripped. Details of how to prevent these accidents are given later under Automatic protection devices. Even the best training, experience, and supervision cannot substitute for well-designed guards and the constant observance of safety practices. (See Figure 11-13.)

Primary and secondary operations

Power press operations consist of primary and secondary operations.

• In primary operations, the operators are not required to place their hands between the punch and the die. Examples are blanking, piercing, corner cutting, and other operations on long-strip stock or in processing a large part. Primary operations should have die enclosures or fixed barrier guards (see Figure 11-14).

• In secondary operations, a preshaped part is further processed by being placed in a nest under the upper die. These operations include coining, drawing, and forming. Secondary operations, which account for most power press accidents, should have the most effective protection within the limitations of the die—if possible, automatic or semiautomatic feeds and ejection and some form of protective guard.

Wherever possible, high-production or long-run dies should be guarded individually. This procedure saves the time involved in setup, and a permanent guard will not be detached or lost.

If die enclosures or fixed barriers cannot be used on secondary operations, an adjustable barrier device, a gate or movable barrier device, or a device that either prevents normal operation of the press until the hands are removed from the point of operation, or the device itself removes the hands from the point of operation, should be used. Unless the press has automatic or semiautomatic feeding and ejection with a die-enclosure or a fixed-barrier guard, hand tools should be used.

These safety devices must be maintained, and their use supervised strictly in accordance with the manufacturer's instructions. If they are not, they may fail. If they do fail, injuries may result and the workers' confidence will be destroyed.

Usually an insurance company safety professional or the state or lo-

Figure 11-14. Fully enclosed die guard is made of preslotted material easily fabricated in the shop.

Figure 11-15. Slide feed allows loading of the die outside the danger zone. Plastic barrier guard permits full visibility of the operation.

cal OSHA representative is willing to assist in the design and installation of the best guard for a specific operation.

A hand-feeding tool is not a point-of-operation guard or protection device, and shall not be used instead of it.

Feeding methods

Automatic or semiautomatic feeds, if they can be used, are generally successful safeguards. In most cases, they either increase production or reduce costs or both. With these feeds, it is unnecessary for operators to place their hands under the slide during ordinary feeding. They may, however, be tempted to do so if a piece sticks, or they may do so inadvertently. Therefore, it is necessary to provide a wood or soft metal stick or pick with which the operators can remove the material, if necessary, and an enclosure to prevent their putting a hand under the slide. Use of an air-ejection jet can help in removing parts from the die. The enclosure should be interlocked with the clutch brake mechanism.

The choice of feed will depend on the design of the die, the shape of the part being processed, the quantity of parts being processed, and the type of equipment available. Feed types include gravity or chute, push, follow, magazine, automatic magazine, dial, roll, reciprocating, hitch, and transfer. Feeds can be automatic, semiautomatic, or manual.

Among the advantages gained with automatic feeding are: (*a*) the operator does not have to reach into the point of operation to feed the press; (*b*) the feeding method usually makes it possible to enclose the die

285

Figure 11-16. Hand tools are used to insert and remove small piece parts formed by this special-purpose press brake. Two-hand control station requires hands to be far away from the danger zone during downward stroke of the press. Note the transparent barrier that guards the unused portion of the press.

Cincinnati Incorporated

completely; and (c) the operator can load the feed mechanism, start the press, and then leave the vicinity of the press for a considerable number of strokes. Sometimes, the operator may be able to run several presses at once. Production volume must be sufficient to justify the expense of automatic feeding.

With semiautomatic feeds, the operator does not have to reach into the point of operation, but usually must manually load the feed mechanism repeatedly or at frequent intervals. The feeding method usually makes it possible to enclose the die completely. Semiautomatic feeding is not adaptable for certain blanking operations or for nesting off-shaped pieces. (See Figure 11-15.)

When manual feeding is required, provision should be made to eliminate the need for operators to place their hands or fingers within the point of operation. If this cannot be done, some method must be employed to protect the employee should the ram descend. Special tools

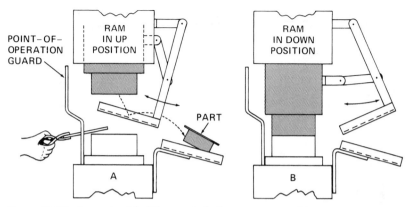

Figure 11-17. Approximately 80 percent of all power press accidents occur on secondary operations. Feeding can be made safe by adequate guarding of the point of operation, combined with gravity unload with mechanical-action chute. When ram goes up (A), formed part is knocked out and next blank is loaded. Mechanical-action chute moves out of the dies with downstroke of press (B).

have been developed and used successfully on operations where automatic feeds or enclosure guards are impractical (see Figure 11-16). Such tools include pushers, pickers, pliers, tweezers, forks, magnets, and suction disks and are usually made of soft metal to protect the die. Strict discipline is necessary to force operators to use them consistently. Such hand tools are not substitutes for guards, but should be used in conjunction with guard devices.

Bear in mind that few kinds of press guards provide complete protection. An automatic or semiautomatic feed may make it unnecessary for operators to place their hands in the danger zone, but may not prevent their doing so. If the operator attempts to straighten a part just before it passes under the slide, this method of safeguarding provides no real protection. Therefore, good practice combines such guards with a two-hand trip (for actuating the clutch) that requires constant pressure or control during the downward stroke of the press (see Figure 11-16 again).

Automatic or semiautomatic methods of feeding can usually be installed on jobs that are fed manually. Automatic feeds should be supplemented by a substantial enclosure at the point of operation, especially on slow-moving equipment, for complete protection. If possible, machine parts should be adjusted to reduce the hazard. For instance, the stroke on a press may be limited so that the fingers cannot enter between the dies. More details are given later in this chapter.

Ejecting material

The safe removal of material is as necessary as safe feeding. Since

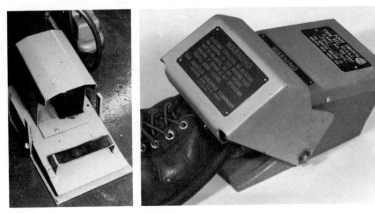

Figure 11-18. Foot pedals must be covered to prevent unintentional tripping of the press by the operator or by falling objects.

the way in which the finished piece is removed from the machine may influence the choice of feeding method, the removal method must be considered at the time an automatic or semiautomatic feed is selected.

Various methods of ejection may be used: compressed air, punch, knockouts, strippers, and gravity. Operators should not be required to remove the finished parts from the die manually. Operators, furthermore, should not be required to remove scrap from the die manually because of the hazards involved. Air blowoff systems, crankshaft-operated scrap cutters, and other devices may be used. (See Figure 11-17.)

Controls

Power presses should have actuating devices that prevent the operator's hands from getting under the slide or ram when the press is operated. Such devices include two-hand switches or levers, treadle bars, pedals, and switches, located away from the point of operation. If two-hand switches or levers are used, relays or interlocks should be installed so that one switch or lever cannot easily be made inoperable and permit the press to be controlled with one hand, thus defeating the safeguard. Pedals, foot switches, and pedal bars should be used only when it is absolutely necessary for the operator to have both hands away from the point of operation when the press is operated (see Figure 11-18).

Press brakes are the source of many accidents because the gaging stops are too low and the piece being processed slips beyond them. Because the motion of the ram is slow, some operators reach through the area between the ram and the die to adjust the work and, in doing so, are

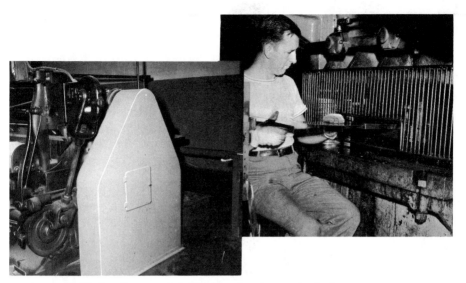

Figure 11-19. Fixed barriers. *Left:* Sheet metal encloses ends of rollers on a papercutter. Door in center of cover facilitates inspection and maintenance; the door must be interlocked. *Right:* Barrier guard for strip- and coil- fed stock has openings designed to keep fingers out of the danger area.

caught. The proper type of starting device will make it impossible for the operator to reach under the ram after the press has begun to operate.

Foot controls should be covered by stirrup-type covers that extend over the entire length of the treadle arm (an inverted U-shaped metal shield above the control) to prevent accidental tripping. When two or more operators run a press, foot controls or hand controls should be connected in series so that each person is in the clear before the press can be operated.

On die-casting machines, two-hand tripping devices have been widely used, but many consider it safer to install a sliding door that covers the die area. As the door closes, protecting the hazardous zone, it activates switches that set the machine in motion. Such a door virtually eliminates burns from splashing material.

It is a prerequisite for a safe die casting that no operator be allowed to place his other hand or arm between the dies at any time. Long-handled pliers or tongs or similar tools should be used to place and remove stock; mechanical feeds and ejectors are even safer. Effective safeguards for these machines include two-hand tripping devices, sliding doors, treadle bars, and electrical or mechanical interlocking devices.

PART III—SAFEGUARD TYPES AND MAINTENANCE

To eliminate the dangers involved in machine operation, enclosures may either be built and installed over the hazardous areas or the equipment may be redesigned to eliminate such exposed parts.

The modern lathe is a good example of machinery made safe through improved design. Its motor drive and gear box are enclosed so that line shafts, pulleys, and belts are dispensed with. The modern power press, in which all the working parts with the exception of the slide (ram) are enclosed, is another good example.

Safeguards used to make machinery safe include the fixed guard or enclosure, the interlocking guard or barrier, and the automatic protection device. Automatic or semiautomatic feeding and ejection methods are also ways of safeguarding machine operations.

Fixed guards or enclosures

The fixed guard or enclosure (see Figure 11-19) is considered preferable to all other types of protection and should be used in every case, unless it has been definitely determined that this type is not at all practical. The principal advantage of the fixed guard is that it prevents access to the dangerous parts of the machine at all times.* Another advantage to this type of guard is that when the production job is finished, the guard remains with the die until it is needed for the next run.

Fixed safeguards may be adjustable to accommodate different sets of tools or various kinds of work. However, once they have been adjusted, they should remain fixed; under no circumstances should they be detached or moved.

Typical examples of the application of fixed safeguards are found on power presses, sheet leveling or flattening machines, milling machines, gear trains, drilling machines, and guillotine cutters. Some fixed barriers are installed at a distance from the danger point in association with remote feeding arrangements that make it unnecessary for the operator to approach the danger point.

Interlocking guards or barriers

Where a fixed safeguard cannot be used, an interlocking guard or

---

*If a fixed barrier is to provide complete protection, the openings in it must be small enough to prevent a person from getting into the danger zone. See the diagram of point-of-operation guard locations in Part I of this chapter.

Figure 11-20. A fixed guard is not practical on this secondary operation. This automatic protection device will stop the ram if the operator's hand is in the danger zone when the press is activated. A tough transparent plastic allows an unobstructed view of the work. An interlock (not shown) prohibits press operation if, for some reason, the device is tampered with or is otherwise not operating properly.

barrier (see Figure 11-20) should be fitted onto the machine as the first alternative. Interlocking may be mechanical, electrical, pneumatic, or a combination of types.

The purpose of the interlock is to prevent operation of the control that sets the machine in motion until the guard or barrier is moved into position. Operators subsequently cannot reach the point of operation, the point of danger.

When the safeguard is open, permitting access to dangerous parts, the starting mechanism is locked to prevent accidental starting, and a locking pin or other safety device is used to prevent the basic mechanism from operating, for example, to prevent the main shaft from turning.

When the machine is in motion, the enclosure cannot be opened. It can be opened only when the machine has come to rest or has reached a fixed position in its travel.

To be effective, an interlocking safeguard must satisfy three requirements. It must:

1. Guard the dangerous part before the machine can be operated.

2. Stay closed until the dangerous part is at rest.

3. Prevent operation of the machine, if the interlocking device fails.

Two-hand tripping devices are incorporated in many types of interlocking controls. These devices require simultaneous and sustained pressure of both hands on switch buttons, air control valves, mechanical levers, or controls interlocked with foot control, to name just a few. Two-hand operating attachments should be connected so that it is impossible to block, tie down, or hold down one button, handle, or lever, and still operate the machine.

When gate devices or hinged barriers are used with interlocks, they should be arranged so that they completely enclose the pinch point or point of operation before the operating clutch can become engaged.

Interlocking controls are often installed on bakery machinery, guillotine cutters, power presses, dough mixers, some kinds of pressure vessels, centrifugal extractors, tumblers, and other machines on which covers or barricades must be in place before the starting control can be operated.

Automatic protection devices

An automatic protection device may be used, subject to certain restrictions, when neither a fixed barrier nor an interlocking safeguard is practicable. Such a device must prevent the operator from coming in contact with the dangerous part of the machine while it is in motion, or must be able to stop the machine in case of danger.

An automatic device functions independently of the operator, and its action is repeated as long as the machine is in motion. The advantage of this type of device is that tripping can occur only after the operator's hands, arms, and body have been removed from the danger zone.

An automatic protection device is usually operated by the machine itself through a system of linkage, through levers, or by electronic means, and there are many variations. It can also be a hand-restraint device or similar device, or a photoelectric relay.

Pull-away or hand-restraint devices are attached to the operator's hands or arms and connected to the slide or ram, plunger, or outer side of the press in such a way that the operator's hands or fingers will be withdrawn from the danger zone as the slide or ram plunger, or outer slide de-

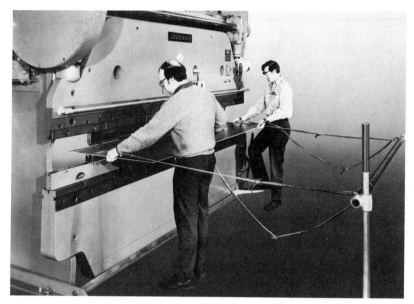

Figure 11-21. Hand-restraint devices safeguard the point of operation of this press brake. The operator at the right controls the manual clutch by means of a foot pedal because the operators' hands are needed to support the work.

Cincinnati Incorporated

scends. These devices should be readjusted at the start of every shift so that they will properly pull the operator's hands clear of the danger zone. (See Figure 11-21.)

All electronic safety devices for power presses are made to perform the same function when energized—they act to interrupt the electric current to the power press (just as if the STOP button had been pushed). Electronic safety devices are effective only on power presses having air, hydraulic, or friction clutches. Such devices are not effective on power presses with positive clutches, because once the operating cycle of this type of power press starts, nothing can prevent completion of the cycle.

To be effective, the electronic device should be operated from a closed electric circuit so that interruption of the current will automatically prevent the press from tripping. It is the supervisor's responsibility to make sure these devices are properly adjusted and maintained in peak operating condition. Many injuries have occurred because of improper adjustments and because parts have been allowed to become worn or need repair.

One advantage claimed for electronic devices is the absence of a mechanism in front of the operator. It is particularly advantageous on large presses. The electric-eye device should be installed far enough away from the danger zone so that it will stop the slide or ram before the operator's hand can get underneath, and sufficient light beams should cover the bad break open area with a curtain of light.

Indexing is another press-shop term used to describe a mechanical method of feeding stock into press dies. One method is by a dial feeder. The dial feed is constructed, as its name implies, in the form of a dial having multiple stations that progress into the die by the indexing motion of the dial. The indexing of the dial should take place in conjunction with the up-stroke of the ram. When hand feeding, the index circuit should be controlled by dual-run buttons. Release of either button, during index, should stop the index cycle by releasing a safety clutch in the table. Safety guards should be connected to switches that stop the crank motion of the press whenever they are bumped. Both of these safety precautions will stop accidents should the operator be tempted to reach into the die area to correct an improperly positioned part on the dial.

Automation

Automation, a somewhat misused term, is defined in this text as the mechanization of processes by the use of automatically controlled conveying equipment. Automation has minimized the hazards associated with manually moving stock in and out of machines and transferring it from one machine to another. It has also minimized exposure to the causes of hernias, back injuries, and foot injuries.

Most finger and hand injuries result from operator exposure to the closing or working parts of a machine in the process of loading and unloading. The use of indexing fingers, sliding dies, and tongs or similar hand tools reduces the hazard from such exposure, but the supervisor still has the problem of making sure that these devices are used consistently and correctly.

Automation represents a giant step forward in preventing injuries since it completely eliminates the need for repetitive exposure of workers at the point of operation. Automatic devices move parts into and out of production equipment, turn them over, rotate them, shunt them to one side, remove scrap and waste, and perform other related functions.

Like most innovations, however, automation has brought not only benefits, but also hazards. Since each automatic operation is dependent on others, machine breakdown or failure must be corrected quickly. Because speed is highly important, maintenance employees may expose themselves, inadvertently perhaps, to working parts of the equipment. It is therefore imperative to have a mandatory policy that equipment must be completely de-energized and locked out at the power source before servicing the machine. A well-defined lockout procedure should be written down and used.

Automated handling also has increased the use of stiles or crossovers. These should be constructed and installed in accordance with the standard.* Automation eliminates or greatly reduces exposure to mechanical and handling hazards. In the single-operation process, however, the basic principles of safeguarding of equipment must still be applied. These principles are:

- Engineer the hazard out of the job insofar as possible.
- Guard the remaining hazards.
- Educate and test the performance of workers.
- Insist on use of safeguards provided.

Robotics

Since robots—machines specifically designed and programmed to perform certain operations—are rapidly becoming a part of the work environment, the supervisor should know that these machines can and have caused accidents to unsuspecting people working in the vicinity.

As early as possible, the supervisor should consult the engineer who designed or worked on the robot, to learn about its capabilities, features, and operation. Allow for proper clearances when the robot is working with peripherals, such as machine tools, presses, transfer lines, palletizers, gaging stations, and so on. Even the robot with the best conceptual design may only be efficient if it has these clearances. Providing clearance for personnel, however, is even a more important factor. Although robots perform repetitive tasks for long periods of time, still they are machines, and thus will require periodic preventive maintenance. Eventually, the robots will require repairs to keep their devices, modules, and/or tooling working properly. Clear spaces and safe areas must be incorporated in the design stage. *(See Figure 11-22.)*

A big hazard of robots is that when an operation is being performed, it may be virtually impossible to shut it off or reverse the cycle because of the programming feature. Therefore, workers should be warned not to get near these machines. In some cases, it may be possible to totally enclose the robot, but in many instances, this may be impractical.

---

*American National Standard A12.1, *Safety Requirements for Floor and Well Openings, Railings, and Toeboards.*

Figure 11-22. Clear spaces and areas for personnel who must maintain and repair robots must be provided for in the design phase. Perimeter is effectively and relatively inexpensively guarded by a chain link fence with gates.

Cincinnati Milacron

Control systems for robots usually work with a priority interrupt scheme. Interrupts of higher priorities are those reserved for hardware devices to signal that personnel are entering the work area, or that tooling needs to be changed or repaired.

The basic rules the supervisor should follow then, are:

1. Get as much information as possible on the operation of the robot.

2. Provide proper clearances and barrier guards around the robot (see Figure 11-22).

3. Discuss all facets of the operation, including safety, with his people. All personnel should be trained.

4. Do not allow workers near robots when they are in operation, but wait for the cycle to be completed and the machine de-energized before approaching.

There may be some jobs that will require work to be done with power "on" (such as alignment and repair of servo systems.) This must be realized in the design stage by the user's engineers. It cannot be assumed that work always will be performed in a power-off state.

Experience shows that those who work with automated equipment must have a thorough knowledge of its hazards and must be trained well in proper work and precautionary methods.

The simplest guarantee that equipment is safe to work on is to insist that repair personnel and the maintenance crew place their company-issued padlocks on the power source. (Lockout procedures are discussed later in this chapter.)

Safe practices

Safeguards are of primary importance in eliminating machine accidents, but they are not enough. The employee who works around mechanical equipment or operates a piece of machinery must have a healthy respect for safeguards.

Before being permitted to run a piece of equipment, operators should be instructed in all the practices required for safe operation of the machine. Even experienced operators should be given refresher training, unless the supervisor is certain that they know the hazards and the necessary precautions to be taken. In addition, employees who do not themselves operate machinery, but who work in machine areas, should also receive instruction in basic safety practices.

Positive procedures should be established to prevent misunderstandings, and the supervisor should enforce the following:

1. No guard, barrier, or enclosure should be adjusted or removed for any reason by anyone unless that person has specific permission from the supervisor, has been specifically trained to do this work, and machine adjustment is considered a normal part of the job.

2. Before safeguards or other guarding devices are removed so that repair or adjustments can be made or equipment can be lubricated or otherwise serviced—the power for the equipment must be turned off and the main switch locked out and tagged.

3. No machine should be started unless the safeguards are in place and in good condition.

4. Defective or missing safeguards should be reported to the supervisor immediately.

5. Employees should not work on or around mechanical equipment while wearing neckties, loose clothing, watches, rings, or other jewelry.

Maintenance of safeguards

The supervisor is responsible for scheduling inspection of machine safeguards as a regular part of machine inspection and maintenance. Such inspections are necessary because employees are inclined to operate their machines without safeguards if they are not functioning properly, if they have been removed for repairs, or if they interfere in any manner with their operations. A guard or enclosure that is difficult to remove or to replace may never be replaced once it has been taken off. An inspection checklist can be developed for each type of machine to simplify the job and to provide a convenient record for followup.

Safeguarding for maintenance and repairs

Machines are subject to wear and deterioration and can become unsafe to operate. Wear cannot be prevented, but it can be reduced to a minimum by controlling loads through proper manufacturing methods, alert supervision, attention of employees, and by good maintenance.

Lubrication is a basic maintenance function. Centralized lubrication will reduce the hazards to which the oiler is subjected when climbing ladders attempting to reach fairly inaccessible points. Perhaps, changes can be made so that most lubrication can be done at floor level.

When oilers must get to the tops of presses to lubricate flywheel bearings, motors, and other parts, and repair crews must also get to such places, good practice suggests that permanent ladders with sturdy enclosures (cages or wells) be installed.

Regardless of the type of lubrication necessary or the method used, it is the supervisor's responsibility to know that the machinery—including driving mechanisms, as well as gears, motors, shafting hangers, and other parts—is being lubricated properly. Where automatic lubrication is not possible or feasible, extension grease or oil pipes should be attached to machines so that the oiler can avoid coming in contact with moving parts. However, automatic lubrication should not be used in cases where the oil or grease can congeal in the pipes.

Lockout procedure

Oilers and maintenance personnel often enter places "where no one ever goes" in order to do a job. As mentioned earlier in this chapter, even though an apparatus may seem safe by virtue of its location, safeguards should be provided on its moving parts (see Figure 11-13). Another problem results when oilers or repair personnel work on machines in operation and fail to replace safeguards after the work is completed. It is a definite responsibility of the supervisor to use all of his or her authority to prevent such lapses.

Maintenance personnel and oilers should be provided with and use padlocks to lockout the power-driven apparatus on machinery or equip-

Figure 11-23. Before working on any machine, its power must be turned off and locked out. Each worker should have his own, company-supplied lock and key, and each person working should personally lock out the power source of equipment he is working on, even if this means that more than one lock is used. Lock extenders (one is shown here) make use of more than one lock practicable.

General Electric Company

ment they are to clean or oil, especially when the working place is some distance from the controls, or hidden from view. Each worker should have his own lock and key, and no two locks or keys should be alike. Only locks bought by the company should be used. Locks can be painted different colors, according to craft, shift, or department, to facilitate identification. The employee's name or clock number should be stamped on the lock, or a metal tag bearing the owner's name should be attached.

Where a lockout system is to be set up, equipment must have built-in locking devices. They must be designed for the insertion of padlocks or

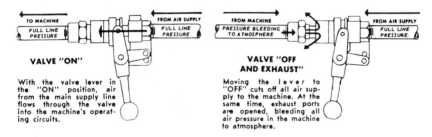

Figure 11-24. This automatic bleeder valve helps prevent an accidental machine stroke by permitting residual pressure to bleed immediately. Valve can be locked in either the "on" or the "off" position.

have attachments on which locks can be placed. Methods include special tongues that hold several locks or sliding rods that can be extended and then locked to prevent operation of control handles (see Figure 11-23). The lockout procedure, however, will be effective only if the supervisor trains employees to follow it, and then watches constantly for deviations. A typical lockout routine for maintenance and repair workers is given here:

1. Notify the operator that repair work is to be done on a machine or piece of equipment.

2. Make sure the machine cannot be set in motion without your permission.

3. Place your padlock on the power disconnect, even though another worker's lock is already on it and blocks the mechanism. Another person's lock will not protect you.

4. Place a MACHINE UNDER REPAIR sign at the control and block the mechanism. Make sure that neither the sign nor the blocking can be easily removed.

5. When the job is finished or the shift has ended, remove your own padlock and blocking. Never let another person remove it for you. Make sure first that you will not expose others to danger by removing your block or sign.

6. If the key to a lock is lost, it must be reported at once to the supervisor who will issue a new set.

If two or more people are to work on a machine or piece of equipment where they might become separated, they should agree upon a foolproof set of signals. It is good practice to have a rule that when a machine or group of machines is stopped, only a specific, authorized person may start them again. In any case, the safe procedure is to give a warning and make sure that everyone is in the clear before power is turned on again.

It is also good practice for the supervisor to check machines back into operation after repairs have been made and before new operations are undertaken. Every worker should be warned not to start the machine unless safeguards are in place. This is the supervisor's responsibility—not only to teach employees this practice, but to check to see that it is complied with constantly.

More details can be found in American National Standard Z244.1, *Safety Requirements for the Lock Out/Tag Out of Energy Sources.*

Replacements

Alerting management whenever replacement of machinery and/or its safeguards is advisable is partly, sometimes entirely, up to the supervisor. Although this may seem like a production problem and not closely related to accident prevention, this is not the case. When machinery, safeguards, and safety devices become worn to the extent that repairs cannot restore them to original operating efficiency, they constitute hazards, often, unfortunately, concealed. For example, if a nonrepeat device on a press becomes so worn that it does not operate at all or fails to operate properly, amputation can result. These hazards can only be eliminated by replacement.

Several methods are used to determine when maintenance or overhaul needs to be done to prevent breakdown, or when replacements are in order. Some supervisors rely on reports of the machine operators; some have occasional inspections made by oilers, machine setters, or similar mechanics; others put inspection on a periodic time basis and do it themselves, or have it done, periodically. The best plan is a system of frequent, regularly spaced inspections.

Safeguarding hazards before accidents

Guarding the hazard is a fundamental principle of accident prevention and not limited to machinery. When you, the supervisor, survey your department solely from the point of view of safeguarding hazards—no matter what kind—you are likely to list a good many potential sources of injury that should be protected by barricades, rails, toeboards, enclosures, or other means. As you list electric switches and equipment, motors, engines, fixed ladders, stairs, platforms, and pits, you might well ask yourself, "Can an accident occur here, or here. . . or here?"

See Chapter 1, "Loss Control for Supervisors," for details on how to eliminate accidents before they happen.

Chapter 12

Hand Tools and Portable Power Tools

A major responsibility of supervisors is to train people in the safe handling of hand and power tools. This chapter discusses ways in which hand and portable power tool injuries can be avoided. But to pinpoint the situation, you, as supervisor, should review the department or company accident records first. Try to find problems and identify specific hazards, and then check to see if there are any employees who have had an unusual number of injuries. They should have additional training and closer supervision.

Training and close supervision are also needed when new tools, processes, and equipment are introduced in the operation. A job safety analysis of each job will serve to clarify tool needs and safe work practices.

SAFE WORK PRACTICES

A supervisor needs to have experience performing each job, so that small changes can be identified as a potential accident cause. To be effective, a program to reduce tool injuries must include training in four basic safe practices.

1. *Select the right tool.*

While there are many tools capable of doing a job, proper selection means choosing the tool that can be most safely used by the employee while adequately performing the task. If power is available, power tools should be considered.

Error, accidents, and damage to the product will result when improper tools are used. For example, an adjustable wrench can tighten a nut, but it would be better if the employee used a box end or a socket wrench of the proper size.

There is usually more than one kind of tool to fit a particular job. Ergonomic-designed tools, of course, provide the best fit for the employee and the job. Tool selection is also related to the job setup, work space available, work height, and so forth, each bearing on the most efficient tool selection. Cost of tools is another factor to consider. Quality needs to be specified on orders. Employers generally are expected to provide the correct tool(s) to do the job safely.

2. *Use tools correctly.*

Employees need to be shown how to use tools safely. Supervisors must insist on their correct usage. It is far too common for employees to use tools that are neither safe nor necessary for the task. Using a screwdriver to pry or using pliers instead of the proper wrench are typical examples.

3. *Keep tools in good condition.*

Tools that have deteriorated should not be used until repaired to meet factory specifications—examples: wrenches with cracked or worn jaws, screwdrivers with broken bits (points) or broken handles, hammers with loose heads, dull saws, and deteriorated extension cords or power cords on electric tools or broken plugs, and improper or removed grounding systems.

All tools need to be replaced from time to time. Employees should know what a tool in good condition looks like and what to do with it if it's not.

However, employees are usually not expected to do tool maintenance work. If they are, they should be trained and supervised. Good housekeeping is closely related to good, clean tools.

4. *Keep tools in a safe place.*

Tools need to be properly stored either in or on the work area or in a common tool crib. If employees own their own tools, safe storage is of equal importance. Good housekeeping is also closely related to safe usage and safety.

Control of tool accidents

A supervisor's program to control accidents should include the following activities:

1. Train employees to select the right tools for each job. Good job safety analysis and job instruction training helps here. See Chapter 5, "Safety Training."

2. Train and supervise employees in the correct use of tools.

Figure 12-1. Accident control starts with tool control. Only tools that are in good condition and that are in proper adjustment should be issued.

3. Establish regular tool inspection procedures (including inspection of employee-owned tools), and provide good repair facilities as insurance that tools are being maintained in safe condition.

4. Establish a procedure for control of company tools. A check-out system at tool cribs is ideal. Provide proper storage facilities in the tool room and on the job. (See Figure 12-1.)

Also make a complete check of operations to determine the need for special tools to do the work more safely. Special tools may require special handling and storage. For example, some tools (like powder-actuated hand tools) should be kept under lock and key.

USE OF HAND TOOLS

The misuse of common hand tools is a prolific source of injury to industrial workers. In many instances, injury results because it is assumed that "anybody knows how to use" common hand tools. Observation and the records of injuries show that this is not the case.

Supervisors should study each job and train new and retrain old employees on correct procedures for using tools. Where employees have the privilege of selecting or providing tools, the supervisor should advise them on the hazards of the job and insist on their using the safest equipment for each job.

Supervisors should enforce all rules. They should frequently check the condition of tools to be sure that they are maintained and sharpened correctly and that guards are not altered or removed. The use and the condition of personal protective equipment should be checked frequently.

Specific rules should be adapted for using hand tools in each operation. So important is this training that considerable attention is given in the following pages to discussing safe practices.

The use of personal protective equipment is often required when using hand tools. Gloves may also be necessary. The hazards identified on a job safety analysis can be useful in setting up personal protective equipment needs.

Metal-cutting tools

Chisels. Factors determining the selection of a cold chisel are (*a*) the materials to be cut, (*b*) the size and shape of the tool, and (*c*) the depth of the cut to be made. The chisel should be heavy enough so that it does not buckle or spring when struck. For best results and for maximum safety, flat and cape chisels should be ground in such a way that the faces form an angle of 70 degrees for working on cast iron, 60 degrees for steel, 50 degrees for brass, and about 40 degrees for babbitt and other soft metals.

A chisel only large enough for the job should be selected so that the blade is used rather than the point or corner. Also, a hammer heavy enough to do the job should be used.

Some workers prefer to hold the chisel lightly in the hollow of their hands with the palms up, supporting the chisel by the thumb and first and second fingers. If the hammer glances from the chisel, it will strike the soft palm rather than the knuckles. Other workers think that a grip with the fist holds the chisel steadier and minimizes the chances of glancing blows. Moreover, in some positions this is the only grip that is natural or even possible.

Hand protection can consist of a rubber pad, forced down over the chisel to provide a hand cushion. Chip in a direction away from the body. When shearing with a cold chisel, the worker should hold the tool at the vertical angle that permits one bevel of the cutting edge to be flat against the shearing plane. Workers should wear safety goggles when using chisels and should set up a shield or screen to prevent injury to other workers from flying chips. If a shield does not afford positive protection to all exposed employees, then they should wear glasses with side protection.

Bull chisels held by one person and struck by another require the use of tongs or a chisel holder to guide the chisel so that the worker is not exposed to injury. Both workers should wear safety goggles and safety hats. The one who swings the sledge should not wear gloves. Safety shoes are also required.

Dress all heads at the first sign of mushrooming, because mushroomed heads often produce flying chips that can be very dangerous to the eyes. It is suggested that when using a $1/2$-in. steel chisel, a hammer with $1 1/2$-in. diameter face be used.

Tap and die work has certain built-in precautions. The work should be firmly mounted in a vise. Only a T-handle wrench or adjustable tap wrench should be used. Steady downward pressure should be applied on the taper tap. Excessive pressure causes the tap to enter the hole at an angle or bind the tap, causing it to break. A proper sized hole must be made for the tap. The tap should be lubricated as necessary.

Keep hands away from broken tap ends. Broken taps should be removed with a tap extractor. If a broken tap is removed by using a prick punch or a chisel and hammer, the worker should wear safety goggles. When threads are being cut with a hand die, the hands and arms should be kept clear of the sharp threads coming through the die, and metal cuttings should be cleared away with a brush.

Hack saws should be adjusted in the frame to prevent buckling and breaking, but should not be so tight that the pins that support the blade break. Install blades with teeth pointing forward.

The preferred blade to be used is shown in Table 12-A. A general rule is that at least two teeth be in the cutting piece.

It is advisable to loosen blades when in storage; retighten before starting work.

Files. Selection of the right kind of file will prevent injuries, lengthen the life of the file, and increase production.

A file-cleaning card or brush should be used to keep the file in peak condition. Files should not be hammered or used as a pry. Such abuse frequently results in the file's chipping or breaking, causing an injury to the user. A file should not be made into a center punch, chisel, or any other type of tool because the hardened steel could fracture.

The correct way to hold a file for light work is to grasp the handle firmly in one hand and use the thumb and forefinger of the other to guide the point, using smooth file strokes. This technique gives good control, and thus produces better and safer work.

A file should never be used without a smooth, crack-free handle;

TABLE 12-A

SELECTOR FOR HACK SAW BLADES

Pitch of Blade (Teeth per Inch)	Stock To Be Cut	Explanation
14	Machine Steel Cold Rolled Steel Structural Steel	The coarse pitch makes saw free and fast cutting
18	Aluminum Babbitt Tool Steel High Speed Steel Cast Iron	Recommended for general use
24	Tubing Tin Brass Copper Channel Iron Sheet Metal (18 gage or over)	Thin stock will tear and strip teeth on a blade of coarser pitch
32	Small Tubing Conduit Sheet Metal (less than 18 gage) **18 gage = 1.27 mm**	

otherwise, if the file binds, the tang may puncture the palm of the hand, the wrist, or other part of the body. Under some conditions, a clamp-on, raised offset handle can provide extra clearance for the hands. Files should not be used on lathe stock turning at high speeds (faster than three turns per file stroke), because the end of the file may strike the chuck, dog, or face plate and throw the file (or metal chip) back at the operator and inflict serious injury. To avoid contact with the turning parts of the lathe, the operator should always cross file. Use a vise, whenever possible, to hold the object being filed.

Tin snips should be heavy enough to cut the material easily so that the worker needs only one hand on the snips and can use the other to hold the material. The material should be well supported before the last cut is made so that the cut edges do not press against the hands. When cutting long sheet-metal pieces, push down the sharp ends next to the hand holding the snips.

Jaws of snips should be kept tight and well lubricated. When not in use, they should be hung up or laid on a shelf. Burrs on the cut usually indicate a need for adjusting or sharpening.

Workers should wear safety goggles when trimming corners or slivers of sheet metal, because small particles often fly with considerable force. They should always wear gloves.

Cutters used on wire, reinforcing rods, or bolts should have ample capacity for the stock; otherwise, the jaws may spring or spread. Also, a chip may fly from the cutting edge and injure the user.

Cutters are designed to cut at right angles only. They should not be "rocked," hammered, or pushed against the floor to facilitate the cut, because they are not designed to take the resulting strain. This practice will nick the cutting edges and result in future problems. A good rule is, "If it doesn't cut with ease, use a larger cutter or use a cutting torch." Cutters require frequent lubrication. To keep cutting edges from becoming nicked or chipped, cutters should not be used as nail pullers or pry bars.

Cutter jaws should have the hardness specified by the manufacturer for the particular kind of material to be cut. By adjustment of the bumper stop behind the jaws, cutting edges should be set to have a clearance of 0.003 in. (0.076 mm) when closed. Cutters should be stored in a safe place.

Punches are used like chisels. They should be held firmly and securely and struck squarely. The tip should be kept shaped as the manufacturer has specified. Punches should be held at right angles to the work.

Wood-cutting tools

Edged tools should be used in such a way that, if a slip occurs, the direction of force will be away from the body. For efficient and safe work, edged tools should be kept sharp and ground to the proper angle. A dull tool does a poor job and may stick or bind. A sudden release may throw the user off balance or cause his or her hand to strike an obstruction. Thus, all cuts should be made along the grain when possible.

Dressing of wood-cutting tools will be discussed under that heading later in this chapter, pages 240 and 241.

Wood chisels. All employees should be instructed in the proper method of holding and using chisels. While molded plastic and metal handles are often available, wood handles are also found on wood chisels. If the handle is wood, it should be free of splinters and cracks. The wood handle of a chisel struck by a mallet should be protected by a metal or leather cap to prevent its splitting.

The work to be cut should be free of nails to avoid damage to the blade or to prevent a chip from flying into the user's face or eye.

The steel in a chisel is hard so that the cutting edge will hold, and is, therefore, brittle enough to break if the chisel is used as a pry. When not in use, the chisel should be kept in a rack, or on a workbench, or in a slotted section of the tool box so that the sharp edges will be out of the way. Sharp edges can be safeguarded as shown in Figure 12-2.

Figure 12-2. Sharp edges of hand tools can be guarded by metal, fiber, or heavy cardboard sleeves that fit over them. Tool boxes should be checked regularly to make sure that tools are stored with sharp edges protected.

Saws should be carefully selected for the work they are to do. For fast crosscut work on green wood, a coarse saw (4 to 5 points per inch) should be used. A fine saw (over 10 points per inch) is better for smooth, accurate cutting in dry wood. Saws should be kept sharp and well set to prevent binding, and when not in use, should be kept in racks. (See Figure 12-3.)

Saw set (the amount of angle or lean of a point from the blade) is needed to properly and cleanly cut wood or other materials. Inspect the material to be cut, to avoid sawing into nails or other metal.

Sawing should be a one-hand operation. When starting a cut, guide the saw with the thumb of your free hand held high on the saw. Don't place a thumb on material being cut. Begin with a short, light stroke toward you. After the cut begins, increase pressure and increase stroke length. Use light shorter strokes as the cut is completed.

Figure 12-3. Dull saws can be frustrating. In the rear is a saw that is in good condition. The one in front has been neglected—teeth are flattened, dull, and badly out of set.

Axes. To use an axe safely, workers must be taught to check the axe head and handle, clear the area for an unobstructed swing, and swing correctly and accurately. Accuracy is attained by practice and proper handhold—and good supervisory training. All other workers must be kept a safe distance away from the direct line of swing.

A narrow axe with a thin blade should be used for hard wood, and a wide axe with a thick blade for soft wood. A sharp, well-honed axe gives better chopping speed and is much safer to use because it bites into the wood. A dull axe will often glance off the wood being cut and strike the user in the foot or leg.

The person using the axe should make sure that there is a clear circle in which to swing before starting to chop. Also vines, brush, and shrubbery within the range, especially overhead vines that may catch or deflect the axe, should be removed.

Axe blades should be protected with a sheath or metal guard wherever possible. When the blade cannot be guarded, it is best to carry the axe at one's side. The blade on a single-edged axe should be pointed down.

Hatchets are used for many purposes and frequently cause injury. For example, when workers attempt to split a small piece of wood while holding it in their hands, they may strike their fingers, hand, or wrist. Hatchets are dangerous tools in the hands of the inexperienced worker. To start the cut, it is a good practice to strike the wood lightly with the hatchet, then force the blade through by striking the wood against a solid block of wood.

Hatchets should not be used for striking hard metal surfaces, because the tempered head may injure the user or others by flying chips. When using a hatchet for cutting or for driving nails in a crowded area, workers should take special care to prevent injury to themselves and others.

Using a hatchet to drive nails is a poor practice. If used, however, the face of a hatchet used for driving nails should be square. Some companies, however, prefer to use a corrugated face to prevent nails from flying.

Miscellaneous cutting tools

Planes, scrapers, bits, and drawknives should be used only by experienced personnel. These tools should be kept sharp and in good condition. When not in use, they should be placed in a rack on the bench, or in a tool box in such a way that will protect the user and prevent damage to the cutting edge.

Knives are more frequently the source of disabling injuries than any other hand tool. In the meatpacking industry, hand knives are the cause of more than 15 percent of all disabling injuries. The principal hazard in the use of knives is that the hands may slip from the handle onto the blade or that the knife may strike the body or the free hand. A handle guard or a finger ring (and swivel) on the handle eliminates these hazards (see Figure 12-4).

The cutting stroke should be away from the body. If that is not possible, then the hands and body should be in the clear, a heavy leather apron or other protective clothing should be worn, and, where possible, a rack or holder should be used for the material to be cut. Jerky motions should be avoided to help maintain balance. Be sure employees are trained and supervised. Training is very important in the food service industry (see Figure 12-5).

Belt repairers and other workers who must carry knives with them on the job should keep them in sheaths or holders. Never carry a sheathed knife on the front part of a belt—always carry it over the right or left hip, toward the back. This will prevent severing a leg artery or vein in case of a fall.

Knives should never be left lying on benches or in other places where

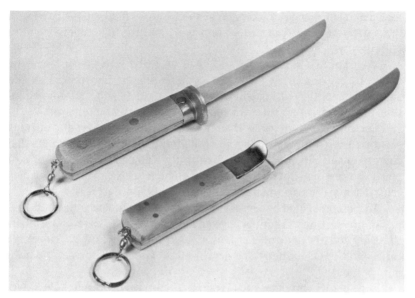

Figure 12-4. Knives equipped with ring-and-swivel guards and handle guards prevent employee's hand from sliding over the handle onto the blade in the event that the knife stubs against a solid object.

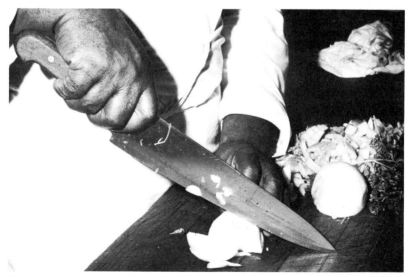

Figure 12-5. Slice vegetables with a rocking motion, rather than chopping or hacking away. Hold the point of the chef's knife against the cutting surface. Fingers that hold the object should be curled back and kept in the clear.

they could cause hand injuries. When not in use, they should be kept in racks with the edges guarded. Safe placing and storing are important to knife safety.

Ring knives—small, hooked knives attached to a finger ring—are used where string or twine must be cut frequently. Supervisors should make sure that the cutting edge is kept outside the hand, not pointed inside. A wall-mounted cutter or blunt-nose scissors would be safer.

Carton cutters are safer than hooked or pocket knives for opening cartons. They not only protect the user, but eliminate the deep cuts that could damage carton contents. Frequently, damage to contents of soft plastic bottles may not be detected immediately; subsequent leakage may cause chemical burns, damage other products, or start a fire.

To cut corrugated paper, a hooked linoleum knife permits good control of pressure on the cutting edge and eliminates the danger of the blade suddenly collapsing as pocket knives can do. Be sure hooked knives are carried in a pouch or heavy leather (or plastic) holder. The sharp tip must not stick out.

Supervisors should make certain that employees who handle knives have ample room in which to work so they are not in danger of being bumped by trucks, the product, overhead equipment, or other employees. For instance, a left-handed worker should not stand close to a right-handed person; the left-handed person might be placed at the end of the bench or otherwise given more room. Workers should be trained to cut away from or out of line with their bodies.

Supervisors should be particularly careful about employees leaving knives hidden under the product, scrap paper, or wiping rags, or among other tools in work boxes or drawers. Knives must be kept separate from tools to protect the cutting edges and the employee.

Work tables should be smooth and free of slivers. Floors and working platforms should have slip-resistant surfaces and be kept unobstructed and clean. If sanitary requirements permit mats or wooden duck boards, they should be in good repair, so workers do not trip or stumble. Conditions that cause slippery floors should be controlled as much as possible by good housekeeping and frequent cleaning.

Careful job and accident analysis may suggest some changes in the operating procedure that will make knives safer to use. For instance, on some jobs, special jigs, racks, or holders may be provided so it is not necessary for the operator to stand close to the piece being cut.

The practice of wiping a dirty or oily knife on the apron or clothing should be discouraged. The blade should be wiped with a towel or cloth with the sharp edge turned away from the wiping hand. Sharp knives should be washed separately from other utensils and in such a way that they will not be hidden under soapy wash water.

Horseplay should be prohibited around knife operations. Throwing, "fencing," trying to cut objects into smaller and smaller pieces, and similar practices are not only dangerous, but reflect inadequate supervision.

Supervisors should make sure that nothing is cut that requires excessive pressure on the knife, for example, frozen meat. Food should be thawed before it is cut or else frozen food should be sawed. Knives should not be used as substitutes for openers, screwdrivers, or ice picks.

Torsion tools

Many tools used to fasten or grip materials are available to facilitate work. Proper tool selection and usage are important if employees are to work safely.

Wrenches. All wrenches should be pulled, not pushed, in operation. Your footing should be secure and allow plenty of clearance for your fingers. Use a short, steady pull. If a nut does not loosen or tighten fully, a larger wrench may be needed. Damaged tools should be removed for service. Open-end and box wrenches (Figure 12-6) should be inspected to

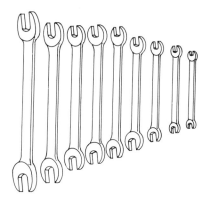

Figure 12-6a. Open-end wrenches, solid nonadjustable wrenches with openings in one or both ends, come in both English and metric systems. Wrenches with openings greater than 1 in. are widely used on pipelines, in marine operations, and on heavy equipment. The smaller the opening, the shorter the length; this proportions the leverage to the size of the bolt or nut and helps reduce the force applied in order to keep the threads from stripping or the bolt from being twisted in two.

Figure 12-6b. Box-end wrenches (also called box wrenches or 12-point wrenches) can be used in close quarters and are best for breaking loose tight nuts. If securely seated, there is little chance of the box wrench slipping off the nut; also the wrench opening cannot spread. The lower drawing shows a combination wrench.

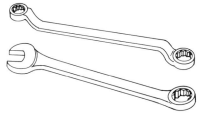

make sure that they fit properly. Wrenches should not be hammered or struck.

Socket wrenches give great flexibility. The use of special types should be encouraged where there is danger of injury. Socket wrenches are safer to use than adjustable or open-end wrenches and protect the bolt head or nut.

Wrench jaws that fit (and are not sprung or cracked) prevent damage to the heads of nuts or bolts, and are not likely to slip and cause injury to the user. (See Figure 12-7.)

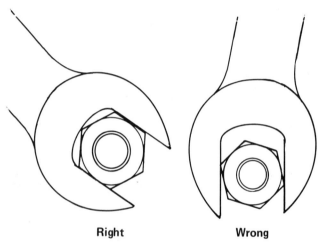

Right   **Wrong**

Figure 12-7. Wrench jaws that fit (and are not sprung or cracked) prevent damage to the head of the nut or bolt, and are not likely to slip and cause injury to the user. (The wrench opening is slightly larger than the size stamped on the wrench so that it will easily slip onto the nut or bolt heads.)

Adjustable wrenches are used for many purposes. They are not intended, however, to take the place of standard open-end, box, or socket wrenches. They are used mainly for nuts and bolts that do not fit a standard wrench. Pressure is always applied to the fixed jaw and the wrench is pulled toward you. (See Figure 12-8.)

Pipe wrenches. Workers, especially those on overhead jobs, have been seriously injured when pipe wrenches slipped on pipes or fittings, causing them to lose their balance and fall. Pipe wrenches, both straight and chain tong, should have sharp jaws and be kept clean to prevent slipping.

The adjusting nut of the wrench should be inspected frequently. If it

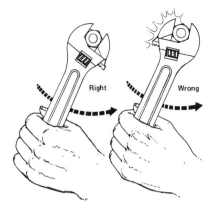

Right Wrong

Figure 12-8. Adjustable (crescent) wrenches are probably the most often misused wrenches; they are made for use on odd-sized nuts and bolts that other wrenches might not fit (such as metric system sizes). To use, the wrench should be placed on the nut so that when the handle is pulled, the moveable jaw is closer to the user's body; the pulling force will then force the wrench onto the nut and apply force to the fixed jaw, which is the stronger of the two.

is cracked, the wrench should be taken out of service. A cracked nut may break under strain, causing complete failure of the wrench and possible injury to the user.

Using a wrench of the wrong length is another source of accidents. A wrench handle too small for the job does not give proper grip or leverage. An oversized wrench handle may strip the threads or break the fitting or the pipe suddenly, causing a slip or fall.

A pipe wrench should never be used on nuts or bolts, the corners of which will break the teeth of the wrench, making it unsafe to use on pipe and fittings. Also a pipe wrench, when used on nuts and bolts, can damage their heads. A pipe wrench should not be used on valves, struck with a hammer, or used as a hammer unless, as with specialized types, it is specifically designed for such use.

Torque wrenches have a scale to indicate the amount of force to be applied to the nut or bolt (usually foot pounds). It is important that a torque wrench be well cared for so that the measurements will be accurate. Cleanliness of the bolt/nut threads is also important.

Tongs are usually bought, but some companies make their own to perform specific jobs. To prevent pinching hands, the end of one handle should be upended toward the other handle, to act as a stop. It is also possible to braze, weld, or bolt bumpers on the handles a short distance behind the pivot point so that the handles cannot close against the fingers.

Pliers. Side-cutting pliers sometimes cause injuries when the short ends of wire are cut. A guard over the cutting edge and the use of safety

317

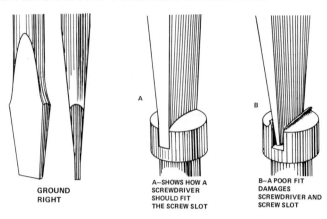

GROUND
RIGHT

A—SHOWS HOW A
SCREWDRIVER
SHOULD FIT
THE SCREW SLOT

B—A POOR FIT
DAMAGES
SCREWDRIVER AND
SCREW SLOT

Figure 12-9. Screwdriver blades must be ground flat in that portion of the tip that enters the screw slot, and then gradually taper out to the diameter of the shank *(left)*. When selecting a screwdriver, make sure the blade makes a good fit in the screw slot *(right)*.

glasses will help to prevent eye injuries.

The handles of electrician's pliers should be insulated. In addition, workers should wear insulated gloves if they are to work on energized lines. Because pliers do not hold the work securely, they should not be used as a substitute for a wrench. Vise-type pliers can be locked on the object. Pinching of the fingers or hand is a danger.

Special cutters include those for cutting banding wire and strap. Claw hammers and pry bars should not be used to snap metal-banding material. Only cutters designed for the work provide safe and effective results.

Nail band crimpers make it possible to keep the top band on kegs and wood barrels after nails or staples have been removed. Use of these tools eliminates injury caused by reaching into kegs or barrels that have projecting nails and staples.

Pipe tongs should be placed on the pipe only after the pipe has been lined up and is ready to be made up. A 3-in. or 4-in. (7.5 or 10 cm) block of wood should be placed near the end of the travel of the tong handle and be parallel to the pipe to prevent injury to the hands or feet in the event the tongs slip.

Workers should neither stand nor jump on the tongs nor place extensions on the handles to obtain more leverage. They should use larger tongs, if necessary, to do the job.

Screwdrivers. The screwdriver is probably the most commonly abused tool. The practice of using screwdrivers for punches, wedges, pinch bars, or pries should be discouraged. If used in such a manner, they become unfit for the work they are intended to do. Furthermore, a broken handle, bent blade, or a dull or twisted tip may cause a screwdriver to slip out of the slot and cause a hand injury. (See Figure 12-9.)

The tip must be kept clean and sharp in order to permit a good grip on the head of the screw. A screwdriver tip should fit the screw snugly. A sharp square-edged bit will not slip as easily as a dull, rounded one, and requires less pressure. The part to be worked upon should never be held in the hands; it should be laid on a bench or flat surface, or held in a vise. This practice will lessen the chance of injury to the hands if the screwdriver should slip from the work.

• No screwdriver should ever be used for electrical work unless it is insulated.

• In wood, make a pilot hole for the screw.

• Don't carry screwdrivers in your pockets.

• Keep screwdriver handles clean.

Screwdrivers used in the shop are best stored in a rack. This layout allows proper selection of the right screwdriver quickly.

Allen wrenches are used like screwdrivers, but having the correct size is most important. It is often easy to apply too much force on small Allen wrenches.

Shock tools

A hammer should have a securely wedged (if of wood) handle suited to the type of head used. The handle, whether glass fiber or metal, should be smooth, free of oil, shaped to fit the hand, and of the specified size and length. Employees should be warned against using a steel hammer on hardened steel surfaces. Instead, a soft-head hammer, ball peen hammer, or one with a plastic, wood, or rawhide head should be used. Safety goggles should be worn to protect against flying chips, nails, or scale.

The chipping or spalling of a hammer varies with four things:

1. The more square the corners of the hammer are, the easier it chips.

2. The harder the hammer is swung, the more likely it is to chip.

3. Chipping increases as the hardness of the object being struck increases.

4. The greater the angles between the surface of the object and the hammer face, the greater are the chances of chipping.

Selection of the proper hammer is important. One that is too light is as unsafe and inefficient as one that is too heavy.

To drive a nail, hold the hammer close to the end of the handle, use a light blow to start, and increase power after setting the nail. The fingers should hold the handle underneath, and alongside or on top of the handle. Hold the hammer so that an angle of the face of the hammer and the surface of the object being hit will be parallel. A nail will drive straighter and there will be less chance for damage. Placing the hammer on the nail before drawing it up to swing may increase the accuracy of the aim.

Sledge hammers have two common unsafe conditions: split handles and loose or chipped heads. Because these tools are used infrequently in some industries, the heads may become loose or chipped and the defect not noticed. Some companies place a steel band around the head and bolt it to the handle to prevent the head from flying off. The heads should be dressed whenever they start to check or mushroom. A sledge hammer so light that it bounces off the work is hazardous; similarly, one that is too heavy is hard to control and may cause body strain.

Riveting hammers, often used by sheet metal workers, should have the same kind of use and care as ball peen hammers and should be watched closely for checked or chipped faces.

Carpenter's or claw hammers are designed primarily for driving and drawing nails. The striking faces should be kept well dressed at all times to reduce the hazard of flying nails while they are being hammered into a piece of wood. A checker-faced head is sometimes used to reduce this hazard.

Eye protection is advisable for all nailers and all employees working in the same area, (*a*) as in a shipping room, (*b*) when blocking and bracing trucks or railway cars, or (*c*) as in carpenter shops and the like.

When a nail is to be drawn from a piece of wood, a block of wood may be used under the hammer head to increase the leverage.

Spark-resistant tools

Spark-resistant tools of nonferrous materials are sometimes advised for use where flammable gases, highly volatile liquids, and explosive materials are stored or used.

320

Other tools

Vises are best used to hold objects being worked. A variety of sizes, jaws, and attachments can be used to properly hold many kinds of materials. Vises should be secured solidly to a bench or similar base. When work is held in the vise for sawing, saw as close to the jaw as possible. If clamping long pieces, there should be support on the other end. Lightly oil all moving parts of a vise.

Clamps of many kinds are used in a variety of operations. Nearly all clamps can be used with pads to reduce marring the work. Too much tightening can damage the product or break the clamp. If there is a swivel, it must be free to turn. Moving parts, like the threads, should be lightly oiled. Clamps should be stored on a rack and not in a drawer.

PORTABLE POWER TOOLS

Portable power tools are divided into four primary groups according to the power source: electric, pneumatic, internal combustion, and explosive (powder actuated). Several types of tools, such as saws, drills, grinders, and wrenches, are common to the first three groups, whereas explosive tools are used exclusively for penetration work and cutting.

A portable power tool presents similar hazards as a stationary machine of the same kind, in addition to the risks of handling power. Typical injuries caused by portable power tools are burns, cuts, and sprains. Sources of injury include electric shock, particles in the eyes, fires, falls, explosion of gases, and falling tools.

Because of the extreme mobility of power-driven tools, they can easily come in contact with the operator's body. At the same time, it is difficult to guard such equipment completely. There is also the possibility of breakage because the tool may be dropped or roughly handled. Furthermore, the source of power (electricity, compressed air, liquid fuel, or explosive cartridge) is brought close to the operator, thus creating additional hazards.

When using powder-actuated tools (explosive cartridge equipment) for driving anchors into concrete, or when using air-driven hammers or jacks, it is imperative that hearing protection and eye and/or face protection be worn by operators, assistants, and adjacent personnel when the tool is in use. All companies and manufacturers of portable power tools attach to each tool a set of operating rules of safe practices. These are meant to supplement the thorough training each power tool operator should have. (More details on using these tools are given below.)

Power-driven tools should be kept in safe places and not left in areas

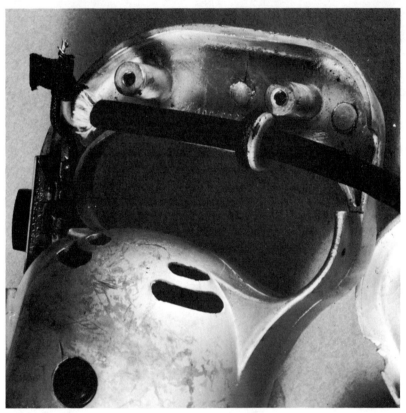

Figure 12-10. Exposed energized wire inside the handle of this tool can contact the metal shell. The tool will still run, but if the operator presents a good ground (such as by touching a water pipe), the flow of current through him could cause death. Many accidents primarily caused by electric shock are not reported as such and are charged against falls, tools dropped on feet, burns, and the like.

where they may be accidentally struck by a passer-by, and be activated. The power cord should always be disconnected before accessories on a portable tool are changed, and guards should be replaced or put in correct adjustment before the tool is used again.

Selection

When you replace a hand tool with a power tool, you may be replacing a less serious hazard with a more serious one. Check with your safety professional to make sure the tools you select meet current safety standards. The tool manufacturer, too, can recommend the best tool to do the job. Describe the job you want accomplished, and also describe the material to be worked on, and the space available in the work area of your shop or plant. Tell the manufacturer if the operation is intermittent or continuous. Too light a tool may fail or cause undue operator fatigue if used over an extensive period.

Electric tools

Electric shock is the chief hazard from electrically powered tools. Injury categories are electric flash burns, minor shock, and shock resulting in death. Serious electric shock is not entirely dependent on the voltage of the power input. Nearly all tools are powered at 110 or 220 volts. As explained in Chapter 13, "Electrical Safety," the ratio of the voltage to the resistance determines the current that will flow and the resultant degree of hazard. The current is regulated by the resistance to the ground of the body of the operator and by the environmental conditions. It is possible for a tool to operate with a defect or short in the wiring (see Figure 12-10); however, the use of a ground wire protects the operator under most conditions.

Insulating platforms, rubber mats, and rubber gloves provide an additional factor of safety when tools are used in damp locations—in tanks or boilers or on wet floors. Safety low voltage of 6, 12, or 24 volts, obtained through portable step-down transformers, will reduce the shock

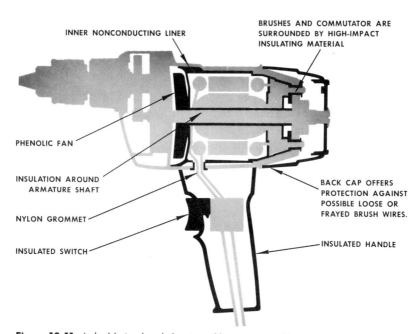

Figure 12-11. A double-insulated electric tool has an internal layer of protective insulation that isolates the electrical components from the outer housing.

hazard in damp locations.

Electric tools used in damp areas or in metal tanks expose the operator to conditions favorable to the flow of current through the body, particularly if it is wet with perspiration. Most electric shocks from tools have been caused by the failure of insulation between the current-carrying parts and the metal frames of the tools. Only tools in good repair that are listed by an authorized testing laboratory should be used.

Double insulated tools. Protection from electric shock, while using portable power tools, has been described as depending upon third-wire protective grounding. "Double insulated" tools, however, are available which provide reliable shock protection (see Figure 12-11) without third-wire grounding or a ground fault circuit interrupter (GFCI). The *National Electrical Code*® permits double insulation for portable tools and appliances. Tools in this category are permanently marked by the words "double insulation" or "double insulated." Units designed in this category that have been tested and listed by Underwriters Laboratories also carry the UL marks. Many manufacturers are also using the symbol

for a variety of tools to denote "double insulation."

This double insulated tool does not require separate ground connections; the third wire or ground wire is not needed and should not be used.

Failure of insulation is harder to detect than worn or broken external wiring, and points up the need for frequent inspection and thorough maintenance. Care in handling the tool and frequent cleaning will help prevent the wear and tear that cause defects.

See Chapter 13, "Electrical Safety," for more details.

Grounding of portable electric tools provides the most convenient way of safeguarding the operator. If there is any defect or short circuit inside the tool, the current is drained from the metal frame through a ground wire and does not pass through the operator's body. All electric power tools should be effectively grounded unless they are double insulated or of the cordless type.

The noncurrent-carrying metal parts of portable and/or cord- and plug-connected equipment required to be grounded may be grounded—either by means of the *metal enclosure* of the conductors feeding such equipment—provided an approved grounding-type attachment plug is used—or by means of a *grounding conductor*. The grounding conductor should be run with the power supply conductors in a cable assembly or flexible cord that is properly terminated in an approved grounding-type attachment plug having a fixed grounding contacting member. The grounding conductor may be noninsulated; if individually covered, however, it must be finished in a continuous green color or a green color with one or more yellow stripes.

By special permission, nonportable cord- and plug-connected equipment can be grounded by a separate flexible wire or strap, insulated or bare, that has been protected (as well as practicable) against physical damage.

Of major concern is the maintenance of the electric power system and especially the ground. Periodic tests of the electric system should be made by an electrician. A ground fault circuit interrupter, GFCI, is a device that protects the tool operator should a ground fault occur. The GFCI is a part of the receptacle or on an extension cord. GFCIs come in a variety of sizes and types. They need to be tested periodically, which is a requirement of the manufacturer. If a GFCI trips, it is often an indicator of a fault someplace in the system. GFCIs are described in detail in Chapter 13, "Electrical Safety."

Electric cords of power tools should be inspected frequently and kept in good condition; they should be of adequate wire size—have this checked by a qualified person. Heavy-duty plugs that clamp to the cord should be used to prevent strain on the current-carrying parts if the cord is accidentally pulled. Employees should be trained not to pull on cords and to protect them from sharp objects, heat, and oil or solvents that might damage or soften the insulation.

Extension cords. Use only three-wire extension cords that have three-prong, grounding-type plugs and three-pole receptacles that accept the tool's plug. Replace or repair damaged or worn cords immediately. An undersized cord will cause a drop in line voltage, resulting in a drop in power and overheating. See discussion in Chapter 13.

Electric drills cause injuries in several ways: a part of the drill may be pushed into the hand, the leg, or other parts of the body; the drill may be dropped when the operator is not actually drilling; or the eyes may be hit either by material being drilled or by parts of a broken drill bit. Although no guards are available for drill bits, some protection is afforded if drill bits are carefully chosen for the work to be done, such as being no longer than necessary to do the work.

When the operator must guide the drill with a hand, the drill should be equipped with a sleeve that fits over the drill bit. The sleeve protects the operator's hands and also serves as a limit stop, if the drill should suddenly plunge through the material.

Oversized bits should not be ground down to fit small electric drills; instead, an adapter should be used that will fit the large bit and provide extra power through a speed reduction gear; however, this again is an indication of improper drill size. When drills are used, the pieces of work should be clamped on or anchored to a sturdy base to prevent whipping.

Electric drills should be of the proper size for the job. A 1/4-in. drill means a maximum 1/4-in. (diameter) drill bit can be used for wood and light metal, whereas a 1/2-in. drill would be needed to pierce heavy steel and masonry. To operate, the chuck key should be attached to the cord, but removed from the chuck before starting the drill. If the drill has a side handle, it should be used. A punch mark should be used to facilitate starting the drill and bit. Hold the drill solidly and at the proper angle, and start it slowly. Increase speed as needed after the start.

Routers operate at a high speed of about 25,000 rpm. Hands should be placed firmly on the handle provided. Do not adjust depth when running. If on wood, it is good practice to try cutting on scrap first so that the dimension of the cut can be determined.

The cutter turns clockwise, with the best cut moving from left to right as you stand facing the work. Keep the cutting pressure constant, but do not crowd. The router bit or cutter must be securely locked in place.

Electric circular saws are usually well guarded by the manufacturer, but employees must be trained to use the guard as the manufacturer intended (see Figure 12-12). The guard should be checked frequently to be sure that it operates freely and encloses the teeth completely when not cutting, and encloses the unused portion of the blade when it is cutting.

Circular saws should not be jammed or crowded into the work. The saw should be started and stopped outside the work. At the beginning and end of the stroke, or when the teeth are exposed, the portable power hand-held circular saw operator must take extra care to keep his or her body and power cord away from the line-of-cut. All saws have a trigger switch to shut off power when pressure is released.

Injuries that occur when using portable circular saws are caused by: contact with the blade; electric shock or burns; tripping over the electric or the extension cord, saws, or debris; losing balance; and kickbacks resulting from the blade being pinched in the cut.

Figure 12-12. Workers should understand potential accidents and injuries involved in the use of portable power tools and known how to use the safeguards that protect them.

Important requirements for safe operation of the portable circular saw are proper use, frequent inspection, and a rigid maintenance schedule. It is equally important that the manufacturer's recommendations for operation and maintenance be followed faithfully and treated as standard procedure.

The importance of wearing eye protective equipment must be stressed, and it should be worn at all times.

Blades should not be changed or adjusted until the cord has been disconnected. The angle of blade or depth of the cut should not be adjusted while the motor is running. Portable electric hand saws with circular blades are well-guarded by the manufacturer. Keep guards in place and in good working condition; never clamp or wedge the guard in the open position.

The saw should be placed on the uncut part of the work. The work should be well secured to prevent its being thrown or dragged by blade action, and both hands should be free to operate the saw. A piece should never be held across the knee or any other part of the body while using the saw.

When the saw is being used in a damp environment, the operator should wear electrical insulating boots and gloves. Insulating gloves and footwear are also recommended when working outdoors. GFCI protection or a double insulated saw is a necessity for outside use.

Cutoff wheels. Do not use any cutoff wheel beyond its rated speed. Check catalog rpm against safe wheel speed. Never try to cut through thick material in one try; make a series of shallow cuts that gradually deepen to the cut desired.

Operators who are exposed to harmful or nuisance dusts should be required to wear approved respirators.

Electric reciprocating saws are of two basic types—the common saber saw and reciprocating saw. Because the blade is almost fully exposed when in use and storage, the tool must be handled with extra care. The blade must be secured. The type of blade will be determined by the material being cut. Hold the shoe as secure as possible against the work. Turn off the tool when the job is completed and hold until the motor has stopped before putting it down.

Abrasive wheels, buffers, and scratch brushes should be guarded as completely as possible. For portable grinding, the maximum angular exposure of the periphery and sides should not exceed 180 degrees and the top portion of the wheel should always be enclosed. Guards should be adjustable so that operators will be inclined to make the correct adjustment rather than remove the guard. However, the guard should be easily removable to facilitate replacement of the wheel. In addition to this mechanical guarding, the operator must wear safety goggles at all times to prevent eye injuries from broken wheels and spokes. (See Figure 12-13.)

The portability of a grinding wheel exposes it to more abuse than that given a stationary grinder. The wheel should be kept away from water and oil, which might affect its balance; the wheel should be protected against blows from other tools; and care should be exercised not to strike the sides of a wheel against objects or to drop the wheel. Cabinets or racks will help to protect the wheel against damage.

The speed and weight of a grinding wheel, particularly a large one, make it more difficult to handle than some other power tools. Since part of the wheel must necessarily be exposed, it is important that employees be trained in the correct way to hold and use the wheel so that it does not touch the clothes or the worker's body.

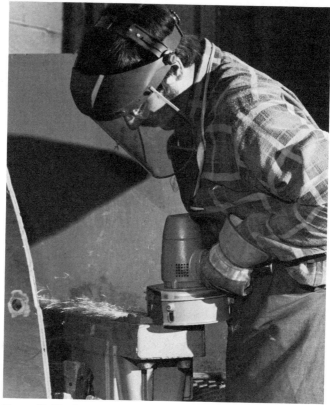

Figure 12-13. The operator of a portable abrasive wheel should wear proper protective equipment and be trained in correct way to hold it so it does not contact his clothes or body.

The wheels should be mounted by trained personnel only, with the wheels and safety guards conforming to American National Standard B7.1, *Safety Requirements for the Use, Care, and Protection of Abrasive Wheels.* Grinders should be marked to show the maximum abrasive wheel size and speed. Abrasive wheels should be sound-tested (ring-tested) before being mounted; for details, see the standard.

Sanders of the belt or disk type cause serious skin burns when the rapidly moving abrasive touches the body. Because it is impossible to guard sanders completely, employees must be thoroughly trained. The motion of the sander should be away from the body, and all clothing should be kept clear of the moving parts.

A vacuum system attached to the sander or an exhaust system must be used to remove the dust from the work area. Dust-type safety goggles or plastic face shields should be worn and, if harmful dusts are created, a respirator certified by the National Institute for Occupational Safety and Health (NIOSH) or the Mine Safety and Health Administration (MSHA) for the exposure should be worn. (See Chapter 9, "Personal Protective Equipment.")

Sanders require especially careful cleaning because of the dusty nature of the work. If a sander is used steadily, it should be dismantled periodically, as well as thoroughly cleaned every day by being blown out with low-pressure air—less than 30 psig (208 kPa). If compressed air is used, the operator should wear safety goggles or work with a transparent chip guard between the body and the air blast.

Because wood dust presents a fire and explosion hazard, keep dust to a minimum; sanders can be equipped with a dust collection or vacuum bag. Electrical equipment should be designed to minimize the explosion hazard. Fire extinguishers approved for Class C (electrical) fires should be available. Employees should be trained in what to do in case of fire.

Soldering irons are the source of burns and of illness resulting from inhalation of fumes. Insulated, noncombustible holders will practically eliminate the fire hazard and the danger of burns from accidental contact. Ordinary metal covering on wood tables is not sufficient because the metal conducts heat and can ignite the wood.

Holders should be designed so that employees cannot accidentally touch the hot irons if they should reach for them without looking. The best holder completely encloses the heated surface and is inclined so that the weight of the iron prevents it from falling out. Such holders must be well ventilated to allow the heat to dissipate, otherwise the life of the tip will be reduced and the wiring or printed circuit may be damaged. Also see NSC Data Sheet 445, *Hand Soldering and Brazing.*

Local and federal regulations may require exhaust facilities if much lead soldering is done. Even if lead fumes are not present in harmful quantities, it is desirable to exhaust the nuisance fumes and smoke. Air samples should be taken to verify that the amount of lead in the air is not harmful.

Lead solder particles should not be allowed to accumulate on the floor and on work tables. If the operation is such that the solder or flux may spatter, employees should wear face shields or do the work under a transparent shield.

Electrically heated glue guns are being increasingly used in industry. Although all guns have insulated handles, there is danger in the high temperature of the glue and tip of the gun. Proper holders and storage can minimize the exposure. Electric shock is also a possibility.

Air-powered tools

Air hose. An air hose presents the same tripping or stumbling hazard as do power cords on electric tools. Persons or material accidentally hitting the hose may unbalance the operator or cause the tool to fall down. An air hose on the floor should be protected against trucks and pedestrians by placing two planks on either side or by building a runway over it. Suspend hoses over aisles and work areas.

Workers should be warned against disconnecting the air hose from the tool and using it for cleaning machines. Air hoses should not be used to remove dust from clothing.

Accidents sometimes occur when the air hose becomes disconnected and whips about. A short chain attached to the hose coupling and to the tool housing will keep the hose from whipping about if the coupling should break; other couplings in the air line should also be safely pinned or chained. Air should be cut off before attempting to disconnect the air hose from the air line. Air pressure inside the line should be released before disconnecting.

A safety check valve installed in the air line at the manifold will shut off the air supply automatically if a fracture occurs anywhere in the line. If kinking or excessive wear of the hose is a problem, it can be protected by a wrapping of strip metal or wire. One objection to metal armored hose is that it may become dented and thus restrict the flow of air.

Tool operation. Operators of air tools should be instructed to:

- Keep hands and clothing away from the working end of the tool.

- Follow safety requirements applicable to the tool being used and the nature of the work being performed.

- Inspect and test the tool, air hose, and coupling, before each use.

Most air powered tools are difficult to guard. Therefore, care must be exercised by the operator to prevent hands, feet, or body from injury in case the machine slips or the tool breaks.

Pistol or doughnut hand grips, or flanges in front of the hand grip, provide protection for the hands and should be used on all twist or percussion tools.

Air power grinders require the same kind of guarding as electric grinders. Maintenance of the speed regulator or governor on these machines is of particular importance in order to avoid overspeeding the wheel (runaway). Hold grinder properly (see Figure 12-13).

331

Regular inspection by qualified personnel at each wheel change is recommended.

Pneumatic impact (percussion) tools, such as riveting guns and jackhammers, are essentially the same in that the tool proper is fitted into the gun and receives its impact from a rapidly moving reciprocating piston driven by compressed air at about 90 psig (625 kPa) pressure.

Two safety devices are needed. The first is a trigger located inside the handle where it is reasonably safe from accidental operation. The machine operates only when the trigger is depressed. The second is a device to hold the tool in place so that it cannot be shot accidentally from the barrel (see Figure 12-14).

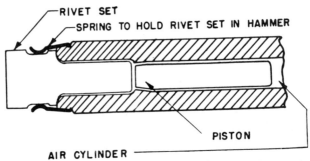

Figure 12-14. A spring clip, like the one shown here, should always be used to prevent a rivet set from falling from a hammer.

On small air hammers not designed to use this device, use a spring clip to prevent the tool and piston from falling from the hammer.

It is essential that employees be thoroughly trained in their proper use. A safety rule to impress on all operators of small air hammers is *Do not squeeze the trigger until the tool is on the work.*

Air percussion tools produce heavy blows or, due to rapid pulsating, vibrate profusely; and tools such as rotary drills, saws, or grinders, especially those rotating at high speeds, cause excessive vibration. Continued use of this equipment may, therefore, cause damage to the body. Precautions should be taken to reduce transmission of this vibration to the operator by using rubber hand grips, air cushion devices, and other vibration dampeners wherever possible. Prolonged use should be avoided.

Jackhammers. Handling of heavy jackhammers causes fatigue and strains. Jackhammer handles should be provided with heavy rubber grips to reduce vibration and fatigue, and operators should wear safety shoes

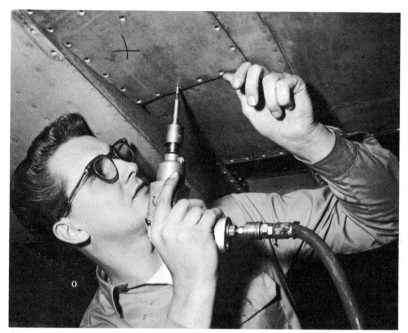

Figure 12-15. Safety glasses save the left eye of this plane overhaul mechanic. While he was using a pneumatic screwdriver to install this plate, the screwdriver tip broke and struck the left lens of his safety glasses. The lens was chipped, but the mechanic's eye was unharmed.

to reduce the possibility of injury should the hammer fall.

Two chippers should work away from each other, that is, back to back, to prevent face cuts from flying chips. Workers should not point a pneumatic hammer at anyone, nor should they stand in front of operators handling pneumatic hammers.

Many accidents are caused by the steel drill breaking because the operator loses balance and falls. Also, if the steel is too hard, a particle of metal may break off and strike the operator. The manufacturer's instructions for sharpening and tempering the steel should be followed.

Air-operated nailers and staplers. The principal hazard from these tools is the accidental discharge of the fastener. In such instances, the fastener can become a dangerous projectile and inflict serious injury at considerable distance. Operators should be trained in the use of these tools and must follow the manufacturer's operating instructions.

Personal protective equipment. As with all pneumatic impact tools, there is, of course, a hazard from flying chips. Operators should wear

333

safety goggles, and, if other employees must be in the vicinity, they should be similarly protected. Where possible, screens should be set up to shield persons nearby where chippers, riveting guns, or air drills are being used.

Eye protection should also be provided when using powered saws, grinding wheels, screwdrivers, buffers, scratch brushes, and sanders (see Figure 12-15).

Special power tools

Flexible shaft tools require the same type of personal protective equipment as do direct power tools of the same type. Abrasive wheels should be installed and operated in conformance with American National Standard B7.1, discussed earlier. The flexible shaft must be protected against denting and kinking, which may damage the inner core and shaft.

It is important that the power be shut off whenever the tool is not in use. When the motor is being started, the tool end should be held with a firm grip to prevent injury from sudden whipping. The abrasive wheel or buffer of the tool is difficult to guard and, because it is more exposed than the wheel or buffer on a stationary grinder, extra care should be exercised to avoid damage. Wheels should be placed on the machine or put on a rack, not on the floor.

Gasoline power tools are used in logging, construction, and other heavy industry. The most ubiquitous is the chain saw. (See OSHA regulations §1910.266(c)(5), Chain saw operations, and NSC Data Sheet 320, *Portable Power Chain Saws.*)

Operators of gasoline power tools must be trained in their proper operation and follow the manufacturer's instructions. They must also be familiar with the fuel hazards. (See Chapter 10, "Materials Handling.")

Powder-actuated fastening tools (see OSHA regulations §1910.243(d) and NSC Data Sheet 236, *Powder-Actuated Hand Tools*) are used for fastening fixtures and materials to metal, precast or prestressed concrete, masonry block, brick, stone, and wood surfaces, tightening rivets, and punching holes. Blank cartridges provide the energy and are ignited by means of a conventional percussion primer.

The hazards encountered in the use of these tools are similar to those encountered with firearms. The handling, storing, and control of explosive cartridges present additional hazards. Therefore, instructions for the use, handling, and storage of both tools and cartridges should be just as rigid as those governing blasting caps and firearms.

Figure 12-16. Worker demonstrates correct use of power-assisted hammer-driven tool to fasten conduit clips to masonry blocks.

Specific hazards are accidental discharge, ricochets, ignition of explosive or combustible atmospheres, projectiles penetrating the work, and flying dirt, scale, and other particles. In case of misfire, the operator should hold the tool in operating position for at least 30 seconds and follow the manufacturer's instructions for removing the load.

Powder-actuated tools can be used safely if special training and proper supervision are provided. Manufacturers of the tools will aid in this training. Only trained and properly qualified personnel should be permitted to operate or handle the tools. A worker, however, may be qualified after a few hours of instruction.

Power-assisted, hammer-driven tools are used for the same purposes as powder-actuated tools and, generally, the same precautions should be followed (see Figure 12-16).

Figure 12-17. Powder-actuated tool drives threaded studs into poured concrete slab. Wearing of eye protection, ear protection, and head protection is "standard operating procedure."

Workers should be trained to use powder charges of the correct size to drive studs into specific surfaces and should be made responsible for safe handling and storing of the cartridges and the tools.

Powder-actuated tools should not be used on concrete less than three times the fastener shank penetration, or into very hard or brittle materials including, but not limited to, cast iron, glazed tile, hardened steel, glass block, natural rock, hollow tile, or smooth brick. Fasteners should not be driven closer than 3 in. (7.5 cm) from an unsupported edge or corner.

Operators should wear adequate eye and face protection when firing the tool. Where the standard shield cannot be used for a particular operation, special shields can be obtained from the tool manufacturer. Hearing protection should also be worn. (See Figure 12-17.) See Chapter 9,

"Personal Protective Equipment," for more details.

Propane torches are commonly used in many industries, but there is danger from the open flame. Proper storage of cylinders is important. Operating instructions are available from the manufacturer.

SUPERVISORY CONSIDERATIONS

Centralized tool control

Centralized tool control helps to assure uniform inspection and maintenance of tools by a trained person. The tool room attendant can promote tool safety by recommending or issuing the right type of tool, by encouraging employees to turn in defective or worn tools, and by encouraging the safe use of tools. The correct protective equipment, such as welder's safety goggles or respirators, can be recommended and issued when the tool is distributed.

Centralized control and careful records of tool failure and other accidents will pinpoint hazardous conditions and unsafe practices.

Some companies issue each employee a set of numbered checks which are exchanged for tools from the tool room. With this system, the attendant knows where each tool is and can recall it for inspection at regular intervals.

A procedure should be set up so that the tool supply room attendant can send tools in need of repair to a department or the manufacturer for a thorough reconditioning.

Companies performing work at scattered locations may find that it is not always practicable to maintain a central tool room. In such cases, the job supervisor should inspect all tools frequently and remove from service those found to be defective. Many companies have supervisors check all tools weekly. A checklist can help.

Personal tools

In trades or operations where employees are required or prefer to have their own personal tools, the supervisor may encounter a serious problem. Personal tools are usually well maintained, but some people may purchase cheap tools, make inadequate repairs, or attempt to use unsafe tools (such as hammers with broken and taped handles, or electrician's pliers with cracked insulation).

To remedy this, the company should spell out the general requirements that tools must meet before they can be used; for example, where applicable, they should meet the appropriate American National Stan-

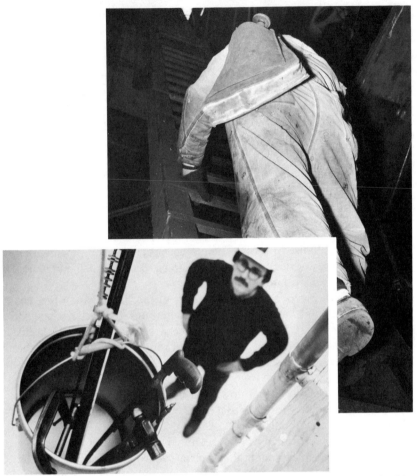

Figure 12-18. To avoid carrying tools in the hand when climbing a ladder, use a shoulder bag *(top)* or a bucket or similar container to hoist or lower tools.

dard(s) and, again if applicable, be listed by a nationally recognized testing firm. Then the supervisor should arrange a thorough inventory and initial inspection of personal tools. Supervisors should inspect and list additional tools that employees buy just as though they were company purchased tools. The supervisor must not permit the use of inferior tools.

Carrying tools

Workers should never carry tools in any way that might interfere with using both hands freely on a ladder, or while climbing on a structure. A strong bag, bucket, or similar container should be used to hoist tools from the ground to the job (see Figure 12-18). Tools should be returned in the same manner, not brought down by hand, carried in pockets, or dropped to the ground.

Mislaid and loose tools cause a substantial portion of hand tool injuries. Tools are put down on scaffolds, on overhead piping, on top of step ladders or in other locations from which they can fall on persons below. Leaving tools overhead is especially hazardous when there is vibration or when people are moving about or walking.

Chisels, screwdrivers, and pointed tools should never be carried in a worker's pocket. They should be carried in a tool box or cart, in a carrying belt (sharp or pointed end down) like that used by electricians and steelworkers, in a pocket tool pouch, or in the hand with points and cutting edges pointing away from the body.

Tools should be handed from one worker to another, never thrown. Edged or pointed tools should be passed, preferably in their carrying cases, with the handles toward the receiver. Workers carrying tools on their shoulders should pay close attention to clearances when turning around and should handle the tools so that they will not strike other people.

MAINTENANCE AND REPAIR

The tool room attendant or tool inspector should be qualified by training and experience to pass judgment on the condition of tools for further use. Dull or damaged tools should not be returned to stock. Sufficient tools of each kind should be on hand so that when a defective or worn tool is removed from service, it can be replaced immediately.

Efficient tool control requires periodic inspections of all tool operations. These inspections should cover housekeeping in the tool supply room, tool maintenance, service, inventory, handling routine, and condition of the tools. Responsibility for such periodic inspections is usually given to the department supervisor. This job should not be delegated. However, all employees need to recognize signs that tell when a tool is damaged, dull, or unsafe so they can report it at once.

Hand tools receiving the heaviest wear—chisels, wrenches, sledges, drills and bits, cold cutters, and screwdrivers—will require regular maintenance.

Proper maintenance and repair of tools require adequate facilities: workbenches, vises, a forge or furnace for hardening and tempering, safety goggles, repair tools, grinders, and good lighting.

Tempering tools

Such tools as chisels, stamps, punches, cutters, hammers, sledges, and rock drills should be made of carefully selected steel and be heat treated so that they are hard enough to withstand blows without excessive mushrooming, and yet not so hard that they chip or crack.

Hardening and tempering of tools require special skills.

Metal fatigue

Metal fatigue is a common problem in or near the polar regions. Metals exposed to sub-zero temperatures undergo cold-soaking. A molecular change takes place that makes steel brittle and easily broken. Pneumatic impact tools, drill bits, and dies for threading conduit have their usefulness shortened.

Ferrous metals, including carbon steel, alloy steel, and cast iron, are characterized by decreased toughness and corresponding brittleness at low temperatures.

Nonferrous metals, such as aluminum and aluminum alloys (nickel, copper and copper alloys, chromium, zinc and zinc alloys, magnesium alloys, and lead) are more resistant to low temperatures and often used in areas of extreme cold.

Safe-ending tools

Such tools as chisels, rock drills, flatters, wedges, punches, cold cutters, and stamping dies should have their heads properly hardened by a qualified worker.

Short sections of tight-fitting rubber hose can be set flush with the striking ends of chisels, hand drills, mauls, and blacksmith's tools to keep chips from flying, since they usually imbed themselves in the rubber sleeve.

Chisels, drift punches, cutters, and marking tools that are claimed not to spall or mushroom are available. This feature is attributed to a combination of alloys, with scientific heat treatment.

Dressing tools

Tools should have regular maintenance of their cutting edges or striking surfaces. In most cases, once the cutting or striking surfaces have been properly hardened and tempered, only an emery wheel, grindstone, or oilstone need be used to keep the tool in good condition. Be sure to grind in easy stages. Keep the tool as cool as possible with water or other cooling medium.

Tools that require a soft or medium-soft head should be dressed as soon as they begin to mushroom. A slight radius ground on the edge of the head, when it is dressed, will enable the tool to stand up better under pounding and will reduce the danger of chips being knocked off. A file or oilstone, rather than an abrasive wheel, is recommended for sharpening pike poles and axes.

A wood-cutting tool, because of its fine-cutting edge, can be initially dressed on a grinder having a wheel recommended by the manufacturer. An oilstone set securely in a wood block placed on a bench should be used to obtain a fine, sharp cutting edge. The oilstone should never be held in the hand because a slip off the face of the stone could cause a severe hand injury. Often a few finishing strokes on a leather strop will produce a keener edge.

Metal cutting tools, because they generally have greater body, can be dressed or sharpened (or both) on an abrasive wheel. Care should be taken so that the tool does not overheat from too much pressure against the wheel.

The manufacturer's recommendations for type and kind of abrasive wheel should be followed. Each cutting edge should have the correct angle according to its use.

Handles

The wooden handles of hand tools should be of the best straight-grained material, preferably hickory, ash, or maple, and should be free from slivers. Make sure that they are properly attached, because poorly fitted or loose handles are unsafe, may damage the material, and also make it difficult for the worker to control.

No matter how tightly a handle may be wedged at the factory, both use and shrinkage will loosen it. Tool inspection should disclose damaged and loose handles. These should be removed from service and repaired, if feasible.

Chapter 13

Electrical Safety

Electricity is the 20th century version of Aladdin's lamp. But just as the genie in the lamp could be put to insidious uses, electricity, handled incorrectly, can kill and cause serious accidents.

Thousands of people are killed or injured each year. Many fatalities go undetected as electrocutions since low alternating current levels going through the chest area can trigger ventricular fibrillation, simulating a heart attack. It has been estimated that 31 percent of the known electrocution fatalities occur in the home, 24 percent occur in general industry, and the remaining in the generation and distribution of electrical power. This means that approximately 55 percent of electrocutions are due to contact with so-called low voltage circuits, 600 volts and under.

Americans use more electricity per person than do citizens of any other country in the world. Because electricity is everywhere, it is often ignored. We can't see, hear, smell, or taste it. Misstatements about electricity abound. Some common myths and misunderstandings of electrical hazards are as follows:

1. Electricity takes the path of least resistance.

2. Electricity wants to go to the ground.

3. If an electrical appliance falls into a sink or tub of water, the appliance will short and trip the circuit breaker.

4. AC reverse polarity is not hazardous.

5. It takes high voltage to kill; 120 volts AC is not dangerous.

6. Double insulated power tools are doubly safe and can be used in wet and damp locations.

Every piece of electrical equipment is a potential source of electrical shock. Even an electrical shock too small to cause injury, in or of itself, can trigger an involuntary reaction causing physical injury, such as a person recoiling from touching a live wire and falling off a ladder. Obviously design, layout, installation, and maintenance of electrical equipment can minimize chance contact with live or "hot" electrical parts. Effective procedures, adequate training, and use of personal protective equipment can further prevent electrical shock.

This chapter provides basic information about electrical hazards that will help you eliminate and/or prevent electrical shock injuries. Be aware of, and make sure that your employees do not believe in, or cling to, any myths and misconceptions about electrical power. Major subjects include a review of electrical fundamentals, typical industrial wiring systems, electrical systems protection and testing methods, plug- and cord-connected equipment, ground fault circuit interrupters, hazardous locations, and electrical inspection techniques.

ELECTRICAL FUNDAMENTALS REVIEW

Ohm's Law

Before discussing electrical hazards, a brief discussion of Ohm's Law is necessary. Important terms are voltage, current, resistance, impedance, and power.

Ohm's Law simply states that one volt will cause a current of one ampere to flow through a resistance of one ohm. As a formula, the relationship is represented by E (volts) = I (amps) times R (resistance). An easy way to remember this formula, and the different ways it can be expressed, is to put the symbols in a circle (Figure 13-1).

1. Put your finger on I—I = E/R.

2. Put your finger on R—R = E/I.

3. Put your finger on E—E = I × R.

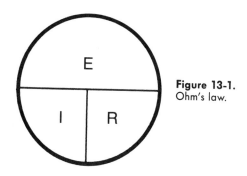

Figure 13-1.
Ohm's law.

With this basic formula, you can better understand and explain the effects electrical current has on the human body.

The above applies to direct current (DC); however, in alternating current usage, Ohm's Law is $E = I \times Z$, where Z is called the impedance. Impedance is the sum of the resistance and the capacitive and inductive reactance, expressed this way:

$$Z = \sqrt{R^2 + (X_L - X_C)^2}.$$

Since the body is essentially resistive, the explanations and examples that follow will treat the body as a resistive factor only.

To demonstrate an understanding of Ohm's Law, try to solve this problem. Assume a person is working and perspiring, and has a hand-to-hand resistance of 1000 ohms. This person contacts 100 volts with one hand and touches a grounded surface with the other, completing a loop to the voltage source. What would be the current going through the body?

$$I = E/R = 100/1000 = 0.1 \text{ amps}$$

If someone asked how many milliamps this was, the answer would be (multiply 0.1 by 1000), 100 ma. Another example of converting amps to milliamps would be to convert a circuit breaker with a rating of 20 amperes to milliamps. To do this, multiply 20 by 1000 and get an equivalent 20,000 ma.

Another important formula is the relationship of voltage, current, and power utilization (watts). Power is measured in watts and is equal to E (volts) $\times$ I (current). In other words, one watt would be equal to one ampere of current flowing through a resistor with one volt of potential difference. Another way to put this relationship to practical use would be to consider a 6-watt electric bulb (about the size of a night light or panelboard light). Determine the current flowing through the filament of a 6-watt bulb that is being used in a 120 volt light socket.

$$I = P/E = 6/120 = 0.05 \text{ amps} = 50 \text{ milliamps (50 ma)}$$

These examples of current levels from 50 ma to 20,000 ma are used to illustrate and clarify misconceptions about electricity and its effect on the human body. For example, a current flowing through the heart area at low levels (in the 50 to 100 ma range) can be fatal.

Body resistance model

The human body impedance has three distinct parts: internal body resistance and the two skin impedances associated with contact with surfaces of different voltage potential. The internal body impedance is reported to be essentially resistive with no reactive components. If the voltage applied is high, the skin impedance can be considered negligible.

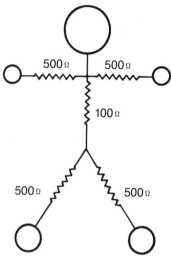

Figure 13-2. Human body resistance model.

TABLE 13-A
CURRENT AND ITS EFFECT ON THE HUMAN BODY

	Current in Milliamperes					
			Alternating			
Effect	*Direct*		*60 Hz*		*10,000 Hz*	
	Men	*Women*	*Men*	*Women*	*Men*	*Women*
Slight sensation on hand	1	0.6	0.4	0.3	7	5
Perception threshold	5.2	3.5	1.1	0.7	12	8
Shock—not painful, muscular control not lost	9	6	1.8	1.2	17	11
Shock—painful, muscular control not lost	69	41	9	6	55	37
Shock—painful, let-go threshold	76	51	16	10.5	75	50
Shock—painful and severe, muscular contractions, breathing difficult	90	60	23	15	94	63
Shock—possible ventricular fibrillation effect from 3-second shocks	500	500	100	100		
Short shocks lasting t seconds			$165/\sqrt{t}$	$165/\sqrt{t}$		
High voltage surges	50*	50*	13.6*	13.6*		

Energy in watt-seconds or joules

Note: Data is based on limited experimental tests, and is not intended to indicate absolute values.

345

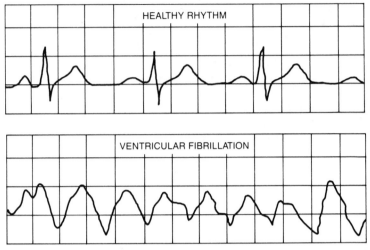

Figure 13-3. Electrocardiograms show (*at top*) rhythm of a healthy heart, and (*bottom*) ventricular fibrillation of the heart.

A body resistance model (Figure 13-2) would indicate approximately 1000 ohms from hand to hand, or about 1100 ohms from hand to foot. It is believed that the greatest number of injurious shocks involve a current pathway that is either hand-to-hand or hand-to-feet.

It is easy to analyze electrical shock hazards today. A small amount of current (50 ma) can cause the heart to go into ventricular fibrillation. The example given, that a 6-watt bulb uses 50 ma of current when energized by 120 volts, simply means that merely the current required to light a 6-watt bulb is capable of causing death.

Look at the resistance model of a person (Figure 13-2). It illustrates that wet contact with an energy source (such as 120 volts AC) in one hand and a ground loop in the other produces current through the chest area equal to: $I = E/R = 120/1000 = 0.12$ amp or 120 ma. This current level is definitely hazardous.

Contrary to many other beliefs, low AC current is dangerous and it doesn't take high voltage to kill, as shown in Table 13-A. A case involving a welder, using an AC-welder, illustrates the fact that less than 120 volts can be hazardous. The welder was kneeling on a metal plate; he was wet with perspiration and used the welding rod to scratch an itch on the back of his head. Although the contact was at the base of the head, current flowed through to both knees. In this case, the current through the neck and torso formed a series/parallel circuit. The resulting current flow would be approximately 228 ma with an 80-volt AC source ($I = E/R = 80/350 = 0.228$ amps $= 228$ ma).

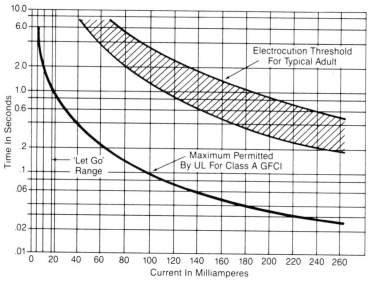

Figure 13-4. Chart shows effects of electric current intensity vs. the time it flows through the human body.

Ventricular fibrillation is defined as repeated, rapid, uncoordinated contractions of the ventricles of the heart resulting in loss of synchronization between heartbeat and pulse beat. Once ventricular fibrillation occurs, death will ensue in a few minutes. Resuscitation techniques, if applied immediately, can save the victim. Electric current flow is one of several things that can cause ventricular fibrillation. Figure 13-3 shows reproductions of electrocardiograms showing the healthy rhythm of the heart and ventricular fibrillation of the heart.

Electrical current danger levels

Since experiments on ventricular fibrillation could obviously not be performed on humans, animals have been substituted. The first work of this type was that of Ferris, Spence, King, and Williams of the Bell Telephone Laboratories in 1936. Since that time, researchers at John Hopkins University and the USSR Academy of Sciences have expanded the knowledge of the effects of electrical currents on humans. As a result, the danger threshold for ventricular fibrillation was established for typical adult workers.

Figure 13-4 plots the range of electrical values that affect humans. Also shown is the requirement of Underwriters Laboratories for a Class A ground-fault circuit interrupter (GFCI) intended for protection. Note the time-current relationship at much lower currents and shorter time

347

periods. The electrical current range, causing freezing (called the "let-go" range), is also illustrated.

From Figure 13-4, one can determine that a 100 milliampere (ma) current flowing for 2 seconds through a human adult body will cause death by electrocution. This doesn't seem like much current when you consider that a small, light-duty portable electric drill draws 30 times that much. But, because a current as small as 3 ma (3/1000 amp) can cause painful shock, it is imperative that all electrical equipment plugs and cords and extension cords be kept in good condition and connected to a properly wired grounded circuit.

Factors enhancing electrical shock

The route that electrical currents take through the human body affects the degree of injury. The voltage determines how much current flows. In cases where individuals come in contact with distribution lines, the high voltage can cause the moisture in the body to heat so rapidly that body parts can literally explode. This extreme expansion is the result of the body fluids changing to steam, with an expansion ratio estimated to be 1 to 1500. This could result in a person's being injured severely, but not electrocuted. When investigating shock incidents—whether near misses or those that have caused injury—these factors can be used as an investigative tool. Any report of a shock hazard should be checked. The combination of one or more of these factors can be analyzed and action taken to eliminate or control the hazard potential. Other factors that enhance electrical shock potential are as follows:

- Wet and/or damp locations
- Ground/grounded objects
- Current loop from source back to source
- Path of current through body/duration of contact
- Area of body contact and pressure of contact
- Physical size/condition/age of person
- Type and/or amount of voltage
- Personal protective equipment/gloves/shoes
- Metal object such as watches, necklaces, rings
- Miscellaneous
  Poor workplace illumination
  Color blindness
  Lack of training/knowledge
  No safe work procedures

Basic rules of electrical action

There are four basic rules of electrical action that everyone should know. They are as follows:

1. Electricity doesn't spring into action until current flows.
2. Electrical current won't flow until there is a complete loop, that is, a loop from the voltage source back to the voltage source.
3. Electrical current always returns to its source.
4. When current flows, work (measured in watts) is accomplished.

Rule 1 explains why faulty power tools with live metal cases can be carried around and be used without causing a shock, that is, until a person comes in contact with a ground loop of low resistance.

Rule 2. The current will then flow since there is a way for the electricity to return to the source or the grounded transformer secondary. If a bird is sitting on a power line, no current flows through the bird's body since there is no loop back to the transformer.

Rule 3 explains the action that current takes when a loop or path returns to the source. In a grounded transformer secondary system, electrical current will not only use the earth as a return path, but any other loop path it can, to get back to its secondary. The water pipes, metal ventilation duct, metal studs in modern wall construction, metal door frames, T-bars holding suspended ceiling panels, and metal ridge roll with a grounded lighting system are examples of other ground loops.

Rule 4 explains the action that current has on the body. Since the body is considered a resistive load, obviously getting in a current loop will cause injury. High voltage and high current can cause irreversible body harm.

Using these factors as an analytical thought process, rationalize why you received a shock hazard (if you have). Can you analyze why you were not injured severely? Use the loop concept to investigate and analyze potential shock hazards in the workplace.

BRANCH CIRCUITS AND GROUNDING CONCEPTS

Single-phase service

A typical pole-mounted transformer (single phase) is shown in Figure 13-5. Industrial plants may have their transformer vaults and the feeder lines and branch circuits distributed throughout the building in

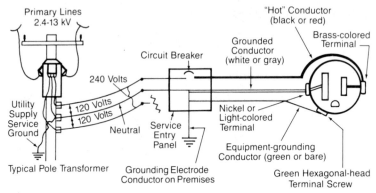

Figure 13-5. Single phase service-branch circuit wiring. Note how the elements are identified.

conduit systems. This system is used in residential, commercial, and industrial operations to provide 120 volts for lighting and small appliances. The 240-volt, single-phase power is used for heavy appliances and small motor loads. It is important that an understanding of the simple, single-phase, 3-element, 120-volt electrical system be understood, and that some misconceptions about grounding, bonding, and reverse polarity be clarified.

The *National Electrical Code*® (NEC) requires that electrical wiring design assure continuity of the system. In Figure 13-5, the ungrounded conductor from the service entrance panel (SEP) is wired to the small slot of the receptacle. The terminal screw and/or the metal connecting to the small slot is required to be a brass color. The insulation on the ungrounded conductor is generally black or red. Remember the phrase "black to brass" or the initials "B & B." The insulation on the grounded conductor is either white or gray. This conductor fastens to the large slot side of the receptacle and is defined by the code as the "grounded conductor." An easy way to remember this wiring method is to think "white to light." It is important that the receptacle be wired in this manner. If it is wired in reverse, that is, the white insulated conductor to the brass screw and the black insulated wire to the silver screw, this condition is called reverse polarity.

Reverse polarity (AC)

Many individuals experienced with electrical wiring and appliances think that reverse polarity is not hazardous. An example of one hazardous situation would be an electric hand lamp. Figure 13-6 illustrates a hand lamp improperly wired and powered.

When the switch is turned off, the shell of the lamp socket is ener-

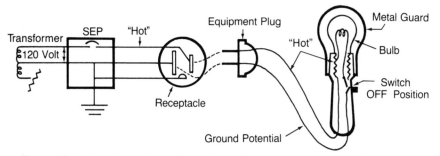

Figure 13-6. Hand lamp plugged in so that polarity is reversed—even with the switch turned OFF, the shell of the lamp socket is still energized. (SEP is the service entrance panel.)

gized. If a person accidentally touched the shell with one hand and a ground loop back to the transformer, a shock could result. If the lamp had no switch and was plugged in as shown, the lamp shell would be energized when the plug was inserted into the receptacle. Most two-prong plugs have blades that are the same size and the situation described is just a matter of chance. If the plug is reversed, Figure 13-7, the voltage is applied to the bulb center terminal and the shell is at ground potential. Contact with the shell and ground would not create a shock hazard in this situation.

Another example is the case of electric hair dryers or other plastic-covered electrical appliances. Figure 13-8 illustrates a hair dryer properly plugged into a receptacle with the correct polarity. You will notice that the switch is a single pole throw (SPST). When the appliance is plugged in with the switch in the hot or 120-volt leg, the voltage stops at the switch when it is in the OFF position. If the hair dryer was accidentally dropped into water, current could flow out of the plastic housing using

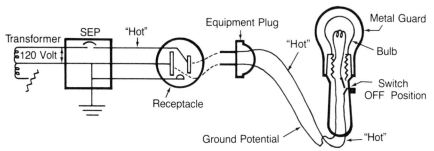

Figure 13-7. Hand lamp with plug in correct polarity. Current flows to center terminal and shell is at ground potential.

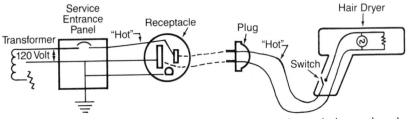

Figure 13-8. Hair dryer plugged in correctly (so that the switch is on the hot conductor).

the water as the conducting medium.

The water does not short the appliance since it has resistance that creates current flow, but in the 100 ma range. This fault current is not sufficient to trip a 20-amp circuit breaker. In order to trip the circuit breaker, there would have to be a line-to-line short that would cause an excess of 20 amps (20,000 ma). When the appliance is polarized or plugged in, as shown in Figure 13-8, the switch connection is the only surface area where the hot conductor is fastened, and is so small that high resistance allows only a small current to be available $(I = E/R)$. Should a person try to retrieve the appliance from the water while it is still plugged into the outlet? In this configuration, the fault current would be extremely low (unless the switch was in the ON position).

If the appliance is plugged in, as shown in Figure 13-9, when the switch is off, voltage will be present throughout all the internal wiring of the appliance. Now if it is dropped into water, the $I = E/R$ ratio will have increased current available in the water, since the heating element has a large surface area, decreasing the resistance and increasing the available fault current. A person who accidentally tries to retrieve the dryer now is in a hazardous position because the voltage in the water could cause current to flow through the body if another part of the body contacts a ground loop. This illustrates the concept that reverse polarity is a prob-

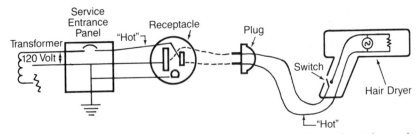

Figure 13-9. Hair dryer plugged in so that polarity is reversed. Even with switch turned off, voltage will be present throughout all the internal wiring of the appliance.

lem whenever appliances are used with plastic housings in areas near sinks, or where rain or water can wet down the appliance. Remember, most motorized appliances have air passages for cooling. Wherever air can go, so can moisture and water.

If the appliance had a double pole-double throw switch (DDPT), then it would make no difference how the plug was positioned in the outlet. The hazard would be minimized since the energized contact surface would be extremely small, resulting in a high resistance contact in the water and a resulting low available fault current. Later, we will see how ground fault circuit interrupters (GFCIs) can be used to protect against shock hazards when using appliances with nonconductive housing around water.

Grounding concepts

The terms "grounded conductor," "equipment grounding conductor," "neutral," and "ground" are probably the cause of many difficulties in understanding basic 120-volt AC system-design concepts. In order to clarify and eliminate confusion, the terms are defined and Figure 13-10 is used to illustrate the concept.

Grounding falls into two safety categories. One of these is systems safety grounding, and the other is equipment safety grounding. *System grounding* provides protection of the power company equipment and the consumer. Lightning strikes and higher voltage lines falling on secondary lines during storms use the system safety grounding loop to activate protective devices. *Equipment safety grounding* provides a system where all noncurrent-carrying metal parts (such as the metal frame of a drill press or electric refrigerator) will be bonded together and kept at the same potential.

Grounding concept definitions are as follows:

Grounded conductor. The NEC defines grounded conductor as "a system or circuit that is intentionally grounded." Figure 13-10 shows the conductor from the SEP to the outlet as the grounded conductor. For 120-volt AC, three-conductor outlets, the grounded conductor (white insulation or gray) is fastened to the silver screw which, in turn, is the large parallel slot (Figure 13-10).

The grounded conductor is a current-carrying conductor, but is also connected to ground at the SEP. From the SEP back to the transformer, the grounded conductor is called neutral. On 120-volt circuits, refer to the grounded conductor from the SEP to the receptacle as just that, the *grounded conductor,* not the neutral.

Neutral. The term "neutral" connotes a neutral conductor that car-

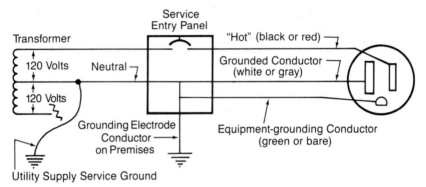

Figure 13-10. Wiring terminology. Note, particularly, the relationship of the *neutral* to the *grounded conductor* and the *equipment grounding conductor*.

ries only unbalanced current from the other conductors in the case of normally balanced circuits of three or more conductors. From the SEP to the transformer, the "neutral" term is used. In circuits from the SEP to large 240-volt AC appliance receptacles, the grounded conductor would also be referred to as the neutral.

Ground. The NEC defines this term as a "conducting connection, whether intentional or accidental, between an electrical circuit or equipment and earth, or to some conducting body that serves in place of earth." Ground, then, means an electrical connection to a water pipe or to a driven ground rod, or, where the pipe is not available, to the rod alone. To "ground" something means to connect it electrically to the ground. Since the secondary of the transformer and the SEP are both connected to ground, the earth or ground loop becomes an electrical loop hazard.

Figure 13-10 illustrates that accidental contact with the hot conductor, while a person is standing on the ground, could allow a current to return to the transformer secondary through the ground loop formed by the person and the earth. This can cause a shock.

Remember that grounded objects are many. The metal studs used in new construction are usually grounded from the electrical conduit system. The T-bar hangers for suspended ceilings can be a ground loop since the electric lighting fixtures are grounded and electrically may cause the T-bars to be ground potential. Ventilation duct work may be ground potential since electric switches, dampers, and other devices may be mounted on the duct work.

Equipment-grounding conductor. Figure 13-10 shows the

equipment-grounding conductor going from the SEP to the appliance outlet. This path is sometimes also called the grounding wire. This grounding conductor, if insulated, has insulation that is colored green or green with a yellow stripe. This conductor may also be a bare wire like those used in plastic sheathed cable. The NEC allows the conduit system to be the grounding conductor path also. The grounding conductor normally does not carry a current. Only when an equipment malfunction occurs—allowing current to flow from the motor or electrical device to the equipment case—then the grounding conductor carries the fault current back to the transformer secondary and keeps the equipment case at ground potential. More on this in the discussion on grounded power tools and equipment.

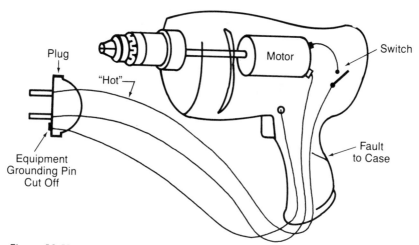

Plug

"Hot"

Equipment
Grounding Pin
Cut Off

Motor

Switch

Fault
to Case

Figure 13-11. Equipment
grounding pin removed.

Portable equipment and portable power tools can be grounded (equipment grounding) by the use of a separate grounding wire from the equipment housing to a *known* ground. This method is satisfactory for stationary equipment as long as conditions do not change; but, is less than satisfactory for portable equipment where the integrity of the grounding wire may be questionable and the quality of the ground is unknown. However, it is better than no grounding provision at all. If used, the grounding wire should be at least one inch longer than the power cord, so that the plug can be removed from the receptacle before the ground is disconnected.

PLUG- AND CORD-CONNECTED EQUIPMENT AND EXTENSION CORDS

Grounded power tools and equipment

The earlier discussion of two-conductor appliances with plastic housings revealed the hazard of dropping ungrounded electrical devices in water. Now, it is important to explain how appliances with metal cases properly grounded provide safety if accidentally immersed in water.

Virtually all portable power tools, except double insulated tools, used in industry and on construction sites are equipped with a 3-prong plug. Unfortunately, not all receptacles are equipped with provisions for the 3-prong plug.

This can lead a worker, who is unwilling to take the time or effort to use an adaptor, to break off the U-blade and defeat the protection of an equipment-grounding circuit. This is a highly dangerous practice on construction sites and in other areas that are often damp and wet. Cutting off the equipment-grounding conductor U-blade not only destroys the grounding path, but also may allow the plug to be inserted in the receptacle in a reverse polarity mode (Figure 13-11).

As shown in Figure 13-11, the grounding pin is cut off. If, in this situation, a fault developed when the power tool was plugged into an outlet, the case would have leakage voltage. The power tool would operate and the person using the power tool would be safe—but only until a ground loop was encountered. Then, current could flow through the person, through the ground loop, and back to the secondary. This would cause an electrical shock to the person, the seriousness of which would be determined by the loop resistance.

Double insulated power tools

Double insulated tools and equipment generally do not have an equipment-grounding conductor. Protection from shock depends upon the dielectric properties of the internal protective insulation and the external housing to insulate the user from the electrical parts. External metal parts, such as chucks and saw blades, are internally insulated from the electrical system.

Today, many electrical power tool manufacturers produce a line of double insulated tools. As a result, many of their advertisements lead us to believe that double insulated power tools are "doubly safe." There are some precautions in using double insulated power tools that you should be aware of. These are as follows:

- Double insulated tools are designed so that the inner electrical

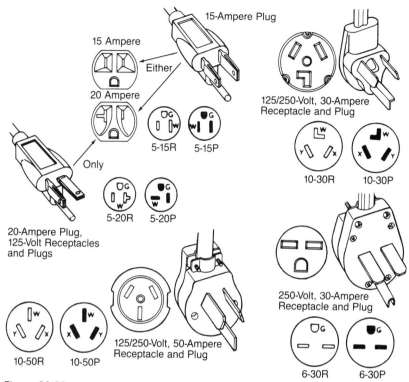

Figure 13-12. Some NEMA plug and receptacle blade configurations.

From OSHA Publication 3073, *An Illustrated Guide to Electrical Safety*

parts are isolated physically and electrically from the outer housing. The housing is nonconductive. Particles of dirt and other foreign matter from the drilling and grinding operations may enter the housing through the cooling vents and become lodged between the two shells, thereby voiding the required insulation properties.

• Double insulation does not protect against defects in the cord, plug, and receptacle. Continuous inspection and maintenance are required.

• A product with a dielectric housing, for example plastic, protects the user from shock if interior wiring contacts the housing. Immersion in water, however, can allow a leakage path that may be either high or low resistance. Handling the product with wet hands, in high humidity, or outdoors after a rain storm can be hazardous. The best indication of the safety of a double insulated tool is the Underwriters Laboratories (or other recognized testing laboratory's) label attached to the housing. The

357

UL listing is evidence that the tools meet minimum standards. A tool marked "double insulated," but without a UL label, may not be safe.

Double insulated tools and equipment should be inspected and tested as is all other electrical equipment. Remember, do not use double insulated power tools or equipment where water and a ground loop are present. They should not be used in any situation where dampness, steam, or potential wetness can occur, unless protected by a GFCI.

Equipment plugs

Attachment plugs are devices that are fastened to the end of a cord so that electrical contact can be made between the conductor in the equipment cord and the conductors in the receptacle. The plugs and receptacles are uniquely designed for different voltages and currents, so that only matching plugs will fit into the correct receptacle. In this way, a piece of equipment rated for one voltage/current combination cannot be plugged into a power system that is of a different voltage or current capacity (see Figure 13-12).

The polarized 3-prong plug is also designed with the equipment-grounding blade slightly longer than the two parallel blades. This provides equipment grounding before the equipment is energized. Conversely, when the plug is removed from the receptacle, the equipment-grounding pin is the last to leave, assuring a grounded case until power is removed. The parallel line blades may be the same width on some appliances since the 3-prong plug can only be inserted in one way.

Figure 13-12 illustrates the National Electrical Manufacturers Association (NEMA) standard plug and receptacle connector blade configurations. Each has been developed to standardize the use of plugs and receptacles for different voltages, amperes, and phases from 115 through 600 volts and from 10 through 60 amps, and for single- and three-phase systems.

BRANCH CIRCUIT AND EQUIPMENT TESTING METHODS

Testing branch circuit wiring

Branch circuit receptacles should be tested periodically. The frequency of testing should be established on outlet usage. In shop areas, quarterly testing may be necessary. Office areas may only need annual testing. A preventive maintenance program should be established. It is not unusual to find outlets as old as the facility. For some reason, a pop-

Figure 13-13. Typical receptacle circuit tester.

Figure 13-14. A receptacle tension tester.

ular belief exists that outlets never wear out. This is obviously false. For example, outlets take severe abuse from employees disconnecting the plug from the outlet by yanking on the cord. This can put severe strain on the contacts inside the outlet, as well as on the plastic face.

The electrical outlet is a critical electrical system component. It must provide for the appliance plug a strong mechanical connection that provides a continuous electrical circuit for each of the prongs. The receptacle must be electrically correct or serious accidents can result. For this reason, a three-step testing procedure is recommended. The first two steps can easily be done by most collateral duty safety inspectors. The third step is one that should be performed by electrical maintenance personnel prior to accepting contractor wiring jobs. Also, the third step should be done on any circuit where electrical maintenance has been performed. Some inspectors use the third step as a spot check of ground loop quality.

Step 1. Plug in a 3-prong receptacle circuit tester and note the combination of indicator lights (Figure 13-13). The tester checks the receptacle for proper connection of ground wire, correct polarity, or fault in any of the three wires. If these check out okay, proceed to the next test. If the tester indicates a wiring problem, contact electrical maintenance and

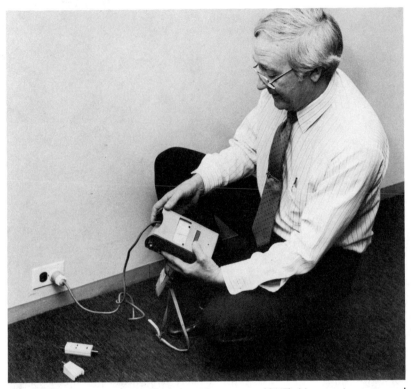

Figure 13-15. Using a ground loop impedance tester (GLIT). Note tension tester and circuit tester at lower left.

have it corrected as soon as possible. Retest after the problem is corrected.

Step 2. After the outlet has been found to be wired electrically correct, the receptacle contact tension test must be made. A typical tension tester is shown in Figure 13-14. The tension should be 8 oz or more. If it is less than 8 oz, have it replaced. The first receptacle function that loses its contact tension is usually the grounding contact circuit. This, because it is a critical circuit, illustrates the importance of checking for receptacle contact tension. In determining the frequency of testing, the interval must be based on receptacle usage. All electrical maintenance personnel should be equipped with receptacle checkers and tension testers. Other maintenance employees could also be equipped with testers and taught how to use them. In this manner, the receptacles can be tested before maintenance workers use them.

Step 3. The ground loop impedance tester (GLIT) should be used next. This step may be used by the electrical maintenance person whenever any electrical circuit is reworked or repaired. An electrical preventive maintenance program could be established to perform annual ground loop testing in high usage areas. The safety inspector can use the GLIT for spot checking (see Figure 13-15).

To perform this test, simply insert the 3-prong plug of the GLIT into the receptacle. Press the grooved portion of the red bar and observe the meter reading. As you have learned in previous sections, a reading of 1 ohm or less is required. Any reading of more than 1 ohm should be reported to electrical maintenance for analysis and corrective action.

WARNING: The GLIT must never be used to test a branch circuit with patient monitoring equipment in use.

The GLIT should not be used until steps 1 and 2 have been completed successfully. The tester will indicate the wiring fault. Prior to making the circuit operational, all wiring faults must be corrected and the circuit retested.

Testing extension cords

Many electrical accidents have been caused by faulty or incorrectly repaired extension cords. Many times the male plug on a 3-conductor extension cord becomes damaged and the repair person installs a 2-prong plug (Figure 13-16). This obviously means the receptacle end has no grounding path. It also means the plug can be inserted with correct polarity or reverse polarity.

Sometimes, the repair may be made in such a way that the hot and ground are interchanged, shown in Figure 13-17. This could happen on repair of the plug or the receptacle. In this configuration, when a grounded appliance is plugged into the extension cord, voltage will be applied to the appliance case. This could cause a dangerous or fatal electrical shock.

The same dangerous condition is illustrated in Figure 13-18. A repair was made replacing the broken 3-prong plug with a 2-prong plug. The repair person connected the white- and green-insulated conductors on one prong, then connected the black-insulated conductor to the other prong. Depending on how the plug was inserted in the outlet, in one mode, the case would be grounded; and in the other mode, the case would be energized.

With a "hot" case, the user would only have to find a ground loop to the source and a fatal shock could occur. Interestingly enough, the appliance would operate in either mode.

Figure 13-19 illustrates a repaired or a jury-rigged extension cord fabricated with a 3-prong plug and receptacle, but the connecting cord is only 2-conductor. This configuration would obviously show an open ground with a tester. Sometimes the cord may look like a three-conductor cord. So the tester should be used to make sure the extension cord is okay.

New extension cords must be tested before being put into service. Many inspectors have found that new extension cords have open ground or reverse polarity. Don't assume that even a new extension cord is good. *Test it.*

Extension cord testing and maintenance is extremely important. The extension cord serves to take the electrical energy from a fixed outlet or source and provides this energy at a remote location. The extension cord must be wired correctly or it can become the critical fault path.

Testing of extension cords must then use the same three steps of electrical outlet testing. These three steps are as follows:

Step 1. Plug the extension cord into an electrical outlet that has successfully passed the 3-step outlet testing procedure. Plug in any 3-prong receptacle circuit tester into the extension receptacle and note the combination of indicator lights. If the tester checks the extension as okay, proceed to the next step. If the tester indicates a faulty condition, return the extension cord to electrical maintenance for repair. Once the extension cord is correctly repaired and passes the 3-prong circuit tester test, the extension cord must be tested according to step 2.

Step 2. Plug a reliable tension tester into the receptacle end. The parallel receptacle contact tension and the grounding contact tension should check out at 8 oz or more. If the tension is less than 8 oz, the receptacle end of the extension cord must be repaired. As with fixed electrical outlets, the receptacle end of an extension cord loses its grounding contact tension first. This path is the critical human protection path and must be both electrically and mechanically in good condition.

Step 3. Once an extension cord has passed steps 1 and 2, the ground loop impedance tester may be used. The extension cord must be plugged into a properly connected outlet (as noted in Step 1). Plug the GLIT into the receptacle end of the extension cord. A reading of 1 ohm or less is required. A reading of more than 1 ohm means that the extension cord must be returned to maintenance for analysis and repair or replacement.

If GLIT is not available, use an ohmmeter to test the continuity from the U-shaped grounding pin to the grounding outlet hole in the receptacle end of the extension cord. This test is done with extension cord de-

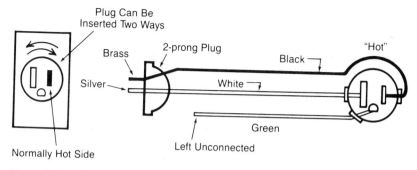

Figure 13-16. Three-conductor extension repaired with a 2-prong plug.

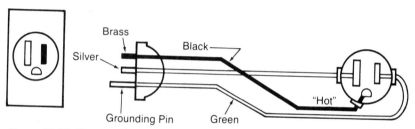

Figure 13-17. Three-conductor extension cord with hot and ground wires interchanged.

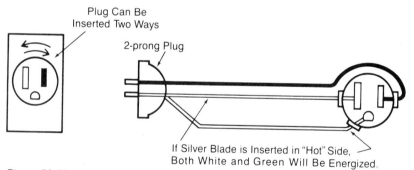

Figure 13-18. Three-conductor extension repaired with 2-prong plug that has the white and green wires tied together.

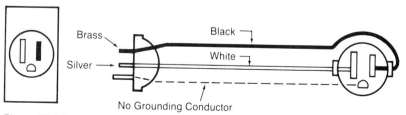

Figure 13-19. Extension cord with 3-prong plugs connected to 2-conductor cord.

energized. *The extension cord should not be plugged into an electrical outlet when using an ohmmeter. Damage to the ohmmeter could result.*

Testing plug- and cord-connected equipment

As part of the electrical system testing sequence, both outlet testing and extension cord testing have been discussed. The last element of the systems test is the cord- and plug-connected equipment.

The electrical inspector should be on the alert for jury-rigged repairs made on electric power tools and appliances. Many times a visual inspection will disclose 3-prong plugs with the grounding prong broken or cut off. Obviously, the grounding path to the equipment case has been destroyed. (The plug can now also be plugged into the outlet in the reverse polarity configuration.)

Double insulated equipment generally has a nonconductive case and will not be tested using the procedures in this section. Some manufacturers that have listed double insulation ratings may also provide the 3-prong plug in order to ground any exposed noncurrent-carrying metal using the grounding path conductor. In these cases, the grounding path continuity can be tested.

A common error from a maintenance standpoint is the installation of a 3-prong plug on a 2-conductor cord to the appliance. Obviously, there will be no grounding path if there are only 2 conductors in the cord. Anything can be jury-rigged, but normally the maintenance error is simply to hook up the black- and white-insulated conductors to the brass and silver screws respectively, and leave the third screw unconnected. Some hospital-grade plugs have transparent bases that allow visual inspection of the electrical connection to each prong. Even in this situation, you should still perform an electrical continuity test.

Field testing using an ohmmeter only. Maintenance shops may have commercial power tool testing equipment. It is not the purpose of this section to discuss this level of electrical equipment testing; it will review field testing procedures using an ohmmeter only. Many electrical power tool testers require the availability of electric power. The ohmmeter can be used in the field and in locations where electric power is not available or is not easily obtained. An additional safety feature is that the plug- and cord-connected equipment tests are made on de-energized equipment. Testing of de-energized equipment in wet and damp locations can also be done safely.

The plug- and cord-connected equipment test using a self-contained battery-powered ohmmeter is simple and straightforward. The two-step testing sequence that can be performed on 3-prong plug grounded equipment is as follows:

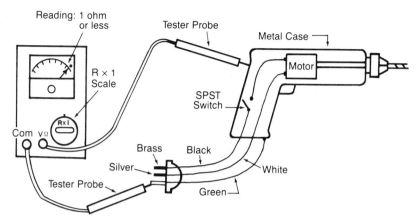

Figure 13-20. Continuity test for checking grounding path of appliance. Reading on ohmmeter should be less than one ohm.

Step 1. Ground pin-to-case test. Put the ohmmeter selector switch to the lowest scale (such as R × 1). Zero the meter. Place one test lead (tester probe) on the grounding pin of the de-energized equipment (Figure 13-20). While holding that test lead steady, take the other test lead and make contact with an unpainted surface on the metal case of the appliance. You should get a reading of less than 1 ohm. If the grounding path is open, the meter will indicate infinity. If no continuity, then the appliance must be tagged out and removed from service. If the appliance

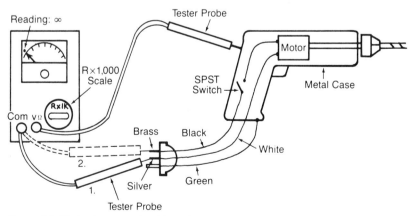

Figure 13-21. Leakage test should read near infinity on ohmmeter when checking appliance for current-to-case leakage.

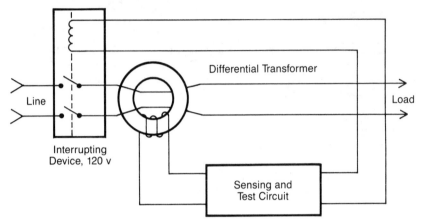

Figure 13-22. Circuit diagram for a ground fault circuit interrupter.

grounding path is okay, proceed to step 2.

Step 2. Appliance leakage test. Place the ohmmeter selector switch on the highest ohm test position (such as R × 1000). Zero the meter. Place one test lead on an unpainted surface of the appliance case, then place the other test lead on one of the plug's parallel blades. Observe the reading. The ideal is close to infinity. (If a reading of less than 1 meg-ohm is noted, return the appliance to maintenance for further testing.) With one test lead still on the case, place the other test lead on the remaining parallel blade and note the ohmmeter reading. A reading approaching infinity is required. (Again, anything less than one meg-ohm should be checked by a maintenance shop.) See Figure 13-21.

GROUND FAULT CIRCUIT INTERRUPTERS

Operational Theory

The ground fault circuit interrupter, or GFCI, (Figure 13-22) is a fast-acting device that senses small leakage current to ground and, in a fraction of a second, shuts off the electrical supply, thereby interrupting the fault current flow to ground. The GFCI, when placed between the electrical supply and the tool or appliance it serves, continually monitors the amount of current going to and from the tool or appliance along the normal path of circuit conductors. Whenever the amount going differs from the amount returning by a set trip level (for personnel protection, 5 ma), the GFCI interrupts the electrical power within 1/40th of a second. This difference in current is called ground fault leakage current. A person's body could be the ground fault leakage current path—in which case, the rapid response of the GFCI is fast enough to prevent electrocution. Protection provided by the GFCI is independent of the condition of the equipment grounding conductor. Thus, the GFCI can provide personnel protection even when the equipment grounding conductor path is broken, loose, or otherwise inoperative.

It is important to remember that a fuse or circuit breaker cannot possibly provide this kind of personnel protection. The fuse or circuit breaker will only trip or open the circuit, if a line-to-line fault occurs that is greater than the circuit protection device rating. For a 15 amp circuit-breaker, a short in excess of 15,000 ma would be required. The GFCI will trip if 0.005 amp starts to flow through a ground fault in a circuit it is protecting. This small amount of current flowing for the extremely short time required to trip the GFCI would not electrocute a person. Figure 13-23 illustrates a GFCI incorporated into a common wall receptacle. The obvious differences between a regular electrical duplex outlet and a GFCI outlet are the presence of the RESET and TEST buttons.

Be aware that a GFCI will not protect the user from line-to-line contact hazards. If a person was standing on an insulated surface and was holding a faulty appliance in one hand with fault from the "hot" (ungrounded conductor) to case, and reached with the other hand to unplug the appliance and contacted a faulty cord with an exposed grounded conductor, a line-to-line contact would be effected and the GFCI would not operate. Assuming a two-prong plug in this case, with no equipment grounding path, a serious shock could result.

The GFCI is not a substitute for good electrical safety work practices and maintenance. An equipment-grounding conductor inspection program should be used in addition to a GFCI program. GFCIs do not replace equipment grounding. They should be considered an additional personnel safety device for protection against the most common form of electrical shock and electrocution, the line ("hot" conductor) to ground fault.

GFCI uses

GFCIs should be used in dairies, breweries, canneries, steam plants, and construction sites; also inside metal tanks and boilers, or when workers are exposed to humid or wet conditions and come in contact with ground or grounded equipment. It is recommended that GFCIs be used in any work environment that is or can become wet, and in other areas that are highly grounded. In hospitals, where patients have sinks in their rooms with electrical outlets nearby, GFCIs should be used.

Off-the-job electrical safety should also be stressed. The *National*

Figure 13-23. Three types of ground fault circuit interrupters.
Left: circuit breaker with GFCI.
Top right: Receptacle-type.
Bottom right: Portable type.

Electrical Code requires GFCIs on 15 and 20 amp, 120 volt, outside receptacles, garage circuits, and bathrooms in residential occupancies. There have been several proposals to amend the NEC to require GFCIs in kitchens and laundries. The proposed change has merit.

Nuisance GFCI tripping

When GFCIs are used in construction activities, the GFCI should be located as close as possible to the electrical equipment it protects. Excessive lengths of electrical temporary wiring or long extension cords can cause ground fault leakage current to flow by capacitive and inductive coupling.

Other nuisance tripping may be due to one or several of the following items:

- Wet electrical extension cord to tool connections
- Wet power tools
- Outdoor GFCIs not protected from rain or water sprays
- Bad electrical equipment with case to hot conductor fault
- Too many power tools on one GFCI branch
- Resistive heaters

- Coiled extension cords (long lengths)
- Poorly installed GFCI
- Defective or damaged GFCI
- Electromagnetic-induced current near high-voltage lines
- Portable GFCI plugged into a GFCI-protected branch circuit.

Summary

A GFCI does not prevent shock. It merely limits the duration so that the heart is not affected. The shock lasts about 1/40 second (0.025 seconds) and can be intense enough to knock a person off a ladder or otherwise cause an accidental injury.

HAZARDOUS LOCATIONS

Overview of classes and divisions

This portion of the chapter provides an overview of hazardous locations. A summary of electrical equipment requirements is provided as a guide for inspection or system analysis of various hazardous locations. For more in-depth design and engineering requirements, refer to subpart S—Electrical, in the OSHA Standards (29 CFR 1910) and Chapter 5 of the *National Electrical Code* (NEC). Hazardous locations are areas where flammable liquids, gases, or vapors, combustible dusts, or other easily ignitable materials exist, or can exist accidentally, in sufficient quantities to produce an explosion or fire. In hazardous locations, specially designed equipment and special installation techniques must be used to protect against the explosive and flammable potential of these substances.

Hazardous locations are classified as Class I, Class II, or Class III, depending on what type of hazardous substance is or may be present. In general, Class I locations are those in which flammable vapors and gases may be present. Class II locations are those in which combustible dusts may be found. Class III locations are those in which there are ignitable fibers and flyings.

Each of these classes is divided into two hazard categories, Division 1 and Division 2, depending on the likelihood of a flammable or ignitable concentration of a substance. Division 1 locations are designated as such because a flammable gas, vapor, dust or easily ignitable material is normally present in hazardous quantities. In Division 2 locations, the existence of hazardous quantities of these materials is not normal, but they

TABLE 13-B. SUMMARY OF CLASS I, II, AND III HAZARDOUS LOCATIONS

| *CLASSES* | *GROUPS* | *DIVISIONS* | |
		1	*2*
I Gases, Vapors, and Liquids (Art. 501)	A: Acetylene B: Hydrogen, etc. C: Ether, etc. D: Hydrocarbons, Fuels, Solvents, etc.	Normally explosive and hazardous	Not normally present in an explosive concentration (but may accidentally exist)
II Dusts (Art. 502)	E: Metal dusts (conductive* and explosive) F: Carbon dusts (some are conductive,* and are all explosive) G: Flour, Starch, Grain, Combustible Plastic or Chemical Dust (explosive)	Ignitable quantities of dust normally is or may be in suspension, or conductive dust may be present	Dust not normally suspended in an ignitible concentration (but may accidentally exist). Dust layers are present.
III Fibers and Flyings (Art. 503)	Textiles, woodworkings, etc. (easily ignitable, but not likely to be explosive)	Handled or used in manufacturing	Stored or handled in storage (exclusive of manufacturing)

*Note: Electrically conductive dusts are dusts with a resistivity less than 10^5 ohm-centimeters.

Source: *An Illustrated Guide to Electrical Safety,* OSHA Pub. No. 3073.

occasionally exist either accidentally or when material in storage is handled. In general, the installation requirements for Division 1 locations are more stringent than for Division 2 locations.

Additionally, Class I and Class II locations are also subdivided into groups of gases, vapors, and dusts having similar properties. Table 13-B summarizes the various hazardous (classified) locations.

Equipment requirements

General-purpose electrical equipment can cause explosions and fires in areas where flammable vapors, liquids, and gases, and combustible dusts for fibers are present. Hazardous areas require special electrical equipment designed for the specific hazard involved. This includes explosion-proof equipment for flammable vapor, liquid, and gas hazards and dust-ignition-proof equipment for combustible dust. Other kinds of equipment are nonsparking equipment, intrinsically safe equipment, and purged and pressurized equipment.

Many pieces of electrical equipment include certain parts that arc, spark, or produce heat under normal operating conditions. For example, circuit controls, switches, and contacts may arc or spark when operated. Motors and lighting fixtures are examples of equipment that may heat up. These energy sources can produce temperatures high enough to cause ignition. Electrical equipment should not be installed in known or potentially hazardous environments unless absolutely necessary. However, when electrical equipment must be installed in these areas, the sparking, arcing, and heating nature of the equipment must be controlled.

Installations in hazardous locations must be: (a) intrinsically safe; (b) approved for the hazardous location; or, (c) of a type and design that provides protection from the hazards arising from the combustibility and flammability of the vapors, liquids, gases, dusts, or fibers present. Installations can have one or any combination of these options. Each option is described in the following paragraphs.

Intrinsically safe. Equipment and wiring approved as intrinsically safe are acceptable in any hazardous (classified) location for which they are designed. Intrinsically safe equipment is not capable of releasing sufficient electrical or thermal energy under normal or abnormal conditions to cause ignition of a specific flammable or combustible atmospheric mixture in its most easily ignitable concentration. To avoid contaminating nonhazardous locations, the passage of flammable gases and vapors through the equipment must be prevented. Additionally, all interconnections between circuits must be evaluated to be sure that an unexpected source of ignition is not introduced through other nonintrinsically safe equipment. Separation of intrinsically safe and nonintrinsically safe wiring may be necessary to make sure that the circuits in hazardous (classified) locations remain safe.

Approved for the hazardous (classified) location. Under this option, equipment must be approved for the class, division, and group of location. There are two types of equipment specifically designed for hazardous (classified) locations—explosion-proof and dust-ignition-proof. Explosion-proof apparatus is intended for Class I locations, while dust-ignition-proof equipment is primarily intended for Class II and III locations. Equipment listed specifically for hazardous locations should have a recognized testing laboratory's label or mark indicating the class, division, and group of locations where it may be installed. Equipment approved for use in a Division 1 location may be installed in a Division 2

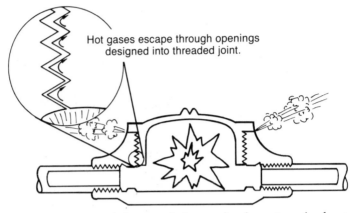

Hot gases escape through openings designed into threaded joint.

Figure 13-24. Threaded-joint explosion-proof enclosure is made of cast metal strong enough to withstand the maximum explosion pressure of a specific group of hazardous gases or vapors. Small openings designed into threaded joint cool hot gases as they escape.

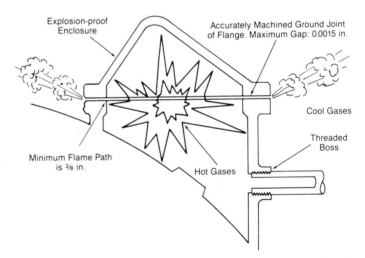

Explosion-proof Enclosure

Accurately Machined Ground Joint of Flange. Maximum Gap: 0.0015 in.

Cool Gases

Threaded Boss

Minimum Flame Path is ⅜ in.

Hot Gases

Figure 13-25. Ground-joint enclosure cools gases as they escape through the ground joint of flanges.

Both figures from OSHA Publication 3073, *An Illustrated Guide to Electrical Safety*

location of the same class and group.

Explosion proof. Generally, equipment installed in Class I locations must be approved as explosion-proof. Since it is impractical to keep flammable gases outside of enclosures, arcing equipment must be installed in enclosures that are designed to withstand an explosion. This minimizes the risk of having an external explosion that occurs when a flammable gas enters the enclosure and is ignited by the arcs. Not only must the equipment be strong enough to withstand an internal explosion, but the enclosures must be designed to vent the resulting explosive gases. This venting must ensure that the gases are cooled to a temperature below that of ignition temperature of the hazardous substance involved before being released into the hazardous atmosphere. There are two common enclosure designs: threaded-joint enclosures (see Figure 13-24) and ground-joint enclosures (see Figure 13-25). When hot gases travel through the small openings in either of these joints, they are cooled before reaching the surrounding hazardous atmosphere.

Other design requirements, for example, sealing, prevent the gases, vapors or fumes from passing into one portion of an electrical system from another. Motors, which typically contain sparking brushes or commutators and tend to heat up, must also be designed to provide for the control of internal explosions.

Dust-ignition-proof equipment. In Class II locations, equipment must generally be dust-ignition proof. Section 502-1 of the *National Electrical Code* defines dust-ignition proof as equipment, "enclosed in a manner that will exclude ignitable amounts of dust or amounts that might affect performance or rating and that, where installed and protected in accordance with the Code, will not permit arcs, sparks, or heat otherwise generated or liberated inside the enclosure to cause ignition of exterior accumulations or atmospheric suspensions of a specified dust on or in the vicinity of the enclosure."

Dust-ignition-proof equipment is designed to keep ignitable amounts of dust from entering the enclosure. In addition, dust can accumulate on electrical equipment, causing overheating as well as dehydration or gradual carbonization of organic dust deposits. Overheated equipment may malfunction and cause a fire. Dust that has carbonized is susceptible to spontaneous ignition or smoldering. Therefore, equipment must also be designed to operate below the ignition temperature of the specific dust involved even when blanketed. The shape of the enclosure must be designed to minimize dust accumulation when fixtures are out of reach of normal housekeeping activities, e.g., lighting fixture canopies.

In Class II hazardous locations, there are three groups—E, F, and G. (See Table 13-B.) Special designs are required to prevent dust from entering the electrical equipment enclosure. Assembly joints and motor shaft openings must be tight enough to prevent dust from entering the enclosure. In addition, the design must take into account the insulating effects of dust layers on equipment and must make sure that the equipment will operate below the ignition temperature of the dust involved. If conductive combustible dusts are present, the design of equipment must take the special nature of these dusts into account.

In general, explosion-proof equipment is not designed for, and is not acceptable for use in Class II locations, unless specifically approved for use in such locations. For example, since grain dust has a lower ignition temperature than that of many flammable vapors, equipment approved for Class I locations may operate at a temperature that is too high for Class II locations. In contrast, equipment that is dust-ignition proof is generally acceptable for use in Class III locations, since the same design considerations are involved.

Safe design for the hazardous location. Under this option, equipment installed in hazardous locations must be of a type and design that provide protection from the hazards arising from the combustibility and flammability of vapors, liquids, gases, dusts, or fibers. The employer has the responsibility of demonstrating that the installation meets this requirement. Guidelines for installing equipment under this option are contained in the *National Electrical Code* in effect at the time of installation of that equipment. Compliance with these guidelines is not the only means of complying with this option; however, the employer must demonstrate that his installation is safe for the hazardous (classified) location.

Equipment marking

Approved equipment must be marked to indicate the class, group, and operating temperature range (based on 40 C ambient temperature) in which it is designed to be used. Furthermore, the temperature marked on the equipment must not be greater than the ignition temperature of the specific gases or vapors in the area. There are, however, four exceptions to this marking requirement.

• First, equipment that produces heat, but that has a maximum surface temperature of less than 100 C (or 212 F), is not required to be marked with operating temperature range. The heat normally released from this equipment cannot ignite gases, liquids, vapors, or dusts.

• Second, any permanent lighting fixtures that are approved and marked for use in Class I, Division 2 locations do not need to be marked to show a specific group. This is because these fixtures are acceptable for use with all of the chemical groups for Class I, that is, for Groups A, B, C, and D.

• Third, general-purpose equipment, other than lighting fixtures, considered acceptable for use in Division 2 locations, does not have to be

TABLE 13-C. INSPECTION CHECKLIST OF COMMON ELECTRICAL DEFICIENCIES

NEC–NFPA 70-1984 Reference	SUBJECT	OSHA STANDARD 29 CFR 1910
110-3	Examination, Identification, Installation and Use of Equipment	.303(b)
110-8	Wiring Methods	_____
110-12	Workmanship	_____
110-14(b)	Splices	.303(c)
110-16	Working Space	.303(g)(1)
110-17	Guarding of Live Parts	.303(g)(2)
110-22	Disconnect and Circuit Identification	.303(f)
200-11	Reverse Polarity	.304(a)(2)
210-7	Grounding-Type Receptacles	.305(j)(2)*
210-8	Ground Fault Circuit Interruptors	_____
250-42	Grounding Fixed Equipment—General	.304(f)(5)(iv)
250-43	Grounding Fixed Equipment—Specific	.304(f)(5)(i)(ii), (iii)(vi)
250-45	Equipment Connected by Cord and Plug	.304(f)(5)(v)
250-51	Effective Grounding Path	.304(f)(4)
250-59	Methods of Grounding Cord-Connected Equipment	.304(f)(6)
400-7	Flexible Cord Uses Permitted	.305(g)(1)(i)
400-8	Flexible Cord Uses Not Permitted	.305(g)(1)(iii)
400-9	Splices	.305(g)(2)(ii)
400-10	Pull at Joints and Terminals	.305(g)(2)(iii)

*Partial coverage

labeled according to class, group, division, or operating temperature. This type of equipment does not contain any devices that might produce arcs or sparks and, therefore, is not a potential ignition source. For example, squirrel-cage induction motors without brushes, switching mechanisms, or similar arc-producing devices are permitted in Class I, Division 2 Locations (see NEC Section 501-8 (b)); therefore, they need no marking.

• Fourth, for Class II, Division 2 and Class III Locations, dust-tight equipment (other than lighting fixtures) is not required to be marked. In these locations, dust-tight equipment does not present a hazard so it need not be identified.

COMMON ELECTRICAL DEFICIENCIES

To aid the new or even experienced inspector to do a more thorough job of electrical inspecting, a listing of common electrical deficiencies is provided; see Table 13-C. This is a compilation of federal and private-sector inspection experience and primarily concerns personnel safety. The average inspector should become adept at recognizing the items in this listing.

Table 13-C summarizes the deficiencies and provides a cross-reference to the *National Electrical Code*—1984 edition, and the OSHA Standard paragraph. Each electrical deficiency noted in the table is discussed below. Consult the *National Electrical Code Handbook* for additional details.

110-3—Examination, identification, installation and use of equipment. Operational characteristics to provide practical employee and facility safeguarding are provided. Suitability, mechanical strength of enclosures, insulation, heating and wiring effects, proper use of listed or labeled equipment, and any other factor that would provide personnel safeguarding should be evaluated.

110-8—Wiring methods. This paragraph states that only wiring methods included in the *National Electrical Code* are recognized as suitable. Using junction boxes designed for permanent wiring as receptacle boxes on the end of an extension cord would not meet this NEC requirement.

110-12—Mechanical execution of work. This reference requires that electrical equipment must be installed in a professional manner. All openings to electrical equipment must be effectively closed to prevent metal objects from entering the enclosure and causing arcing or shorting of the supply conductors. Personnel protection is also provided.

110-14—Splices. Splices are required to be joined by suitable splicing devices or by brazing, welding, or soldering with a fusible metal or alloy. The three important elements of a good splice are mechanical strength, electrical quality, and insulation. These factors must be at least equivalent to the conductors being spliced.

110-16—Working space around electrical equipment (600 volts, nominal, or less). This paragraph requires that sufficient access and working space be provided and maintained around all electrical equipment. Electrical equipment clearance space must never become storage space. It may be necessary to make the space obvious by using floor stripes or other methods.

110-17—Guarding of live parts (600 volts, nominal or less). This reference requires that the live parts of electrical equipment operating at 50 volts or more shall be guarded against accidental contact. Approved enclosures are recommended. When the alternatives of location are used, employee safeguarding should be carefully evaluated.

110-22—Identification of disconnecting means. This reference requires that the disconnecting means for motors and appliances, and each service, feeder, or branch circuit, be legibly marked at its point of origin. Many times, a contractor will install new wiring and leave circuit breaker panels with blank circuit identification cards. Motor disconnects must also be obvious, or specific labels should be placed on the box to identify what it electrically disconnects.

200-11—Polarity of connections. No grounded conductor shall be attached to any terminal or lead that reverses designated polarity. This can usually be determined by using the 3-prong circuit tester.

210-7—Receptacles and cord connectors. This reference requires receptacles installed on 15- and 20-amp branch circuits to be of the grounding type. Older nongrounded receptacles should be evaluated and proper branch circuits installed.

210-8—Ground-fault protection for personnel. Whereas this paragraph applies to dwelling units and hotels and motels, a general statement after paragraph (a) (3) states "Such ground-fault circuit interrupter protection may be provided for other circuits, locations, and occupancies, and, where used, will provide additional protection against line-to-ground shock hazard." The NEC is a minimal standard and the inspector should look for potential line-to-ground shock hazards and recommend GFCIs accordingly.

250-42—Grounding fixed equipment—General. This paragraph requires that exposed noncurrent carrying metal parts of fixed equipment be grounded.

250-43—Grounding fixed equipment—Specific. Switchboard frames, motor frames, motor controller enclosures, elevators, cranes, electric signs, and other specific electrical equipment are required to have exposed noncurrent-carrying metal parts grounded.

250-45—Equipment connected by cord and plug. This paragraph requires that exposed noncurrent-carrying metal parts of cord- and plug-connected equipment (listed) shall be grounded.

250-51—Effective grounding path. The path to ground from circuits, equipment, and conductor enclosures shall: (*a*) be permanent and continuous: (*b*) have capacity to conduct safely any fault current likely to be imposed on it; and (*c*) have sufficiently low impedance to limit the voltage to ground and to facilitate the operation of the circuit protective devices in the circuit. If portable power tools had the equipment grounding prong broken off, requirement 250-41(1) would not be met since the grounding path was not continuous. Extension cords being used with defects in the grounding path would also not meet this requirement. If the grounding path tested out at more than 10 ohms, obviously 250-51(3) would not be met.

250-59—Cord- and plug-connected equipment. Noncurrent carrying metal parts of cord- and plug-connected equipment may be grounded by several methods. These methods include by means of the metal enclosure of the conductors supplying the equipment, a grounding conductor in the flexible cord, or a separate flexible wire or strap.

400-7—Uses permitted (flexible cords and cables). Specific applications where flexible cords and cables are permitted include pendants, wiring of fixtures, portable lamps and appliances, and stationary equipment that may have to be moved frequently. Other uses are specified including prevention of transmission of noise or vibration.

400-8—Uses not permitted (flexible cords and cables). Flexible cords must not be used as a substitute for fixed wiring. Flexible cord must not be used to provide power to appliances by running through holes in walls, ceilings, or floors, or through windows or doorways.

400-9—Splices. This paragraph prohibits the use of flexible cords that have been spliced or taped.

400-10—Pull at joints and terminals. This reference requires that flexible cords be connected to devices and to fittings so that tension will not be transmitted to joints or terminal screws.

The above list is not intended to be comprehensive, but rather identifies the most obvious electrical safety problem areas. The description included with each reference is, of necessity, brief; to find the exact requirements, consult the *National Electrical Code.*

Electrical extension cords

Electrical extension cords are used in manufacturing maintenance, construction, and even in office operations. Defective, worn, or damaged extension cords have been the cause of electrical equipment damage, injury, fire, and even deaths. Often the rush to meet schedules, cost considerations, or the red tape entailed to obtain new cords result in jury-rigged cords being fabricated and used. Other problems of overloading, cutting off the grounding prong, and repairing a damaged receptacle with a two-slot receptacle (on a 3-conductor cord) endanger the user. The following safety criteria should be strictly observed and used for training and inspecting:

• A visual and electrical inspection should be made of the extension cord each time it is used. Cords with cracked or worn insulation or damaged ends should be removed from service immediately. Cords with the grounding prong missing or cut off must also be removed from service.

• Extension cords that are procured must be listed by a recognized testing laboratory (such as Underwriters Laboratories Inc.). If extension cords are fabricated, only qualified electricians shall do the work. The use of jury-rigged receptacles fabricated from J-boxes is prohibited. Only listed ends and cords shall be used when fabricating extension cords.

• Only the 3-conductor grounding-type extension cords shall be used.

• Power extension cords on the floor create a stumbling or tripping hazard. They should be suspended over aisles or work areas, where possible. The cord should be suspended in such a way that it will not be struck by other objects or by material being handled or moved.

• When cords must cross passageways, whether vehicular and/or personnel, the cord shall be protected and identified with appropriate warning. Cords will only be used in this manner for temporary or emergency use. They must never be used through doorways that serve as exits, hazardous storage areas, smoke barriers, or fire barriers.

• Extension cords shall be of continuous length without splices or taps.

• Extension cords must not be connected or disconnected until all electrical load has been removed from the outlet end.

• Extension cords used in hazardous locations must be approved for the applicable hazardous location. (See details under the heading, Hazardous Locations—Equipment requirements, earlier in this chapter.)

• When the extension cord is not in use, it should be disconnected and neatly stored. A cord holder is recommended.

• Never overload an extension cord (electrically). If it is hot to the touch, have it and/or the appliance being used checked by a qualified person to determine the problem. The wire size may be too small for the cord length and amperage required.

• Extension cords must not be draped over hot surfaces, such as steam lines, space heaters, radiators, or other heat sources.

• Extension cords must not be run through standing water, on wet floors, or in other wet areas.

• Extension cords for outdoor use should be listed and marked for outdoor use.

SAFEGUARDS FOR HOME APPLIANCES

When using electrical appliances, especially when children are present, safety precautions should always be followed. Appliance manufacturers provide written procedures for safe use of their appliances. Their instructions should be read by adults and children alike. Safety precautions must also be understood. The following list is provided to form the basic common sense baseline to safe handling, use, and storage of electrical appliances in the home.

DANGER
To reduce risk of electrocution:

• Always unplug appliance after using.

• Do not use any electrical appliance while bathing. For warning labels, see Figure 13-26.

• Do not place or store appliance where it can fall or be pulled into a tub or sink.

• Do not place or drop any appliance into water or other liquid.

• Do not reach for an appliance that has fallen into water; unplug the electrical cord immediately.

WARNING
To reduce the risk of burns, electrocution, fire, or injury:

• An appliance should never be left unattended when plugged in.

• Close supervision is necessary when an appliance is used by, on, or near children or invalids.

• Use the appliance only for its intended use as described in the manufacturer's manual. Do not use attachments that are not recommended by the manufacturer.

• Never operate an appliance if it has a damaged cord or plug, if it is not working properly, if it has been dropped or damaged, or dropped into water. Return the appliance for examination, electrical or mechanical adjustment, and repair.

• Keep the cord away from heated surfaces.

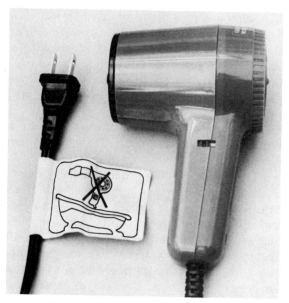

Figure 13-26. When hair dryers carry labels warning against using them in bathtubs, labels should not be removed.

• Never block the air openings of the appliance or place it on a soft surface, such as a bed or couch, where the air openings may be blocked. Keep the air openings free of lint and hair.

• Never use while sleeping.

• Never drop or insert any object into any appliance opening.

• Do not use outdoors or operate appliances where aerosol (spray) products are being used or where oxygen is being administered.

• Small electrical appliances do not lend themselves to normal repair procedures. Therefore, repairs should not be attempted by the consumer.

• Keep your appliance in a cool dry place and out of the reach of children. When storing your unit, do not put any stress on the line cord and the point where it enters the unit. Excessive stress could cause the cord to fray or to break.

SAFETY PROGRAM POLICY AND PROCEDURES

Policy

Each facility should have an electrical safety program policy. The policy should cover the responsibilities of all employees including supervisors, employers, and the specialists who inspect, install, and maintain the electrical systems and equipment. The policy should stress management's concern with and support of the policy. Individuals who are responsible for applying and enforcing the electrical policy should have standards of performance that include periodic assessment of their electrical safety performance.

In addition to policy and implementation procedures, an electrical safety program should also include four basic areas of concern—training and education, hazardous condition reporting, work practices, and housekeeping. The National Safety Council Data Sheets (Table 13-D) provide an excellent source of technical and training information to support all electrical safety programs. Additionally, the professional electrical person responsible for installing, repairing, and maintaining electrical equipment and systems should be familiar with NFPA 70E-1983, *Electrical Safety Requirements for Employee Workplaces*. Suggestions for improving any electrical safety program would include the aforementioned and additional items in this section. All employees must recognize and report unsafe electrical equipment. The following discussion provides suggestions for assuring that these responsibilities are carried out effectively.

Supervisory responsibilities

Training and education. Supervisors should be given training courses to assist them in discharging their electrical safety program responsibilities for their specific administrative functional areas. If any employees under their supervision use, install, repair, or modify electrical equipment and/or appliances, the supervisor must know that they have first received the proper training. The supervisor should also monitor employees and assess their performance against the established facility safety program policy.

Hazardous condition reporting. A written procedure promoting the observation and reporting of electrical hazards should be implemented. It is suggested that an employee-recognition program also be included in conjunction with the hazard-reporting program. This will give recognition to employees who help locate electrical hazards so that the hazards may be eliminated in a timely manner.

Work practices. The supervisor is responsible for employees following safe work practices. A sample of suggested work practices is included here under Employee Responsibilities, next employees should be rated on their thoroughness in following safe work practices. The supervisor should also be familiar with OSHA regulations as they apply to that portion of the workplace under his or her responsibility.

**TABLE 13-D. NATIONAL SAFETY COUNCIL DATA SHEETS
THAT PERTAIN TO ELECTRICAL SAFETY PROGRAMS**

Data Sheet No.	Title
I-316	Low-voltage Extension Light Cords and Systems
I-385	Electric Cords and Fittings
I-498	Live Line Tools
I-515	Temporary Electric Wiring for Construction Sites
I-544	Electrical Switching Practices
I-546	Maintenance of Electric Motors for Hazardous Locations
I-547	Static Electricity
I-579	Applications of Electric Plug and Receptacle Configurations
I-607	Direct Buried Utility Cables
I-624	Electrical Controls for Mechanical Power Presses
I-635	Lead-Acid Storage Batteries
I-636	GFCIs for Personnel Protection
I-641	Electrical Testing Installations
I-644	Treatment of Extraneous Electricity in Electric Blasting
I-657	Underground Residential Distribution of Electricity
I-660	Electrical Safety in Health Care Facilities
I-675	Electric Hand Saws, Circular Blade Type
I-684	Equipment Grounding

Housekeeping. It is important that housekeeping be monitored closely by the supervisor. Space problems always present challenges. Areas around electrical equipment, such as circuit breaker panels, disconnects, and fixed power tools, should be kept free from stored items, debris, and liquids or other material that would create slippery floors. When hazards of this nature are reported to the supervisor, they should be logged in and necessary work orders issued for corrective action.

Employee responsibilities

Training and education. It's obvious that employees should receive training relating to electrical safety work practices and equipment operation. Any changes in job duties will require additional safety training. Many accidents are caused by employees simply lacking the knowledge of equipment or its operation. Sometimes blame for accidents is placed on employees when, in reality, specific training was not provided to the employee.

Hazardous condition reporting. Employees should always be encouraged to report unsafe equipment, conditions, or procedures immediately. A team effort is required by both the employee and the supervisor. Getting equipment repaired should receive priority, even if it requires rescheduling a process or project. It may seem too obvious to stress, but under no condition should electrical equipment that is causing electrical shocks to employees be used to get a job done. The electrical safety policy, below, should be followed, and deviations reported at once.

Work practices. Employees are responsible for following safe work practices, procedures, and safety policies established by their employers. The employee should also be familiar with OSHA regulations as they apply to workplace safety.

Housekeeping. In the process of getting a job done, employees should be observant and report conditions that could cause virtually any type of accident. Good housekeeping requires all employees to observe activities that could cause electrical shock hazards. Using electrical equipment that is not properly grounded in areas that have water on the floor can create shock hazards. Storing tools or other materials around electrical panels or equipment disconnects can create hazards for others, as well as prevent immediate access to electrical equipment for disconnection in an emergency. Cleaning tools and electrical equipment with solvents can create health and physical safety problems. Discarding these rags into trash could create fire hazards as well.

Electrical safety policy

Supervisors must know all facets of their employers' electrical safety policy well and assure that the employees are also knowledgeable of these expectations. These suggested items can be of help:

- Power equipment should be plugged into wall receptacles with power switches in the off position.

- Unplug electrical equipment by grasping the plug and pulling. Do not pull the cord or drape the power cord on pipes, radiators, or any other metal objects.

- Check for frayed, cracked, broken, or exposed wires and cords before plugging in equipment. Report any such hazards, also damaged or loose parts.

- Flexible AC power-line cords should not exceed 10 ft (0.9 m) in length.

- "Cheater plugs," extension cords, or jury-rigged equipment should not be used.

- Home-type electrical equipment or appliances should not be used if not properly grounded.

- Personnel should know the location of electrical circuit breaker panels that control equipment and lighting. Circuits must be identified. Equipment disconnects must also be identified.

- Temporary or permanent storage of materials will not be allowed within 3 ft of any electrical panel or electrical equipment.

- When defective equipment is discovered or identified, it shall be immediately tagged and removed, repaired, or replaced.

- Any electrical equipment causing shocks or that has high leakage potential, must be tagged with a DANGER—DO NOT USE label or equivalent.

ELECTRICAL DISTRIBUTION SYSTEM REVIEW

The electrical distribution system should be designed, installed, operated, and maintained in a safe and reliable manner. The facility should be analyzed to determine that the following requirements are documented and followed, as regards the overall electrical system operation and maintenance. The checklist below can be used to determine compliance with OSHA and *National Electrical Code* requirements. If there are any NO answers, professional engineering or other appropriate services should be obtained.

- There is a program of preventive maintenance and periodic inspection to assure that the electrical distribution system operates safely and reliably. Inspections and corrective actions are documented:

Yes _____ No _____

- The facility identifies components of the electrical distribution system to be included in the program. Consideration is given to reliability of receptacles, electrical feeds and transformers, and so forth.

Yes _____ No _____

385

• There is an up-to-date set of documents that indicate the distribution of the controls for partial or complete shut-down of each electrical system.

Yes _____ No _____

• Electrical maintenance and operating personnel are given appropriate job training.

Yes _____ No _____

• The capacity of electrical feeds and transformers is adequate for the electrical demands of the facility.

Yes _____ No _____

• Any special-purpose electrical subsystems or devices installed are maintained as required.

Yes _____ No _____

• The electrical distribution system is designed with enough receptacles and circuits to power devices used in each area of the facility.

Yes _____ No _____

SUMMARY

This chapter contains basic information about how to recognize electrical hazards. Use of the Loop concept will aid the supervisor to analyze potential as well as actual electrical hazards. It also allows for the proper analysis of shock hazards reported by employees and for deciding on the corrective action to eliminate them. The effectiveness of electrical inspections will be enhanced though a better understanding of testing and recognizing conditions that can cause electrical shock.

Testing methods also allow employees to locate defective equipment and tag it for repair and/or replacement. Electrical program policy gives the supervisor basic elements that can be used for monitoring effectiveness of the electrical hazard recognition program. Additional assistance can be obtained through the National Safety Council data sheets.

Chapter 14

Fire
Safety

An effective fire protection program must, in the long run, depend on you, the supervisor. Although the overall program may be under the director of safety, fire protection, security, engineering, or maintenance—each supervisor has a direct interest in, and responsibility for, the program.

Fire protection is a science in itself. This manual obviously cannot cover all aspects of fire prevention and extinguishment, but this chapter does present condensed, basic information to help supervisors conduct fire-safe operations. More specialized information is available; sources are cited throughout this chapter.

BASIC PRINCIPLES

Supervisors, because of their knowledge of day-to-day operations, are in an excellent position to determine necessary fire prevention measures. You should be able to recognize the need for specific fire protection equipment and take the necessary steps to see that such equipment is provided. Supervisors must become thoroughly familiar with the use of fire equipment suited to their particular operations.

Departmental housekeeping is also under the supervisor's control. Make sure that your employees follow safe housekeeping practices with regard to preventing fires (see Figure 14-1). Continuous training in fire-safe work procedures, regular inspections of work areas, and close supervision of the employee job performance are requisites of a successful fire prevention program.

Although fire protection equipment may be maintained by others, the ultimate responsibility for the safety of employees, materials used in processes, and production equipment rightfully belongs to supervision.

Figure 14-1. It is apparent from this photo of a fire in a building under construction that better housekeeping could probably have averted it.

Understanding fire chemistry

Supervisory expertise, in regard to fire prevention and control problems, begins with an understanding of basic fire chemistry. Every ordinary fire (one that does not produce its own oxygen supply) results when a substance (fuel) in the presence of air (oxygen) is heated to a critical temperature, called its "ignition temperature."

This important concept is best illustrated by the fire triangle. This diagram (Figure 14-2, on facing page) is an excellent visual aid. The absence of any one of the sides of the fire triangle can eliminate the possibility of a fire.

• *Oxygen removal*—Taking oxygen away is difficult since a fire needs about the same amount for burning (percentage of oxygen in the air) that humans need for breathing. In some cases, oxygen levels can be reduced below the minimum percentage needed for combustion by purging and inerting the atmosphere in closed containers or processing sys-

Figure 14-2. Normally, the elements of oxygen and fuel are always present; therefore, eliminating and/or controlling heat (ignition) sources is of primary importance in preventing fires.

tems. Firefighting foam extinguishes fires by smothering (and cooling) action.

• *Fuel Removal*—In many cases, it is neither possible nor practical to remove all fuels (solids and liquids). However, try to keep the quantity of stored combustible materials at a minimum. Storage containers must be placed in orderly piles with adequate aisle space. Good housekeeping, with the frequent removal of waste materials, is also a crucial factor in keeping a small, accidental fire from rapidly spreading.

• *Heat source control*—Eliminating and controlling heat sources also are elementary steps in fire prevention. The use of welding and cutting equipment, torches, heating equipment, spark-producing equipment, electricity, and smoking materials can be controlled by conscientious workers. The time to stop a fire is *before it starts*—keep heat and ignition sources away from fuel.

Table 14-A lists the major sources of ignition that cause industrial fires, gives examples in each case, and suggests preventive measures. A following section, Causes of Fire, discusses each in detail.

For many years, the principle of extinguishment centered around the fire triangle and the removal of any of its three sides, representative of three components.

Remodeling the fire triangle into a fire pyramid (Figure 14-3) presents a more realistic concept of extinguishment because it also takes into consideration the chemical chain reaction needed to sustain combustion. The pyramid has four sides or faces, one for each of the ways to extinguish a fire. Because each face is directly adjacent to and connected to the other, a pyramid accurately represents their interdependency. Removing one or more of the faces will put out the fire.

TABLE 14-A. HOW TO CONTROL SOURCES OF IGNITION IN INDUSTRIAL FIRES

SOURCES OF IGNITION (Descending order of frequency)	EXAMPLES	PREVENTIVE MEASURES
Electrical equipment	Electrical defects, generally due to poor maintenance, mostly in wiring, motors, switches, lamps, and hot elements.	Use only approved equipment. Follow *National Electrical Code*. Establish regular maintenance.
Friction	Hot bearings, misaligned or broken machine parts, choking or jamming of material, poor adjustment.	Follow a regular schedule of inspection, maintenance, and lubrication.
Foreign substances	Tramp metal, which produces sparks when struck by rapidly revolving machinery (a common cause in textile industry).	Keep foreign material from stock. Use magnetic or other separators to remove tramp metal.
Open flames	Cutting and welding torches (chief offenders). Gas and oil burners. Misuse of gasoline torches.	Follow established welding precautions. Keep burners clean and properly adjusted. Do not use open flames near combustibles.
Smoking and matches	Dangerous near flammable liquids and in areas where combustibles are used or stored.	Smoke only in permitted areas. Use prescribed receptacles. Make sure matches are out.
Spontaneous ignition	Deposits in ducts and flues. Low-grade storage. Industrial wastes. Oily waste and rubbish.	Clean ducts and flues frequently. Remove waste daily. Isolate stored materials likely to heat spontaneously.
Hot surfaces	Exposure of combustibles to furnaces, hot ducts or flues, electric lamps or irons, hot metal being processed.	Provide ample clearances, insulation, air circulation. Check heating apparatus before leaving it unattended.
Combustion sparks	Rubbish-burning, foundry cupolas, furnaces and fireboxes, and process equipment.	Use incinerators of approved design. Provide spark arresters on stacks. Operate equipment carefully.
Overheated materials	Abnormal process temperatures. Materials in driers. Overheating of flammable liquids.	Have careful supervision and competent operators, supplemented by well-maintained automatic temperature controls.
Static electricity	Dangerous in presence of flammable vapors. Occurs at spreading and coating rolls or where liquid flows from pipes.	Ground equipment. Use static eliminators. Humidify the atmosphere.

Adapted from *Factory Mutual Record*

Figure 14-3. The "fire pyramid" shows the four components necessary to produce ordinary burning. Remove any one, and the fire goes out.

Consequently, to extinguish a fire, the following steps should be taken:

1. Exclude the air by smothering (for example, by shutting the lid over a tank of burning solvent or by covering it with foam) or by dilution (replacing the air with an inert gas such as carbon dioxide).

2. Remove or seal off the fuel by mechanical means, or divert or shut off the flow of liquids or gases that are fueling the fire.

3. Cool the burning material below its ignition point with a suitable cooling agent (hose streams or water extinguishers).

4. Interrupt the chemical chain reaction of the fire (using dry chemical or Halon extinguishing agents).

Once people understand the fire pyramid and its practical application, they will be more alert to, and aware of, fire prevention and control methods.

Determining fire hazards

To best contribute to a fire protection program, the supervisor must, first, identify the existing fire problems and, second, take action to solve

Figure 14-4. Be sure that fire protection measures are adequate and are in ready condition to handle any of the existing fire problems that you have identified.

them. To do this, seek the best technical advice available from experts.

If you have not already done so, draw up an inspection checklist that specifies as many places, materials procedures, classes of equipment, conditions, and circumstances where fire hazards are likely to exist, as possible. Under such category names, used as headings on the list, specific fire-safe practices that must be followed should be written down precisely. Personnel with responsibilities relative to the practices and installations might be specified, for example, machine operator, electrician, maintenance crew, or porter. (See discussion of inspections in Chapter 8.)

When, after a tour of inspection, you have made brief notations beside each of the described safe practices, you will have a detailed picture of how many or how few fire protection measures are actually in effect. You will be able to spot neglected precautions readily. The sample fire prevention checklist shown in Figure 14-5 can serve as a guide, but you should make your own and include special points for conditions that are not listed in this broad example. A fuller discussion is given in the next session.

When conducting an inspection, some points may have previously escaped your notice. Unless you have had considerable experience in fire prevention, you should ask your superior and your company's fire safety personnel, or the fire insurance company engineer, to help you conduct inspections and to make recommendations for eliminating fire hazards. If company policy permits, you usually can ask the local fire department for help too.

It is important that all fire inspections be made with a critical eye. Every shortcoming should be listed. You should not hedge in listing certain hazards with the thought that they might reflect poor supervision. Omission of a pertinent detail might result in a fire later; such an outcome would reflect poor supervision.

The National Fire Protection Association (NFPA) *Inspection Manual*, a pocket-sized book, is a valuable reference for the beginner, as well as the experienced inspector. It covers both common and special fire hazards, their elimination or safeguarding, and human safety in all types of properties.

Informing the work force

Periodic inspections are an important part of any fire protection program. However, your responsibilities, under a complete program, extend further. As you become acquainted with actual or potential fire hazards, and after all physical corrections possible have been made, you should familiarize the personnel in your department with each hazard and explain how it relates to them individually.

You should inform your people of your own and management's desire for fire-safe operations. You should call their attention to all the physical safeguards that have been provided to prevent injury and destruction by fire. You should stress to individuals the precautions necessary for their jobs—the safe practices that complement mechanical protection.

If the individuals on the job understand the reason for precautions and the possible consequences if not followed, they are much more likely to comply. Patient explanation and persistent enforcement, in every case, are important fire prevention duties of the supervisor.

FIRE PREVENTION CHECKLIST

ELECTRICAL EQUIPMENT

- ☐ No makeshift wiring
- ☐ Extension cords serviceable
- ☐ Motors and tools free of dirt and grease
- ☐ Lights clear of combustible materials
- ☐ Safest cleaning solvents used
- ☐ Fuse and control boxes clean and closed
- ☐ Circuits properly fused or otherwise protected
- ☐ Equipment approved for use in hazardous areas (if required)
- ☐ Ground connections clean and tight and have electrical continuity

FRICTION

- ☐ Machinery properly lubricated
- ☐ Machinery properly adjusted and/or aligned

SPECIAL FIRE-HAZARD MATERIALS

- ☐ Storage of special flammables isolated
- ☐ Nonmetal stock free of tramp metal

WELDING AND CUTTING

- ☐ Area surveyed for fire safety
- ☐ Combustibles removed or covered
- ☐ Permit issued

OPEN FLAMES

- ☐ Kept away from spray rooms and booths
- ☐ Portable torches clear of flammable surfaces
- ☐ No gas leaks

PORTABLE HEATERS

- ☐ Set up with ample horizontal and overhead clearances
- ☐ Secured against tipping or upset
- ☐ Combustibles removed or covered
- ☐ Safely mounted on noncombustible surface
- ☐ Not used as rubbish burners
- ☐ Use of steel drums prohibited

HOT SURFACES

- ☐ Hot pipes clear of combustible materials
- ☐ Ample clearance around boilers and furnaces
- ☐ Soldering irons kept off combustible surfaces
- ☐ Ashes in metal containers

SMOKING AND MATCHES

- ☐ "No smoking" and "smoking" areas clearly marked
- ☐ Butt containers available and serviceable
- ☐ No discarded smoking materials in prohibited areas

SPONTANEOUS IGNITION

- ☐ Flammable waste material in closed, metal containers
- ☐ Flammable waste material containers emptied frequently
- ☐ Piled material, cool, dry, and well ventilated
- ☐ Trash receptacles emptied daily

STATIC ELECTRICITY

- ☐ Flammable liquid dispensing vessels grounded or bonded
- ☐ Moving machinery grounded
- ☐ Proper humidity maintained

HOUSEKEEPING

- ☐ No accumulations of rubbish
- ☐ Safe storage of flammables
- ☐ Passageways clear of obstacles
- ☐ Automatic sprinklers unobstructed
- ☐ Premises free of unnecessary combustible materials
- ☐ No leaks or dripping of flammables and floor free of spills
- ☐ Fire doors unblocked and operating freely with fusible links intact

EXTINGUISHING EQUIPMENT

- ☐ Proper type
- ☐ In proper location
- ☐ Access unobstructed
- ☐ Clearly marked
- ☐ In working order
- ☐ Service date current
- ☐ Personnel trained in use of equipment

Figure 14-5. Sample checklist serves as guide for supervisor in drawing up an inspection list. It should be reviewed regularly to keep it up-to-date.

CAUSES OF FIRE

The supervisor should be alert for potential causes of fire. The principal ones shown in Table 14-A, on page 390, are discussed below.

Electrical equipment

Electrical motors, switches, lights, and other electrical equipment exposed to flammable vapors, dusts, gases, or fibers present special problems. The NFPA's code and standard pamphlets designate the standard governing a particular hazard and indicate the special protective equipment needed. The *National Electrical Code*®, ANSI/NFPA 70, (the NEC), gives the specifications for the protective equipment required. Substandard substitutions or replacements must not be made.

Haphazard wiring, poor connects, and temporary repairs must be brought up to standard. Fuses should be of the proper type and size. Circuit breakers should be checked to see that they have not been blocked in the closed position (which results in overloading), and to see that moving parts do not stick.

Cleaning electrical equipment with solvents can be hazardous because many solvents are flammable and toxic. It is, of course, of utmost importance to use the safest cleaning solvents available.

A solvent may be safe with respect to fire hazards, but unsafe with respect to health hazards. For example, carbon tetrachloride is nonflammable, but its vapors are extremely toxic. Before a solvent is used, therefore, it is necessary to determine both its toxic and flammable properties.

A satisfactory solvent is inhibited methyl chloroform, or a blend of Stoddard solvent and perchloroethylene. These solvents are commonly used in industry since they are relatively nonflammable and have a relatively high Threshold Limit Value with respect to toxicity. (See Chapter 6, "Industrial Hygiene and Noise Control," for a discussion.)

Many of the cleaning solvents encountered in industry are not single substances, but mixtures of different chemicals, usually marketed under nondescriptive trade names or code numbers. Currently, there are no absolutely safe cleaning solvents. Therefore, before any commercially available solvent is used, it is essential to know its chemical composition. Without such knowledge, the hazards cannot be evaluated, nor the required safety controls be used. (Again, see Chapter 6.)

Friction

Overhead transmission bearings and shafting—where dust and lint accumulate in locations, such as grain elevators, cereal and textile mills, and plastic, woodworking, and metalworking plants—are frequent sources of ignition. Bearings should be kept lubricated so that they do not run hot, and accumulations of combustible dust should be removed as part of a rigid housekeeping routine. Pressure lubrication fittings should be kept in place, and oil holes of bearings should be kept covered to prevent combustible dust and grit from entering the bearings and causing overheating.

Special fire-hazard materials

Flammable liquids are not really a *cause* of fire, although they are often referred to as such. More correctly, they are contributing factors because a spark or minor source of ignition, which might otherwise be harmless, can result in a fire or explosive forces when flammable vapors, given off by the liquids and then mixed with air, are present.

Almost all industrial plants use flammable liquids. It is thus the responsibility of the supervisor to see that the safe practices are followed in the storage, handling, and dispensing of such liquids.*

Because all flammable liquids are volatile, they are continually giving off invisible vapors.

• Flammable liquids should be stored in, and dispensed from, approved safety containers equipped with vapor-tight, self-closing caps or covers.

• Flammable liquids should be used only in rooms or areas having adequate and, if possible, positive ventilation. If the solvent hazard is especially high, solvents should be used only in places having local exhaust ventilation.

• When highly volatile and dangerous liquids are being used, a warning placard or sign should be placed near the operation, notifying other personnel and giving warning that all open flames are hazardous and must be kept away.

• Vapors of flammable liquids are heavier than air and will seek the floor or other lowest possible level where they may not be easily detected. This mandates adequate ventilation and the elimination of ignition sources.

• Wherever flammable liquids are used, it is essential that ignition sources—open flames and sparks—be eliminated or alternative preventative measures taken.

---

*Detailed information is contained in NSC Data Sheet I-532 on the storage, handling, and use of small quantities of flammable liquids. NFPA 30, *Flammable and Combustible Liquids*, published by the National Fire Protection Association, is also an excellent source of detailed information on this subject.

There are many other types of materials that must be kept isolated to prevent fire. For example, some chemicals, such as sodium and potassium, decompose violently in the presence of water, evolve hydrogen, and ignite spontaneously. Yellow phosphorus may also ignite spontaneously on exposure to air. Other combinations, too numerous to mention here, may react with the evolution of heat and produce fire or explosion—in some cases, without air or oxygen being present. These materials must, of course, be handled in a special manner. NFPA 49, *Hazardous Chemicals Data*, lists about 100 such items and provides information on unusual shipping containers, fire hazards, life hazards, storage, firefighting phases, and additional data, where applicable. (Check NFPA for other publications relating to hazardous materials.)

Some materials, principally the ethers, during long periods of storage may become unstable and eventually explosive. In such cases, using the oldest stock first contributes to both fire safety and good housekeeping—and seeing that this principle is followed is part of the supervisor's job.

Whatever materials are used or stored in the department, it is important to know whether they explode when heated, react with water, heat spontaneously, yield hazardous decomposition products, or otherwise react in combination with other materials.

The supervisor's best course of action is to obtain detailed information and be guided accordingly. The company's fire insurance carrier can be asked to help.

Welding and cutting

Welding and cutting operations should ideally be conducted in a separate, well-ventilated room with a fire-resistant floor. This safety measure is not, of course, always practical.

If welding and cutting must be carried on in other locations, these operations must not be performed until (*a*) the areas have been surveyed for fire safety by persons who know the hazards; (*b*) the necessary precautions to prevent fires have been taken; and (*c*) a permit has been issued. This permit must not be stretched to cover an area or an item or a time not originally specified—no matter how small the job may seem, or how little time may be required to do it. (For more information on hot work permit programs, see NSC's *Accident Prevention Manual for Industrial Operations—Engineering and Technology* volume.)

If welding must be done over wood floors, they should be swept clean, wet down, and then covered with fire-retardent blankets, metal, or other noncombustible covering. Pieces of hot metal and sparks must be kept from falling through floor openings onto combustible materials.

Sheet metal or flame-resistant canvas or curtains should be used around welding operations to keep sparks from reaching combustible materials. Welding or cutting should not be permitted in or near rooms containing flammable or combustible liquids, vapors, or combustible dusts. These operations should not be done in or near closed tanks that contain—or have contained—flammable liquids, until the tanks have been thoroughly drained and purged, and tested free from flammable gases or vapors.

No welding or cutting should be done on a surface until combustible coverings or deposits have been removed. It is important that combustible dusts or vapors not be created concurrently during the welding operation. Fire extinguishing equipment should be provided at each welding or cutting operation. A water pump tank unit is recommended for Class A fires, and a dry chemical extinguisher for Class B and C fires; both are discussed later in the chapter. Where extra-hazardous conditions cannot be completely eliminated or protected by isolation, the additional back-up protection of a fire hose should be considered.

A watcher should be stationed to prevent stray sparks or slag from starting fires, or to immediately extinguish fires that do start while they are small, no matter how many precautions are taken. The area should be under fire surveillance for at least one-half hour after welding or cutting has been completed because many fires are not detected as soon as they ignite.

Open flames

No open flames are allowed in or near spray rooms or spray booths. Occasionally, it may be necessary to do indoor spray-painting or spray-cleaning outside of a standard spray room or booth. In such cases, adequate ventilation must be provided and possible ignition sources, such as spark-producing devices and open flames, must be eliminated.

Gasoline, kerosene, or alcohol torches when used, should be placed so that their flames are at least 18 in. (46 cm) from wood surfaces. They should not be used in the presence of dusts or vapors, near flammable or combustible liquids, paper, excelsior, or similar material. Torches should never be left unattended while they are burning.

Portable heaters

Gasoline furnaces, portable heaters, and salamanders always present a serious fire hazard. Their use should be discouraged as much as possible. Upright models of fuel oil salamanders have been involved in numerous accidents. It is recommended that they be replaced with other types of low-profile heaters.

Fuel used in portable heaters should be restricted to liquified petroleum gas, coal, coke, fuel oil, or kerosene. The area in which they are burned must be well ventilated, since the products of combustion contain carbon monoxide.

All these heating devices require special attention with respect to clearances and mounting. A clearance of 2 ft (0.6 m) horizontally and 6 ft (1.8 m) vertically should be maintained between a heater and any combustible material.

If coal or coke is used, the heater should be supported on legs 6 in. (15 cm) high or on 4 in. (10 cm) of tile blocks and set on a noncombustible surface.

Combustible material overhead should be removed or shielded by noncombustible insulating board or sheet material with an air space between it and the combustible material. A natural-draft hood and flue of noncombustible material should be installed.

As a fire precaution, each unit must be carefully watched. Heaters should be shut down and allowed to cool off before being refueled. Coal and coke salamanders should not be moved until the fire is out.

All portable heating devices should be equipped with suitable handles for safe and easy carrying. They also should be secured or protected against tipping or upsetting.

The most serious fire hazard occurs when heaters are improvised from old steel drums or empty paint containers, with scrap wood, tar paper, or other waste used as fuel. This practice should be prohibited.

Rubbish should be burned in rubbish burners with wire mesh-screen covers. The burners should be placed at least 50 ft (15 m) from combustible stores and equipment. In view of stringent antipollution laws, make sure that no violation of clean air ordinances is being committed. Portable heaters must not be used to burn rubbish.

Hot surfaces

If possible, smoke pipes from heating appliances should not pass through ceilings or floors. If a smoke pipe must be run through a combustible wall, a galvanized double-thimble with clearance, equal to the diameter of the pipe and ventilated on both sides of the wall, must be provided.

Soldering irons must not be placed directly upon wood benches or other combustibles. Rests, which will prevent dangerous heat transfer, can be used instead.

Smoking and matches

Management usually has a specific policy about cigarette/cigar/pipe smoking. Smoking areas, as well as no smoking areas, must be clearly defined and marked off with conspicuous signs. Reasons for these restrictions must be clearly explained to the employees, and rigid enforcement must be maintained *all* of the time.

Fire-safe, metal containers should be provided in places where smoking is permitted. Safety ash trays in offices, lounges, and lunchrooms should be installed. If carrying matches is prohibited, special lighter equipment should be kept in service in smoking areas.

"No smoking" areas, especially when they include stairways and other out-of-the-way places, should be watched for evidence of discarded smoking materials.

Spontaneous combustion

Spontaneous heating is a chemical action in which there is a slow generation of heat from the oxidation of a fuel. When adjacent materials provide sufficient insulating properties, the heating process can continue until spontaneous ignition occurs. Conditions leading to spontaneous ignition exist where there is sufficient air for oxidation, but not enough ventilation to carry away the heat generated by the oxidation. Any factor that accelerates the oxidation while other conditions remain constant obviously increases the likelihood of such ignition.

Materials like unslaked lime and sodium chlorate are susceptible to spontaneous ignition, especially when wet. Such chemicals should be kept cool and dry, away from combustible material. Rags and waste saturated with linseed oil, paint, or petroleum products often cause fires because no provision is made for the generated heat to escape. By keeping such refuse in air-tight metal containers with self-closing covers (see Figure 14-6), the oxygen supply is limited and a fire will quickly extinguish itself. These containers should be emptied daily.

The good precautions against spontaneous ignition are total exclusion of air or good ventilation. The former is practicable with small quantities of material through the use of air-tight containers. Ventilation can best be assured by storing material in small piles or by turning over a large pile at regular intervals.

To determine the progress of spontaneous heating, temperatures should be taken in the interior of a mass of material. Various locations within the mass should be checked. Exterior temperatures are not likely to provide a good index.

Static electricity

Sparks due to static electricity may be a hazard wherever there are flammable vapors or gases or combustible dusts. Precautions against static electricity are required in such areas. Static charges result from

Figure 14-6. Check containers for oily waste to make sure the lid closes snugly against the top.

friction between small particles or from the contact and separation of two unlike substances, one or both of which are nonconductive.

Static charges can be produced in many ways—by the flow of gasoline through a nonconductive hose, or by the passing of dry and powdered materials down a nonconductive chute, or through the action of a machine.

It is impossible to prevent the generation of static electricity under the above circumstances, but the hazard of static sparks can be avoided by preventing the accumulation of static charges. One or more of the following methods can be used:

- Grounding

Figure 14-7. Grounds and bonds should be constructed of bare flexible wire in order to prevent broken wires from being concealed. Wires must be attached securely.

- Bonding
- Maintaining the relative humidity at a predetermined level
- Ionization of the atmosphere.

A combination of these methods may be advisable in some instances where the accumulation of static charges presents a severe hazard. The National Fire Protection Association's Publication No. 77, *Recommended Practice on Static Electricity,* gives additional information and guidance on this subject.

Grounding is accomplished by mechanically connecting a conductive machine or vessel (in which the generation of static may be a hazard) to ground by means of a low resistance conductor. Another method is to make the entire floor and structure of the building conductive so that all equipment in contact with it will be grounded. When the first method is used, the supervisor must check the continuity of the ground circuit. Connections must be clean and the conductor unbroken. (See Figure 14-7.) With the second method, it is important that the floor be free of wax, oil, or other insulating films.

As many people have learned from walking across a rug and then touching a doorknob or other conductive object, the human body can also carry an electric charge. The use of conductive shoes with a floor of conductive material is a common means of controlling this hazard by the grounding method. The parts of such shoes that are designed to render them conductive should be made of nonferrous metal. As an added measure of safety, the conductive flooring may be made of spark-resistant metal. Ferrous contacts increase the risk of friction sparks.

When humidity is low, the hazard of static is greatest. When humidity is high, the moisture content of the air serves as a conductor to drain off static charges as they are formed. Where humidification is utilized to prevent the accumulation of static charges, the supervisor must see that an effective relative humidity—usually 60 to 70 percent—is maintained. However, the minimum humidity required for safety may vary over a considerable range under different conditions, and under some conditions the static charge cannot be controlled by humidification. Engineering authorities should be consulted.

When air is ionized, it has sufficient conductivity to prevent static accumulation. Ionization is produced by electrical discharges, radiation from radioactive substances, or gas flames. Only an electrostatic neutralizer designed for use in hazardous locations should be used; otherwise, the neutralizer may itself be a source of ignition of flammable vapor or dust. Neutralizers must be kept in good condition.

FIRE-SAFE HOUSEKEEPING

Good housekeeping is another important part of an effective fire protection program. It is imperative that the supervisor maintain a positive attitude with the crew and enforce housekeeping rules at *all* times. Each person should be held personally responsible for preventing the accumulation of unnecessary combustible materials in the work area. Workers should be held accountable for their areas at the end of their shift. Here are the precautions to take.

• Combustible materials should be present in work areas only in quantities required for the job, and should be removed to a designated, safe storage area at the end of each work day.

• Quick-burning and flammable materials should be stored only in designated locations. Such locations always should be away from ignition sources and have special fire extinguishing provisions. Covered metal receptacles are best.

- Vessels or pipes containing flammable liquids or gases must be airtight and have no leaks. Any spills should be cleaned up immediately.

- Workers should be required to guard against their clothing's becoming contaminated with flammable liquids. If contamination does occur, these individuals must be required to change their clothing before continuing to work.

- Passageways and fire doors should be kept clear and unobstructed.

- Material must never obstruct automatic sprinklers or be piled around fire extinguisher locations or sprinkler and standpipe controls. To obtain proper distribution of water, a minimum of 18 in. (46 cm) of clear space is required below sprinkler deflectors. However, clearance of 24 to 36 in. (60 to 90 cm) is recommended. If there are no sprinklers, clearance of 3 ft (0.9 m) between piled material and the ceiling is required to permit use of hose streams. Double these distances when stock is piled more than 15 ft (4.5 m) high.

Be sure to check applicable codes, especially *Code for Safety to Life from Fire in Buildings and Structures,* ANSI/NFPA 101.

ALARMS, EQUIPMENT, AND EVACUATION

A fully effective fire protection program, of course, includes fire extinguishment. Despite the best laid plans, a fire may occur. Whenever a fire occurs, it is important to:

1. Turn in the fire alarm right away—regardless of the size of the fire.

2. Attempt to extinguish or control the fire with appropriate fire extinguishing equipment.

Fire alarms

Plants in areas where municipal fire departments are available usually have an alarm box close to the plant entrance or located in one of their buildings. Others may have auxiliary alarm boxes, connected to the municipal fire alarm system, at various points in the plant. Another system often used is a direct connection to the nearest fire station that may register water flow alarms in the sprinkler system, be activated by fire detectors, or be set off manually. In some cases, the telephone may be the only means for signaling a fire alarm.

Whatever the alarm system used, all employees should be carefully

Figure 14-8. Fire alarm boxes and firefighting equipment must be clearly marked and free of obstruction. Fire doors must be kept clear.

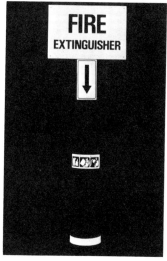

instructed in (a) how to report a fire, (b) when, and (c) where. These three items are extremely important since many fires progress beyond control simply because someone did not know how, when or where to give the alarm.

What about extinguishers?

The supervisor should, of course, be aware of what class or classes of fires might be expected. Before the employees can effectively combat fires in their incipient stages, they must be familiar with and understand the four classes of fires. Briefly, they are:

ORDINARY
COMBUSTIBLES

Class A—Fires in ordinary combustible materials, such as wood, paper, cloth, rubber, and many plastics, where the quenching and cooling effects of water or of solutions containing large percentages of water are of prime importance.

FLAMMABLE
LIQUIDS

Class B—Fires in flammable liquids, greases, oils, tars, oil-base paints, lacquers, and similar materials, where smothering or exclusion of air, and interrupting the chemical chain reaction are most effective. This class also includes flammable gases.

ELECTRICAL
EQUIPMENT

Class C—Fires in or near live electrical equipment, where the use of a nonconductive extinguishing agent is of first importance. The material that is burning is, however, either Class A or Class B in nature.

COMBUSTIBLE
METALS

Class D—Fires that occur in combustible metals, such as magnesium, lithium, and sodium. Special extinguishing agents and techniques are needed for fires of this type.

Each of the fire extinguishers in the department or at a job location should have on it a plate identifying the class of fire for which it is intended (see Figure 14-9), operating instructions, and servicing instructions. The data plate should have the identifying symbol/name of a recognized testing facility to indicate that the unit has been listed or approved. Equipment that does not bear an approval label should be brought to the attention of management. Only listed or approved equip-

Figure 14-9. Picture-symbol labels promulgated by the National Association of Fire Equipment Distributors show class of fire that a specific extinguisher is meant for. The symbols shown here would be on a Class A extinguisher (for extinguishing fires in trash, wood, or paper). Symbol at left is in blue. Because this extinguisher is not meant for use on a Class B or C fires, these two illustrations (center and right) are in black, with a diagonal red line through them. A Class A/B extinguisher would have the first two illustrations in blue; the third would be black with a red diagonal. For use on a Class B/C, the last two would be in blue; on a Class A/B/C, all three would be in blue.

ment should be furnished.*

The information on these data plates can assist the supervisor in teaching employees how to operate the extinguishing equipment. The supervisor must see that every worker knows the important details about each of the fire extinguishing agents provided for use in the particular job area or shop. (See Table 14-B) Fire extinguisher manufacturers and distributors can be contacted for additional training materials. Local fire departments may be able to provide training assistance. Information on selection, installation, use, inspection, and maintenance can be obtained from the National Fire Protection Association.**

Normally, the location and installation of portable fire extinguishers, fire blankets, stretchers, and other fire safety equipment at strategic places about the plant, shop, or job site are the responsibility of higher management. However, the supervisor should know the location of units in his area, and should be quick to recommend relocation of them or obtaining additional units when such changes will afford more adequate protection.

---

*"Fire Protection Equipment List" (Underwriters Laboratories Inc., Northbrook, Ill. 60062). "Approved Equipment for Industrial Fire Protection" (Factory Mutual Research Corp., Norwood, Mass. 02062).

**NFPA Publication 10, *Portable Fire Extinguishers,* is an authorative source of information and should be made available to all supervisors for reference use.

TABLE 14B. FIRE EXTINGUISHER SELECTION CHART

	CLASS A					CLASS A/B	CLASS B/C			
	WATER TYPES		MULTIPURPOSE DRY CHEMICAL		HALON 1211	AFFF FOAM	CARBON DIOXIDE	DRY CHEMICAL TYPES		HALON 1211
	STORED PRESSURE*	PUMP TANK*	STORED PRESSURE	CARTRIDGE OPERATED	STORED PRESSURE	STORED PRESSURE*	SELF EXPELLING	STORED PRESSURE	CARTRIDGE OPERATED	STORED PRESSURE
SIZES AVAILABLE	2½ gal	2½ and 5-gal	2½-30 lb ALSO (Wheeled 150-350 lb)	5-30 lb ALSO (Wheeled 50-350 lb)	9 to 22 lb	2½ gal	5-20 lb ALSO Wheeled 50-100 lb	2½-30 lb ALSO Wheeled 150-350 lb	4-30 lb ALSO Wheeled 50-350 lb	2 to 22 lb
HORIZONTAL RANGE (APPROX.)	30 to 40 ft	30 to 40 ft	10-15 ft (Wheeled-15-45 ft)	10-20 ft (Wheeled-15-45 ft)	14 to 16 ft	20 to 25 ft	3-8 ft (Wheeled-10 ft)	10-15 ft (Wheeled-15-45 ft)	10-20 ft (Wheeled-15-45 ft)	10 to 16 ft
DISCHARGE TIME (APPROX.)	1 min.	1 to 2 min.	8-25 seconds (Wheeled-30-60 s)	8-25 seconds (Wheeled-20-60 s)	10 to 18 seconds	50 seconds	8-15 seconds (Wheeled-8-30 s)	8-25 seconds (Wheeled-30-60 s)	8-25 seconds (Wheeled-20-60 s)	8 to 18 seconds

	CLASS/A/B/C			CLASS D
	MULTIPURPOSE DRY CHEMICAL		HALON 1211	DRY POWDER
	STORED PRESSURE	CARTRIDGE OPERATED	STORED PRESSURE	CARTRIDGE OPERATED
SIZES AVAILABLE	2½-30 lb ALSO Wheeled 150-350 lb	5-30 lb ALSO Wheeled 50-350 lb	9 to 22 lb	30 lb ALSO Wheeled 150-350 lb
HORIZONTAL RANGE (APPROX.)	10-15 ft (Wheeled-15-45 ft)	10-20 ft (Wheeled-14-45 ft)	14-16 ft	5 ft (Wheeled-15 ft)
DISCHARGE TIME (APPROX.)	8-25 seconds (Wheeled-30-60 s)	8-25 seconds (Wheeled-20-60 s)	10 to 18 seconds	20 seconds (Wheeled-150 lb to 70 s, 350 lb 1¾ min.)

*Must be protected from freezing

Courtesy of the National Association of Fire Equipment Distributors

Figure 14-10. Employees are being trained to use extinguishers not only so they won't panic if an emergency arises, but also so they will use the most effective techniques.

From NSC *Air Transport Newsletter*

Extinguishers must not be blocked by material or equipment, and signs indicating their location must remain legible and conspicuous. (See Figure 14-8.) Many companies have found that marking the area of the floor directly under the fire extinguisher is an excellent way to keep employees from placing obstructions in front of the equipment.

The location of extinguishers can be identified by painting the housing, wall area, column, or other support of the extinguisher with standard fire-protection red. Fire protection equipment itself, such as sprinkler system piping, is sometimes painted or marked in red.

The supervisor should make sure that each worker knows the location of the nearest unit and that each individual is impressed with the importance of keeping areas around extinguisher units clear.

It is advisable for the supervisor to schedule fire drills during which workers use extinguishers applicable to their particular work areas. (See Figure 14-10.) The company's safety professional or fire chief, the insurance company's safety engineer, or the local fire department representative will assist in conducting such drills.

Every organization should have a specific program for periodic inspection and servicing of portable fire extinguishing equipment. This routine work is usually outside the scope of the department supervisor and/or maintenance personnel. However, you can do some things to assist in this program. For example, during regular department inspections, you should doublecheck each data card to determine when each extinguisher was last inspected and serviced. Management should be notified when inspection dates have been missed or are outdated. If the seal is broken, the pressure gage reads below normal, or another unsatisfactory condition is observed, the extinguisher may not operate properly. These conditions should also be promptly reported.

Fire extinguishers must meet the following requirements:

- Be kept fully charged and in their designated places.

- Be located along normal paths of travel where practical.

- Not be obstructed or obscured from view.

- Not be mounted higher than 5 ft (1.5 m) (to the top of the extinguisher) if they weigh 40 lb (18 kg) or less. If heavier than 40 lb, extinguishers must not be mounted higher than 3 1/2 ft (1 m). There shall be a clearance of at least 4 in. (10 cm) between the bottom of the extinguisher and the floor.

- Be inspected by management or a designated employee, at least monthly, to make sure that they are in their designated places, have not been tampered with or actuated, and do not have corrosion or other impairment.

- Be examined at least yearly and/or recharged or repaired to ensure operability and safety. A tag must be attached to show the maintenance or recharge date and signature or initials of the person performing the service.

- Be hydrostatically tested. Extinguisher servicing agencies should be contacted to perform this service at appropriate intervals.

- Be selected on the basis of type of hazard, degree of hazard, and area to be protected.

- Be placed so that the maximum travel (walking) distances between extinguishers, unless there are extremely hazardous conditions, do not exceed 75 ft (23 m) for Class A extinguishers or 50 ft (15 m) where Class B extinguishers are used for hazardous area protection. The travel distance requirement does not apply when Class B extinguishers are used for spot-hazard protection.

Follow up for fire safety

Frequent inspections of the area, correction of hazardous conditions, and indoctrination of the workers in fire prevention and extinguishment measures are still not enough to assure a fire-safe work area.

Figure 14-11. Fire brigade members undergo training in simulated environment requiring use of self-contained breathing apparatus.

Survivair Division of U.S. Divers

The supervisor must follow up relentlessly. Constant alertness to assure a continuous fire-safe attitude on the part of personnel and their observance of safe work practices is required.

It is recommended that fire prevention and extinguishment be the subject of frequent safety talks between the supervisor and each worker. Fire prevention and extinguishment should also be discussed in safety meetings so that each worker will be fully indoctrinated that it is a definite part of the overall departmental safety program.

Fire brigades

Many plants and construction job sites have organized fire brigades. The organization of such a brigade would not normally be the responsibility of the supervisors. However, they should be well enough acquainted with the form and activities of a fire brigade to carry out the responsibilities likely to occur in the brigade's operations.

In some fire brigades, a supervisor or foreman is designated a brigade chief or company captain. Whether or not the supervisors are named to this job, they should know the fire brigade assignments for which their workers are responsible.

On the basis of this information, the supervisor should then organize the work in his or her department so that brigade members may attend brigade training and drills as designated by their brigade chief. (See Figure 14-11.)

Regardless of the role in fire brigade organization, the supervisor should be familiar with the location and operation of the following items in and adjacent to his department—standpipes and valves, sprinkler system valves, electric switches for fans and lights, fire-alarm boxes and telephones, fire doors, and emergency power for equipment and/or lighting.

Enclosed stairway doors are especially important. For life safety, they must be kept closed, and it is a direct and serious responsibility of the supervisor to see that they are kept closed. Such doors are provided to keep out smoke, combustion gases, and heat from the exit passageways and stairs, as well as to help prevent the rapid spread of fire. Doors should be equipped with self-closing devices and not blocked in the open position. In those cases where the exitway is frequently used, doors may be held in the open position with fire-actuated detectors that will automatically release the door.

To gain familiarity with the items listed above, the supervisor should take every opportunity to accompany the fire inspector on inspection tours to learn how the items operate.

Whether or not supervisors operate this equipment will depend upon the particular situation and specific policy and procedure in the plant. In some instances, it may be desirable for supervisors to operate this equipment if they know the system thoroughly. However, some cases in the records of the National Fire Protection Association indicate that it may be extremely dangerous for anyone to operate the equipment without full knowledge of it. Operation at the wrong time or inaccurate operation might seriously affect the protective measures.

Special fire protection problems

Construction. When building construction is going on at an existing plant site, fire protection problems are compounded. The plant department supervisor and the construction supervisor should work together in determining the hazards in each field of operations and in maintaining awareness of firefighting limitations. Definite fire prevention steps should be taken.

Such practices as use of temporary wiring and of portable heaters and gasoline engines that have to be refueled on the spot are likely to be

Figure 14-12. Whenever a sprinkler system must be shut down, special precautions must be taken to assure maximum fire safety during the protection impairment. All preliminary work is completed, extra firefighting equipment is set out, and firefighting units are informed as toi what areas will be without sprinkler protection. One procedure that is used requires that a bright red tag be attached to the sprinkler valve when it is closed and that the insurance carrier be notified. The work is completed as quickly as possible, at which time the tag is removed and the insurance company notified that service is restored. To make certain that the valve is left wide open, it is tested and then locked in the open position. All sprinkler valves should be checked regularly to make sure they are not unlocked, tampered with, or even shut.

From NSC *Fertilizer and Agricultural Chemical Newsletter*

required in the construction activities. Manufacturing processes, normally not hazardous, may become so under these conditions. The supervisor for the plant department should see that employees are aware of additional ignition sources created by the construction operations. The construction supervisor should inform workers of the additional exposures present from the plant activity.

When the construction work involves plumbing, the water supply available for fire extinguishment may be decreased or need to be shut off. To offset this possible shortage of water, additional auxiliary fire extinguishing equipment should be available. Either temporary hose lines or water tank trucks can be used.

Sprinkler system shutdown. Whenever a sprinkler system must be shut down, special precautions must be taken to assure maximum fire safety during the protection impairment. All preliminary work is completed, extra firefighting equipment is set out, and firefighting units are informed as to what areas will be without sprinkler protection. One procedure requires that a bright red tag be attached to the sprinkler valve when it is closed (see Figure 14-12) and that the insurance carrier be notified. The work is completed as quickly as possible, at which time the tag is removed and the insurance company notified that service is restored. To make certain that the valve is left wide open, it is tested and then locked in the open position. All sprinkler valves should be checked regularly to make sure they are not unlocked, tampered with, or shut.

Whenever the sprinkler system must be shut down for alterations or repairs, the supervisor and the maintenance people should do their best to plan such operations so that they can be handled outside normal working hours. If work must be done during the interval of danger, special precautions may have to be taken, such as having hose lines laid and furnishing extra patrols.

Some plant and construction supervisors have made a practice of attending each other's safety meetings in order to benefit from an exchange of their respective points of view and to learn about each other's problems. This joint approach to common exposures is recommended.

Radioactive materials. The use of radioactive materials for various purposes in manufacturing processes has become more common, and their presence requires special understanding and control in the event of fire or other emergency.

In view of the potential contamination hazards to employees, supervisors in the areas or departments having radioactive materials should be thoroughly familiar with the procedures to be followed in such areas or departments in case of fire or other emergency, and should rigidly en-

Figure 14-13. General emergency and/or fire alarm system is part of industrial security system. By use of closed circuit television, one officer can monitor several different areas at once.

force compliance with that procedure. Access to the contaminated area following the emergency should be prohibited until authorized personnel have recovered the sources of radiation and have determined that the contamination is below the safe levels.

Valuable information on this problem can be secured from the Nuclear Regulatory Commission, 1717 H. Street, N.W., Washington, D.C. 20555.

Evacuation

Prevention of fire is the primary objective of any fire protection program. Nevertheless, each program must include provisions to assure the safety of employees in the event of a fire. Essential among such provisions are those that will chart and facilitate the quick and orderly evacuation of personnel. Security personnel must be included in the overall plan (see Figure 14-13).

You can do much to prepare for the safety of employees in the event of a serious fire. As a matter of routine, you should make sure that each man and woman knows the evacuation alarms, both primary and alternate exit and escape routes, as well as what to do and where to be during and after an evacuation.

You should make sure that each person knows that he or she, upon being alerted, must proceed *at a fast walking pace*—not a run—to an assigned exit or, if it is blocked, to the nearest clear one. Day in and day out, you should emphasize that the exit routes and any fire doors must be kept unobstructed. Furthermore, you should make it clear that your employees, upon a signal for evacuation, shut down machines before leaving.

Such essential steps in emergency procedures will best be instilled by periodic fire drills. If company policy assigns the responsibility to you, plan and conduct practice evacuations at regular intervals. You should also do everything possible to integrate fire emergency training with plant-wide drills and the company's overall evacuation plan. When it is impossible to hold drills, you should give oral instructions regarding evacuation conduct, and distribute printed information to all employees.*

REVIEWING THE SUPERVISOR'S FIRE JOB

The supervisor's prime responsibility with regard to fire prevention and control is summarized below:

1. Know the fire hazards and promote installation of engineered safeguards in every instance practicable.

2. Conduct regular, periodic inspections of work areas to assure that they remain in fire-safe condition.

3. Instill in each employee a fire-conscious attitude for elimination of hazards and observance of safe practices—then keep checking his performance.

4. Keep well informed on fire brigade activity and evacuation plans. Inform employees immediately of any changes in procedure.

A supervisor will rightfully feel that the prime reason for being in charge of a group of workers is to get out production—to get a job done safely. Yet, a vital element of that overall job is fire prevention and extinguishment.

---

*Details are given in the NSC Data Sheet No. 588, *Fire Brigades.*

Appendix

Conversion Factors

All physical units of measurement can be reduced to three basic dimensions—mass, length, and time. Not only does reducing units to these basic dimensions simplify the solution of problems, but standardization of units makes comparison between operations (and between operations and standards) easier.

For example, air flows are usually measured in liters per minute, cubic meters per second, or cubic feet per minute. The total volume of air sampled can be easily converted to cubic meters or cubic feet. In another situation, the results of atmospheric pollution studies and stack sampling surveys are often reported as grains per cubic foot, grams per cubic foot, or pounds per cubic foot. The degree of contamination is usually reported as parts of contaminant per million parts of air.

If physical measurements are made, or reported in different units, they must be converted to the standard units if any comparisons are to be meaningful.

To save time and space in reporting data, many units have standard abbreviations. Because the metric system is becoming more frequently used, conversion factors are given for the standard units of measurement.

It is the purpose of this appendix to show the standard abbreviations used in this book, and used generally in the practice of industrial hygiene. Conversion factors are provided for use when data is reported in "nonstandard" units.

FUNDAMENTAL UNITS

Conversion factors for various measurement units are listed in this appendix. Each group—length, area, flow, for example—has its own table showing the interrelationship of the units.

To use the table to find the numerical value of the quantity desired, locate the unit to be converted in the first column. Then multiply this value by the number appearing at the intersection of the row and the column containing the desired unit. The answer will be the numerical value in the desired unit. Various English system and metric system units are given for the reader's convenience.

The new system of measurement is called the International System of Units (SI). The official conversion factors and an explanation of the system are given to 6- or 7-place accuracy, in ANSI/IEEE Standard 268–1982, *Metric Practice*. In Canada, refer to the *Canadian Metric Practice Guide,* CAN3–Z234.1–79, published by the Canadian Standards Association.

Briefly, the SI System, now being adopted throughout the world, is a modern version of the MKSA (meter, kilogram, second, ampere) system. Its details are published and controlled by an international treaty organization, the International Bureau of Weights and Measures (BIPM), set up by the Metre Convention signed in Paris, France, on May 20, 1875. The United States and Canada are member states of this Convention.

To Obtain→ Multiply Number of ↓ By →	meter (m)	centimeter (cm)	millimeter (mm)	micron (μm) or micrometer	angstrom unit, A	inch (in.)	foot (ft)
meter	1	100	1000	10^6	10^{10}	39.37	3.28
centimeter	0.01	1	10	10^4	10^8	0.394	0.0328
millimeter	0.001	0.1	1	10^3	10^7	0.0394	0.00328
micron	10^{-6}	10^{-4}	10^{-3}	1	10^4	3.94×10^{-5}	3.28×10^{-6}
angstrom	10^{-10}	10^{-8}	10^{-7}	10^{-4}	1	3.94×10^{-9}	3.28×10^{-10}
inch	0.0254	2.540	25.40	2.54×10^4	2.54×10^8	1	0.0833
foot	0.305	30.48	304.8	304,800	3.048×10^9	12	1

AREA

To Obtain → Multiply Number of ↓	square meter (m^2)	square inch $(sq\ in)$	square foot $(sq\ ft)$	square centimeter (cm^2)	square millimeter (mm^2)
square meter	1	1,550	10.76	10,000	10^6
square inch	6.452×10^{-4}	1	6.94×10^{-3}	6.452	645.2
square foot	0.0929	144	1	929.0	92,903
square centimeter	0.0001	0.155	0.001	1	100
square millimeter	10^{-6}	0.00155	0.00001	0.01	1

VOLUME

To Obtain → $\rightarrow$ Multiply Number of $\downarrow$ By $\rightarrow$	cu ft	gallon (U.S. liquid)	liters	cm^3	m^3
cubic foot	1	7.481	28.32	28,320	0.0283
gallon (U.S. liquid)	0.1337	1	3.785	3,785	3.79×10^{-3}
liter	0.03531	0.2642	1	1,000	1×10^{-3}
cubic centimeter	3.531×10^{-5}	2.64×10^{-4}	0.001	1	10^{-6}
cubic meter	35.31	264.2	1,000	10^6	1

VELOCITY

To Obtain → Multiply Number of By →	cm/s	m/s	km/h	ft/s	ft/min	mph
centimeter/second	1	0.01	0.036	0.0328	1.968	0.02237
meter/second	100	1	3.6	3.281	196.85	2.237
kilometer/hour	27.78	0.2778	1	0.9113	54.68	0.6214
foot/second	30.48	0.3048	18.29	1	60	0.6818
foot/minute	0.5080	0.00508	0.0183	0.0166	1	0.01136
miles per hour	44.70	0.4470	1.609	1.467	88	1

FLOW RATES

Multiply Number of By →	Liters/min	m^3/s	m^3/hr	gal/min	cu ft/min	cu ft/sec
To Obtain →						
Liter/minute	1	1.67×10^{-5}	0.06	0.2640	0.0353	5.89×10^{-4}
Cubic meter/second	4.63×10^{-3}	1	2.77×10^{-4}	1.22×10^{-3}	1.63×10^{-4}	2.7×10^{-6}
Cubic meter/hour	16.67	2.78×10^{-4}	1	4.4	0.588	9.89×10^{-3}
Gallon (U.S.)/minute	3.78	6.3×10^{-5}	0.277	1	0.1338	2.23×10^{-3}
Cubic foot/minute	28.32	4.71×10^{-4}	1.699	7.50	1	0.01667
Cubic foot/second	1.69×10^3	2.83×10^{-3}	1.02×10^2	448.8	60	1

MASS

To Obtain → / Multiply Number of / By ↗	gram (gm)	kilogram (kg)	grains (gr)	ounce (avoir) (oz)	pound (avoir) (lb)
gram	1	0.001	15.432	0.03527	0.00220
kilogram	1,000	1	15,432	35.27	2.205
grain	0.0648	6.480×10^{-5}	1	2.286×10^{-3}	1.429×10^{-4}
ounce	28.35	0.02835	437.5	1	0.0625
pound	453.59	0.4536	7,000	16	1

FORCE

To Obtain → Multiply Number of *By* → ↓	*dyne*	*newton* (N)	*kilogram-force* (kg-f)	*pound-force* (lb-f)
dyne	1	1.0×10^{-5}	1.02×10^{4}	2.248×10^{4}
newton	1.0×10^{5}	1	0.1020	0.2248
kilogram-force	9.807×10^{-5}	9.807	1	2.205
pound-force	4.448×10^{-5}	4.448	0.4536	1

425

EMISSION RATES

To Obtain → $\quad$ Multiply Number of $\quad$ By →	gm/s	gm/min	kg/h	kg/day	lb/min	lb/h	lb/day
gram/second	1.0	60.0	3.6	86.40	0.13228	7.9367	190.48
gram/minute	0.016667	1.0	0.06	1.4400	2.2046×10^{-3}	0.13228	3.1747
kilogram/hour	0.27778	16.667	1.0	24.000	0.036744	2.2046	52.911
kilogram/day	0.011574	0.69444	0.041667	1.0	1.5310×10^{-3}	9.1860×10^{-2}	2.2046
pound/minute	7.5598	453.59	27.215	653.17	1.0	60.0	1440.
pound/hour	0.12600	7.5598	0.45359	10.886	1.6667×10^{-2}	1.0	24.0
pound/day	5.2499×10^{-3}	0.31499	1.8900×10^{-2}	0.45359	6.9444×10^{-4}	4.1667×10^{-2}	1.0

PRESSURE

To Obtain → Multiply Number of ↓ By →	lb/sq in (psi)	Atm	in.(Hg) 32 F 0 C	mm(Hg) 32 F 0 C	kPa (kN/m²)	ft(H₂O) 60 F 15 C	lb/sq ft
pound/square inch	1	0.068	2.036	51.71	6.895	2.309	144
atmospheres	14.696	1	29.92	760.0	101.32	33.93	2,116
inch (Hg)	0.4912	0.033	1	25.40	3.386	1.134	70.73
millimeter (Hg)	0.01934	0.0013	0.039	1	0.1333	0.04464	2.785
kilopascals	0.1450	9.87×10^{-3}	0.2953	7.502	1	0.3460*	20.89
foot (H₂O)(15 C)	0.4332	0.0294	0.8819	22.40	2.989*	1	62.37
pound/square foot	0.0069	4.72×10^{-4}	0.014	0.359	0.04788	0.016	1

* at 4 C

HEAT, ENERGY, OR WORK

Multiply Number of By → / To Obtain →	joule	ft-lb	kwh	hp-hour	kcal	cal	Btu
joules	1	0.737	2.773×10^{-7}	3.725×10^{-7}	2.39×10^{-4}	0.2390	9.478×10^{-4}
foot-pound	1.356	1	3.766×10^{-7}	5.05×10^{-7}	3.24×10^{-4}	0.3241	1.285×10^{-3}
kilowatt-hour	3.6×10^6	2.66×10^6	1	1.341	860.57	860,565	3,412
hp-hour	2.68×10^6	1.98×10^6	0.7455	1	641.62	641,615	2,545
kilocalorie	4,184	3,086	1.162×10^{-3}	1.558×10^{-3}	1	1,000	3.9657
calorie	4.184	3.086	1.162×10^{-6}	1.558×10^{-6}	0.001	1	.00397
British thermal unit	1,055	778.16	2.930×10^{-4}	3.93×10^{-4}	0.252	252	1

RADIANT ENERGY UNITS

To Obtain → Multiply ↓ By →	erg	joule	W-s	μW-s	gm-cal
erg	1	10^{-7}	10^{-7}	0.1	2.39×10^{-8}
joule	10^7	1	1	10^6	0.239
watt-second	10^7	1	1	10^6	0.239
microwatt-second	10	10^{-6}	10^{-6}	1	2.39×10^{-7}
gram-calorie	4.19×10^7	4.19	4.19	4.19×10^6	1

ENERGY/UNIT AREA
(Dose units)

To Obtain → Multiply ↓	By → erg/cm^2	$joule/cm^2$	$W\text{-}s/cm^2$	$\mu W\text{-}s/cm^2$	$gm\text{-}cal/cm^2$
erg/square centimeter	1	10^{-7}	10^{-7}	0.1	2.39×10^{-8}
joule/square centimeter	10^7	1	1	10^6	0.239
watt-second/square centimeter	10^7	1	1	10^6	0.239
microwatt-second/square centimeter	10	10^{-6}	10^{-6}	1	2.39×10^{-7}
gram-calorie/square centimeter	4.19×10^7	4.19	4.19	4.19×10^6	1

DENSITY

To Obtain → Multiply Number of ↓ By ↘	gm/cm³	lb/cu ft	lb/gal
gram/cubic centimeters	1	62.43	8.345
pound/cubic foot	0.01602	1	0.1337
pound/gallon (U.S.)	0.1198	7.481	1

1 grain/cu ft = 2.28 mg/m³

TEMPERATURE EQUIVALENTS

To convert from "degrees Fahrenheit" to "degrees Celsius" (formerly called "degrees centigrade"), use the formula:

$$t_c = \frac{(t_f - 32)}{1.8} \text{ or } \frac{5}{9}(t_f - 32)$$

Conversely,
$$t_f = 1.8\, t_c + 32 \text{ or } \frac{9}{5} t_c + 32$$

Examples: (1) Convert the boiling point of water in F to C:

$$212\,F - 32 = 180$$
$$\frac{5}{9}(180) = 100\,C$$

(2) Convert 25 C to F:

$$\frac{9}{5}(25) + 32 = 45 + 32$$
$$= 77\,F$$

Useful
References

American Conference of Governmental Industrial Hygienists, 6500 Glenway Ave., Building D-5, Cincinnati, Ohio 45211. "Threshold Limit Values for Chemical Substances and Physical Agents in the Workroom Environment." (Issued annually.)

_____. Committee on Industrial Ventilation, P.O. Box 16153, Lansing, Mich. 48901. *Industrial Ventilation—A Manual of Recommended Practice.* (Latest edition.)

American Industrial Hygiene Association, 475 Wolf Ledges Parkway, Akron, Ohio 44311.
Heating and Cooling for Man in Industry. 1975.
Industrial Noise Manual. 1975.

American National Red Cross, 17th and D Streets NW. Washington, D.C. 20006. *First Aid Textbook.* (Latest edition.)

American National Standards Institute, 1430 Broadway, New York, N.Y. 10018. "American National Standards" (catalog available).

American Society for Training and Development, 1630 Duke St., P.O. Box 1443, Alexandria, Va. 22313. *Training and Development Handbook,* 1976.

American National Standards Institute, 1430 Broadway, New York, N.Y. 10018. "Catalog of American National Standards." (Issued annually.)

USEFUL REFERENCES

American Welding Society, 2501 NW. 7th Street, Miami, Fla. 33125. *Welding Handbook.*

Bird, Frank E., Jr. *Management Guide to Loss Control.* Loganville, Ga.: Institute Press. 1974.

Bird, Frank E., Jr., and Robert G. Loftus. *Loss Control Management.* Loganville, Ga.: Institute Press. 1976.

Blanchard, Kenneth, and Spencer Johnson. *The One Minute Manager.* New York, N.Y.: Berkley Publishing Group. 1982.

"Care and Operating Instructions for Various Electric Tools." Milwaukee Electric Tool Corp., 13171 W. Lisbon Rd., Brookfield, Wis. 53005.

DeCristofores, R. J. *Complete Book of Power Tools.* New York, N.Y.: Harper & Roe. 1973.

Factory Mutual Engineering Corporation of the Factory Mutual System, 1151 Boston-Providence Turnpike, Norwood, Mass. 02062.
Approval Guide.
Handbook of Property Conservation.
Loss Prevention Data.

Fallon, William K., ed. *Leadership on the Job: Guide to Good Supervision,* 3rd ed. New York, N.Y.: AMACOM. 1981.

Feldman, Edwin B. *Housekeeping Handbook for Institutions, Business and Industry.* New York, N.Y.: Frederick Fell, Inc. 1969.

Ferry, Ted S. *Elements of Accident Investigation.* Springfield, Ill.: Charles C Thomas. 1978.

_____. Modern Accident Investigation and Analysis: *An Executive Guide to Accident Investigation.* New York, N.Y.: John Wiley & Sons. 1981.

Firenze, Robert J. *The Process of Hazard Control.* Dubuque, Iowa: Kendall/Hunt Publishing Co. 1978.

Hammer, Willie. *Handbook of System and Product Safety.* Englewood Cliffs, N.J.: Prentice-Hall, Inc. 1972.

"Hand Tool Safety: A Guide to Selection and Proper Use." Hand Tool Institute, 707 Westchester Ave., White Plains, N.Y. 10604. 1976.

Hannaford, Earle S. *Supervisors Guide to Human Relations.* Chicago, Ill.: National Safety Council. 1976.

Heinrich, Herbert W., Dan Petersen, and Nestor Roos. *Industrial Accident Prevention*, 5th ed. New York, N.Y.: McGraw-Hill Book Co. 1978.

Herzberg, Frederick. *Work and the Nature of Man.* New York, N.Y.: Thomas Y. Crowell Co. 1966.

Illuminating Engineering Society, 345 East 47th Street, New York, N.Y. 10017.
  IES Lighting Handbook (The Standard Lighting Guide).
  Practice for Industrial Lighting (ANSI/IES RP7).

International Labor Office, 1750 New York Ave., Suite 330, Washington, D.C. 20006. *Encyclopedia of Occupational Health and Safety.* 1983.

Johnson, William G. *MORT Safety Assurance Systems.* New York, N.Y.: Marcel Dekker. 1980.

Kirkpatrick, Donald L. *Supervisory Training and Development.* Reading, Mass.: Addison-Wesley Publishing Co. 1971.

Maslow, Abraham H. *Motivation and Personality.* New York, N.Y.: Harper & Row. 1970.

Matwes, George and Helen. *Loss Control: A Safety Guidebook for Trades and Services.* New York, N.Y.: Van Nostrand Reinhold Co. 1973.

McGregor, Douglas. *The Human Side of Enterprise.* New York, N.Y.: McGraw-Hill Book Co. 1960.

Montgomery, Robert L. *Listening Made Easy.* New York, N.Y.: AMACOM. 1981.

National Association of Suggestion Systems, 230 N. Michigan Ave., Chicago, Ill. 60601. *Journal* (quarterly).

USEFUL REFERENCES

National Fire Protection Association, Batterymarch Park, Quincy, Mass. 02269.

Fire Protection Handbook, 15th ed. 1981.
Fire Protection Guide on Hazardous Materials, 8th ed.
Flammable and Combustible Liquids Code Handbook, 2nd ed. 1984.
Industrial Fire Hazards Handbook, 2nd ed. 1984.
Inspection Manual, 5th ed. 1982.
Life Safety Code® Handbook. 1985.
National Electrical Code® Handbook, 1984.
"Standards and Recommended Practices" (catalog available).

National Institute of Occupational Safety and Health, U.S. Department of Health, Education, and Welfare, 5600 Fishers Lane, Rockville, Md. 20857.

Certified Personal Protective Equipment.
"Criteria Documents."
The Industrial Environment: Its Evaluation and Control.
Machine Guarding—Assessment of Need.
"Publications Catalog"
Safety Program Practices in High Versus Low Accident Rate Companies.
Toxic Substances List.
"Welding Safely."

National Safety Council, 444 N. Michigan Ave., Chicago, Ill. 60611.

Accident Facts (annually).
Accident Investigation: A New Approach.
Accident Prevention for Industrial Manual Operations (2 volumes).
Communications for the Safety Professional.
"Electrical Inspection Illustrated."
Family Safety and Health Magazine (quarterly).
"5 Minute Safety Talks" (a series).
Fundamentals of Industrial Hygiene.
"Guards Illustrated."
"Industrial Data Sheets" (listing available).
Industrial Noise and Hearing Conservation.
National Safety and Health News (monthly).
"Pocket Guide to First Aid."
"Power Press Safety Manual."
Safety Guide for Health Care Institutions.
"Safety Slides" (a series).
"Successful Supervision."

"Supervisors Safety Observation Handbook."
"You Are the Safety and Health Committee."

National Society to Prevent Blindness, 79 Madison Ave., New York, N.Y. 10016. *Eyesight in Industry.*

Nichols, Ralph, and Leonard A. Stevens. *Are You Listening?* New York, N.Y.: McGraw-Hill Book Co. 1957.

Ottoboni, M. Alice. *The Dose Makes the Poison: A Plain Language Guide to Toxicology.* Berkeley, Calif.: Vincente Books. 1984.

Peters, Thomas J., and R. B. Waterman. *In Search of Excellence.* New York, N.Y.: Harper & Row. 1982.

Petersen, Dan C. *Techniques of Safety Management,* 2nd ed. New York, N.Y.: McGraw-Hill Book Co. 1978.

Planer, Robert G. *Fire Loss Control: A Management Guide.* New York, N.Y.: Marcel Dekker. 1979.

Sax, N.I. *Dangerous Properties of Industrial Materials.* New York, N.Y.: VanNostrand Reinhold. 1968.

Simonds, Rollin H., and Grimaldi, John V. *Safety Management: Accident and Cost Control.* Homewood, Ill.: Richard D. Irwin, Inc. 1963.

Steil, Lyman, *et al. Listening: It Can Change Your Life.* New York, N.Y.: John Wiley & Sons. 1984.

Underwriters Laboratories Inc., 333 Pfingsten Rd., Northbrook, Ill. 60062. "Product Directories."

U.S. Department of Labor, Occupational Safety and Health Administration, 200 Constitution Ave., Washington, D.C. 20210.
An Illustrated Guide to Electrical Safety, Pub. 3073. 1983.
"Recordkeeping Requirements Under the OSHAct of 1970."

U.S. General Services Administration, National Archives and Records Service, Office of the Federal Register, Washington, DC.
Code of Federal Regulations:
Title 10—"Energy."

USEFUL REFERENCES

Title 29—"Labor."
Title 40—"Protection of the Environment."
Title 49—"Transportation."

Note. Government publications are available from Superintendent of Documents, U.S. Government Printing Office, Washington, D.C. 20402.

Watkins, William S., ed. *An Illustrated Guide to Electrical Safety.* American Society of Safety Engineers, 850 Busse Highway, Park Ridge, Ill. 60068. 1984.

Wolvin, Andrew D., and Carolyn Coakley. *Listening.* Wm. C. Brown Co., Publishers, 2460 Kemper Blvd., Dubuque, Ia. 52001. 1982.

Index

INDEX

440

INDEX

443

INDEX